Social Studies
in Elementary Education

JOHN JAROLIMEK

University of Washington, Seattle

The Macmillan Company, New York
Collier-Macmillan Limited, London

Fourth

*Social Studies
in Elementary
Education*

Edition

The Macmillan Company
866 Third Avenue, New York, New York 10022
COLLIER-MACMILLAN CANADA, LTD., TORONTO, ONTARIO

LIBRARY OF CONGRESS CATALOG CARD NUMBER: 70–126186

PRINTING   456789   YEAR   456789

Preface

More than ten years have passed since the first edition of this book was published. These have been dynamic years for social studies education—so much so that a number of authors have used the term *ferment* to describe what has been happening in this part of the curriculum. Whether this fermentation will ultimately yield a social studies curriculum wine of rare vintage is yet to be determined, for the process continues. What has happened in the last decade has been a vigorous exploration of various approaches to social studies education through many large and generously funded projects. The emphasis has been largely, but not entirely, on the cognitive components of the social studies curriculum and on inquiry as a teaching strategy.

As we move into the 1970's these additional developments in social studies education seem to be most significant: (1) there is a close tie-up between the social studies and the parent disciplines, the social sciences; (2) the social scientist is more involved in curriculum development; (3) there is an increased use of a broader range of the social sciences as sources of social studies content; (4) conceptually oriented curriculums are receiving greater attention, with a corresponding emphasis on inductive, inquiry-centered teaching methods; (5) there is a search for realism in programs, an effort to find ways to bring social studies education more into line with the social realities of life outside school; (6) an increased concern for the teaching of values and valuing is apparent; (7) there is greater emphasis on cross-cultural studies to build world understanding; (8) the critical role of skills in social studies is being recognized; (9) there is concern for more efficient and more effective teaching procedures to reach greater numbers of pupils from various environments; and (10) depth studies of fewer topics, as opposed to survey approaches covering vast amounts of subject matter, are receiving favorable consideration. These and other developing trends are reflected in the revision of this book.

But even though social studies education is changing rapidly, a certain amount of stability must be maintained. Programs that incorporate all new ideas, under the mistaken assumption that because they are new they are good, are in constant chaos. New approaches need careful trial and evaluation before they can be accepted on a mass scale. Therefore, although this book has undergone extensive revision, its original and central purpose is unchanged: to present preservice and in-service teachers with reliable, basic principles, ideas, and procedures that will lead to sound instructional practices in teaching the social studies at the elementary school level. No matter what happens on the forefront of curriculum reform, successful elementary teachers of social studies must (1) know the children they teach; (2) know subject matter, how to organize it, and how to translate it for pupils; (3) know learning resources and how to use them; and (4) know how to apply appropriate teaching procedures. These are central concerns of teachers as they meet with their pupils day after day and month after month in the many thousands of elementary school classrooms across the country. Likewise, these are the primary concerns of this text.

The readers who are familiar with the three previous editions of this book will notice a number of changes in this edition. The text has been reorganized to bring the chapters dealing with the substantive elements of the curriculum physically closer to the chapters that treat planning processes. Throughout the book the treatment of inquiry has been updated and given more emphasis. There is much greater attention given to the wide range of ethnic backgrounds of pupils and to the implications of this for social studies education. A new full chapter has been included on ecology and environment because of the increasing importance of this topic to society and to social studies education.

In the revision of this text the author has relied on his friends and professional associates for criticism, comments, and helpful suggestions. He is particularly indebted to Dr. Elmer Williams of the University of Georgia for his thorough and meticulous assistance. The author wishes to thank the many individuals and school districts who assisted in securing photographs for the book: Mrs. Rachel Bold, Seattle Public Schools; Mr. Raymond Braga, Northshore School District, Bothell, Washington; Mr. William C. Frederick, Shoreline Public Schools, Seattle; Mr. John B. Hughes, *Northshore Citizen*,

Bothell, Washington; Mr. Lowell R. Jackson, Seattle Public Schools; Mrs. Zita Lichtenberg, Washington State Office of Public Instruction, Olympia; Mr. Larry Sears, Colorado State College, Greeley; and Mr. Robert A. Sethre, Highline School District, Seattle. As was the case in the three previous editions, the author has depended heavily on the expert technical assistance and substantive contributions of his wife, Mildred Fleming Jarolimek, to whom and for whom he is deeply grateful. To all who assisted with the fourth edition of this text the author expresses his sincere appreciation.

J. J.

Contents

ix

The Social Studies Curriculum: Its Nature and Objectives

The prophets of doomsday have always enjoyed a good audience in the Western world. The modern Western man, whether his data source is a Biblical passage, extrasensory stimuli resulting from a psychedelic experience, or a sophisticated scientific report on environmental contamination, continues to be fascinated by the notion that the sky is falling, that California is soon to drop into the Pacific Ocean, and that the earth and all its inhabitants are soon to become no more than a few flecks of dust in the vast expanse of infinity and nothingness of the universe.

Social studies education has as its particular mission the task of helping young people grow in their understanding of and sensitivity to the physical and

1

social forces at work around them in order that they may shape their lives in harmony with those forces. Modern social studies education must be based on wisdom, reason, and rational processes, not on myth, superstition, and ignorance. It must help young people generate hope in the future and confidence in their ability to solve social problems and must not contribute to the despair of a doomsday mentality.

When one thinks of social studies, he commonly thinks of history and geography, perhaps even of economics or civics. This is because the social sciences are the parent disciplines of the social studies. But more fundamentally, social studies education concerns itself with man himself: man the culture maker, man being shaped by his culture; man in historical perspective, man in the contemporary world; man, that most fascinating of all creatures who can make his home anywhere on this planet or even beyond this planet and who in a variety of ingenious ways can devise means of meeting his basic needs and of developing a social system. Learning about man, how and where he lives, how he forms and structures societies, how he governs himself and provides for his material and psychological needs, how and why he loves and hates his fellow men, how he uses and misuses the resources of the planet that is his home—all this is what social studies education is really about.

What a challenge faces the teacher who is serious about his responsibility for teaching social studies! Almost any newspaper of the past decade carried stories about riots, confrontations, pollution, racism, war, assassination, moon landings, international intrigue, violence, and demands. These are familiar to us all because they are some of the realities of the times in which we live. In one way or another, meaningful social studies programs need to deal with these realities. This does not mean that social studies programs should deal only with the unpleasant, seamy side of life. However, it also does not mean that the unpleasant should be overlooked. Boys and girls should get honest pictures of the world in which they live, not make-believe ones.

The children the elementary teacher of today sees before him are a part of the human family that will be confronted with these realities for the next six to eight decades. These children—not all but most of them—are more fortunate than the bulk of humanity. They have the advantages of material well-being, good medical attention, long life expectancy, and opportunities for self-realization. They are a part of that minority of the human population surrounding the North Atlantic that has developed a high standard of living. The difference between their way of life and that of the rest of the world is vast and is central to some of the most severe human problems and conflicts these youngsters will encounter in their lifetimes.

The social studies curriculum is an important part of the education they will need to understand the world in which they live and to enable them to lead productive, happy lives in it. The social studies, along with the remainder of the curriculum, are part of an educational program that is increasingly emphasizing the rational process as an approach to the solution of human problems. Education today attempts to help pupils fashion enduring values from man's past experiences and apply them to life in today's world. It is a program of instruction that helps pupils accept change and deal with it thoughtfully and intelligently.

Social Studies, a Curriculum Area

It has long been recognized that a republic based on democratic principles demands high standards of education if it is to function. Through the years, numerous national leaders have addressed themselves to this need. In a nation where any voter can hold public office and where there has been a continual extension of the franchise, a common education for the masses is more than a matter of individual and personal choice; it is a concern of society as a whole. The American people have always expected the schools to contribute directly to the development of loyalty to the democratic ideal, good citizenship, civic responsibility, and human relationships. These represent the broader goals of all education, but the social studies have historically assumed a special responsibility toward the attainment of those goals.

The part of the elementary school curriculum now called the social studies was traditionally designated and taught as separate subjects. Those most commonly included were history and geography—conventionally, history and geography of the local area, the home state, and the nation. Old World history and geography and that of the Western Hemisphere were also popular. Until recently little attention was given the non-Western world. Civics, the study of the role and structure of government, was the third subject frequently included. Sometimes the subject-matter lines were exceedingly rigid, as in the case of schools where "History of the United States" was taught at one time during the day and "Geography of the United States" was taught at another time of the same day to the same children. Today some schools organize and teach the social studies according to subjects; but, where this is done, subject-matter lines are usually not as inflexible as they once were.

Educators are coming to realize that there are a variety of formats that social studies programs can take. Many believe that for the elementary school pupil some type of interdisciplinary or multidisciplinary arrangement is best. A multidisciplinary plan would include content and concepts from more than one discipline but would maintain the identity and integrity of the disciplines that are included. That is, there would be elements of history, geography, economics, and so on in the program, but they would be clearly recognized and taught as history, geography, and economics. An interdisciplinary arrangement, on the other hand, would include content and concepts from more than one discipline, but the particular discipline would not necessarily be identified in the study. This latter arrangement is illustrated in Figure 1. Under this scheme significant ideas from several disciplines are brought together in a single study of a topic, as illustrated in Figure 2.

The interdisciplinary pattern is consistent with the well-established practice of moving from the general to the particular—from gaining a general background of information before becoming a specialist. This arrangement also has the advantage of presenting a more realistic picture and a more accurate explanation of social phenomena than is often possible in single-subject approaches. Peoples' ways of living simply cannot be explained adequately or accurately in terms of a single discipline such as history or geography. In the elementary grades this is frequently attempted, and misunderstandings result because the explanations omit significant factors. For example, explanations of the way of life of nomadic desert people based only on geographic phenomena are probably inaccurate or at best incomplete because they fail to recognize the importance of historical, economic, and other cultural factors. For this reason, if programs are to be really effective they must be interdisciplinary to some extent, no matter what they are called. It is safe to say that good teachers of history, geography, economics, or political science have always utilized concepts from closely related disciplines even though the subject label was that of a particular discipline.

The term *social studies* can be applied to programs of a single-subject type as well as to those of the unified variety. In fact, there may be specific social studies units in the elementary grades that do have a special subject emphasis, even though the total program is conceived of as interdisciplinary. There might, for example, be a place for units that have an economics orientation or a geographical emphasis or that are primarily historical. There could be very good reasons why a program would call for such units: to ensure systematic treatment of important learnings, to highlight a particular historical period, to provide for experience in a way of thinking about a subject, and so on. But this does not mean that all the units must have the same emphasis or be organized in the same way. Attention is again called to Figure 1. Instead of *social studies* occupying the center rectangle, the reader might substitute a unit on *geography, history,* or *economics.* This

SOCIAL STUDIES CONTENT INCLUDES BASIC CONCEPTS FROM MANY OF THE SOCIAL SCIENCES

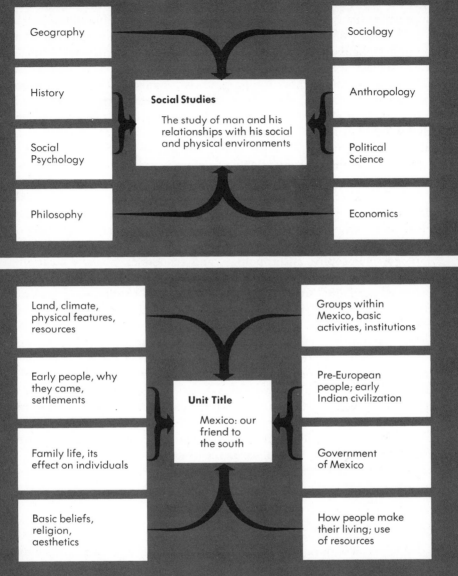

Geography

Sociology

History

Anthropology

Social Studies

The study of man and his relationships with his social and physical environments

Social Psychology

Political Science

Philosophy

Economics

Land, climate, physical features, resources

Groups within Mexico, basic activities, institutions

Early people, why they came, settlements

Pre-European people; early Indian civilization

Unit Title

Mexico: our friend to the south

Family life, its effect on individuals

Government of Mexico

Basic beliefs, religion, aesthetics

How people make their living; use of resources

Figures 1, 2. The diagram in **Figure 1** (top) represents an interdisciplinary approach to social studies. In some cases a single discipline might occupy the position of central importance but would draw upon the other related disciplines for concepts to illuminate the topic under study. The diagram in **Figure 2** (bottom) parallels **Figure 1** and shows how the various social sciences might contribute to a specific topic.

would indicate that in that particular unit special stress was being given a single discipline, but the same relationship between it and the supporting disciplines, as represented in the figure, would obtain.

The point of view expressed here is that an interdisciplinary or a multidisciplinary arrangement is preferable for the elementary grades. Nevertheless, it is recognized that good teaching *or* poor teaching can take place no matter how the program is organized. There is little to be gained by insisting that one organizational format is better for all purposes than another organizational format. Experience has shown that good instruction can result under either a separate subject or a unified arrangement. As Drummond has pointed out, what is more important than the organizational structure is the quality of the learning experiences the pupils are having.[1]

The social studies should not be thought of as the same as social education. As was noted earlier, the social studies as a part of the elementary school curriculum draw subject matter from the social sciences: history, geography, sociology, political science, social psychology, philosophy, anthropology, and economics. *Social education,* on the other hand, is a more inclusive, broader concept embracing the entire interpersonal social life of the child. Social studies as an area of the curriculum is a regularly scheduled part of the school day; social education takes place whenever the child is in a social situation. This can occur during a mathematics lesson, in the school lunchroom, on the playground, in and out of school. It is true that the social studies make an important contribution to the social education of children and have, indeed, a special responsibility to assist children to learn social-living skills. But a distinction should be made between the broad term *social education* and the specific area of the elementary school curriculum referred to as the social studies. This is not to say that desirable social education will take place if the child is left unguided. It suggests, rather, that the task is beyond the scope of the social studies program.

Objectives of the Social Studies

The perpetuation of our way of life, its values and ideals, depends almost entirely on the success of society in educating its members in democratic principles and democratic action as defined by this society. "The maintenance of any particular form of human social organization not only requires provision for the addition of new individuals by reproduction but also ways and means of structuralizing the psychological field of the individual in a manner that *will induce him to act in*

1. Harold D. Drummond, "Separate or Merged—Sound Experiences Are Vital," *The National Elementary Principal,* 42, No. 4, April, 1963, pp. 27–30.

We have here an excellent sample of the diversity of ethnic backgrounds represented by American school children. These pupils and their counterparts throughout the world will be decision makers of the twenty-first century. (Courtesy of the Seattle Public Schools and the Clover Park Schools, Tacoma, Washington)

certain predictable ways." [2] As instruments of society, schools play a major role in the process of the democratization of young citizens.

Although the development of good citizenship is often accepted as a major objective of the social studies, there is a considerable difference of opinion as to what constitutes the "good citizen" and what behavior characterizes such a person. This is to be expected, because the good citizen is always an idealized type whose behavior reflects a set of values preferred by those making the construct. There is some objection to the use of *good citizenship* as an objective of social studies instruction because it implies a single qualitative standard designed by the dominant cultural group in our society and imposed on others. Those who share this point of view would argue that *good citizenship* is an elusive concept at best and that it includes a broad range of acceptable behavior. The adjectives *good* and *bad* as applied to citizenship are meaningful only in the context of the subcultural group within which one finds himself. What is good citizenship behavior in white, middle-class society may or may not be good citizenship in other groups.

Within limits, however, it is important to understand that social studies education is legally charged with the responsibility of dealing with learnings related to citizenship in this society.

In the legal or political sense, one obtains citizenship through birth or through the naturalization process. The requirements for legal citizenship obtained through naturalization are fairly clear-cut because they are defined by law. They include an understanding of the English language, the basic elements of national history, and the fundamental principles and form of the government of the United States. The person applying for citizenship cannot be opposed to the government or laws of the United States, nor can he favor totalitarian forms of government. He must meet certain requirements of residence, be of good moral character, be attached to the principles of the Constitution, and be favorably disposed to the United States. He is examined in court and required to give the oath of renunciation and allegiance. This is usually accomplished by a dignified and solemn ceremony to impress the candidate with the serious responsibilities of the citizen in a democratic nation. *It is approximately correct to say that many of the same understandings and attitudes are expected of persons who secure citizenship through birth, these being learned through the medium of public education.* For this reason the states have laws that make mandatory the inclusion of various aspects of the social studies in the elementary school curriculum.

2. A. Irving Hallowell, "Culture and Personality," *Cultural and Social Anthropology, Selected Readings,* Peter B. Hammond, ed., New York: The Macmillan Company, 1964, p. 453.

But the legal and political requirements for citizenship are the barest minimum essentials. Surely there is a qualitative aspect of citizenship that goes beyond meeting a few legal requirements. It is conceivable that one could meet the legal requirements for citizenship and fall far short of his responsibilities as a worthy member of a democratic society. Through the years a number of lists have been compiled that state or describe qualities characterizing the behavior of the good citizen. These lists have not been altogether satisfactory as guidelines for the development of social studies programs. Such lists often result in a long enumeration of discrete and fragmented parts that lack cohesiveness. The feeling is that good citizenship is a global concept and loses meaning when broken down into a long list of components.

The Civic Education Project team sponsored by the National Council for the Social Studies and financed by the Danforth Foundation was asked to visit schools throughout the United States and to identify the most promising practices in the making of citizens. In its report, the project team lists eleven citizenship goals for a new age. They are listed here:

1. Knowledge and skills to assist in solving the problems of our times
2. Awareness of the effects of science on civilization and its use to improve the quality of life
3. Readiness for effective economic life
4. Ability to make value judgments for effective life in a changing world
5. Recognition that we live in an open-ended world which requires receptivity to new facts, new ideas, and new ways of life
6. Participation in the process of decision-making through expression of views to representatives, experts, and specialists
7. Belief in both liberty for the individual and equality for all, as guaranteed by the Constitution of the United States
8. Pride in the achievements of the United States, appreciation of the contributions of other peoples, and support for international peace and cooperation
9. Use of the creative arts to sensitize oneself to universal human experience and to the uniqueness of the individual
10. Compassion and sensitivity for the needs, feelings, and aspirations of other human beings
11. Development of democratic principles and application [of these] to daily life [3]

In 1961, the Educational Policies Commission issued a statement entitled *The Central Purpose of American Education*. The most widely publicized and quoted sentence in the document states, "The purpose

3. Donald W. Robinson *et al.*, *Promising Practices in Civic Education*, Washington, D.C.: National Council for the Social Studies, 1967, pp. 16–17.

which runs through and strengthens all other educational purposes—the common thread of education—is the development of the ability to think." [4] Thinking in the social studies involves the expression of preferences, the consideration of alternatives, and the making of decisions. Because there is no direct way of assessing the nature and quality of another's thought processes, appraisals are made of a man's thinking by what he says and what he does. Thus, it follows that one of the best tests of the quality of a man's thinking is in the kinds of decisions he makes when dealing with social and civic issues.

If the statement of the Educational Policies Commission and the goals identified by the Civic Education Project team are taken seriously as guides to building social studies programs to improve citizenship, objectives can be classified into three categories: (1) understandings—those that deal with knowledge and knowing, (2) attitudes—those that deal with values, appreciations, ideals, and feelings, and (3) skills—those that deal with using and applying social studies learnings and the ability to gain new learnings.

UNDERSTANDINGS

It would be difficult to defend a position suggesting that a poorly informed person can consistently make wise decisions on social and civic affairs. We assume that a good citizen is a person who is informed, that he has at his command a background of knowledge and information needed to consider social problems and issues intelligently. The need for information is great in the world today; and, from his first day in school, the child needs to be building his background of functional information about the world and its people. Better social studies programs recognize this need and plan accordingly for it. The programs make certain the child has the opportunity to extend his understanding of basic and elementary concepts of geography, history, government, economics, and sociology as they bear on the study of people and their struggle to solve the perennial problems of mankind. This knowledge and understanding provides the child with the raw material to give meaning and depth to his thinking about and discussion of the problems he encounters in social studies. Class discussions, reports, and problem-solving situations will be both more stimulating and more profitable when based on sound, factual, authentic, and functional information.

It should be emphasized that the building of understandings begins in the primary grades. Child-growth and development research and common sense advise against presenting children with problems,

4. Educational Policies Commission, *The Central Purpose of American Education,* Washington, D.C.: National Education Association, 1961, p. 12.

topics, and materials for which they are not ready; but concepts can be simplified to suit the developmental level of children. Ideas are presented in simple forms at the primary levels and are extended and given depth as the child moves through the grades. It has been repeatedly demonstrated in recent years that young children are able to profit from programs having strong substantive content.

ATTITUDES

This second category of objectives includes values, ideals, appreciations, and, in general, the *feeling* dimension of social studies education. There is not now, nor has there been in the past, any clear or consistent policy regarding the role of the school in inculcating certain preferred values in pupils. It should arouse, therefore, little wonder that there is disagreement among those who address themselves to this complicated issue. There are those who believe the school should play a forceful and positive role in teaching attitudes, values, and beliefs that characterize the "American way of life." Quite naturally they would insist that such teaching be done in accordance with the "American way of life" as they perceive it. Others take serious exception to this approach because they see the procedure conflicting with some of the values presumably being promoted. That is, they would insist that the school should not tell pupils what to believe or value, that these are individual and personal affairs. The issue is further complicated because statements of beliefs, values, or attitudes are subject to a variety of interpretations.

In spite of these difficulties, social studies programs are expected to and do teach certain attitudes, values, beliefs, ideals, and appreciations. This is because the school is an instrument of a society that is based on a particular value system. These values are the ethical guidelines of society, and helping pupils to gain an understanding of them is a responsibility the school shares with other agencies. This is not to say that children are to be taught in dogmatic ways or in ways that violate the values being taught.

There may not be total agreement on what these values and their meanings are, but this is not the same as saying that there are no values at all. A value orientation is a basic requirement for normal living. The value system serves as the conscience of society and assures that the application of knowledge and understanding will be to worthwhile and positive ends. One of the great challenges of social studies teaching today is not to *give* values to pupils but to help them understand the value system, learn the sources of some of our values, recognize and deal with the value components of civic and social issues, and form their own value systems on a rational basis.

SKILLS

The third group of objectives deals with the development of a variety of *abilities* and *skills* associated with the social studies. There are many such abilities and skills; and, for purposes of clarity, these may be grouped as follows:

Social Skills. Social skills include living and working together, learning to give and take, assuming responsibility, taking turns, respecting the rights of others, and building social awareness. They embrace the entire area of social living and social sensitivity and give the child the opportunity to develop self-control and self-direction. Teaching social skills, of course, is not limited to the social studies but is an important part of the entire school program and should be taught in every contact the school has with the child. The development of the skills of social living represents an exceedingly important outcome of the social studies, especially at the primary level. It should not, however, entirely dominate the program.

Study Skills and Work Habits. There are a number of study skills and work habits that children should be developing as a part of their social studies instruction. Some of these are general skills and abilities included and taught in other areas of the curriculum as well: skill in locating and collecting data, making reports, speaking before a group, using reference material, outlining, summarizing, and other skills. Children are taught how to apply these skills and abilities to the social studies and are provided with situations that give them genuine reasons to apply the skills and abilities. Another group of study skills and work habits is more or less peculiar to the social studies: the ability to read social studies materials for a variety of purposes; facility in the use of maps, globes, charts, graphs; the use of special references, such as an atlas or the *World Almanac.* Because these skills, abilities, and/or work habits are not ordinarily included in the school program, except in the social studies, they must be carefully planned and taught.

Group-Work Skills. Included in the category of group-work skills are skills and abilities needed for group planning, to lead and participate in group discussions, and to function effectively in situations demanding cooperative efforts in planning, working, and evaluating. Group-work skills do not appear full-blown when the individual comes of age, but they are developed gradually with experience and instruction in group action over a period of several years. The elementary social studies program has the responsibility of providing a good beginning for these important skills.

Intellectual Skills. These skills are associated with various aspects of thinking and include the use and application of a rational approach to the solution of problems. The need for the development of critical thinking on the part of youngsters is a clearly recognized goal of all sound social studies programs. However, skills involving the use of inductive procedures need greater application in the teaching of social studies than is commonly found.

It is apparent that the responsibility for teaching many of these skills overlaps other curriculum areas. This means that the social studies can reinforce such teaching by providing opportunities for practical use of the skill and by showing the pupils how a general skill is applied to a specific subject area. For example, outlining as a skill for organizing information might be taught in the language arts. In the social studies, however, the pupil could make practical application of it by organizing social studies content. Also, by making an outline based on social studies material he would learn how outlining is applied to social studies. Careful coordination and reinforcement of teaching in the various subject areas that overlap in their concern for certain skills can do much to strengthen the overall skill development of children.

In the 33rd Yearbook of the National Council for the Social Studies, skills are grouped to show those that are shared with other curriculum areas and those that are the major responsibility of the social studies:

Skills which are a definite but shared responsibility of the social studies:

    I. Locating information
   II. Organizing information
  III. Evaluating information
  IV. Acquiring information through reading
   V. Acquiring information through listening and observing
  VI. Communicating orally and in writing
 VII. Interpreting pictures, charts, graphs, tables
VIII. Working with others

Skills which are a major responsibility of the social studies:

    I. Reading social studies materials
   II. Applying problem-solving and critical-thinking skills to social issues
  III. Interpreting maps and globes
  IV. Understanding time and chronology [5]

The rationale for social studies education developed here is summarized in Figure 3. Content and content-related skills are defended on the basis of their contribution to rational behavior. A knowledgeable and informed citizen is likely to approach social and civic affairs more thoughtfully, critically, and intelligently than one who does not

5. Helen McCracken Carpenter, ed., *Skill Development in Social Studies*, Washington, D.C.: National Council for the Social Studies, 1963, pp. 310–311.

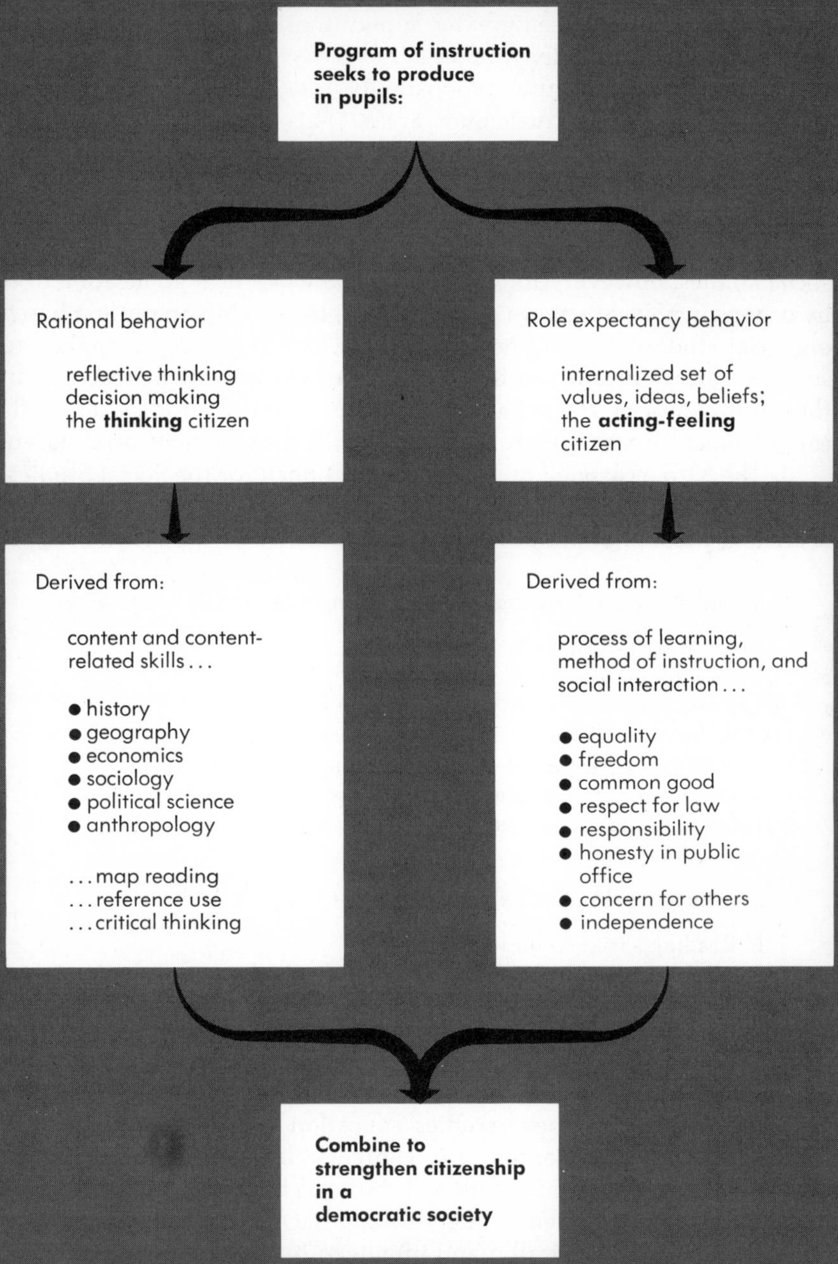

Program of instruction seeks to produce in pupils:

Rational behavior

reflective thinking
decision making
the **thinking** citizen

Role expectancy behavior

internalized set of
values, ideas, beliefs;
the **acting-feeling**
citizen

Derived from:

content and content-
related skills . . .

- history
- geography
- economics
- sociology
- political science
- anthropology

. . . map reading
. . . reference use
. . . critical thinking

Derived from:

process of learning,
method of instruction, and
social interaction . . .

- equality
- freedom
- common good
- respect for law
- responsibility
- honesty in public
  office
- concern for others
- independence

**Combine to
strengthen citizenship
in a
democratic society**

Figure 3

have these qualities. Programs that provide adequately for this dimension of social studies education begin introducing in the early grades basic ideas from the social sciences along with related skills. Simple variations are introduced and more complex variations are presented later. This type of spiraling curriculum arrangement is widely accepted today.

But along with knowledge and the tools (skills) available to gain and use it, the individual needs a value base to serve as a guide for its use. Unless one uses his knowledge in accordance with the values accepted by society, he may actually be a dangerous person. This stresses the importance of the second dimension of social studies education, *role expectancy behavior*. It is based on a set of internalized values, beliefs, ideals, and attitudes that the individual develops through the years. He does not learn these entirely from social studies instruction, of course, but they are an important component of elementary social studies. For example, let us assume that a class is engaged in a unit on elementary economics in the primary grades. Attention is directed to such concepts as *producer* and *consumer*. A child not only should learn something about the meaning of these concepts but also should learn that society expects certain behavior from consumers and producers: it is expected that the head of a family will find and hold a job to support his family; it is expected that consumption will not be done wastefully. Much social and civic behavior is learned and performed in this way. People behave and act in certain ways because they have come to believe that they are expected to behave and act in those ways.

The vital role of elementary social studies education in developing role-expectancy behavior is not always fully appreciated. Herein lies the value of having young pupils encounter idealized types—persons who illustrate by their way of life the values society rewards and likes to see in its citizens. From these role models, young pupils learn to know what society expects of its citizens. In this connection, biographical material is often helpful in acquainting pupils with role-expectancy behavior. Similarly, the conduct of the teacher and his methods of instruction have much to do with the development of such behavior.

Good instructional programs blend and balance these two dimensions of social studies education. Too great an emphasis on role-expectancy behavior results in overconformity, lack of originality, no creative endeavors, and too much concern for what others think about one's behavior. Overemphasis on the rational dimension, on the other hand, depends too heavily on the transfer of knowledge into action or, worse, disassociates knowledge from behavior. It should be apparent, too, that good instruction will interrelate these two components of social studies education in ways that make it possible for them to strengthen and enrich each other.

The major objectives of social studies programs, therefore, may be identified as the development of the understandings, attitudes, and skills necessary for effective and responsible democratic citizenship. Careful study of the objectives of social studies points to the importance of instructional procedures; for, if attitudes and skills are to be learned beyond the verbal level, the child must be given practice in in their application and use over an extended period of time. The objectives of the social studies are not achieved completely in any one grade or any group of grades; rather, they indicate the *direction* in which growth is anticipated, and each year should help the child make progress and growth in the desired direction. The outcomes of social studies, as in any other instruction, are many and varied; and the best programs are the ones that give indication of a good balance in the intensity of efforts in the development of understandings, attitudes, and skills.

Citizenship Education and the Social Studies

One of the realities of the world today is the basic conflict in philosophy between peoples of the free world and those who embrace communism as a way of life. It is for this reason that developing citizenship for life in a free society has been a dominant concern of those who plan educational programs for the children of America. Serious-minded Americans, persons who are concerned that freedom from tyranny be preserved, look to the schools to instill in the young people of the nation an understanding of and deep commitment to the principles that inhere in the concepts of freedom and dignity for the individual.

Although the social studies have a unique responsibility to help children develop understandings, attitudes, and skills prerequisite to responsible citizenship, citizenship itself cannot be taught entirely within the social studies. It must be a part of the entire school life of the child. Schools that teach citizenship during the social studies period but teach mathematics and ignore citizenship during the mathematics period have very shallow programs of citizenship education. Good teachers have recognized the need to place children in activities that will allow them to begin experimenting with the responsibilities involved in democratic group living at an early age. Children everywhere are assuming more and more responsibility for many of the routines of classroom life. Today it is not uncommon to see elementary classrooms where children bring themselves to order in the morning, go through the flag ceremony, morning song, and sharing time in an orderly and efficient manner almost entirely unassisted by the teacher. First-graders pass out books, collect papers, straighten up the library corner, feed the animals or birds, water the plants, act as mail carriers between their room and the office, put the playhouse in order, greet visitors at the door, gather up playground equipment after recess, and work together in remarkably responsible ways. Many elementary schools have organized student councils to give young children experience in exercising habits of responsible citizenship. Although the social studies deal directly with citizenship education, such learnings must be supported by the practice of democratic living throughout the school day if they are to be effective.

Earlier in this chapter reference was made to the importance of attitudes as an ingredient of responsible citizenship. Even though there is yet much to be learned about the development of attitudes, there is a growing volume of evidence to indicate that one's attitudes are quite directly related to emotional well-being and balance. That is to say, a person who is unable to meet satisfactorily his personal-social needs develops inner conflicts that bear on his ability to perceive and deal with his social environment. For example, the young child who is rejected by his classmates in play situations is not likely to be favorably disposed toward cooperative behavior and good will toward others. The child who comes from a family that suffers economic privation, rejection, fear of unemployment, victimization, discrimination, or disparagement presents a fertile field for the growth of prejudice, rebellion, hate, distrust, selfishness, and lack of concern for others. It seems that the school's task of building responsible citizenship is much more complex than teaching children a few elements of American history and reciting the pledge of allegiance each morning.

With the recognition of emotional stability as a primary dimension of citizenship, more and more schools are organizing their instructional programs with the thought of helping children meet their basic personal-social needs in socially acceptable ways. It is not likely that any school program can assist all children to meet all their personal-social needs entirely. The child relates and identifies himself psychologically first of all with his family, and it is the family that is the wellspring of his emotional tendencies. But the school can help, and its contributions ought to be in positive rather than negative directions. Teachers, therefore, need to give careful thought to meeting the psychological needs of children, not only while teaching the social studies, but throughout the entire school day. It is becoming increasingly clear that the citizen is first and foremost a person, and the quality of citizenship depends on the balance of emotional forces within that person. To this end teachers today must make careful studies of individual children, take a broader view of their teaching task, and concern themselves with more than the intellectual development of children, important as that is.

Child Development and Social Studies

Since the mid-1950's there has been a growing concern to strengthen content and content-related skills in social studies. Educators and scholars from several of the academic disciplines—especially geography, anthropology, and economics—have studied ways of improving the teaching of these subjects in elementary schools. There is much in this emphasis that is desirable and necessary. Nonetheless, these new directions have the potential of violating sound principles of child development. Programs always need to be planned in terms of the background, ability, maturity, interests, and developmental characteristics of children. In the past, the application of knowledge about children has contributed substantially to improved teaching and learning. It is just as necessary today to apply knowledge about children to the teaching process. The essential point here is that just because programs are soundly based in subject matter does not make it any less necessary to be concerned about the needs of children who are to receive the instruction.

Through the years, growth and developmental characteristics of children have been important considerations in selecting suitable topics for study at various grade levels. This is particularly noticeable in the primary grades. The primary program must of necessity be designed in terms of the things, places, persons, and processes that are psychologically close to the child. Here one finds units dealing with orientation to the school, home and family living, the neighborhood and the community. Because the primary grade child's ability to use vicarious experiences is more limited than it will be later on, many of the concepts and generalizations developed deal with the child's firsthand experiences. As the child grows and matures, he begins reaching out physically and intellectually beyond his immediate environment. He refines his ability to perceive relationships and to integrate previous learnings. He gains greater skill in the use of language and reading as helpful tools in learning about the aspects of the world environment that he cannot experience directly. This expanding interest and concern on the part of the child is known as *widening of horizons* and has been a fundamental principle in planning experiences for children.[6] It has its roots in a knowledge of children and how they grow and develop.

A visit to elementary school classrooms in which pupils are en-

6. For a criticism of an overly rigid application of the *widening-horizon principle*, see pp. 49–50.

For very young children even simple motor tasks necessitate a high degree of concentration to be performed. (Courtesy of the Washington State Office of Public Instruction, Olympia)

gaged in social studies units will illustrate the influence of the child-development approach in the teaching procedures used and the activities performed by the children. There is likely to be a good balance between activities that demand sustained attention and "quiet time" and those that allow children more physical freedom. There will be flexibility in requirements rather than a uniform standard of achievement that all are expected to attain. In the primary grades there will be more overt physical activity, larger illustrative materials, more dramatic play, and more concrete firsthand experiences than in the middle and upper grades. The middle- and upper-grade classrooms will provide for the wide range of abilities and achievement that characterizes those grades and will take into account the changing interests and values of growing children. Modern teaching procedures in the social studies are not possible unless the teacher has a substantial knowledge of the psychological and physiological characteristics of the learner.

Most teacher-preparation institutions require the preteacher to take courses designed to acquaint him with the growth patterns of children and their implications for teaching.

As we compare current teaching practices with those of earlier times, we find greater application of sound and workable principles of human learning today. Teachers are less preoccupied with "keeping school" than they are with helping children learn. They are more sensitive than teachers were a generation ago to such concepts as readiness for learning, motivation, development of interest, need for backgrounds of experience, and the relationship of the basic needs of children to learning. Good teachers help children clarify their goals of learning; they give children the opportunity to identify purposes of classroom activities by involving them in some of the planning.

Throughout social studies units there is a heavy emphasis on meaning and understanding. Teachers are more concerned with essential meanings that underlie facts than they are in having children master the facts alone. Because language is a primary vehicle of learning, there is a greater awareness of the need to clarify the difficult words and concepts that are so often used without meaning in social studies. In teaching children to generalize, teachers are becoming more alert to the hazards of easy generalizations and overgeneralizations, both of which lead to misunderstanding. Increasingly there is recognition of the affective dimension of many social studies topics, resulting in greater attention to the neocognitive components of social studies education.

Relationship of Social Studies to Other Areas of the Curriculum

There are differing points of view regarding the proper relationship of the social studies to the other areas of the elementary school curriculum, but most schools make some effort to relate social studies activities to the remainder of the school program. Social studies units are viewed as presenting many situations in which the child can use related learnings in a functional setting. For example, good programs make provision for the direct teaching of developmental aspects of reading during some part of the school day and will then provide the child with many situations in which he must use reading skills. Responsible teachers do not expect all children to become proficient readers by having them read in connection with social studies, although they know some children could be taught to read in this manner. The social studies provide a natural setting for the application and use of basic skills in solving problems. Social studies units should not therefore be completely responsible for the total development of reading, writing, speaking, spelling, or number skills, although there will be many opportunities for the use of such skills throughout the unit.

It is important to emphasize that if the teacher is to take advantage of opportunities to teach and reinforce related learnings within social studies units, careful planning will be needed. Often incidental learnings are opportunistic and accidental rather than built into the program in a systematic way. When teachers have the goals of their total program in mind, they can more easily plan their teaching to bring related learnings together, thereby providing necessary reinforcement in many settings.

There is a very close relationship between science and social studies, and the two are frequently combined in the primary grades. Units dealing with food, clothing, shelter, weather, transportation, and communication all have science as well as social studies aspects. A unit developed around the topic of food may be taken as a good example. When units of this type are undertaken in the primary grades, teachers usually help children gain some understanding and appreciation of the complexities involved in the production, marketing, and distribution of various foods. Concepts such as interdependence, cooperation, cleanliness, and work are stressed. It is likely that the unit will deal also with social conventions associated with the consumption of food such as table manners, pleasant conversation, and the use of eating utensils. Differences in foods may be studied and discussed by young children—party foods, picnic foods, breakfast foods, school lunches, foods from other lands, and so on. All these learnings and others similar to them deal almost entirely with concepts related to social studies. In the course of the unit, the teacher may also desire to include experiences that help children understand the conditions needed to grow certain kinds of plants; the need for good food in maintaining health; health hazards in the careless or unsanitary production of foods; elementary physiological effects of certain foods, such as taste buds in determining food flavors; the various edible parts of plants, such as the roots of some, fruits or leaves of others; and so on. It is apparent that this second group of learnings is more closely related to science concepts than to social studies. In the development of the unit, however, both the science and the social studies concepts are included because they help children gain a better understanding of the topic under study, and no effort is made to single them out as "science" or "social studies." Although the same relationship exists in the upper grades, the two areas are ordinarily taught separately. But at any level it is often impossible to distinguish precisely between what is science content and what is social studies because the application of science to living frequently affects social relations. When this occurs, the material should be taught as it contributes to a better understanding of the topic at hand. Even though the inclusion of pure science or experimental science in the social studies program is not recommended, concepts that demonstrate the effects of science on human relationships are appropriate for study within a social studies unit. Units such as Tidepool Science, The Solar System, Aerodynamics, Prehistoric Animals, and Electricity and Magnetism should not be taught as *social studies*, because they are science topics.

Reading and the social studies likewise are closely related. The child uses reading as a helpful tool in social studies and, as he applies his reading skills and abilities in social studies, becomes more proficient as a reader. This is especially true beyond the second grade, where there is greater dependence on printed materials as a source of information. It cannot be assumed that the child learns to read in the basic developmental reading program and simply applies these skills and abilities in the social studies. Reading and social studies are related to the extent that the child needs to be taught reading skills as a part of social studies instruction. This is necessary because of the special types of reading tasks confronting the child in the social studies. Reading social studies content is discussed in greater detail in Chapter 11.

The extent to which oral and written expression, number experiences, and music and art activities can be related to social studies is limited only by the resourcefulness of the teacher. There are reports to share, distances to measure, pictures to draw, plays to write, problems to discuss, songs to sing, and other activities that any group will plan and execute if given the opportunity and the leadership of an imaginative teacher. These are the activities that hold meaning and purpose for the child and are among the ones having the most satisfying outcomes for him. They are the ones he will remember after many of the other specifics have been forgotten. In summary, the teacher will find many opportunities in social studies units for the child to use and apply in a purposeful manner the proficiencies he has learned in other areas of the curriculum, but important skills are systematically taught apart from the social studies.

Discussion Questions and Suggested Activities

1. Select a unit topic for a grade level of your choice and identify the the understandings, attitudes, and skills that would be your objectives of instruction.
2. Identify four specific objectives of the social studies that are achieved through the *content* of the social studies and an equal number that are achieved through the *process of learning*.

3. Identify five role expectancy behaviors of effective citizens in a democracy.
4. What topics do you believe lend themselves well to both social studies teaching and science teaching? Can you identify concepts that are definitely science and others that are definitely social studies?
5. What implications for social studies instruction in the elementary school can be found in the foreign policy of the United States?
6. Talk to an elementary school teacher concerning his social studies program. Cite examples of how his program applies principles of child growth and development in the selection and organization of content and learning experiences.
7. Prepare a short statement defining the role of the social studies in the total elementary school curriculum that you might use with a group of parents.
8. Explain why good social studies instruction is interdisciplinary even in the programs that are nominally single subject.
9. Cite instances of change in social studies knowledge that have occurred since your own school experience.
10. Visit the curriculum laboratory on your campus and study the objectives listed for social studies in the curriculum guides from school systems throughout the country. Make certain to include the curriculum guide for your state and community. Note any interesting differences and similarities among them. How would you account for the differences and similarities?

Selected References

Clements, H. Millard, William R. Fielder, and B. Robert Tabachnick. *Social Study: Inquiry in Elementary Classrooms.* Indianapolis: The Bobbs-Merrill Co., Inc., 1966.

Cordier, Ralph W. "Needed Perspectives in the Social Studies," *Social Education, XXXIII*, No. 1 (January, 1969), pp. 41–47.

Cox, C. Benjamin, and Byron G. Massialas. *Social Studies in the United States: A Critical Appraisal.* New York: Harcourt, Brace & World, Inc., 1967.

Engle, Shirley H. "Objectives of the Social Studies," in *New Challenges in the Social Studies*, Byron G. Massialas and Frederick R. Smith, eds. Belmont, Calif.: Wadsworth Publishing Company, Inc., 1965, pp. 1–19.

Feldman, Martin, and Eli Seifman, eds. *Social Studies: Structure, Models, and Strategies.* Englewood Cliffs, N.J.: Prentice-Hall, Inc., 1969.

Gibson, John S. *New Frontiers in the Social Sciences: Goals for Stu-

dents—Means for Teachers, Vol. 1. New York: Citation Press, 1967.

Gross, Richard E., Walter E. McPhie, and Jack R. Fraenkel, eds. *Teaching the Social Studies: What, Why, and How.* Scranton, Pa.: International Textbook Company, 1969.

Jarolimek, John. *Guidelines for Elementary School Social Studies.* Washington, D.C.: Association for Supervision and Curriculum Development, National Education Association, 1967.

Jarolimek, John, and Huber M. Walsh. *Readings for Social Studies in Elementary Education.* New York: The Macmillan Company, 1968.

McAulay, John D. "Social Responsibility: A Modern Need of the Social Studies," *The Social Studies,* LVIII, No. 3 (March, 1967), pp. 120–122+.

Massialas, Byron G., and Frederick R. Smith, eds. *New Challenges in the Social Studies: Implications of Research for Learning.* Belmont, Calif.: Wadsworth Publishing Company, Inc., 1965.

Michaelis, John U. *Social Studies for Children in a Democracy.* 4th ed. Englewood Cliffs, N.J.: Prentice-Hall, Inc., 1968.

Michaelis, John U., ed., *Social Studies in Elementary Schools,* 32nd Yearbook. Washington, D.C.: National Council for the Social Studies, 1962.

Muessig, Raymond H., and Vincent R. Rogers, eds. *Social Science Seminar Series* (6 vols.). Columbus, Ohio: Charles E. Merrill Books, Inc., 1965.

Patterson, Franklin, ed. *Citizenship and a Free Society: Education for the Future,* 30th Yearbook. Washington, D.C.: National Council for the Social Studies, 1960.

Preston, Ralph C. *Teaching Social Studies in the Elementary School.* New York: Holt, Rinehart & Winston, Inc., 1968.

Roselle, Daniel. "Citizenship Goals for a New Age," *Social Education,* XXX, No. 6 (October, 1966), pp. 415–420.

Shaver, James P. "Social Studies: The Need for Redefinition," *Social Education,* XXXI, No. 7 (November, 1967), pp. 588–592+.

Wesley, Edgar Bruce, and William H. Cartwright. *Teaching Social Studies in Elementary Schools,* Boston: D. C. Heath & Company, 1968.

The Social Studies Program: Directions for Change

There have been dramatic shifts in social studies program planning as a result of the wave of curriculum reform that has been sweeping across America for more than a decade. Conceptions of social studies education that were accepted only a few years ago are now being challenged, revised, or even discarded as we move into the 1970's. There have been disappointments as well as successes in our efforts to reform social studies curricula. Massive projects in curriculum development in which educators had such high hopes have had only limited success.

Curriculum redevelopment in social studies is far from over. Indeed, it may be just beginning. The teacher may well expect to participate in the development

2

of new curriculums or in the revision of existing ones as a regular part of his job. It is important, therefore, that he have an understanding of the problems, issues, and procedures involved in social studies curriculum planning.

A teacher's first concern is for the particular grade he teaches, and he wants and needs to know what its curriculum requirements are. But a single grade is only a small part of the total social studies curriculum. Most learnings in social studies are developmental and are spread over several years of the child's school life. Elementary concepts of geography, economics, and sociology may be introduced in the primary grades, but they lead to advanced courses in those subjects in the high school. Simple map-reading skills are often introduced in the primary grades, but no one would claim that a child can read a map sufficiently well by the time he completes the fourth grade. Concepts and skills are taught, retaught, extended, and enriched throughout several grades of the elementary, junior, and senior high schools. Consequently, the teacher not only needs to have a thorough understanding of the program of the grade he teaches, but he must also have some familiarity with the total program—its point of view, its major goals, its organizational plan, its sequence of content, and so on. When the teacher understands the contribution and place of the program in the grade he teaches to the total framework of the social studies curriculum, he is in a better position to plan his own curriculum.

Some of the curriculum practices in social studies are an inheritance from the time when the eighth grade was the terminal grade for most pupils. Today organizational patterns are changing. We hear more about middle schools than we did a decade ago. The preschool programs are growing, as are post-secondary school enrollments. As increasing numbers of pupils continue their education to include high school and post-high school work, more school districts are planning their social studies programs on a kindergarten-grade twelve, or even a kindergarten-grade fourteen, basis. This practice has much to recommend it because many social studies learnings take several years to develop. Moreover, problems relating to sequence, continuity, maintenance of learnings, and unwarranted duplication of topics can be more easily handled if curriculums are planned over the full range of grades the child spends in school. Social studies learnings are at best difficult for children. The school can remove some of the obstacles to learning by presenting pupils with a carefully planned program that enhances the possibility of achieving the purposes believed to be important.

Planning instructional programs in the area of social studies occurs at a variety of levels: the nation, the state, the community, the school, and the classroom. The effectiveness of classroom instruction will depend ultimately on the comprehensiveness of planning done on each of these levels. Furthermore, there must be a reasonable balance between the amount and the extent of planning done at each level. A carefully outlined program, for example, in a large city system may be so completely filled with prescription regarding when, how, and what is to be taught that it leaves little opportunity for the teacher and pupils to do much planning. On the other hand, a program that offers no more than a page or two of mimeographed suggestions concerning content allocations does not give the teacher the guidance and direction for planning that he has a right to expect. Both these situations are something less than desirable. Let us examine the proper relationship of the various levels of planning to one another.

Planning at the National Level

In the United States, education is legally the responsibility of the various states, and school programs are not subject to official supervision and review by the national government. Nevertheless, there are a variety of agencies and organizations at the national level that have a considerable impact on the planning and teaching of social studies in the nation's schools. The Office of Education within the United States Department of Health, Education, and Welfare has, for example, been very active in assisting with the planning and implementing of improved curriculums in social studies for the nation's schools. It has been particularly helpful in facilitating training programs for inservice teachers and for the teachers of teachers.

In a variety of ways the national government is playing a more active role in the development of educational programs than it once did. During the 1950's, education came to be accepted as an instrument of national defense. As such, it qualified for federal financial assistance. The National Defense Education Act was passed by Congress in 1958. Initially, this act authorized the expenditure of federal funds for science, mathematics, and foreign languages. Gradually, its provisions became liberalized to include several of the curriculum areas, including some elements of the social studies. Under NDEA, state departments of education were able to get funds on a matching basis to enrich and improve their programs in history, geography, and civics. Teachers attended institutes in geography and history where these were offered on college and university campuses. School districts were able to get funds for supplies and equipment to strengthen certain aspects of their social studies offerings.

Federal financial assistance also aided in the improvement of social studies through "Project Social Studies," which was a part of the Cooperative Research Program of the United States Office of Education. Project Social Studies was initiated in 1962. It provided for the stimulation of research and development through curriculum study centers, research projects, and developmental activities.

Curriculum improvement is being encouraged additionally through the allocation of funds made available by the Elementary and Secondary Education Act of 1965, Public Law 89–10. Although not limited to or specific to social studies, its broad-gauge provisions will have a long-term impact on social studies instruction through increased instructional materials, by providing for educational laboratories, by encouraging experimentation and development of programs for culturally handicapped children, and so on. In all cases, requests for federal funds for education are processed through the United States Office of Education.

Through the years several national professional organizations have concerned themselves with the social studies. The Association for Supervision and Curriculum Development has been particularly active in the social studies field. In 1967 it issued a special bulletin stating guidelines for elementary social studies. This document was distributed nationally and was used extensively in program development. The twelve guidelines are listed below:

1. Are the major purposes of the program clearly stated in terms of pupil behavior, realistically attainable, and consistent with the philosophy of a democratic society?
2. Is the program psychologically sound?
3. Does the program show evidence of providing balance in its attention to cognitive, affective, and skills objectives?
4. Does the program provide for sequential and systematic development of concepts and skills that are believed to be important?
5. Are the criteria for the selection of substantive content clearly specified in the program?
6. Is the program of instruction relevant to the lives of the pupils?
7. Is the scope of the program realistic in terms of the contemporary world and the backgrounds of today's pupils?
8. Are the learning activities and instructional resources consistent with the stated purposes of the program?
9. Does the program provide adequately for differentiated instruction?
10. Is the program one that teachers will understand and be able to implement and support?
11. Are the curriculum documents sufficiently structured to provide the teacher with direction, yet flexible enough to allow individual teacher initiative and creativity?
12. Is it possible to evaluate the program in order to establish with some degree of confidence the extent to which major purposes have been achieved? [1]

1. John Jarolimek, *Guidelines for Elementary Social Studies*, Washington, D.C.: Association for Supervision and Curriculum Development, NEA, 1967.

The American Association of School Administrators and the National Society for the Study of Education have each published yearbooks dealing with this area of the curriculum. The monthly journals of many organizations often carry articles relating to the social studies. The American Historical Association has had a long-standing interest in the teaching of history in the lower schools. The National Council for Geographic Education has been particularly vigorous in recent years in improving the teaching of geography in elementary and secondary schools. Its publication, *The Journal of Geography*, often includes articles of interest to elementary teachers.

The National Council for the Social Studies, an affiliate of the National Education Association, has given much leadership and direction to social studies planning at the national level. Its several committees study problems relating to the social studies on a continuing basis. Its monthly journal, *Social Education*, its yearbooks, and its numerous other publications have been widely circulated and have been valuable aids to teachers and social studies curriculum planners throughout the nation. Membership in the National Council for the Social Studies is open to anyone who has special interest in any of the facets of the social studies at any teaching level.

National lay organizations also help shape the social studies curriculum. Such groups as the National Congress of Parents and Teachers and the American Legion, for example, take positions on educational issues and disseminate those views. Although such organizations operate completely unofficially with respect to the actual direction of school programs, their views are felt and reflected in the planning of the social studies.

From time to time there have been proposals for a national curriculum committee in order to ensure a degree of uniformity from state to state in learnings that are vital to the welfare of the nation as a whole. Such a committee or commission would have no legal power to supervise or regulate school curriculums but would function as an advisory group and make recommendations relative to curriculum content and emphasis. A number of social conditions have called attention to this issue again in recent years: high mobility of pupils, conflicts between groups within society, fragmentation of the school curriculum through experimentation and innovation, and pressure on schools by extremist groups.[2] Whatever the merits or limitations of such a national committee may be, there can be little doubt that (1) the deficiencies of

2. Paul R. Hanna, "Design for a National Curriculum," *The Nation's Schools*, 62, September, 1958 pp. 54–56; Allen A. Siemers, "A National Curriculum?" *Social Education*, XXIV, November, 1960 pp. 305–306; Richard E. Gross and Dwight W. Allen, "Time for a National Effort to Develop the Social Studies Curriculum," *Phi Delta Kappan*, 34, May, 1963 pp. 360–366; Richard Wisniewski *et al.*, "Task Force Report." (Recommendation 17: National Commission on Social Studies), *Social Education*, XXXIII, October, 1969 p. 695.

social studies education in one area contribute to the problems of other areas because of the mobility of pupils; (2) the sequence of social studies learnings for individual pupils cannot be achieved if they move in and out of programs that are fundamentally different; and (3) there does need to be some emphasis on common values and common understandings if the nation is to maintain a degree of cohesiveness. In the past there has been some uniformity in social studies programs, despite local and state authority, in curriculum affairs—probably largely as a result of the massive adoptions of textbooks that are marketed nationally.

Those who oppose a national curriculum committee argue that this would represent a dangerous step toward centralization and control of a critical and sensitive curriculum area. They believe that even though such a committee would have advisory functions only, the prestige and status of such a group would give it great *de facto* power. Furthermore, it is argued that such a practice violates the principle of local curriculum planning that is deeply embedded in the American education tradition. Thus, there are convincing arguments on both sides of this important issue, and one can only speculate as to how it will eventually be resolved.

Planning at the State Level

Individual states have the major responsibility for directing educational programs of public schools. Although it is customary for states to delegate much of this responsibility to local school districts, local programs must always be consistent with the principles, laws, or policies of the state. This means that states have retained authority and control over public schools and may intervene in cases where school policies and practices are at variance with the philosophy and recommendations of the state education code.

In the past the states have been somewhat rigid in setting down curricular requirements in the social studies. Many have state laws that require the teaching of the Constitution, United States history, holiday observances, state history, and other topics usually identified with good citizenship. A survey conducted in 1963 by the Robert A. Taft Institute of Government found that "47 of the 50 states participating in the survey have made some statutory provision for required instruction in citizenship." [3] The policy of issuing state courses of study that included very specific instructions to the teachers regarding the subject matter, time to be devoted to each topic, dates to be memorized, events to learn, men to identify, methods to be used, and a great

3. The Robert A. Taft Institute of Government, *Citizenship Education: A Survey for Citizenship Education Among the 50 States*, New York, 1963.

many very specific details was fairly common some thirty-five years ago.

Although slow in coming, there has been a trend toward greater flexibility in curriculum requirements established at the state level. It has been recognized that statutory provisions and state courses of study requiring the teaching of various aspects of social studies indicate a degree of specificity that is not necessary and that, in fact, may be undesirable from the standpoint of sound curriculum practice. A common practice today is for state departments of education to issue *curriculum guides* or *curriculum bulletins*. The curriculum guides outline the broad objectives of social studies instruction in the state, suggest appropriate topics for study at various grade levels, and offer guidelines for program development and desirable teaching procedures. Local schools are advised to use the materials as a *guide* and within that established framework to develop a social studies program that will be most appropriate in terms of local needs.

The role of the state, then, appears to be one of establishing in a general way the objectives toward which the schools of the state should move and of offering leadership in organizing, planning, and evaluating social studies programs at the local level. The state curriculum plan may properly be thought of as a framework on which schools may shape their programs. It indicates the understandings, attitudes, and skills that are thought to be important for every citizen of the state, but the exact nature of the classroom experiences in social studies is left to the local schools. An example of how a state office provides leadership in curriculum development is furnished by the curriculum document issued by Washington State. The guidelines are reprinted here:

WASHINGTON'S NEW GUIDELINES FOR THE SOCIAL STUDIES [4]

Purposes

1. The social studies program should develop the ability to make a critical analysis of enduring social issues through the application of the social sciences in an interdisciplinary manner.
2. The social studies program should develop the academic and social skills necessary for the development of a positive self-concept, the fulfillment of civic responsibility, and the growth of social identity.

4. Anna Ochoa and Gary Manson, "New Directions in Social Studies Education," *Washington Education, 81,* No. 3, December, 1969, pp. 4–6.

THE SOCIAL STUDIES PROGRAM

3. The social studies program should develop responsible divergent thinking.
4. The social studies program should enable the individual to develop his own values rationally.

Content

5. The content selected should be based on general concepts and methods of investigation derived largely from the social sciences and organized around enduring and pervasive social issues.
6. The content selected should be representative of man's experience, cultures, activities, and beliefs.
7. The content selected should be consistent with the current knowledge, theories, and interpretations commonly accepted by the appropriate social science disciplines.
8. The content selected for use in the curriculum should have a direct relationship to the concerns of the students.
9. The content selected for use in the classroom and the learning experience sequence should be planned and modified with regard for the impact on the total K–12 program.

Strategies

10. Instructional strategies should establish learning objectives that describe desired student competencies in specific terms.
11. Instructional strategies should engage the student directly and actively in the learning process.
12. Instructional strategies should emphasize the individualization of expectations, methods, and evaluation.
13. Instructional strategies should rely on a broad range of instructional materials and media.
14. Instructional strategies should use evaluation procedures that are systematic, comprehensive, and in accord with the stated purposes of the program.
15. Instructional strategies should insure opportunities for students to observe and participate in the affairs of the community.
16. Social studies programs should receive vigorous support from the community and the school administration.

Planning at the Community Level

The feeling that the schools belong to the people of the local community and that the local community should have a great deal to say about the operation of its schools, is fundamental to our educational planning. Because there is great diversity among communities in wealth, density of population, socioeconomic status, and occupations, each one has somewhat different educational needs. Even though there would be *basic similarities* in the purposes of social studies programs in a rural community and in a metropolitan community, there might be very great differences in how those purposes were achieved. A study of pollution would necessarily be planned differently for farm children attending a rural school in central Nebraska than it would be if planned for children attending a city school in Omaha. The local community, therefore, must design its social studies program in terms of the backgrounds of the boys and girls who live there.

Operating within the broad framework established at the state level, the local community fashions a pattern of organization to be followed. In smaller systems this is frequently done by using the state guidelines as a starting point and making whatever adjustments are necessary to meet local needs. Some communities, on the other hand, independently develop complete and comprehensive social studies curriculum guides that are suited to the community but that are consistent with the objectives and philosophy of the state social studies program. Most city systems have developed curricular materials of this type. Such projects ordinarily represent careful study and a considerable amount of teacher involvement in the actual planning and preparation of the social studies curriculum. This means that in modern curriculum planning such materials as teaching guides, curriculum guides, and courses of study are not prepared in the central office of the school system and handed down to teachers for their use. It means that teachers themselves shoulder much of the responsibility for their preparation. This approach to social studies curriculum construction is resulting in materials that are more usable than they were formerly, because teachers are able to contribute their knowledge of the teaching process and of the boys and girls of the community to curriculum planning.

School systems now have teachers participate in curriculum planning and revision at the community level in any of the following ways:

1. *Serving on curriculum committees* for such purposes as to select textbooks, to recommend the purchase of audio-visual aids or other instructional resources, to develop teaching guides, to prepare resource units, to determine specific goals for each grade, or to study ways to improve some aspects of the social studies curriculum such as urban studies, environmental contamination, and world understanding.
2. *Participating in workshops* to develop new materials, to learn how

to use a new curriculum guide, to become acquainted with new instructional resources, to plan ways of improving instruction, to learn how to deal with special problems of gifted or slow learning children, and others.

3. *Grade-level meetings* to make recommendations for the purchase of materials, to suggest goals to be achieved, to study suitability of textbooks or other instructional resources, to study ways of utilizing community resources, and so on.

4. *Professional growth conferences, institutes, and meetings* to become familiar with latest trends, practices, or procedures in teaching social studies.

5. *Attending college and university classes and seminars* to become familiar with the latest research on methods of instruction, child growth and development, different models of curriculum revision, and effective strategies for the diffusion of ideas and products.

6. *Visiting school systems* that have recently completed effective and efficient revision of their social studies programs.

7. *Cooperative research activities* to try out tentatively prepared guides or instructional material, to experiment with new units, to evaluate books or instructional resources. The testing of ideas and materials under classroom conditions has become a very important role of teachers in recent years as more and more schools are trying bold, imaginative approaches to social studies education.

Social studies planning at the community level should provide for a smooth transition in learning as the pupils move from one level of schooling to the next. A good learning program shows evidence of systematic development of knowledge, abilities, and skills. This means there must be decisions made at the community level regarding the use of textbooks, audio-visual aids, major topics to be studied, use of instructional materials, areas of major emphasis, and a basic, overall point of view. When experiences are planned in terms of the child's past experiences as well as planned with regard to what is yet to come, learnings follow one another naturally and smoothly, grade by grade, as the child progresses through the elementary, junior, and senior high schools. As was noted earlier, the curriculum should be planned as a twelve- or thirteen-year program of instruction in the social studies in order to do as much as possible to ensure the well-articulated, sequential development of important learnings.

Planning at the School Level

Some amount of planning at the level of the neighborhood school is always necessary, even when there has been extensive planning at the community level. In smaller systems, where there is but one school, community- and school-level planning, of course, are synonymous. The larger the system becomes, or the more heterogeneous the community, with respect to wealth, density of population, socioeconomic status, or occupations, the greater is the need for planning at the school level. The diversity of socioeconomic status found within many if not most large communities has serious implications for local planning of social studies experiences for children. The need for school-level planning is particularly apparent as the nation devotes more of its attention and financial resources to the poor and educationally disadvantaged children.

The planning that occurs at the local school level must be consistent with the social studies program of the larger community in which the school is located. It is at the school level, however, that the program of instruction becomes a reality. This being the case, its largest task is to translate the purposes, content, activities, and experiences suggested at the community level into a program of action that will best suit the pupils who attend the school. The common purposes of a social studies program would necessarily have to be achieved in different ways in a school where the children's parents are almost entirely professional people or high level businessmen than they would in one where the parents are day laborers, foreign born, or not regularly employed. In some schools the children have had the advantages of good language development, books in the home, travel, intellectual stimulation from parents, and cultural contacts that children in another part of town may not have had. These differences are important considerations in planning the methods, procedures, and activities to be used in achieving purposes. It is this aspect of planning that must be done at the level of the neighborhood school.

The local school also has a primary responsibility for establishing continuity in the child's learning. To this end some schools have teachers keep a log of their social studies program that includes the topics studied, the major books and supplementary materials used, the concepts and generalizations taught, the films and film strips utilized, the field trips taken, a brief summary of major activities performed, and the amount of time spent on topics. This information is turned in to the principal's office at the end of the year and is available to the teachers who have the same group of children the following year. Some procedure similar to the one described helps teachers plan social studies units in terms of the program and experiences children have had during the previous year. This does not take into account, however, the fact that groups may not be the same from year to year and that some children have transferred into the group from other schools. For this reason, it is necessary for the teacher to find out from the children themselves the nature of the experiences they had in social studies during the previous year and to plan the program accordingly.

Finally, the local school must provide an atmosphere to encourage and enhance the development of long-term social skills characteristic of democratic citizenship. There needs to be congruity in instructional policies and procedures to hold over from year to year as the child advances through school. In other words, the child should be confronted with a consistent set of policies from year to year. He should not be given a permissive situation one year, a rigid one the next, and an ambivalent one the third.

Planning at the Room Level

When the classroom teacher begins to design his social studies program for the year, he thinks in terms of the planning that has occurred at the school, community, and state levels. He examines the state social studies bulletin, if there is one, for suggestions and recommendations. He likewise consults the local curriculum guide. He finds out as much as he can about the social studies program in the school from his principal, fellow teachers, files, permanent records, and other sources. He finds out what the children have done in social studies during the previous year. He inquires about the nature of the social studies program that will follow in succeeding grades. He studies his group carefully and begins to formulate the major objectives he hopes to work toward during the year ahead.

Armed with this information, the teacher will plan some possibilities for units throughout the year. In this connection he will consider seasonal changes, holidays, various "weeks" (United Nations Week, Fire Prevention Week, Book Week), resource materials available, local events of interest (celebration of a local community centennial, for example), state and national events of interest (elections), and other similar situations or circumstances that can be anticipated and that will have a bearing on the social studies activities during the year. With reference to the specific unit titles or topics, he may in some cases decide in advance what these will be, or he may prefer to wait and involve the youngsters in deciding the exact unit to be taught. Policies vary from one district to the next as to the amount of teacher preplanning required. Whenever possible, the teacher should allow for plenty of flexibility in the details of his planning in order to involve pupils in some decision making when the study is underway. Social studies teaching necessitates continuous day-to-day planning at the classroom level. The manner in which this is handled is discussed in detail in Chapter 3.

We have seen thus far that much planning is required at several

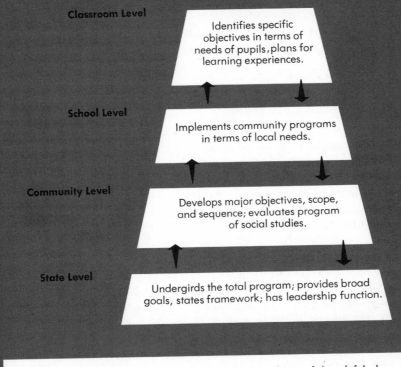

Classroom Level — Identifies specific objectives in terms of needs of pupils, plans for learning experiences.

School Level — Implements community programs in terms of local needs.

Community Level — Develops major objectives, scope, and sequence; evaluates program of social studies.

State Level — Undergirds the total program; provides broad goals, states framework; has leadership function.

Figure 4. Social studies programs should show evidence of thoughtful planning at several levels. Plans become more specific as the classroom level is approached. Planning at the national level is not included on the chart because it is entirely advisory and unofficial.

levels if good social studies programs are to result. This is illustrated in Figure 4. A properly designed social studies curriculum will focus attention on the understandings, attitudes, and skills that ought to be learned by every citizen, irrespective of who he is or where he lives. These purposes are stated in a general way at the state level and become the common threads woven throughout the entire curriculum at all levels. Curriculum planning must necessarily become more specific and detailed as the classroom level is approached, because each school, each class, each child presents some degree of uniqueness in background, interests, and special needs. Good curriculum planning will avoid rigidity and excessive prescription in order that these differences may be taken into account in planning specific experiences for children. In fact, children themselves may and should have some hand in planning *specific* experiences they are to have. But such planning must be done within the context of the overall curriculum design that has been drawn at the state, community, and school levels.

Current Developments Affecting the Planning of Social Studies Programs

The successes of social studies curriculum reformers of the past decade have given us some clear leads as to the direction social studies planning is likely to take in the years ahead. These trends undoubtedly will have a profound effect on the development of new programs, the preparation of teachers, the generation of new learning resources, and the redesigning of conventional instructional material. Each development will be discussed briefly.

CONCEPTUAL APPROACHES

A major shortcoming of past programs in social studies has been the seeming lack of focus on major, profound organizing ideas that provide the learner with organizing frameworks within which he can fit related specific information as he encounters it. These "idea-centered" programs, whether they focus on concepts, generalizations, constructs, basic ideas, main ideas, or major understandings, can be referred to generically as *conceptual approaches* to the organization and implementation of social studies programs. Typical scope and sequence charts of the past showed which topics, subjects, or units were to be studied at specific grades. These were and to some extent still are little more than content allocations for the various grades. But today's more imaginative and forward-looking programs are less concerned with topics, subjects, and units and give attention to the identification of the learnings that are to be stressed. The topics, subjects, and units are regarded only as the vehicles that make it possible for children to learn. Increasingly, schools are defining the scope of their social studies curriculums in terms of key or main ideas selected from the social science disciplines. These main ideas are most frequently expressed as concepts and generalizations and represent conceptual approaches to the selection and organization of content. Conceptual organizations are not unique to the social studies. They have been widely applied in other subject fields, especially in science and mathematics. Organizing knowledge around a few significant main ideas having high transfer value is important in any field with an overwhelming amount of specific information.

In ordinary language, the term *concept* is used to mean idea, as when someone says, "My concept of leisure is not the same as yours." In curriculum development the term has a specialized meaning. Concepts inhere in the universal or common properties of objects, institutions, or experiences. They are categories of meanings and provide a way for the human intellect to organize and classify a vast amount of specific knowledge in a systematic fashion. Verbal symbols are used to identify the categories of meanings that make it possible to deal with meanings at the intellectual, nonsensory level. It is not likely that conceptual thought would be possible without a highly developed symbol system.

As far as is known, the ability to conceptualize is a distinctly human characteristic, as is explained by White in the following passage:

> There are many things that man can do that no other creature is capable of. Only man can appreciate the difference between holy water and ordinary water; no ape, rat, dog, or any other subhuman animal can have the slightest conception of the meaning of holy water. Many primitive peoples distinguish parallel cousins from cross-cousins; all peoples classify their relatives, distinguishing cousin from sibling, uncle from grandfather, etc. No subhuman animal can do this; no monkey can tell an uncle from a cousin. No nonhuman animal can remember the Sabbath to keep it holy; in fact he cannot distinguish the Sabbath from any other day, and he can have no conception whatsoever of holiness. No animal other than man can grasp the meaning or value of fetishes. The lower animals can ascertain the intrinsic properties of commodities, but they can know nothing at all about their prices. . . . It is not that man has a greater, the ape a lesser conception of sin, or that man has merely a superior appreciation of the significance of holy water, or a better understanding of prices. The lower animals are utterly and completely incapable of any of the acts and conceptions cited above.[5]

This material underscores the importance of distinguishing between words and concepts. Concepts *always* have to do with meanings; words are simply verbal symbols. Animals can be taught to respond to words and some can be taught to speak words. But they can never conceptualize the meanings for which the word is a referent. Concepts may deal with concrete places, objects, or institutions or with more or less abstract ways of thinking, feeling, and behaving. Examples of concepts of the first type are mountain, plateau, home, country, state, flood, famine, the dairy, community helpers, valley, ocean, harbor, desert, Chinese, and so forth. The second group includes such concepts as cooperation, adaptation, responsibility, honesty, loyalty, interdependence, justice, fairness, democracy, freedom, liberty,

5. Leslie A. White, "Man and Culture," *The Evolution of Culture*, New York: McGraw-Hill, 1959, p. 4.

tolerance, and rights. Concepts that can be related to concrete reality are more easily understood by young children than are those that are wholly abstract.

Generalizations are similar to concepts in that they, too, help the individual order his physical and social environment. Rather than being represented by a single word or expression, however, generalizations involve the statement of a general law or principle that may be applied to several situations having common characteristics. Generalizations constitute the guidelines by which individuals govern their actions, and many have been handed down through the ages in the form of proverbs or wise statements for good living. They are more complex than are concepts or simple statements of fact. The following are examples of generalizations that have applicability in the social studies:

1. New inventions lead to changes in ways of living.
2. Man changes (adapts) his living to existing conditions.
3. Peoples of the world are interdependent.
4. Members of families help one another.
5. Man influences his environment and is influenced by it.
6. Many peoples have contributed to our present civilization.
7. Basically, all people are very much alike, although they differ in their ways of living because of geographical and historical factors.
8. Man lives in a continually changing world.
9. Workers in our neighborhood help one another.

Generalizations vary in the amount of knowledge they summarize. Compare, for example, the magnitude of the following two generalizations: (1) Members of families help one another. (2) Culture is socially learned and serves as a potential guide for human behavior in any given society. It is apparent that generalizations are not all of the same order. Some are gross, all-encompassing statements that can be applied to many topics, subjects, or units. Others are more specific to a discipline, a region, or a topic. "Geographical factors influence the ways of living of people" is a generalization that might apply to any unit dealing with people, but "Early settlers in the English colonies in America migrated to the New World for a variety of reasons" can only be applied to a unit on colonial life in America. From a practical standpoint, generalizations selected for study should not be so all-inclusive and general that they cannot easily be related to specific content. Neither should they be so specific that they have little transfer value.

During the 1960's a great deal was made of the so-called structure of the disciplines as a way of organizing social studies content for instructional purposes. A considerable amount of controversy surrounds the idea of structure as applied to the parent disciplines of the social studies. Not all scholars agree that the disciplines have a structure; nor is there agreement among scholars as to what constitutes the structure.

The position taken here is that until there is some agreement among historians and social scientists that there actually is a structure to these disciplines and that there is some consensus among these scholars on what the structure is, it is a fruitless exercise to attempt to build a curriculum and teaching plans on the "structure of the disciplines." We are suggesting, therefore, that study units based in the disciplines should simply focus on ideas fundamental to those fields rather than attempt to teach a "structure." These basic ideas are frequently stated as concepts and generalizations.

The use of concepts and generalizations as a system of organizing a social studies curriculum assumes something in the way of inductive teaching procedures. Pupils themselves have to develop the meanings of concepts through many specific experiences and contact with facts and supporting data. One does not learn the meaning of a concept by memorizing its dictionary definition. A child will remember only a small fraction of the factual material he encounters in social studies. Nevertheless, factual information is essential in building conceptual meanings and must be kept in its proper perspective. How many adults, for example, can recall specific facts and data surrounding the concept *colonialism*? Yet, how could the concept have meaning unless one had at some time considerable experience with data associated with it? Dr. Fred Wilhelms has used the example of a lengthy book to illustrate this point.[6] After completing a thousand-page book, who can recall more than a small fraction of the specifics contained in it? But, if the supporting facts and details were not necessary, why would one have read the book? Why not read a ten-page digest of it instead? The reason, of course, is that facts and supporting details build and clarify meanings, even though they will not be remembered and even though the reader is aware of this while he is doing the reading. So, too, facts and specifics are needed in order to build concepts in the social studies. So, too, many of them will not be long remembered. Therefore, a program that spends time hammering away at details and that insists the pupils "remember the facts," is misplacing emphasis.

Growth in the development of concepts and generalizations will proceed more successfully if the teacher bears in mind the manner in which they are learned. Important in this connection is the knowledge that they can be handled at varying levels of complexity. Concepts

6. Fred T. Wilhelms, then Associate Secretary, National Association of Secondary School Principals, in an address delivered at Kelso, Washington, March, 1965.

related to the home, for example, can be studied in first grade, but it is also possible to take courses in home and family life in college. Early in the grades the children learn that "Workers in our community help one another," but the children will continue to expand and refine the meaning of this generalization as they proceed toward maturity and learn of the complexities of marketing, distributing, merchandising, and financing necessary to maintain the modern community. Furthermore, growth in the understanding of concepts and generalizations is directly related to general intelligence and varied personal experience. Concepts introduced and taught at a level of complexity for which the learner is not ready in terms of mental maturity or experiential background inevitably lead to lack of understanding, misunderstanding, or verbalism. The need for many firsthand experiences in teaching concepts and generalizations is of inestimable importance and cannot be overemphasized. This need will be pointed out repeatedly in various contexts in the remainder of this book.

Schools are giving much attention to the possibilities surrounding the use of concepts and generalizations in social studies planning. A necessary first step is to identify the key concepts and generalizations the school is seeking to develop. These may then be broken down into levels of difficulty and placed at appropriate grade levels. This is necessary because, as has already been noted, one does not ever understand a concept or generalization completely, but gradually develops a more mature understanding of it. The concept *responsibility* can and should be taught to first-graders in a way that can be understood by six-year-old children. They will learn more about the meaning of this concept as second-graders, third-graders, sixth-graders, or for that matter, as college seniors. The school must, therefore, operationally define such concepts in the light of the maturity and experience background of the pupils involved.

PERSONALIZING LEARNING

When school learnings are far removed from the personal concerns of learners, they are said to lack relevance—a word commonly heard during the past decade. This problem has been dealt with in the past under the general heading of "Providing for Individual Differences." But personalizing the learning is a more demanding requirement than providing for individual differences. It means more than getting simpler materials for slower learners and getting complex materials for faster learners. It goes beyond what we ordinarily discuss under providing a variety of avenues to learning. This concept—personalizing learning—means that whatever is learned has to make sense to and be vital to individual pupils.

The experiences of the past decade provide us with overwhelm-

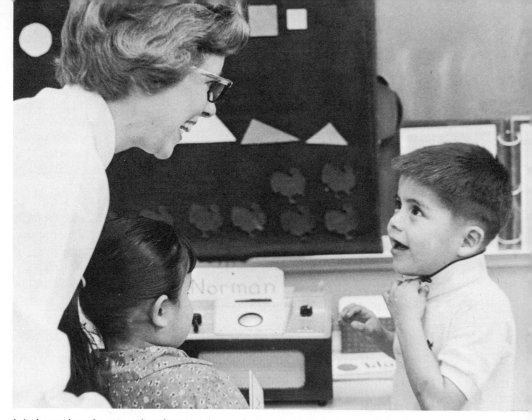

It is the teacher who personalizes learnings for pupils. A first step toward personalizing learning is to develop the kind of trust relationship between the pupil and his teacher that is represented in this photograph. (Courtesy of the Washington State Office of Public Instruction, Olympia)

ingly convincing evidence that our school programs in general and social studies programs in particular are not getting through to a large segment of our school population. The materials of instruction do not relate to the personal backgrounds of boys and girls. The teacher may be out of touch with the ordinary realities of the everyday life of the pupils he teaches. The curriculum content may be similarly out of touch with the personal lives of the children who study it.

Curriculum planning today must take these matters into serious account. The usual conventional criteria for the selection of content and experiences need to be set aside for now, and teachers and curriculum planners must give the highest priority to whether these programs make any sense in terms of the personal out-of-school lives of children. This means that the curriculum must be kept flexible, allowing individual teachers great freedom in adapting the program to pupils. It means, too, that teachers will have to talk with pupils and, conversely, listen—and hear—what the pupils say in return.

Inquiry Orientation

The terms *inquiry, discovery, problem solving, critical thinking, reflective thinking, induction,* and *investigation* have become commonplace in the conversations of teachers. These terms do not all mean precisely the same thing, but they all concern themselves with similar matters. They suggest (1) an emphasis on pupil thinking, (2) an involvement on the part of the learner in the learning process, and (3) a reaction against the idea that teaching is telling and that an education is an accumulation of information.

Basically, there are two teaching styles a teacher may use. One of these is expository and the other is inquiry. There is a place for both in good elementary social studies. It is a mistake to suggest that inquiry strategies are all and always good and that expository strategies are all and always bad. Unquestionably, social studies education has suffered because there has been too much exposition and not enough inquiry. This imbalance needs to be corrected. Inquiry strategies that place a high premium on the pupil's finding things out for himself must become much more common in elementary schools than has been the case in the past.

Multiple Learning Resources

There was a time when a school district or a state changed its social studies curriculum by adopting a new textbook. Today no sophisticated school system would perceive one textbook as an adequate source of idea inputs for social studies. The idea of providing a multimedia program is generally accepted, at least in principle. This has important implications for planning social studies programs, because a greater number of doors can be opened to learning when multiple resources are available.

Valuing

Early efforts to revise social studies curriculums dealt almost entirely with cognitive components. Scholars were asked to identify concepts and generalizations from their disciplines. Much attention was given to the structure of the disciplines and to the ordering of ideas on some continuum of complexity. After a decade of this, we have come to the realization that an important ingredient is missing from our programs. The ingredient is a concern for values and for the valuing process. Knowledge, no matter how well it is organized and taught, comes to the learner through a value screen that he himself has internalized. The learner projects his feelings and values on the data with which he is confronted.

Social studies program planning for the 1970's and beyond will need to come to grips with the values question. These programs must provide pupils with an opportunity to develop and examine their own value system. Additionally, the programs will need to help pupils understand the value systems that guide the lives of people in other societies and in the various subcultures of our own society. To achieve these goals, programs must be characterized by openness, flexibility, and choice making rather than by closure, rigidity, and "find the right answer" procedures.

CONCERN FOR INTELLECTUAL SKILLS

Instructional strategies that stress valuing and thinking have much in common. Both deal with the development of high-level intellectual skills related to thinking: contrasting, comparing, analyzing, evaluating, synthesizing. Indeed, as was noted in Chapter 1, the development of thinking abilities has become one of the high-priority objectives of American education.

With the strong thrust being given to the development of intellectual skills, there is some danger that programs may become abstract, academic, sterile in their appeal to the natural interests of young children. What is needed are strong activity-oriented programs that involve pupils in doing-type exercises that require a high level of intellectual effort. Such programs combine the best of active pupil involvement with the corresponding development of thinking abilities.

THE SEARCH FOR REALISM

The previous chapter stressed the need to present pupils with honest pictures of the kind of world in which they live. The popular expression "Tell it like it is" symbolizes this search for realism. Once we taught children that our country was like a huge melting pot into which people from all over the world came and were converted into idealized-type Americans. Today we recognize that some groups did not "melt" as readily as others and that to pretend there are not identifiable ethnic subgroups within our society is simply contrary to reality. Thus, in the study of our own nation as well as in the study of other people around the world, a greater effort needs to be made to tell the truth and to avoid perpetuating popular myths that do a disservice to certain specific groups.

Occasionally a teacher can be found who, in the name of realism, says things and does things that tend to undermine the confidence of young people in their government, its institutions, or its leaders. It is hard to know what good is served by this kind of cynicism. Sometimes teachers defend such practices on the basis of making pupils aware that historical figures were, after all, human beings and were confronted with many of the same problems of human living that everyone else faces. There is, of course, some merit to this point of view if it does not assume that pupils at all levels of maturity are equally capable of handling such information.

Action Orientation

In past generations the common complaint of adults about the younger generation was their passive, apathetic attitude. This is hardly true today! Now everyone wants to get involved. Everyone wants to "do his own thing." It is the young adult, not the elder, who is impatient with inaction. The young adult who is "turned off" by what he calls the "phoney games played by the Establishment" was probably first "turned off" somewhere down in the elementary grades, probably in social studies.

It seems clear that the social studies programs of the immediate future will be judged inadequate by the students unless they provide for involvement in social action. Certainly, programs must have substantive content and must contribute to valuing and thinking processes. But these components fall short of the mark unless they convert to social action. The elementary school child is not too young to begin applying knowledge to action, thereby making school learning a part of real life for him.

Broad Range of Sources of Content

One of the significant developments of the past decade in social studies education has been the extension of the number of disciplines that contribute subject matter to the social studies program. History and geography remain important, but with increasing frequency one sees economics, anthropology, political science, and sociology in elementary school programs. Some of our nation's most prestigious historians and social scientists have been involved in selecting concepts, ideas, and methods of inquiry from their disciplines for use in social studies curriculums of elementary and secondary schools.

It is immediately apparent that vastly different subject matter can be used to teach the same basic concepts and generalizations. Thus, to a very great extent teacher judgment is involved in selecting subject matter for the social studies. Even in cases where specific units are indicated by the curriculum guide, it is the teacher who makes the final decisions concerning the particular aspects of the topic that are to be emphasized. In the day-to-day work of the classroom, he is constantly making decisions relative to the importance of subject matter—giving priority to some dimensions of a topic, rejecting or depressing the importance of others, and so on.

The subject matter selected should help the instructional program achieve its goals. If social studies curriculums are designed to help pupils develop certain basic ideas, the subject matter selected should be such as to provide the best vehicle for the development of those ideas. If the program intends to develop certain thought processes in pupils, as for example, learning to think geographically, an appropriate topic should be indicated. Or, if the program seeks to teach for generalization and transfer, the units selected should be representative of those to which the ideas are to be transferred.

Topics suggested for various grades do not in themselves tell very much about the instructional program to be built around them. Any topic can be developed in several ways, and the right way to develop it is the one most consistent with and appropriate to the background of experience and knowledge of the pupils engaged in the study. Although many children in the primary grades have a readiness to go far beyond their local areas in their study of topics, one cannot assume that all children will profit from such studies. One group of first-grade pupils may successfully extend its study of "Homes and Families" to homes and families of other lands and cultures. But for another group of first-graders the same study would be inappropirate if the children's knowledge of their immediate world were insufficient—as, for instance, with children who have not ever traveled more than a few blocks from their own homes. The topics listed on pages 50–54 are commonly found in the various grades, but how they are developed in classrooms across the country should and does vary considerably depending on pupil background and teacher skill.

Subject matter in the social studies is vital, interesting, and necessary. Perhaps the reason it sometimes seems to lack these qualities for children is that it serves no real purpose for them. They cannot apply it to the solution of problems because no problems have been identified to which it is related. If subject matter is viewed as a vehicle for the solution of problems, as a tool in gaining a better understanding of the world as the home of man, there is a greater possibility that it will be given the proper emphasis it deserves and that it will have greater appeal for children. Fundamentally, subject matter provides the topics to be used as models or exemplars to get across basic learnings that can be widely applied in new situations yet to be encountered by the pupils.

Achieving Sequence in Learnings

If one assumes that decisions have been made concerning the basic ideas to be developed and concerning the subject matter to be used to develop them, there is still the problem of deciding the order in which

Good program planning takes into account the needs of learners. Every boy the age of these two needs a good buddy, a new pair of boots now and then, and most important, an understanding teacher. (Courtesy of the Washington State Office of Public Instruction, Olympia)

the topics will be taught or the order in which various learning experiences are to take place. In good curriculum-planning, careful attention is given to sequence to avoid unnecessary duplication, repetitions of units, and to ensure continuity of learning from one unit to the next and from grade to grade.

A principle of sequence development that has been widely used in social studies is that of *widening horizons* or *expanding environment.* It is supposed to parallel the natural growth and development of young children. The child's early experiences in school deal with things close to him in the spatial and temporal sense. He first studies things that are happening in the here-and-now. As he matures, his horizons widen; consequently, the program of study also widens to include places and people more remote from him in time and space. This process is often represented by a series of ever widening concentric circles.

The expanding-environment principle was conceived of several years ago when children had fewer opportunities to learn about the world than they do today. Television, radio, travel, and visitors from abroad have done much to push the horizons of the young child out very rapidly. People, places, and topics once thought to be remote from the child might today be psychologically close to him. For example, in one first-grade class, the father of one of the children is a jet pilot who makes regular flights to Japan. Another child spent the last summer in Europe with his family. Most of the others have traveled outside their home state on many occasions. A few have lived in other parts of the United States. All of them watch television regularly. Children with such backgrounds are better prepared to move out of the small circle of their home, school, and neighborhood sooner than children were a generation ago. The expanding-environment principle, therefore, needs to be more flexibly applied today than it was in the past.

Schools have often prided themselves on the orderly sequence of their social studies programs. Scope and sequence charts were prepared to show *what* was to be taught *when.* This tight sequence arrangement rarely worked as well in practice as it did on the charts. The chief difficulty with it is that there is no way of controlling what the child learns about any given topic outside of school. It may be that Mexico is not supposed to be taught until fourth grade, but this will not stop children from reading about Mexico, viewing programs about Mexico on television, visiting Mexico, or, for that matter, having lived in Mexico. Neither will the tight, orderly sequence take care of the transfer pupils. A child may enter the school from another state where Mexico was studied in the third grade.

The backgrounds of children today are such that it is not likely that one could think of any topic appropriate for study in a particular grade that would be entirely unfamiliar to every pupil in the class.[7] This being the case, teachers should not be disturbed when they find that children already have some knowledge of the topic to be studied. What is important is that teachers explore the topic sufficiently with the pupils to find out *how much* they already know. After making this status appraisal, the teacher can plan a program of instruction that is *psychologically sequential* for individual learners. This is possible because most topics can be made as complex or as simple as the teacher desires. Thus, even though a pupil is already familiar with a topic, the teacher can plan the program in such a way as to have him extend and deepen his knowledge of it.

The preceding discussion is not intended to suggest that there is no place for designating a sequence of topics to be studied in the various grades. Some degree of logical ordering based on a knowledge of children and the nature of the subject matter is essential, but such a sequence should not be regarded as sacrosanct. The important point is not that the course of study be logically sequential, for that is easy enough to achieve. What is important is that the learnings are psychologically sequential for individual pupils. If we are to have such psychologically sound sequences, individual teachers must expect to shoulder much of the responsibility in planning for continuity of learning in the program.

EXAMPLES OF UNIT TOPICS FOR EACH GRADE LEVEL [8]

Kindergarten

> Learning About Myself
> School Living
> Learning How My Family Buys Goods and Services
> Differences Among People
> Working Together at School
> Continents and the Globe
> Man Changes the Earth

7. *See* Theodore Kaltsounis, "A Modification of the 'Expanding Environment' Approach," *The Social Studies*, 55, March, 1964, pp. 99–102; Ron O. Smith and Charles F. Cardinell, "Challenging the Expanding-Environment Theory," *Social Education*, XXVIII, March, 1964, pp. 141–142; Dorothy J. Mugge, "Precocity of Today's Young Children: Real or Wishful?" *Social Education*, XXVII, December, 1963, pp. 436–439.

8. This material should not be interpreted as a model curriculum pattern, because it is simply a listing of representative units included in programs across the nation.

Comment: Units for kindergarten ordinarily deal with topics that help to familiarize the child with the world immediately surrounding him. The home and school provide the setting for these studies. With some kindergarten children it is possible to include, in a simple way, references to the world beyond the immediate environment.

Grade One

> The Shopping Center
> Families at Work
> Systems of Action
> Great Americans
> A Japanese Family (comparative study)
> Scarcity and Demand
> Families: Size and Structure
> Families and Their Needs
> Dividing the Work

Comment: The units for grade one are based in the local area, such as the neighborhood, but provision should be made to associate the local area with the larger world. A major criticism of first-grade units in particular and primary units in general has been that they have tended to be too confining and that their content has been thin and inconsequential. Units should provide for easy transition from the near-at-hand to the faraway and back again at frequent intervals—when it is established that the backgrounds of pupils warrant such movement. Neighborhood and community services can be stressed in this grade.

Grade Two

> Suburban Neighborhoods
> Transportation and Communication
> Rural and Urban Communities
> Where and How We Get Our Food
> Soviet Family in Urban Moscow (comparative study)
> How Neighborhoods Change
> Development of Man and His Culture

Comment: The grade-two program should provide for frequent and systematic contact with the world beyond the neighborhood. Through the study of transportation, communication, food distribution, and travel, the child begins to learn how his part of the world is connected to other places on earth.

Grade Three

Our City's Government
Food for the Community
Keeping Cities Up to Date—Change
Communities at Home and Abroad (comparative cultures study)
Life in Early American Settlements
Why a City Is Where It Is
The Parts of a City
Natural Surroundings and People's Actions
The Person: Wants, Actions, Feelings

Comment: The grade-three program often emphasizes the larger community concept: what a community is, types of communities, why some communities grow while others do not, how communities provide for basic needs. Many programs include an outside community for purposes of comparison. Increasingly, schools are giving greater attention to the large, urban community.

Grade Four

Historical Growth and Change of the State
The Beef State (state study)
The Pacific Northwest (regional study)
The Story of Agriculture in the Midwest
Others Who Share Our World (comparative cultures study)
The Story of Industry
India, a Society in Transition (comparative study)
Different Cultures of the World

Comment: In grade four the world as the home of man, showing various geographical features of the earth along with variety in ways of living, is often stressed. These studies help pupils understand some of the adaptive and innovative qualities of man. Home-state studies are popular in grade four; often they are included to meet legislative requirements. Comparative studies are commonly recommended.

Grade Five

Founding of the New World
Indian America
The Making of Our Nation
The War Between the States
An Early American Mining Community
History of the Great Plains

Completion of National Expansion
Four World Views

Comment: Almost everywhere the fifth-grade program includes the geography, history, early development, and growth of the United States. The program may focus on the United States alone or on the United States and Canada or on the United States, Canada, and Latin America. The latter option makes the fifth-grade program a very heavy one. The fifth-grade emphasis should be coordinated with the eighth and eleventh grades in order to avoid redundancy.

Grade Six

Western Hemisphere Emphasis

    Cooperation in the Americas
    The Prairie Provinces
    Three Inca Countries
    The St. Lawrence Seaway and Its Effect on Canadian Growth
    The Organization of American States

Eastern Hemisphere Emphasis

    Ancient, Classical, and Medieval Civilizations
    The Birthplace of Three Faiths
    The U.S.S.R. and Eastern Europe in Recent Times
    Great Discoveries
    The Renaissance and Reformation
    Empires and Revolutions

Comment: The sixth-grade program may include the study of Latin America and Canada or of cultures of the Eastern Hemisphere. Both these patterns are in common use. A major limitation of sixth-grade programs is that they attempt to deal with too many topics. Often this results in a smattering of exposures without the pupil's developing any degree of understanding of anything. The same criticism applies to the seventh grade. Stronger programs emerge where teachers carefully select a few units that are representative of basic concepts having wide and broad applicability. For example, a class need not study all the new African nations to develop some understanding of the problems of newly developing countries.

Grade Seven

    Rise of Modern Civilization
    Africa South of the Sahara

The Home State
International Organizations
The Challenges of Our Times
Developing World Resources
The Age of Technology—Its Effects on Man
Environmental Problems
Principles of Geography

Comment: The nature of the seventh-grade program depends on the content of grade six. Either Latin America or culture regions of the Eastern Hemisphere are popular choices of study for this grade. Some schools are developing exciting programs in anthropology in grade seven. World geography is also included in some districts as are studies of the home state.

Grade Eight

Units relating to the American heritage; the United States, its growth and development

Comment: The study of the United States and of the American heritage is widespread in grade eight. The program usually stresses the development of American political institutions and the development of nationality. The approach typically consists of a series of units arranged chronologically. This program should be planned in the context of the fifth and eleventh grades—which also include elements of American history —in order to avoid unwarranted duplication in the three grades. Defining the emphasis for each of these grades and differentiating appropriately among them in terms of content and approach have constituted a major problem for many schools.

Construction and Use of Social Studies Curriculum Guides

In years past, schools were presented with courses of study by city, county, or state departments of education that spelled out with considerable exactness the precise nature of how, when, and what was to be taught in the classrooms. For reasons already noted, courses of study have to a large extent been replaced by *curriculum guides* intended to help the classroom teacher in planning social studies experiences for children. Today it is standard practice for state departments of education to issue curriculum guides in the various areas of the school program, and these, in turn, have been supplemented by guides prepared by the county, district, city, or school personnel at the local level and under the guidance and direction of local leadership. This arrangement helps keep each level of planning in its proper relationship to the next and makes possible adjustments in the program due to differing educational needs of individual localities. The teacher today is also a curriculum-builder—either formally by serving on curriculum committees, or informally by planning classroom learning experiences for children. In either case the teacher is directly involved and should be familiar with the construction and use of curriculum guides.

There are many types of guides in use today, and even a casual examination of a few will indicate the great variation in their quality and worth. The best ones have the following characteristics: flexibility; comprehensiveness; based on sound principles of child growth and development, human learning, and school-society relationships; and present an overall, balanced plan for growth in human relationships.

Flexibility. The term *guide* is ordinarily used because it is intended to be used only as a guide to the teacher in planning classroom experiences with and for children. Guides are not meant to be followed slavishly or as rigidly as one follows survival procedures in an emergency. They are based on the assumption that the teacher is professionally competent and that he is capable of planning an instructional sequence. Moreover, better schools expect their teachers to be creative and imaginative in their teaching rather than to fall into fixed patterns. It is taken for granted that some adjustment will be made in any program, no matter how well it is planned and prepared, in accordance with the individual differences of children. Beginning teachers frequently feel guides are not specific enough but, as they gain in experience, grow to appreciate the lack of specificity in them. A sound guide is one that will indicate the limits within which the teacher may exercise freedom and choice. It should be a helpful tool to the teacher as he plans the work of his class. In any case, the philosophy underlying any guide is, or should be, *suggestive* rather than *prescriptive*.

Comprehensiveness. Social studies guides vary greatly in their completeness. Some are simply a page or two of mimeographed material; others take on the dimensions of a mail-order catalogue. Even a page or two is better than none at all, but to be helpful to the teacher the guide should be comprehensive. As a minimum, the following ought to be included:

1. A statement of a basic point of view
2. A statement and clarification of the major objectives of the program of instruction
3. An explanation of the organization and content of the curriculum to include
   a. Suggestions relative to the way the guide is to be used

b. A discussion of the overall plan

c. Suggested topics (scope and sequence) for each grade

d. Suggested or sample learning experiences

4. Recommended instructional procedures and practices, such as

a. Use of units

b. The place of textbooks

c. Growth and development characteristics of children and methods of dealing with individual differences

d. Teacher-pupil planning procedures

e. Use of a variety of resources

5. Listing of instructional materials and resources, such as

a. Basic text material

b. Supplementary reading titles

c. Recommended maps, globes, charts, and so on

d. Appropriate audio-visual titles

e. Out-of-school resources available

6. Suggestions concerning the manner in which outcomes of learning are to be evaluated

Based on Sound Principles of Child Growth and Development, Human Learning, and School-Society Relationships. These principles are the foundation of any good instructional program and to ignore them or to design a program contrary to them would weaken the entire curriculum structure. A curriculum guide based on these principles is not likely to go overboard for any one method, approach, or practice. It will contribute to the upgrading of educational practice because it will assist the teacher in applying these principles to classroom activities. Properly constructed, the guide will be practical and usable, consistent with modern educational theory.

Present an Overall, Balanced Plan for Growth in Human Relationships. Social studies education includes a vast number of possibilities for growth in human relationships. Those responsible for the preparation of a guide should recognize the multiplicity of outcomes possible in social studies activities. The program presented should not concern itself solely with the placement of topics in an orderly sequence; neither should it deal only with the social development of children. Those who prepare guides must recognize that children are in school for many years and should envision the child's growth in human relationships through the entire span of those years. A well-prepared guide will show good balance in emphasis on outcomes concerned with information and knowledge as well as skill and attitudinal development extending throughout the child's life in school.

Tentative Rather Than Final. Guides should be inexpensively printed in order that they may be changed frequently without excessive cost. It would, of course, not be reasonable or sensible to have the curriculum in constant turmoil—there will be many constants that will hold year in and year out. In fact, most of the content of a well-prepared guide will wear well and can be used for several years. There will, however, be need for some changes, deletions, or additions as the program is in operation and is evaluated. Unless schools are willing to make a continuous study of their guides and make the appropriate changes following such a study, they will most certainly be faced at about ten-year intervals with making a complete revision, involving much time, effort, and expense. Meanwhile, they have labored and lived with a guide that is apt to become inadequate through lack of revision.

Discussion Questions and Suggested Activities

1. What are some of the advantages and disadvantages of legislative requirements relating to teaching social studies in public schools? What legislative requirements have been formulated for elementary social studies in your state?

2. Show by illustration the differences between a fact, a concept, and a generalization. How are facts, concepts, and generalizations related to one another in teaching and learning in the social studies?

3. Interview an experienced teacher and discuss with him the methods he uses to plan his social studies program. What sources does he use? What persons assist him in planning his program, or is he left entirely on his own?

4. Make lists of the special needs of children living in the central city as compared with children living in a suburban neighborhood. How do you account for any similarities or differences that may be apparent?

5. Study the scope and sequence of a major publishing company's social studies textbook series. How do you think the content was selected? What might have been some of the reasons for the content's being arranged in that sequence?

6. After a social studies guide or program has been revised, it must then be implemented before it can make a difference in the quality of instruction. What strategies might a school system employ to facilitate effective and efficient implementation of a new program?

7. Suggest ways that the expanding-environment principle might be modified in terms of the backgrounds of today's children.

8. Evaluate the following statement made by a teacher: "We have the best teaching guides in our system. They are so complete and tell you just what to do—right down to the very last detail."

9. Why might a sequence that is well organized in terms of the logic of the subject matter fail to be sequential for the learner?
10. Go to the curriculum library on your campus and study one of the social studies projects described in this chapter. How does it differ from the traditional social studies program?
11. What advantages and limitations can you cite for a national curriculum in the social studies?

Selected References

Allen, Jack. "Assessing Recent Developments in the Social Studies," *Social Education*, XXXI, No. 2 (February, 1967), pp. 99–103.

Bruner, Jerome S. *The Process of Education*. Cambridge, Mass.: Harvard University Press, 1960.

Engle, Shirley H. "Thoughts in Regard to Revision," *Social Education*, XXVII, No. 4 (April, 1963), pp. 182–184.

Fraenkel, Jack R. "Curriculum Model for the Social Studies—The Taba Curriculum Development Project," *Social Education*, XXXIII, No. 1 (January, 1969), pp. 41–47.

Fraenkel, Jack R., *et al*. "Improving Elementary School Social Studies—An Idea-Oriented Approach," *Elementary School Journal*, 70, No. 3 (December, 1969), pp. 154–163.

Fraser, Dorothy McClure, ed. *Social Studies Curriculum Development: Prospects and Problems*, 39th Yearbook. Washington, D.C.: National Council for the Social Studies, 1969.

Fraser, Dorothy McClure, and Samuel P. McCutcheon. *Social Studies in Transition: Guidelines for Change*. Washington, D.C.: National Council for the Social Studies, 1965.

Hunkins, Francis P. "Organizing Concept-Based Curricula," *Social Education*, XXX, No. 7 (November, 1966), pp. 545–547.

Jarolimek, John. "Conceptual Approaches: Their Meaning for Elementary Social Studies," *Social Education*, XXX, No. 7 (November, 1966), pp. 534–536+.

Jarolimek, John. "Curriculum Content and the Child in the Elementary School," *Social Education*, XXVI, No. 2 (February, 1962), p. 58–62+.

Jarolimek, John. *Guidelines for Elementary Social Studies*. Washington, D.C.: Association for Supervision and Curriculum Development, NEA, 1967.

Jarvis, O. T., and C. R. Berryman. "Emerging Discipline-Centered Elementary Social Studies Curriculum," *Education*, 88 (November, 1967), pp. 106–111.

Kaltsounis, Theodore. "A Modification of the 'Expanding Environment' Approach," *The Social Studies*, 55, No. 3 (March, 1964), pp. 99–102.

Kenworthy, Leonard. "Changing the Social Studies Curriculum: Some Guidelines and a Proposal," *Social Education*, XXXII, No. 5 (May, 1968), pp. 481–486.

Kurfman, Dana. "National Assessment of Social Studies Education," *Social Education*, XXXI, No. 3 (March, 1967), pp. 209–211.

McAuley, John D. "Criteria for Elementary Social Studies," *Educational Leadership*, 25 (April, 1968), pp. 651–653+.

McNaughton, A. H. "A Generalization Is a Generalization," *The Teachers College Record*, 70, No. 8 (May, 1969), pp. 715–727.

Michaelis, John U. "The Social Studies," *Using Current Curriculum Developments*, rev. ed. Washington, D.C.: Association for Supervision and Curriculum Development, 1965.

Muessig, Raymond H. *Social Studies Curriculum Improvement: A Guide for Local Committees*. Washington, D.C.: National Council for the Social Studies, 1965.

Preston, Ralph C. "Familiarity and Contrast as Curriculum Principles," *Social Education*, XXXI, No. 6 (October, 1967), pp. 491–493.

Skretting, J. R., and J. E. Sundeen, "Social Studies Education," *Encyclopedia of Educational Research*, 4th ed. New York: The Macmillan Company, 1969.

Sowards, G. Wesley, ed. *The Social Studies: Curriculum Proposals for the Future*. Chicago: Scott, Foresman and Company, 1963.

Planning
for Teaching
the Social Studies

The elementary school teacher cannot successfully teach the social studies unless he is able to plan his teaching skillfully. A well-planned lesson will not, in and of itself, ensure a successfully taught one, but careful planning will do much to give the teacher an additional margin of confidence as he approaches his class. Because good planning is basic to good teaching, the beginning teacher owes it to himself to become thoroughly familiar with planning procedures.

Many experienced teachers find it helpful to utilize three types of teaching plans for the social studies. The first type is long-range, covering a period of six to ten weeks or more, during which time the class studies some broad topic, such as "Our Good Neighbor to the

3

North—Canada." A parcel of work such as this is referred to as a *unit* or a *unit of work*. The unit represents a way of organizing materials and activities for instructional purposes. The main purpose of unit planning is to relate learnings to one another and to avoid a program that is highly fragmented by discrete daily lessons. Certain teaching procedures have become associated with units, but because a teacher organizes his instruction on a unit basis does not, thereby, guarantee good teaching.

Because the unit covers a sizable amount of subject matter as well as time, it is often helpful to make additional plans that include shorter blocks of work within the unit. For example, the teacher may want to sketch out the work of the class for a week in advance. Such plans are not necessarily prepared in great detail; perhaps all that is included is the purpose of each day's work and some probable activities. This kind of planning helps the teacher to look ahead and anticipate the direction the unit is to take.

Finally, the teacher needs to plan in detail the work of each day. Daily plans are not to be regarded as separate and distinct "lessons," although the term *lesson plan* is commonly used to designate daily planning. It may also be called a *teaching strategy*, and some teachers prefer that term to the more traditional *lesson plan*. Daily lesson plans should, of course, be made within the context of the overall unit plan and should be continuous from one day to the next. That is, the work of each day is an extension and continuation of the previous day's work.

This chapter is concerned with all three of the types of planning just described. The focus is on the unit because the practice of organizing social studies teaching on a unit basis has won general acceptance in the elementary school. However, the beginning teacher not only will need to know how to plan a unit but also must be able to plan shorter blocks of work and do daily planning. Careful attention to each of these will get the beginning teacher off to a good start in his teaching. Before discussing the structure of the unit plan, however, let us examine more closely some of the learnings with which social studies units are concerned and how these are taught.

Developing Understandings, Attitudes, and Skills

A considerable amount of confusion in teaching social studies could be avoided if teachers would more clearly differentiate the teaching of understandings, attitudes, and skills. Each of these involves different mental processes and is learned differently by the pupils. Therefore, each is taught in a different way from the other two and is also evaluated differently. This is not to say that these learnings should not be taught concurrently; a good lesson in social studies might very well include all three of them. Serious instructional inconsistencies arise, however, when an attempt is made to teach understandings or attitudes as if they were skills, or to teach skills as if they were understandings or attitudes.

Teaching Understandings. Understandings have to deal with knowledge and knowing, in other words with cognitive processes. Understandings involve the acquisition of knowledge of facts, special vocabulary, concepts, and generalizations. It is apparent that understandings vary in their degree of complexity. Knowledge of facts per se requires no more than simple recall and can be acquired by memorization. However, such factual knowledge alone would be of little use to the learner. In order to be useful, a knowledge of facts must be related to some larger, more significant framework. If this is to occur, the learner cannot depend entirely on simple recall but must use higher thinking processes. Consequently, the learner must be confronted with situations that will enable him to obtain wide and varied experience with the ideas concerning the topic under study.

The condemnation of the teaching of facts that occasionally appears in the educational literature can be misleading to the beginning teacher. Facts can be regarded as building blocks that help form some larger idea structure and, as such, are a vital part of the development of understandings. What educators object to is the accumulation of facts that are largely nonfunctional in promoting the growth of understandings. For example, it is a fact of geography that the Andes Mountains extend the full north-south length of South America. A middle-grade teacher might have his pupils learn this as a fact because "it is something everyone ought to know." Possibly so, but this fact would have greater relevance if pupils learned it in terms of the effect these mountains have on the transportation systems of South America and on climate and in terms of the effect they had on the shape of some of the South American countries, on its early history and settlement. We need to recognize that facts are essential to clear thinking about a problem, but when they are taught, we should make sure that they do, in fact, contribute in this way. It is discouraging to visit elementary classrooms and observe class discussions and other activities that are not solidly based on accurate factual information. These practices cannot possibly lead to sound habits of thought in the social studies or engender in the pupils any sense of appreciation for valid sources of information.

Growth in understandings occurs as the individual is able to systematize his thousands of perceptions of the world. From this mass of contact with the world, he sorts, differentiates, relates, generalizes, and organizes his information and uses it to gain new insights. The new learnings that fit into a pattern of something he already knows are likely to be remembered. Learnings that are isolated, unrelated, or considered to be unimportant are easily forgotten. Thus, in a unit on the food market, the primary-grade child learns to differentiate between a butcher shop, a corner grocery, a delicatessen, and a supermarket; but in the process he learns that all serve a purpose, and he may conclude that "a community needs many kinds of food stores." When this occurs, we know his concept of stores is growing and that he is learning to generalize through his observation of the common elements among these stores.

Thus, in order to solve new problems or to do creative thinking in the social studies, the learner must be able to assemble individual pieces of information and relate them to one another to comprehend the connection between what he already knows and the problem confronting him. In this way, he is able to formulate hypotheses that can be tested. Hence, showing the pupils how knowledge already at hand applies to new and novel situations is an important part of the development of understandings. This procedure is fundamental to conceptual approaches to teaching and learning in the social studies.

If we are to teach for generalized knowledge that can be useful in new situations, pupils must be given as many broad and varied experiences with ideas as is possible. They need to view the ideas in a variety of contexts. Citing single examples should be avoided whenever possible, because this presents too narrow an experience for the pupil. When pictures or illustrations are used, several should be presented. Tests of understandings should not be cast in the exact context as presented in the instruction but should be placed in new settings. The teacher needs to ask frequently such questions as these: "Where else do we see this happening?" "How is this like or different from the problem we discussed at newstime?" "Can you give another example of that?" It cannot be assumed that pupils will apply knowledge from one situation to another if left unaided by the teacher. A skillful teacher will pave the way for transfer to take place and, in so doing, will be teaching understandings with wide application. In teaching understandings, the need is not to repeat, drill, and practice. Rather, it is, to enable the pupil to encounter the idea in many settings, each slightly different from the next.

Teaching Attitudes and Values. An attitude may be defined as a predisposition to react in a certain way to objects, persons, or ideas. It may be conscious and willful or may be subconscious; it may be rational or irrational. Attitudes are related to knowledge, although by no means entirely so. One may be fully aware that an attitude is contrary to the facts of the case and may yet persist in it. Attitudes have to deal mainly with feelings and emotions, in short, with affective processes. Because attitudes and values are affective rather than cognitive, there is some considerable question as to the effectiveness of teaching them *directly*. For example, class lessons on "consideration for others" are not likely to be fruitful if this is the only means used to teach this particular value. Children can easily verbalize about desired behavior with respect to consideration for others without reflecting the value in their own relationships. Correct verbal response is an inadequate or inappropriate indication that the pupil has internalized an attitude or value to the point where it is a guide to his own conduct.

Research on attitude development indicates that children are likely to reflect the attitudes of high-status adults with whom they associate and that attitudes are related to the general emotional make-up of the individual. Thus, attitudes and values being promoted by the school may be destroyed by powerful influences on the child from sources outside the school. Many children experience value conflicts in their lives in and outside the school. These conflicts must eventually be resolved on an individual basis, and it is not the responsibility of the school to attempt to get everyone to subscribe to the same set of values. It is the responsibility of the school to help children understand the source of values, attitudes, and beliefs and to alert them to alternatives.

Whether planned or unplanned, attitudes are always an important by-product of the instructional process. A casual, informal remark by a highly regarded teacher is likely to be more effective than a class lesson on a particular attitude. It happens that the social studies area is highly sensitive with respect to attitudes; thus, the teacher needs to exercise care in what is said and how it is said. An unguarded comment by the teacher, no matter how unintentional, might have an adverse and long-lasting effect on the attitudes of pupils.

Because attitudes are related to emotions, the emotional climate of the classroom must foster their growth. Classroom atmospheres that frustrate children by not meeting their social and emotional needs will offer little to the development of wholesome attitudes. Teaching practices that encourage destructive criticism of others, devalue individual worth, and engender hostility and aggression do not provide a satisfactory setting within which desirable attitudes and values can be assimilated. This point is discussed additionally on pages 345–347 of this text.

If attitude- and value-learning are to constitute an important outcome of social studies instruction, unplanned and incidental experiences alone cannot be relied on as a satisfactory means of teaching them. Instead, a planned program of teaching situations needs to be devised. In this connection, Raths, Harmin, and Simon advise adults who seek to help children develop values to

1. Encourage children to make choices and to make them freely
2. Help them discover and examine available alternatives when faced with choices
3. Help children weigh alternatives thoughtfully reflecting on the consequences of each
4. Encourage children to consider what it is they prize and cherish
5. Give them opportunities to make public affirmations of their choices
6. Encourage them to act, behave, live in accordance with their choices
7. Help them to examine repeated behaviors or patterns in their own lives [1]

Teaching Skills. The systematic and sequential development of skills is of utmost importance to children because skills are the tools with which they continue their learning. Consequently, inadequately developed skills tend to retard learning and growth in many areas of the elementary school curriculum. The social studies are no exception in this respect. Inadequate achievement in the social studies can, in most cases, be traced to poorly developed reading skills, inability to handle the vocabulary of the social studies, failure to be able to read maps and globes, poor work-study skills, inability to use reference materials, or retarded language skills. Therefore, a well-balanced program in the social studies must provide for systematic and planned instruction to ensure the development of these skills.

Skill implies proficiency, the capability of doing something well. To have a skill is ordinarily taken to mean that a person is able to respond more or less habitually in an efficient manner. Skills are commonly classified as motor, intellectual, and social. The particular skills with which the social studies are concerned are identified in Chapter 1.

All skills have two characteristics in common: they are developmental and they require practice if they are to be learned. To speak of skills as being developmental means that they are learned through a gradual growth process over a period of years. They are never really learned to completion, although there usually comes a time when the learner feels he has mastered them sufficiently for most purposes. However, one could continue refining his skills throughout his lifetime. Thus, teachers should not assume that skills are taught and learned only once in some particular grade. As the developmental nature of skills becomes better understood, all teachers will assume responsibility for the teaching and maintenance of social studies skills.

1. Louis E. Raths, Merrill Harmin, and Sidney B. Simon, *Values and Teaching: Working with Values in the Classroom,* Columbus, Ohio: Charles E. Merrill, 1966, pp. 38–39.

No amount of explanation or meaningful teaching will make pupils proficient in skills. They must practice and use them in order to build facility. This does not mean repetition or drill in the traditional sense, where a response was repeated over and over in exactly the same way. Instead, it is hoped that pupils will practice skills with the intention of improving their mastery of them. Neither does this mean that skills would be practiced wholly out of their functional setting, although there might be occasions when this would be necessary. In the ordinary work of the unit, there will be numerous opportunities to practice skills in the daily work-study activities of the class. In this way, the child improves his skills *as* he develops understandings. Skills are learned more effectively when they are closely related to actual situations in which they will be used.

Procedures in skills teaching are fairly clear-cut. The pupil should first understand what is involved in the skill, how it is used, and what it means. Providing a good model of its use is helpful at this point. Second, the pupil needs to work through a simple use of the skill under careful teacher guidance. This is essential to verify that the pupil understands what is involved and is making a correct response. Third, the pupil needs additional practice in increasingly complex variations of the skill, applied in functional settings. He needs to use it in solving problems, thus demonstrating its value as a learning tool. Finally, he needs continued practice in its use over an extended period of time, to maintain and improve his facility with it.

Teachers who hope to help children develop skills do not depend entirely on skills teaching to "grow out of something" or be "incidental to something." Rather, the skills are carefully identified, systematically taught, thoroughly practiced, and widely used and applied. This principle applies to such intellectual skills as critical and reflective thinking, coming to valid conclusions based on evidence, evaluating sources of information, and interpreting data as well as to work-study and group-process skills.

In preparing the unit, the teacher will need to take into account the differences in the way understandings, attitudes, and skills are learned and will select instructional activities accordingly. For example, a construction activity might be selected for young children, not because it makes a great contribution to their understanding, but because it provides them with opportunities to develop skill in thinking, planning, and working together. An appreciation experience in art or music relating to social studies might be selected because the teacher feels it has emotional overtones and will enhance desirable attitudes. A field trip might be used because it broadens the pupils' experience and, thereby, contributes to greater depth of understanding. Of course, many activities selected will be multipurpose—they will contribute to the development of understandings and attitudes as well as to the development of skills.

Resource Units

In very general terms, units may be classified into two groups—resource units and teaching units. Resource units may properly be thought of as collections of suggested teaching materials and activities organized around large topics such as "Life in Colonial America," "Nigeria: A New Nation in Africa," "Transportation," or "Conservation." They are frequently prepared by committees of teachers, curriculum workers, state departments of education, graduate classes, workshops, institutes, or commercial agencies. Resource units are not developed with any particular group of children in mind; in fact, the materials may be used in several grades. They cover broad areas of content and always contain more information and suggestions than could be used with any one class. Because they represent general rather than specific procedures, they suggest a variety of ways of achieving the same goal. In a very real sense, resource units should serve as a source of material and suggestions for the teacher when he is planning his teaching unit. The teacher may draw from the resource unit what is appropriate in terms of a specific situation and a particular group of children.

The structure of resource units takes a variety of forms, but the one presented here is fairly representative of the form usually followed. It is an adaptation of one developed by the Wisconsin Cooperative Educational Planning Program.

OUTLINE OF A RESOURCE UNIT

I. *Significance of the topic.* This is a short statement explaining why the particular topic is of importance in the education of pupils. Aspects of the topic to be emphasized and highlighted are noted.

II. *Brief outline of the topic.* Indicates the subject-matter scope of the unit. This may be a conventional outline, a list of questions and problems, or an outline in terms of major and related understandings to be developed.

III. *Possible outcomes.* These should be stated in terms of the understandings, attitudes, and skills *that would be possible* to achieve in the unit. The list will be long; teachers will choose only a few from this list for use in preparing a teaching unit.

IV. *Inventory of possible activities.* This section is the main body of a resource unit and is often the most helpful to the teacher for use in planning a teaching unit.

    A. *Suggested introductory activities.* These are included to help the teacher initiate the unit in a way that will be meaningful and purposeful and that will allow for exploration of pupil interest and are included to facilitate teacher-guided pupil planning. For example, the resource unit might suggest the use of

        1. An arranged room environment: bulletin boards, display table, real objects, books
        2. Films, filmstrips, or other visual aids
        3. A field trip or a resource person
        4. Exploratory reading
        5. Exploratory dramatic representation
        6. Pretest to discover backgrounds

    B. *Suggested developmental activities.* These are designed to help the teacher guide the work after the children get started. They include such types as the following:

        1. *Research-type activities* (reading, interviewing, listening to the radio, seeing motion pictures, and other visual aids)
        2. *Presentation-type activities* (reports, panel and round table discussions, showing of visual aids, making graphs and charts)
        3. *Creative expression activities* (handwork, drawing pictures, writing stories, plays, and poems, singing and playing music)
        4. *Drill activities* (used when students in the group encounter obstacles to further progress. For example, a class might need special work on use of references, map reading, or other skills)
        5. *Appreciation activities* (listening to music, reading for fun, looking at pictures)
        6. *Observation and listening activities* (sharpening the senses of the pupils as an aid to learning)
        7. *Group cooperation activities* (training in democratic group procedures, division of labor among groups leading to cooperation in carrying out plans)
        8. *Experimentation* (learning to try out new ways of doing things, laboratory work, with emphasis on equipment the pupils can make as well as on more elaborate types of equipment)
        9. *Organizing and evaluating activities* (discriminating among and selecting, ordering, and appraising the work done by themselves)

    C. *Culminating or continuing activities.* This section should offer suggestions to the teacher as to how the unit should be brought to a successful conclusion. This would include summary, review, transfer of learnings, sharing with others, and suggestions for continuing study. Several suggestions should be presented in order that the teacher have a wide choice of appropriate culminating activities.

V. *Evaluation suggestions.* These include sample tests, pupil self-analysis inventories, rating scales, and observation techniques to be used *throughout* a unit of work. Stress should be placed on trying to find evaluation techniques that bring out not only what the students *learn* about a topic but also what they *do* about it.

VI. *Listing of materials for reference purposes.* This part of the resource unit should include lists of readings (books, magazines, newspapers), audio-visual aids, community resources, art and music materials, and the like, whenever they are appropriate to the topic under consideration in the resource unit.

Well-prepared resource units help conserve a teacher's time, energy, and effort. Instead of the teacher's having to spend valuable time perusing the library for books dealing with some aspect of community life, for example, he could find appropriate graded titles in a resource unit dealing with the topic under study. Similar examples could be cited for the use of audio-visual materials, community resources, maps, globes, stories, poems, records, and other instructional materials. The resource unit also serves as a storehouse of suggested instructional practices and activities, making it less necessary for the teacher himself to attempt to think of the many opportunities for good teaching that are possible in most units. This in no sense need curtail the teacher's originality or imagination, because ideas usually need to be modified to fit specific situations. Failure to consult the resource unit simply means that a teacher is likely to overlook some good possibilities for teaching as he plans his unit at the end of a busy day in the classroom. In this respect, well-constructed resource units contribute directly to the improvement of instruction in a school.

Obtaining a large supply of resource units on many topics is no small task. Some systems require each teacher to develop one resource unit each year. Other systems have committees of teachers responsible for the preparation of resource units on a variety of topics. Units prepared in this manner are then reproduced in multiple and made available to all schools in the system. Resource units can be obtained from commercial agencies, usually for a nominal fee. Some large school districts, as well as colleges and universities through their campus

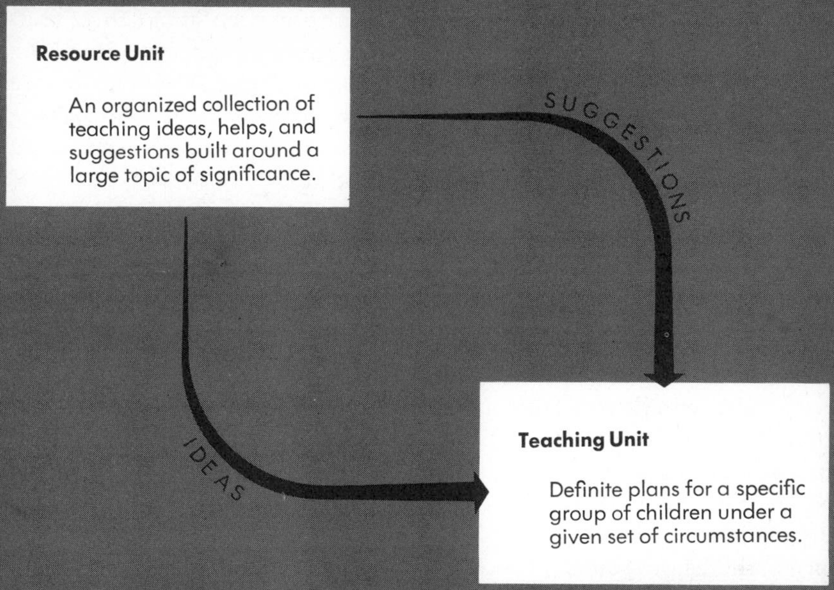

Resource Unit

An organized collection of teaching ideas, helps, and suggestions built around a large topic of significance.

SUGGESTIONS

IDEAS

Teaching Unit

Definite plans for a specific group of children under a given set of circumstances.

Figure 5. The resource unit is a reserve from which the teacher may draw ideas, suggestions, and aids when he plans the teaching unit.

laboratory schools, prepare and are willing to distribute resource units for a small charge. The school that fully recognizes the value of resource units, both as timesavers for teachers and as a means of improving instruction, will utilize many methods to build its supply of them.[2]

School districts may have curriculum materials that are much like resource units but call them by another name: Resource Kits, Resource Collections, and Teaching Guides are designations often used. Whatever they are called, the basic idea is the same in any case. The intention is to pull together into a single source a great many ideas to help the classroom teacher in his organizing, planning, and teaching.

Teaching Units

Teaching units differ from resource units in several respects. Ordinarily, the teacher preparing the unit has a specific group of children in

2. Wilhelmina Hill, "Elementary Social Studies," *Selected Resource Units*, Washington, D.C.: National Council for the Social Studies, 1961.

**PLANNING FOR TEACHING
THE SOCIAL STUDIES**

mind and has at his disposal a wealth of information about their abilities, interests, levels of reading, special weaknesses and strengths. The teaching unit is planned in terms of the known characteristics of the particular class involved in the unit. The topic under study in teaching units is not as broad as it is in resource units. Whereas resource units are general in nature, teaching units are specific.

The term *unit* is one of the terms in education that has taken on a variety of meanings. It is unlikely that there is a single definition of the unit that would be acceptable to everyone, although most authors who use it in the educational literature define it. For the purposes of this text, a unit will refer to a way of organizing materials and activities around some broad topic and will (1) include significant subject-matter content drawn from one or more of the social sciences, (2) involve pupils in learning activities through active participation both intellectually and physically, (3) modify the pupils' behavior to the extent that they are able to cope with new problems and situations more competently, and (4) achieve goals thought to be important in the social studies program.

If the teacher wishes, he may distinguish subject-matter units from experience units by the degree of emphasis placed on subject matter in the first case and the child's interests, needs, and problems in the latter case. Good social studies units will strike a balance between these two emphases. All units contain subject matter of some nature, and it is incumbent on the teacher to make certain that what is selected is worthy of concentrated study. On the other hand, good teaching always takes into account the interests, needs, and educational status of the learner. Whether a unit should be subject centered or learner centered is, therefore, not a fair question, because both are important; proper attention to one does not necessarily preclude attention to the other.

FOUNDATIONS OF UNIT PLANNING

The central idea of the unit plan is to design a series of learning experiences that help the child better understand the interrelatedness of various facets of his social and physical environment, as well as to give him experience in processes of thought involved in meeting new learning situations. This immediately suggests that the unit should deal with a sizable topic, one that is really of some significance to his life in today's world. It suggests, too, that plans extend over longer periods of time than a day or two. Prior to the time when units were used in schools, social studies instruction was often given on a day-to-day lesson basis.

The question of the length of the unit and the time that should be devoted to social studies units is frequently asked. Neither of these questions can be answered precisely because much depends on the age of the children, the nature of the topic, the type of curriculum in the school, the degree to which children maintain a high level of interest, the amount of reference material, and other factors. Certainly in the primary grades, units will be of shorter duration than those in the middle and upper grades. Whereas primary-grade children may engage in social studies units that last a few days to a week or two, upper-grade children may study a single unit for several weeks and continue to find themselves in challenging, interesting material. It is safe to say that when interest lags and/or the planned activities are near completion, the teacher should terminate the unit shortly. Ideally, a unit will end prior to the time the children begin to tire of it. The teacher will have to exercise his best judgment in this matter.

Much the same can be said with reference to the amount of time that should be spent on social studies work each day. Many systems require minimum amounts of time that must be devoted to the social studies in each of the grades. Certainly in middle and upper grades the teacher will need to think in terms of an hour to an hour and a half, at least, for the social studies unit. In primary grades this would, of course, be somewhat less. The best arrangement is to schedule a definite amount of time for the social studies but allow for some flexibility in order that the period need not be cut short or overextended simply to meet the requirements of a rigid schedule. If the class has spent most of the period discussing and developing an idea, an additional five minutes may be all that is needed to get an important point across. In other words, five minutes at a critical time might be more valuable to the teacher and to the pupils than a half hour at another time.

The time of day that social studies is scheduled has little to do with the effectiveness of the program. However, teachers often like to have social studies during the first period in the morning because children may bring objects, books, or news stories that relate to the social studies, and they want to share these with the class immediately. As a matter of principle, it is better to schedule the social studies period in one large block of time than two or three shorter ones. Reasons for this are obvious: In unit work, it takes time to organize, to get out the materials such as books, paints, or construction materials before getting into the work itself. Furthermore, these materials must be put away at the close of the period. If time is short, so much of it is used in getting started and cleaning up that little time is devoted to the actual work at hand.

The unit gains its strength from the variety of outcomes that are possible when it is well planned and skillfully executed. Although it is recognized that the unit is not solely responsible for the development of skills, it does provide a functional setting for the application of many basic skills. The unit offers possibilities for the development of critical thinking, problem solving, planning, consideration for others, responsible habits of work, reading, listening, reporting, and experimenting. The extension of knowledge and the development of skills, abilities, and attitudes are all possible outcomes of good units.

The unit also has the advantage of providing a natural situation in which to teach the skills of democratic group action. Development and growth of socialization skills are recognized as basic to unit work. Unless there is opportunity to teach and apply these skills, the units become little more than chapters in books or little more than logically organized segments of subject matter. Teachers who do not allow group work ostensibly because "the children do not know how to work in groups" fail to recognize that the only way children will learn to work in groups is in group situations. This is very much like the beginning kindergarten teacher who instructed her five-year-olds that they could not use the scissors until they knew how to use them.

A third major advantage of the unit is its flexibility in adapting instruction to individual differences of children. Unit planning rejects the notion of fixed, uniform standards of achievement that all must attain and substitutes the concept of continuous progress and growth for individual children. Children have a hand in certain aspects of the planning, which in itself focuses attention on the individual child, his chief concerns, problems, and interests. In units that are well planned and well taught, standards of achievement are kept at a high level, but they are also different for each child. The structure of the unit facilitates this kind of approach to meeting the educational needs of individual children.

Planning and Executing the Unit

A teaching unit is unique to a specific teaching situation and should not be used over again with succeeding groups in just the same way it was originally planned and used. Part of the reason for this is that it is impossible to plan units entirely in advance of teaching them. Units develop and grow under teacher guidance and direction as the class pursues the study of a topic. In a good unit there is continuous planning, evaluating, and replanning throughout its development. This does not mean, however, that there is no need for considerable planning by the teacher prior to the time the unit is undertaken.

Selection of the Unit Topic. In preparing to teach a unit, the first step must be the selection of the title or topic that will serve as the central theme of the study. Schools vary in the degree of freedom they allow teachers in selecting topics for social studies units. In some cases, there is a required list of units to be studied each year, which may or may not have to be taught in a prescribed order. In other situations, there may be a list of suggested units from which the teacher can select those he and the children wish to study. It may be possible, too, that the curriculum suggests centers of interest for each grade, and the teacher can select units that would be appropriate to such a center of interest or theme. Or, there may be no suggested or required units at all—the teacher and children being completely free to select any unit for study suitable to the interests, needs, and status of the class. The precise manner in which the unit will be selected must be done within the framework of the existing social studies curriculum. At this point the teacher will want to make good use of the curriculum guide as discussed in the previous chapter.

When the teacher can exercise some choice in the selection of units to be studied, he needs to think carefully about whether or not a unit is suitable for study for a given group of children. Several sets of criteria for selection of units may be found in educational literature. Most include such considerations as these:

1. Does the unit topic provide a good vehicle for the development of concepts and skills that are important to the social studies program?
2. Is the unit suitable to the maturity of the pupils?
3. Is the experience background of the children adequate for such a study?
4. Is the unit of sufficient comprehensiveness to provide for a variety of outcomes?
5. Is the material of sufficient significance to warrant study?
6. Is there a sufficient amount of books and other learning material available to make possible such a study?
7. Is the material of appropriate difficulty in terms of the child's understandings, interests, and capabilities?
8. Is the unit suitable in terms of the continuity of learning taking place in the classroom, season of the year, and total school program?

Careful attention to the selection of the topic will help eliminate difficulties when the unit is underway. It would not be easy, for example, to study a topic in the middle grades for which there was no reading or other learning material available. Teachers must be able to anticipate problems of this type that may occur in the development of the unit. The use of a set of standards such as those suggested here in the selection of a topic will help to avoid pitfalls later.

Through the years there has been a tendency to cover a great deal of ground in social studies instruction, resulting in broad, survey-type studies. There has been considerable criticism of this practice in recent years. Survey treatments encourage "covering" topics or books, often emphasizing inconsequential or even trivial factual information that is of little lasting value to the pupils. For example, if pupils are to study all of the Latin American nations—one after another—in a five- or six-week period, it is inevitable that data dealing with capitals, products, rivers, capes, and bays will be stressed because there is insufficient time to develop more relevant concepts. Moreover, such shallow study is likely to result in stereotyping people and places because the study is made on a limited information sampling of the area. The development of accurate and authentic concepts takes time—a great deal of time—and survey studies usually are not planned to make room for this needed time. These criticisms and others have led to the recommendation that fewer topics be selected for study and they should be studied intensively. The term *depth study* has been used to designate approaches of this type.

In order to capitalize on the value of a depth study, the topic has to be carefully chosen. It must be one that provides a good vehicle for the development of selected concepts. In addition, the topic should be representative to allow for the transfer of concepts from the situations studied to others to note similarities and distinctive differences. Depth studies require even greater information sources than do surveys. It is assumed that the study will allow and encourage much pupil exploration, comparison of data, and the application of styles of inquiry appropriate to the nature of the topic and to the disciplines inherent in it. Such an approach requires a high level of competence on the part of the teacher to skillfully manage the procedures of instruction. Depth studies are not any more immune to some of the shortcomings of poor teaching than are any other kind of studies.

Organizing Subject-Matter Content. One of the most critical tasks confronting the teacher in unit planning is organizing the subject matter to ensure the achievement of goals believed to be important. When subject matter is carefully organized it is not only easier for pupils to learn informational and conceptual material, but it also becomes easier to teach related skills and related attitudes and appreciations in appropriate and meaningful ways. A major difficulty in much social studies teaching is that the content is often not organized sufficiently well to clarify what it is that pupils are supposed to *learn* in the way of important understandings, attitudes, and skills. In the following discussion, it is suggested that subject matter should be organized around (1) *organizing ideas from the disciplines,* which provide a basic emphasis or focus for the unit, and (2) *main ideas related to the topic,* which serve as the basis for the informational learnings that are to result.

In social studies curriculum planning today an attempt is made to build into the instructional program an emphasis on basic ideas from the various contributing disciplines. These are usually called major generalizations, basic concepts, key ideas, or other similar designations, depending on the preference of the district. Examples of such ideas are listed in various parts of this text where the disciplines are discussed, and a list is also provided in the Appendix on pages 513–518. An examination of these ideas will indicate that they apply to the *discipline* and not to specific topics or subject matter. For example, an idea from anthropology such as "Every society, however primitive, has formed its own systems of beliefs, knowledge, values, traditions, and skills that may be called its culture" could be developed equally well through the study of several different topics. There might be common-sense reasons why one topic would be selected over another, but from the standpoint of the development of the idea cited, the unit could deal with any society. Such statements help define the focus of the unit; they do not specify what subject matter is to be included. The subject matter will, in a sense, be filtered through these organizing ideas from the disciplines. For example, notice the difference in emphasis in these two units, each of which is dealing with the same topic, Japan:

JAPAN: ISLAND COUNTRY OF THE PACIFIC

Organizing Ideas from the Disciplines

1. The art, music, architecture, food, clothing, sports, and customs of a people help to produce a national identity. (*Anthropology*)
2. The economy of a country is related to available resources, investment capital, and the educational development of its people. (*Economics*)
3. Areas of the earth develop bonds, interconnections, and relations with other areas. (*Geography*)

JAPAN: ISLAND COUNTRY OF THE PACIFIC

Organizing Ideas from the Disciplines

1. Geographic factors influence where and how people live, and what they do; man adapts, shapes, utilizes, and exploits the earth to his own ends. (*Geography*)
2. Human societies have undergone and are undergoing continual, though perhaps gradual, change in response to various forces. (*History*)
3. The interdependence of peoples of the world makes exchange and trade a necessity in the modern world. (*Economics*)

PLANNING FOR TEACHING
THE SOCIAL STUDIES

It is apparent that the emphasis in these two units is very different. Moreover, the units could be equally interesting and valuable to pupils. One cannot say that one unit presents a better emphasis than the other —one can only say they are different.

In organizing subject matter the teacher should begin by identifying a few—perhaps two or three—such organizing ideas from the disciplines, keeping in mind that they will provide the focus for the unit. These organizing ideas should be significant, inclusive statements of a general nature that have relevance to one or more of the social sciences. In addition, organizing ideas should be helpful in explaining or predicting natural or social events; they should have broad applicability; they should be general and representative rather than unique; they should express an idea or relationship that the child is not apt to learn through ordinary living outside of school. These ideas will usually be stated as generalizations and will ordinarily be selected by the teacher from the curriculum guide or some other prepared list.

Even after the teacher has identified the organizing ideas from the disciplines providing the focus for the unit, he is still a long way from organizing the subject matter in a way suitable for teaching. In the examples cited here, for instance, we still do not know which ideas about Japan are to be included in the unit. It is, therefore, necessary for the teacher to identify six to eight main ideas *relating to the topic* that will represent what the pupils are to learn. To be internally consistent the main ideas selected must reflect the emphasis suggested by the organizing ideas from the chosen disciplines. To continue the cited example of the unit on Japan, notice how the main ideas reflect the emphasis suggested by the organizing ideas from the disciplines.

JAPAN: ISLAND COUNTRY OF THE PACIFIC

Organizing Ideas from the Disciplines

1. The art, music, architecture, food, clothing, sports, and customs of a people help to produce a national identity. (*Anthropology*)
2. The economy of a country is related to available resources, investment capital, and the educational development of its people. (*Economics*)
3. Areas of the earth develop bonds, interconnections, and relations with other areas. (*Geography*)

Main Ideas to Be Developed

1. Although the Japanese are of a mixed racial background and their cultural origins come from diverse mainland sources (mainland of

Asia), they have developed as an insular nation and have created their own characteristic culture.
2. Agriculture has been the backbone of Japan's economic life.
3. As Japan's population grew, her agriculture was increasingly unable to provide food, cotton, and other raw materials to sustain her growing industries.
4. Japan's progress to an industrially advanced nation was founded on expanding contacts with the outside world.
5. An understanding of Japanese cultural patterns and family organization is important to our understanding of the Japanese people.
6. Japanese art, music, architecture, and food have enriched our lives.
7. Western culture has influenced Japanese culture directly and indirectly.
8. People of the Western world are learning more about Japan and its people through travel, international relations, and increased contact with Japanese people.

The same plan applied to a primary-grade unit might be organized as follows:

COMMUNITIES NEAR AND FAR

Organizing Ideas from the Disciplines

1. In any society the number of consumers outnumbers producers of goods and services. (*Economics*)
2. Increased specialization in production has led to interdependence among individuals, communities, states, and nations. (*Economics*)
3. Certain social functions such as communicating, producing, distributing, and consuming goods and services are primary activities of all organized societies. (*Anthropology*)

Main Ideas to Be Developed

1. People fulfill most of their common needs and desires in the community in which they live.
2. The world is composed of many thousands of communities.
3. Communities establish certain institutions to meet particular human needs.
4. In most communities there are people who work to produce goods for others.
5. In most communities there are people who work to provide services for others.

6. Community living necessitates the establishment of rules and regulations for group conduct.
7. Communities all over the world are changing.
8. Communities of the world are linked by transportation.

The following is an example of a middle-grade unit:

PIONEER LIFE

Organizing Ideas from the Disciplines

1. The early history of a country has a definite bearing on the culture, traditions, beliefs, attitudes, and ways of living of its people. (*History*)
2. Successive or continuing occupance by groups of people, as well as natural processes and forces, results in changing and changed landscapes. (*Geography*)
3. The decisions, policies, and laws that have been made for a given society reflect and are based on the values, beliefs, and traditions of that society. (*Political Science*)

Main Ideas to Be Developed

1. The pioneers were adventuresome people who helped expand our country westward.
2. The pioneers traveled westward on several different routes, all of which confronted them with danger and with natural barriers.
3. Pioneer families were often self-sufficient, cooperative, and tightly knit groups.
4. The pioneers experienced many hardships due to their dependence on their immediate surroundings for much of their food, clothing, and shelter.
5. The pioneers often started whole new communities, establishing governments, schools, and churches similar to those in the places from which they came.
6. Gathering with neighbors was a happy occasion and a chief source of entertainment for early settlers.
7. There were many outstanding leaders among the pioneers who influenced the development of our country.
8. Modern pioneers who are exploring new frontiers in medicine, science, space, and welfare often face some of the same problems and dangers faced by the early pioneers, even though their ways of living are different.

Now that the main ideas are identified, the teacher has circumscribed in a general way the subject-matter scope of the unit. He now knows what the direction and content emphasis of the unit are to be. This procedure will prevent his planning from wandering in several directions without focusing on well-considered generalizations.

A necessary next step in planning is to identify subideas related to each of the main ideas. These can be listed in an instructional sequence, although this is not necessary. In any case, these related ideas will constitute the backbone of the understandings to be developed in specific daily work. Using the first main idea listed here, related ideas might be specified as follows:

COMMUNITIES NEAR AND FAR

Main Idea

People fulfill most of their common needs and desires in the community in which they live.

Related Ideas

1. Man in early times learned the benefits and advantages to be gained in living together.
2. People who live and work together form a community.
3. The ways in which people work together to help one another often influence the development of a community.
4. All communities are alike in some ways but no one community can be a model to all other communities.
5. The community helps its members supply their daily needs of food, clothing, shelter, protection, and recreation.

PIONEER LIFE

Main Idea

The pioneers traveled westward on several different routes, all of which confronted them with danger and natural barriers.

Related Ideas

1. The most frequent modes of traveling were flatboat, Conestoga wagons, prairie schooners, and stagecoaches.
2. Pioneers usually traveled in caravans, with armed men at the front and rear, and at the most favorable time of the year.

3. The chief routes were those that followed favorable landscape features, such as mountain passes, river routes, and lakes.
4. Personal qualities of perseverance and courage were important in the life of the pioneer.
5. As the settlers moved west, the Indians were pushed out of their land and increasingly resented and resisted the encroachment.

The teacher may want to further analyze each of the related ideas into concepts, special terms, facts, and other ideas to be included. This eventually becomes necessary when he prepares his daily plans. Naturally, he does not make an analysis of the type described by pulling ideas out of the air. He would consult his curriculum guide, his teaching materials, the texts he will use, a resource unit (if there is one), commercially prepared unit outlines, and any other relevant resource he can procure.

Establishing Objectives. A most important aspect of unit planning is to determine the instructional purposes or objectives to be achieved. The teacher and class may not always achieve the objectives as completely as planned, but stating them in advance will ensure that the instruction moves with purpose in the desired direction. The pupils themselves may not necessarily be informed of the broad unit objectives, because the function of the objectives is to guide the teacher in his planning. However, when the unit actually begins, it is quite necessary to have the pupils establish goals, too. This is done through teacher-guided planning and helps orient the pupils to the work that lies ahead for them. Such pupil definition of objectives provides the basis for pupil inquiry and will contribute toward providing meaning and purpose for the study. There can be little pupil inquiry as long as the study is perceived as something done to meet teacher requirements. When the pupils themselves seek to find out something, the study more nearly resembles an inquiry setting.

Not all teachers write their objectives, but all good teachers have goals in mind. Insufficient goal clarity, either on the part of the teacher or the child, is apt to lead to the performance of activities that have neither purpose nor meaning. It makes little sense for teachers and pupils to try to solve a problem when no one seems to know what the problem is. Establishing goals for oneself and helping children identify theirs is a primary and continuing responsibility of the teacher.

There are two mistakes often made in stating unit goals. The first is to list too many specific objectives. In some cases, as many as thirty to forty objectives are listed for a single unit; this is unrealistic and impossible to accomplish. Second, the objectives are sometimes stated in

SOCIAL STUDIES UNIT PLAN USING MAIN IDEAS

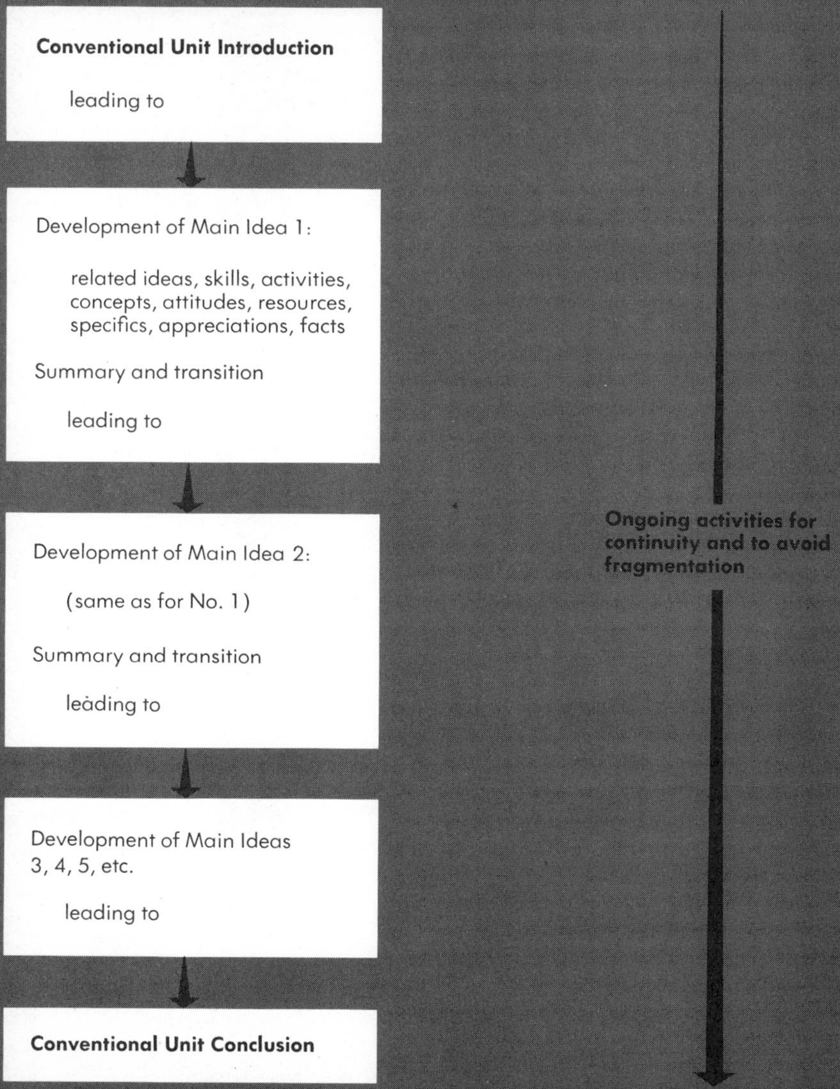
Conventional Unit Introduction
leading to
Development of Main Idea 1:
related ideas, skills, activities, concepts, attitudes, resources, specifics, appreciations, facts
Summary and transition
leading to
Development of Main Idea 2:
(same as for No. 1)
Summary and transition
leading to
Development of Main Ideas 3, 4, 5, etc.
leading to
Conventional Unit Conclusion
Ongoing activities for continuity and to avoid fragmentation

Figure 6. Each of the main ideas needs to be planned by the teacher as is explained in this chapter. Plans can be summarized in chart form such as the one shown in **Figure 7.** Each main idea would take about four to seven days of class instruction. Larger, on-going activities, such as research projects, committee work, construction, art, or dramatic activities are started early in the unit and are continued from one main idea to the next until completed. Daily lesson plans are constructed from the plans for the unit using related ideas as the focus for daily lessons.

SOCIAL STUDIES UNIT PLANNING

Unit Title _____ Grade _____

Learnings to be achieved

Main idea to be developed	Special concepts and vocabulary	Related skills	Related attitudes, values, and appreciation

Resources and activities needed to achieve learnings

Text references	Supplemental references	Audiovisual materials	Community resources	Construction activities	Dramatic representation	Oral and written language

Questions to stimulate reflective thinking

Related curriculum activities

Science	Arithmetic	Art	Music

Note: A plan such as this should be developed for each Main Idea included in the unit.

Figure 7

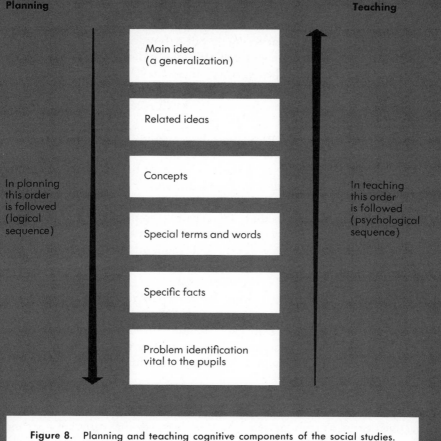

Main idea
(a generalization)

Related ideas

Concepts

Special terms and words

Specific facts

Problem identification
vital to the pupils

In planning
this order
is followed
(logical
sequence)

In teaching
this order
is followed
(psychological
sequence)

Figure 8. Planning and teaching cognitive components of the social studies.

such a general and vague way that they lack directive quality. Objectives stated in such general terms might be applied equally well to an arithmetic lesson, to a reading activity, or to almost any other school experience. For most purposes, five or six well-stated objectives, bearing directly on the topic at hand, will be adequate for the social studies teaching units.

If the teacher has organized and analyzed the subject-matter content as described earlier, he will have already identified the objectives that fall into the category of understandings. If one of the main ideas is "Farms are the source of much of the food we need," this is stated as a unit objective in this way: "Children understand that farms are a source of much of the food we need." This same objective, translated into the children's purpose and placed in problem form, might read, "To find out where most of the food we need comes from."

Of course, unit objectives should not deal with understandings alone. There are important attitudes and skills that need attention, too, and the teacher will want to single out a few for special attention in each unit. This does not mean that attitudes and skills other than these will be ignored. Quite the contrary; there may be, and probably will be, a great many attitudes and skills that become an important part of every unit. However, the ones identified will receive primary attention in the instructional plan.

The three types of objectives—understandings, attitudes, and skills —may not be emphasized to an equal degree in every unit taught. In one unit the chief concern of the teacher may be the development of new knowledge and understandings. In another, he may be less concerned with the development of understandings and may place the emphasis on developing skill in the use of references. On another occasion, he may desire to give the children as much experience as is possible in group and committee work. Most frequently the teacher will have in mind several types of goals to be developed simultaneously as the unit progresses.

The difficulty with not stating definite goals and setting them down in writing is that (1) the unit may proceed aimlessly without getting anywhere, resulting in disorganized and unrelated experiences; (2) there is a tendency to emphasize subject-matter goals to the exclusion of others; and (3) it results in impromptu teaching—sometimes effective but more often not.

In recent years there has been increased interest in stating instructional objectives in terms of learner behavior. Because behavioral objectives focus sharply on what is to be learned, they provide a strong directive function for both teaching and evaluation. That is, the objective identifies the learning outcome in terms of what the pupil will be able to do. What he is able to do must be observable behavior that came about as a result of specific instruction. In writing such objectives, one can indicate specific behaviors that are expected to come under the influence of instruction. For example, the learner

1. Identifies five sources of power used to do work
2. Uses the World Almanac to get specific information
3. Orients a map in terms of cardinal directions
4. Gives an example of division of labor

Notice that these objectives begin with a verb that indicates what the learner will be expected to do, that is, identifies, uses, orients, and gives. A distinguishing characteristic of behavioral objectives is that they begin with a verb. If one states objectives in terms of specific behavior, it is clear that (1) the list will be very long for complex learnings such as social studies and (2) it is not possible to include all the important learning outcomes when one deals with complex learnings. It is possible to write objectives that will define high-level intellectual behavior by (1) stating a broad general objective using the behavioral emphasis, as for example,

a. Understands the meaning of specialized social studies terms
b. Appreciates the contribution of the Spanish to our culture
c. Reads social studies material with comprehension

and (2) citing specific sample behaviors that give evidence of the achievement of the broad general objective, as for example,

Broad, general objective

a. Understands the meaning of specialized social studies terms

Samples of specific behavior

   (1) Cites five examples of technical terms
   (2) Uses the figurative term *iron curtain* correctly in a declarative sentence
   (3) Writes alternative meanings to words with multiple meanings such as *belt, bill, mouth,* and *fork*
   (4) Provides a synonym for terms peculiar to a locality, such as *gandy, draw,* and *coulee*

In some cases it may be appropriate to state the conditions under which the sample of specific behaviors will be observed. In the example that follows notice that (1) a specific passage was to be read, (2) the time limit was set in advance, and (3) the reader was asked to give *four* basic ideas. These three requirements state the *conditions* under which the behavior will be accepted as evidence of the achievement of the behavioral objective:

a. Reads social studies material with comprehension
   Five consecutive pages from a fifth-grade social studies text are selected at random. Given twenty minutes to read these pages, the pupil can
   (1) State six basic ideas discussed in the passage
   (2) Explain in detail one of those ideas
   (3) Illustrate the relationship between two or more ideas

Beginning the Study. Initiation, approach, motivation, or the beginning of a new unit is essentially a matter of building a readiness and interest for the work to follow. Rarely does one find children, or adults for that matter, expressing great interest in a new topic until they have had an opportunity to acquaint themselves with it. The concept of planning experiences in terms of interests and needs of children carries with it the responsibility on the part of the teacher to build interest where none exists and to help children understand their needs.

This phase of unit planning is more than merely getting the unit started. It implies arousing the curiosity of the youngsters, exploring some of the possibilities of the topic, and, in general, setting the stage for learning to take place. In advance of the time the unit is actually undertaken, the teacher will post material about the room that will arouse interest in the anticipated study. He may indicate in class discussions the relationship of the new topic to previous work the class has had. He will have books and other appropriate materials in the room through which the youngsters may browse. He may bring materials to class that will stimulate the thinking of the children. All these activities and others, which the imaginative teacher will use, serve to create interest and will help cause the children to want to learn more about the topic. Through procedures such as these the children will have an opportunity to discover the new material gradually and will be ready to engage in genuine teacher-guided pupil planning. This is quite different from springing a new topic on a group of children and expecting them to identify problems and to make plans for learning activities about a topic that is unfamiliar to them. Unless a readiness has been built for the new material, the teacher-guided pupil-planning sessions are disappointing to the teacher as well as to the children. Time spent at this stage of the study will pay dividends later when learning activities are being planned.

Some teachers use dramatic representation successfully in the initial stages of the unit. Let us assume that a primary class is beginning a unit on transportation. The teacher interests the pupils in having them show through creative dramatics what the workers at an airline terminal do. The children become excited about this and want to start immediately, which the teacher allows. Under the teacher's guidance they begin to plan and to play the representation, but they soon discover that they do not really know enough about the situation to present it accurately. They do not know who the workers are at the terminal, let alone what each worker does. Now they have identified a problem they can understand and can go about their research and problem solving with genuine purpose. This situation also demonstrates the difference between pupil purposes and teacher purposes. Although the example given applies to a primary grade, the procedure can be used at any level in the elementary school.

Other activities can be used in a similar fashion to motivate work, to develop purposes, and to give pupils reasons for doing the things

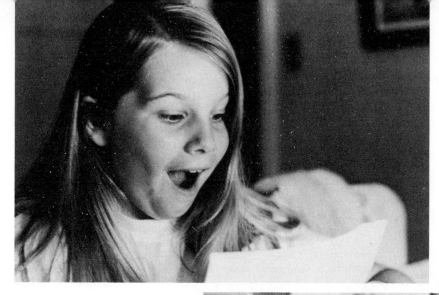

Discovery learning often elicits unexpected expressions of enthusiasm. (Courtesy of the Washington State Office of Public Instruction, Olympia)

they do. The projects, in themselves, are unimportant except as they are able to provide a childlike vehicle for learning. Construction activities are often used in this way. If individual pupils or a class is to build something, they have to learn what goes into it, how it functions, and how it is or was used. One has to be careful, of course, to make certain the time taken in such endeavors is justified by the learnings that result and that it is an instructionally efficient procedure. Much time can be wasted on elaborate projects that involve learnings so simple that a normally intelligent child could understand them after a simple three-minute explanation.

Michaelis describes the initiation of a unit, in part, as follows:

> The classroom is attractively arranged with pictures, realia, maps, books, pamphlets, and other materials related to the first problems to be considered. Children are given an opportunity to examine the materials and to raise questions about them, and so are able to actively participate in the initiation. A film, story, or recording also may be used. During discussion, questions and problems are clarified and may be listed on the chalkboard or on a chart. The teacher may raise further questions to make sure that important points are not overlooked and to guide thinking in directions that he considers most profitable for the group.[3]

Properly understood, this phase of unit development consists of a *group* or *series* of experiences rather than a single experience. Sometimes teachers plan to initiate a unit through the viewing of a film. This single experience is referred to as the "approach." The viewing of a film may be used in the introductory stages of a unit, but this experience should be supported by many others of the type previously described. In one sense, this unfolding process is continued throughout the unit in that each new learning is a readiness for the next. Teachers, therefore, have a continuing responsibility for the development and maintenance of interest and readiness. Time to become familiar with the new topic and building the experience backgrounds of the children are both important in the matter of interest development.

Development: Problems, Experiences, or Activities. A distinguishing characteristic of a good elementary school teacher of social studies is his ability to engage pupils in an interested way in activities that help them achieve learnings believed to be important to the social studies curriculum. One of the unfortunate practices in elementary social studies is using activities without relating them carefully to social studies purposes. This applies to traditional activities such as reading textbook assignments and giving reports as it does to the more in-

3. John U. Michaelis, *Social Studies for Children in a Democracy*, 4th ed., Englewood Cliffs, N.J.: Prentice-Hall, 1968, p. 216.

formal activities such as committee work or some type of expressive experience. Activities are means to ends—they are used to help pupils learn something. This is why it is imperative that the teacher set purposes and know clearly what it is that pupils are supposed to learn *before* he decides what activities are to be used.

Good unit development always makes provision for pupil involvement in the planning of instructional activities. Having pupils participate in planning can do more to overcome the resentful feeling on the part of the pupils that they are "doing assignments for the teacher" than any other teaching procedure. It assists in clarifying goals of learning for the children and allows them to identify psychologically with the unit activities. The many values of teacher-guided pupil planning have been demonstrated in thousands of classrooms for the past thirty years. It is now generally recognized as sound teaching procedure by good teachers everywhere.

Teachers frequently ask about the kinds of activities that can be planned with children. In general, it can be said that pupils can and should plan many of the specific learning tasks undertaken in the unit. Pupil-teacher planning most certainly does not mean that the responsibility for determining the social studies curriculum is placed in the hands of the pupils. As was noted in Chapter 2, a considerable amount of planning occurs at many levels prior to the time the teacher and pupils even begin to plan the specifics of the unit. Some helpful suggestions concerning the kinds of things teachers can plan with their pupils may be found in the Denver Social Studies Program:

1. They find out what they already know about the unit.
2. They list questions and organize them in terms of specific problems which they wish to solve.
3. They set up objectives in terms of behavior changes toward which to work.
4. They set up definite ways of evaluating their progress toward their objectives.
5. They consider experiences which will help to solve their problems.
6. They discuss materials that may be available and where they can get them.
7. They discuss possibilities for culminating the unit.
8. They decide upon their ways of working.[4]

A third-grade teacher and her children summarized their plans for work on a portion of their shopping center unit on an experience chart as follows:

4. *The Social Studies Program of the Denver Public Schools*, Denver, Colorado: Department of Instruction, p. 7.

OUR SHOPPING CENTER

We are going to make a shopping center.
We are making it out of cardboard boxes.
Some boxes will be big; some will be small.
These will be some of the things in our shopping center:

Clothing stores	Furniture store
Parking lots	Restaurant
Children's playground	Jewelry store
Candy shop	Grocery stores
Theater	Large department store

OUR PLANS

Decide what store each box will be.
Put names on the boxes.
Arrange boxes in place.
Paint the parking lots.
Draw roads around the shopping center.

They listed the following items that they wanted to find out about shopping centers:

WHAT WE WANT TO FIND OUT

1. When was the first shopping center built?
2. What different ways can the stores of the shopping center be arranged and still make sense?
3. Why do some shopping centers sometimes stay open later than the downtown stores?
4. Why do some people like to go to shopping centers instead of to the downtown stores?
5. Who owns and operates the shopping center? Do the different stores pay rent?
6. How do the different goods get to the shopping center?
7. Why do some stores have credit cards while others don't?
8. How far do people travel to go to shopping centers? How could we find out?
9. Why is the shopping center located where it is?
10. How do you know or determine how big a certain type of store might be?
11. Why are the different stores where they are in a shopping center?

The teacher can be sure the pupils will benefit from such activities as listing questions on which information is desired, making charts of what to do, finding and listing sources of informational materials, appointing committees, reporting progress, pooling suggestions, making plans for a construction activity, and other similar details. These are the procedures that give real meaning and purpose to the learnings presented in the unit. The pupils will plan, work, evaluate, revise plans, and replan frequently—possibly daily.

Teacher-guided pupil planning can perhaps best be described as an *attitude* on the part of the teacher. It is an attitude of wanting to share ideas with pupils, of sincerely wanting to involve pupils in the work of the classroom, of sensitivity to and respect for the feelings of others. The teacher who approaches his work with such positive attitudes toward children will not need to be told how to involve pupils in planning—he will find opportunities presenting themselves continually throughout the day. He in turn uses these wellsprings of ideas to add freshness, vitality, and interest to his teaching. On the other hand, the teacher who must always be giving assignments and telling children what to do and when to do it will find it quite difficult to do much planning with children. Such teachers usually say they have tried teacher-pupil planning and find "it just doesn't work."

The important elements in sound teacher-pupil planning can be summarized as follows:

1. *Teacher factors.* Teacher is secure with pupils and assumes a nonthreatening posture with respect to himself *or* the pupils. Accepts, clarifies, and restates what pupils contribute as opposed to making a preponderance of evaluative statements. Teacher and pupils seem comfortable with each other.
2. *Types of decisions made by pupils.* Some decisions are clearly the responsibility of the teacher, such as meeting curriculum requirements and selecting units to be studied; others deal with matters of procedure: what information to seek, what resources to use, how to organize for action. Pupils should be involved in these latter matters. They should not be asked to make decisions on questions where there are no alternatives from which to choose.
3. *Classroom climate.* Pupil planning does not work well in a hostile classroom climate. Hostility can be alleviated by reducing negative, destructively critical statements by pupils or teacher. Destructive criticism of others, complaining, disrespect or disregard of others may be inadvertently encouraged even by well-meaning teachers.
4. *Organizing information or planning for action.* If planning sessions are to be more than opportunities for small talk, something

definite must result from them. After the planning session is over, clear-cut plans for next steps need to be made.

5. *Pupil involvement.* Successful planning sessions mean pupil involvement. The planning session cannot be a monologue by the teacher or a conversation between the teacher and a few pupils. It is not necessary that *all* pupils say something, but it is essential that contributions represent a wide sampling of the class and that all pupils are left with the feeling that they have been involved, whether they actually said anything or not.

The exact nature of procedure beyond this point in the unit depends on the age of the children, their past experiences in unit work, their maturity with respect to group functioning, and a number of other variables. It is impossible to describe, therefore, what procedures should be followed except in a general way. The practices described here will have to be accepted in principle and modified to fit specific situations and groups.

A unit is usually begun with a series of exploratory activities—common among these are class discussion, exploring an arranged room environment, reading, or a combination of these. If the group has had some exposure to the topic previously, or if the introductory activities the teacher has used have been extensive, the class may begin immediately to identify problems, list questions on which information is wanted, set up objectives toward which to work, find and list sources of information, and so on. As frequently happens, however, the class is not yet ready for these activities and will want to explore the topic through reading and discussion to determine their course of action. Obviously, a class cannot list questions they want to find out about if they know nothing about the possibilities presented by the topic. When the unit is functioning well, the processes of problem identification, planning, carrying out plans, sharing, evaluating, and replanning will go on continually.

For purposes of explanation and clarity, the unit is usually described in a series of stages or steps, that is, establishing objectives, the approach, and problem solving. In practice, these various phases of the unit blend into each other. For example, as a part of the introductory activity, the teacher may read an interesting and provocative selection to the children that deals with the topic of the unit about to be studied. The teacher is using this as *one* means of building readiness and creating interest. From time to time he stops and raises questions that are discussed, the pupils raise other questions that may or may not be answered, and suggestions are made relative to ways in which the class might learn more about the topic. At this point the unit has moved from the introductory phase to the planning phase. However, the teacher has not yet completed building readiness and will engage the class in many other activities for that purpose, even though the group has already involved itself in preliminary problem-solving activities related to the unit. Similarly, evaluation is ordinarily associated with the final phases of the unit, but in practice the teacher and pupils should begin evaluating progress from the outset of the unit.

In general, the development of a unit consists of a sequence of procedures, each one emerging from the preceding one. In its simplest form, this pattern might be described as follows:

1. *Problem identification* and related information-getting, problem-solving activities such as reading, interviewing, listening, viewing, collecting, using references, doing map work
2. *Application* through expressive activities such as discussing, illustrating, exhibiting, dramatizing, constructing, drawing, and writing
3. *Summarizing, generalizing,* and *transferring* to new situations resulting in identification of new problems of a more complex nature; the cycle is then repeated

This procedure includes both intake and outgo activities on the part of the pupils. They not only take in knowledge in terms of problems vital to them but also must act on knowledge so obtained. Moreover, the pupils must generalize and apply their knowledge to unknown problems and situations. This allows for the widest use of a variety of activities and provides for studies that can be developed in some depth.

As the unit moves into the development phase, each class period or "lesson" should provide for three distinct instructional operations, as shown in Figure 9. Teachers usually begin each day's unit period with the entire class in one group. At this time the previous day's progress is reviewed, plans for the day's work are outlined, work goals are clarified, and the evaluation of the previous day's work may be reviewed. The children then turn to their various tasks while the teacher moves from one child to the next or from one group to another, guiding, helping, clarifying, encouraging, and suggesting. The teacher will terminate the work period sufficiently early to assemble the entire group once again to discuss progress, to evaluate work, and to identify tasks left undone that must be continued the next day. As the children complete their various work projects and are ready to share them with the class, time will be arranged for them to do so. On some days the children may spend the entire period sharing, presenting reports, discussing, and planning. Other days may be spent entirely in reading and research or on work sheets the teacher has prepared because of a special need of the class. (This might occur in a situation where the class

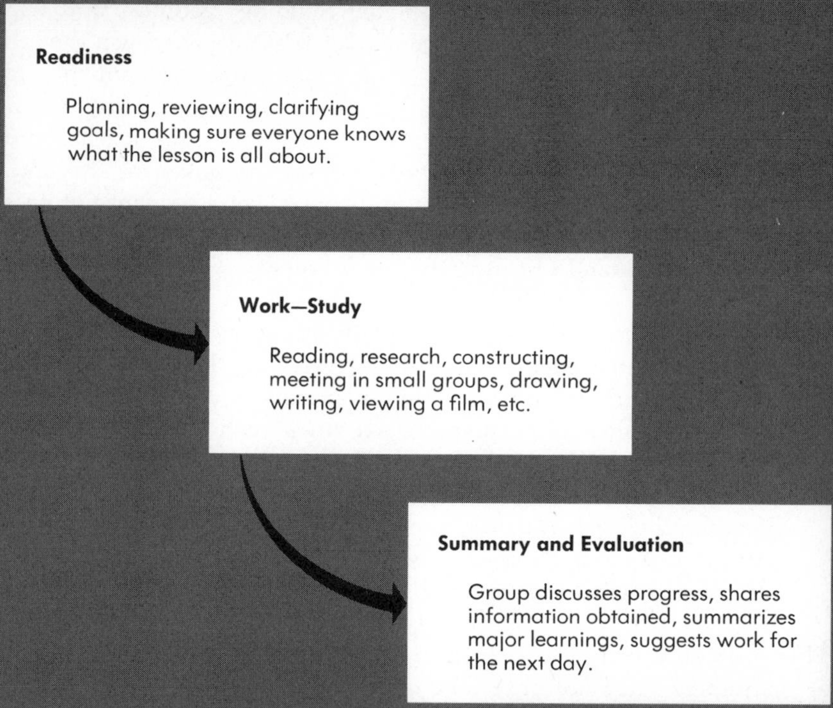

Readiness

Planning, reviewing, clarifying goals, making sure everyone knows what the lesson is all about.

Work—Study

Reading, research, constructing, meeting in small groups, drawing, writing, viewing a film, etc.

Summary and Evaluation

Group discusses progress, shares information obtained, summarizes major learnings, suggests work for the next day.

Figure 9. Three phases of the daily social studies period. The daily social studies period should include three phases as shown by this diagram. Time limits for each phase should be kept flexible because every lesson is unique and some may require more time in one phase than in another.

needed assistance with map-reading skills.) Some days part of the group may be reading while others are preparing a mural and still others are planning a report to be given to the class.

The need for taking time at the end of the work period to summarize what has been learned or to review work that has been accomplished should be underscored and double-checked. Having a clear understanding of the goal or purpose of a learning activity and having knowledge of the progress made in the direction of that goal go hand in hand and are exceedingly important aspects of a good learning situation. Unless the teacher spends some time in helping crystallize what has been accomplished or learned, the children may work for days on end without feeling that they have learned anything or that they are getting anywhere. The teacher should, therefore, take time at the end of the social studies period to have children summarize what they have learned or to evaluate the progress they have made that day. These summary statements should be written on the chalkboard for all to see. Some teachers find it worthwhile to place these daily summaries on charts that serve as a log of the unit work as it progresses. Such logs are helpful in the culmination and final evaluation of the unit.

The work-study or problem-solving phase of the unit is handled somewhat differently in the primary grades than it is in the middle and upper grades. Although children of all ages need many firsthand experiences to extend their understanding of social studies concepts, the older child has a greater familiarity with the world of things and people and can, therefore, profit from vicarious experiences to a much greater extent than the primary-grade child can. Furthermore, the older child can make use of reading as a tool for learning in the social studies, whereas the young child is less able to do so. The physiological and psychological make-up of the primary-grade child makes necessary the utilization of learning activities that involve the child actively on a firsthand experience basis. There are many ways this can be achieved; a few examples are given below:

1. *Sharing with one another.* Miss Sally's first-graders had a table in their room that they used as their "dry dock" in their unit on the harbor. Children brought in toy models of various ships and boats that they told their classmates about and displayed in the dry dock for closer examination.

2. *Construction.* Miss Beth had her class construct a food market in their room. Children accepted responsibilities on various committees that were needed—constructing shelves, the freezer, refrigerator, awning, meat counter, scales. The pupils brought empty food cartons from home for use in the store. The construction was used for creative play activities when it was completed.

3. *Experimenting.* Miss Beaver's class was studying food when the topic of food tastes was discussed. Miss Beaver arranged to get small samples of various foods—coconut, dates, prunes, raisins, pineapple, avocado—and had a "food-tasting party."

4. *Listening.* Miss Jack's second-graders listened attentively when Officer Ray talked to the class on bicycle safety. She has taught them to listen carefully when someone is speaking or when she reads to them.

5. *Discussion.* Mrs. Orr spent most of one social studies period discussing plans for a new bulletin board display on "Winter Fun." Her class contributed many good ideas and observed proper con-

sideration for one another. Mrs. Orr has taught them how to solve problems through discussion and provides some time for discussion of problems each day.

6. *Written-language experience.* Mr. Jones likes to have his class do cooperative group compositions. These may be a poem, a short story, or a very short play. Sometimes they write invitations to other grades, a thank-you note to someone who has done something for them, or a short note to a sick friend. Very often they write about the experiences they are having in their social studies unit.

7. *Dramatic activities.* Miss Mac finds creative dramatics helpful in clarifying ideas as well as promoting social growth among her second-graders. In the train unit, children took turns role playing the ticket agent, the conductor, the passengers, the engineer, or the station master.

8. *Art experiences.* Miss Cook has her first-graders draw or paint pictures that tell a story about the unit they are studying. The children show these to their classmates and tell the story of their pictures. Sometimes these are taken home to show mother and father, and other times they are displayed in the room. One time they made their own picture book and everyone's picture told a part of the story.

9. *Field trips.* Mr. Lee found his third-graders using such terms as blanch, pressurized, sealed, net weight, and jams after their visit to the canning factory.

10. *Processing.* Mrs. Johnson helps her second-grade children understand certain processes by having the children experience them in class. During the years, she has had her class make butter, do simple weaving, make popcorn, make jelly, mold and paint pottery, and bake cookies.

It should be clear to the reader that the work periods in the unit may be handled in a variety of ways. Some of the activities will involve the entire group, whereas others will be individual and/or small-group endeavors. In carrying out this part of the unit, the teacher always makes certain that each child knows what is expected of him and what he is to do. Classrooms operating in this way are places where children are doing things; consequently, they will be moving about, asking questions, and communicating with one another, and a generally informal atmosphere will prevail. But the children are also hard at work and the classroom is an orderly one. The point at which disorderliness and rowdyism take over is the point at which positive results end and at which the many values of the unit are lost. It requires skillful handling by the teacher; and, therefore, one inexperi-

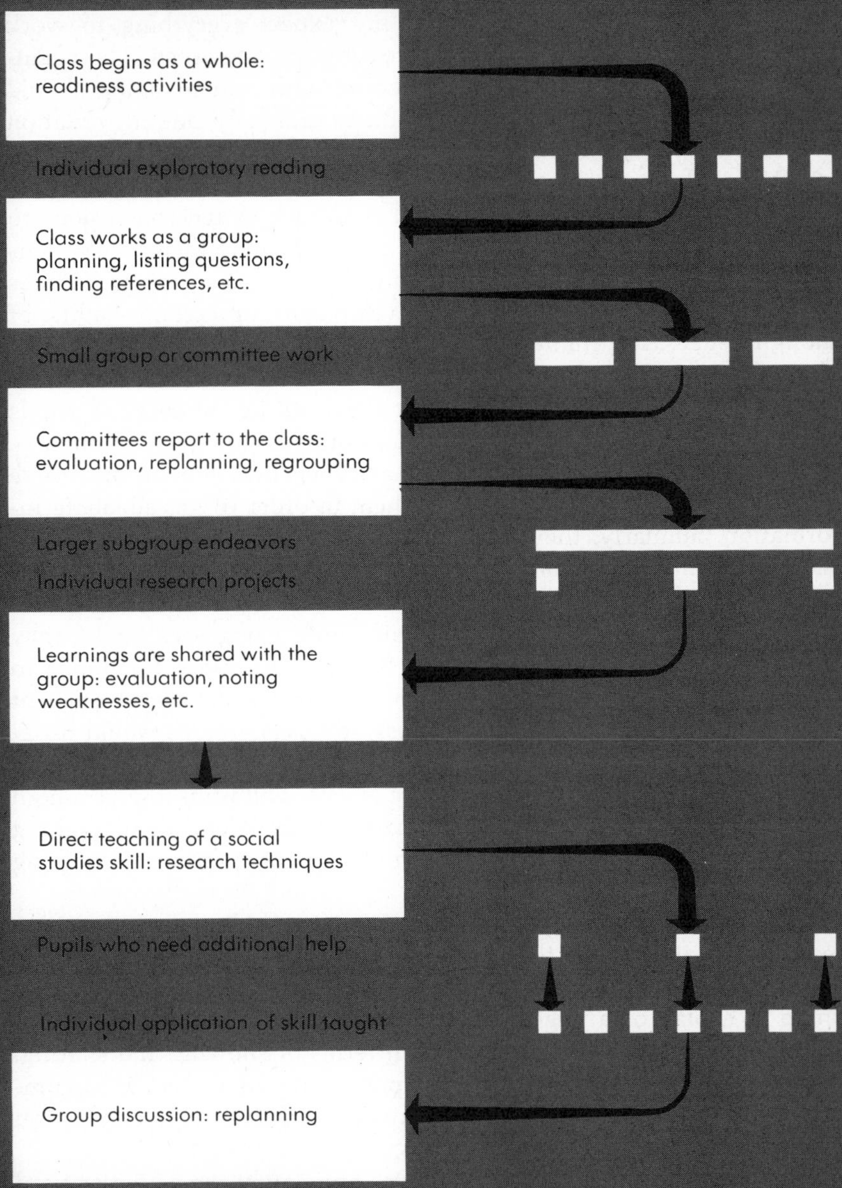

Class begins as a whole:
readiness activities

Individual exploratory reading

Class works as a group:
planning, listing questions,
finding references, etc.

Small group or committee work

Committees report to the class:
evaluation, replanning, regrouping

Larger subgroup endeavors

Individual research projects

Learnings are shared with the
group: evaluation, noting
weaknesses, etc.

Direct teaching of a social
studies skill: research techniques

Pupils who need additional help

Individual application of skill taught

Group discussion: replanning

Figure 10. Possible grouping arrangements as the social studies progresses. There is no set pattern of grouping in the execution of social studies
units. The unit presents the opportunity for a great variety of group situations,
depending upon the purpose of the activity to be performed. Some learnings
can best occur in the group as a whole, others in small groups, while some are
achieved best through independent study.

enced with unit procedures should not expect everything to work perfectly the first few times unit procedures are attempted. The beginning teacher or the teacher inexperienced with unit planning should be well advised to institute unit procedures gradually, adding variation as he feels more secure with it.

One of the weaknesses of prevailing practices in social studies instruction is the tendency of the teacher to give or tell conclusions to pupils rather than have them arrive at conclusions themselves. This tendency is inconsistent with inquiry and discovery teaching procedures so widely recommended. If the development of certain habits of thought, such as openmindedness, testing and checking ideas against alternatives, and so on, are regarded as important outcomes of social studies instruction, it is unlikely that they will be enhanced if pupils are expected to accept the conclusions of others without question.

When pupils are encouraged to make their own conclusions, there must be sufficient data available to them in order to get adequate information. Similarly, they must be led to consider alternatives, even though the alternative may not be the preferred or best response to a situation. If pupils do not consider alternatives and if their data sources are limited (as for example, using only a single textbook), they may come to erroneous conclusions. It is not necessary for pupils to discover everything they need to know—there are other more efficient ways to learn some things. Nonetheless, most classrooms would benefit from more rather than less emphasis on discovery procedures. In planning the activities for the unit, the teacher will want to give a high priority to those that lead pupils to careful and independent thinking and thereby allow them the satisfaction that comes from discovering something for oneself.

Concluding the Study. In years past, concluding activities were much larger affairs than they are today. The class would invite parents and other classes into the room to examine the work displayed and to share in a play or a pageant the class had prepared, and the entire culminating activity was thought of in terms of showing and sharing. Although these procedures may be appropriate under certain circumstances, the trend recently has been away from elaborate exhibits and performances for the benefit of others.

Culminating or concluding activities are simply the activities used to pull together the various learnings that have taken place throughout the unit. This involves coming to conclusions, stating warranted generalizations, evaluating progress, and suggesting areas in which additional study is needed. Unless the culmination is effective, much of the work undertaken during the developmental stages of the unit is left partially undone. The culminating activity serves as a summary— a procedure used to cast various aspects of the unit into relationship with one another and place a capstone on the entire project. Whatever is displayed or shared with others outside the class group is of secondary importance. The value of the culminating activity should first and foremost accrue to the class engaged in the unit.

Culminating activities should include a suggestion of the various interesting facets of the topic left unexplored and about which the children may wish to read and study independently. It is not sound practice to leave the child with the idea that he has learned all there is to know about a given topic. The best education is the one that will encourage and permit the child to continue learning. Culminating activities can and should serve as bridges to new intellectual pursuits.

Evaluation. As was suggested earlier, a class should engage in evaluative procedures frequently throughout the unit. The stopping and taking stock of "How well are we doing?" is one form that evaluation takes. It was suggested, too, that evaluation is a part of the culminating activity because it is here that the class determines the extent to which it has achieved its objectives. Evaluation, therefore, is done by the children themselves within the limits imposed by their degree of maturity and sophistication. Teachers should not underestimate children on their ability to appraise the progress they have made. With help, children can learn to become good judges of whether they have "learned anything." These daily evaluations will help the pupils and teachers identify new avenues of learning to pursue. Many times these goals that emerge as a part of the ongoing study become some of the most important of all. Good teachers are constantly on the alert for these leads to pupil interest and concern.

In addition to whatever evaluation of learning is made by the pupils under the guidance of the teacher, the teacher will independently evaluate the effectiveness of the unit. A sound evaluation of learning cannot be made without knowing what objectives were set up for the unit. It is inconsistent to establish objectives dealing with the development of attitudes, appreciations, ability to work in groups, or concern for others and then to base the final evaluation entirely on subject-matter mastery. Evaluation is made in terms of the objectives established at the outset of the unit and in terms of changes in behavior of children in the direction of those goals.

It frequently happens that the final outcomes of a unit are not synonymous with the objects planned, and it is important to draw a distinction between these two terms. An objective is a desired outcome, the latter being a result of the former. Objectives are determined at the very beginning, even before the teaching is begun, and are foremost in the mind of the teacher throughout the development of the unit. They are the goals the teacher consciously strives to attain. The oucomes are the resultant changes in behavior in the pupils that have occurred through the instructional process. The teacher, therefore, will compare the observable outcomes with the established objectives and will make value judgments accordingly.

Although teacher evaluation is ordinarily associated with the end of a unit, it occurs throughout the unit as does teacher-pupil evaluation. The methods and devices used to assist in this process may be decided on fairly early in the unit, and a variety of methods should be used to observe outcomes. These might include paper-and-pencil tests as well as personal observations by the teacher of such things as improved proficiency in a skill, change in attitude, fewer playground incidents, increased responsibility for self-management, and many other behaviors. A detailed discussion of evaluation is found in Chapter 17.

List of Instructional Resources. Much difficulty is avoided in securing and using instructional materials when teachers plan well in advance what will be needed for the unit. Books, recordings, pictures, films, and filmstrips cannot be secured on a moment's notice and must be requested early enough to ensure their arrival at the time they are needed. In the initial stages of the unit, it is well for the teacher to inventory the available materials needed by the class as they move into the work stages of the unit. Just such a simple matter as knowing what maps will be used and having them in the classroom may make the difference between the use of those materials or not. The teacher will want to make sure that the books, stories, poems, reference materials, fictional materials, maps, charts, globes, newspapers and magazine articles, films, filmstrips, and other audio-visual materials are on hand for the children in the class to use.

Preparing Daily Plans

Because the unit plan of organizing materials for instructional purposes is a flexible one, the teacher will need to make *specific* plans on a day-to-day basis. Unit planning does not preclude the need for daily planning. Each day the teacher must make definite plans for the following day's work. To be sure, some of this is done with the assistance of the pupils—identifying uncompleted tasks, getting additional information on some topic, putting the finishing touches on a mural, having Sarah's group give its report, and so on. But it is the teacher who has the responsibility of pulling together the loose ends and making certain everything is set and ready for the next class period. Good organization will ensure that every child will have a worthwhile task, that everyone knows what he will do, that books, resources, pictures, films, and other materials are available, that needed work is placed on the chalkboard, that appropriate exhibits are placed on the bulletin boards, and that the map Dick's group will need is displayed properly on the map rail. There is no plan that is a substitute for good daily planning—it should take place within the context of the overall unit plan.

Every lesson should have a specific purpose. The purpose should indicate what the pupils are to *learn* rather than what they will do as an instructional activity. For example:

Right: To learn ways in which the same physical environment has been used by people with different backgrounds.

Right: To learn ways that the circle graph can be used to present information.

Right: To learn to use the card catalogue in locating reference books.

Wrong: To make papier-mâché for the piñata. (Wrong because the social studies are not concerned with teaching pupils to make papier-mâché, piñatas, and so on. This is a procedure, not a purpose.)

Wrong: To listen attentively to the guest speaker. (Wrong because this tells what children will do rather than what they will learn.)

Wrong: To independently read library material on the history of Canada. (This, too, tells what children will do in order to learn something but does not tell precisely what it is they will learn.)

Within the body of the lesson, the teacher needs to plan carefully how the lesson is to begin, how the ideas and concepts will be developed in work-study activities, and how the lesson is to close. These three parts of the lesson are included in Figure 9. The lesson plan should also specify which materials will be needed to ensure that they will be available for pupil use. The specific components of a lesson are shown in Figure 11.

Pacing, or gauging the proper time to allow for teaching a lesson, is often difficult for the beginning teacher. Experience in working with children will help the teacher develop skill in pacing lessons properly. As a general rule, a beginning teacher will go through a lesson more rapidly than will a more experienced one. Often, beginners do not realize how long it takes young children to grasp ideas and concepts and as a result rush through the teaching process. Consequently, it is wise for the beginner to prepare more than he thinks can be included, then eliminate some if it is not needed when the lesson is actually taught. This spares him the embarrassment of having his lesson completed when the period is half over.

1) Purpose .... What children will **learn.**

2) Building readiness and interest .... How the lesson is to **begin.**

3) Work-study activities .... What pupils will **do** to help them learn.

4) Summary and evaluation .... How the lesson will **close.**

5) Materials and resources .... What instructional materials will be **needed** to teach the lesson.

Figure 11

Social Studies Units in Multigrade and Nongraded Classrooms

In recent years many schools have placed children from more than one grade in a single classroom. There are several reasons why this is done, one being large enrollments, another being an attempt to place less stress on the "grade" concept, another to take advantage of multiage pupils' teaching one another, and still another to get pupils who are achieving at about the same level grouped together regardless of age. Multigrade or nongraded classrooms present some instructional problems in social studies, although they are not as serious as is usually thought. The extent to which these situations pose serious teaching problems depends on (1) the manner in which children are selected for the multigrade room, (2) the extent to which the school finds it necessary for all children in a given grade to study the same topics, and (3) the length of time children will remain in the multigrade situation. The three examples given below will illustrate how differently social studies programs would have to be planned in each case:

The Rock Spring school is a typical four-teacher elementary school, having two grades in each room. In social studies the children are taught as a single grade, with appropriate adjustments made for individual differences. The required units are placed on an odd-even year schedule to avoid repetition. Over and above the required units, teachers and pupils may select other suitable units in terms of the needs and interests of particular groups.

Last fall the Starr Elementary School found its enrollments in grades one and two disproportionately high. The school census indicates this same situation will not continue in the future, but it appears that the enrollments in these two groups will remain high as long as the children are in school. From each of the two grades an equal number of children are selected at random to form a third room that will be a first-second grade combination. It is expected that this room will continue as a unit as the children progress through the elementary school.

Mr. Smith, principal of Pine School, found he had ten more sixth-graders than his two classes could comfortably accommodate, but the enrollments in the two fifth-grade classes were such that the children could easily be placed in those rooms. He thought first of placing the five slowest learning sixth-graders in each of the two fifth-grade classes but later rejected that plan. Instead, he moved five fifth-grade children to one class and placed all ten of the sixth-graders in the other. The sixth-graders selected were average in intelligence and achievement and were well-adjusted, adaptable children.

The three examples given here indicate that there are about as many ways to form a multigrade classroom as there are situations in which such classrooms are formed. Every multigrade situation is in a sense unique, and one's course of action in planning a social studies program, therefore, must be guided by principles rather than by specifics. The following guidelines are suggested for this purpose:

1. Whenever possible, teach the class as a single group rather than have parallel social studies programs operating within the same room. The range of individual differences in a single grade is of such magnitude that the achievement of children in two successive grades overlaps substantially. The problem of differences in the range of achievement is increased only negligibly when successive grades are combined. (This, of course, does not hold if the children are selected for the combination grade because they are slow learners, poor readers, or some similar criterion.) Teachers of combination grades will soon learn that many children of the lower grade do better work than the average children in the upper grade. Conversely, many children in the upper grade will do work of poorer quality than the average children in the lower-grade group. Teaching the same unit to both grades at the same time poses no serious instructional problem in this regard. In fact, some rural schools teach selected units to the entire school at the same time—all eight grades. This can be done profitably because individual differences are obvious and pronounced and the teacher makes allowances for them in the instructional program.

2. Guard against selecting a unit that some of the children have studied the previous year. If this cannot be avoided, the children who have been through the topic before must be provided with fresh

reading material, be allowed to pursue unfamiliar facets of the problem, be encouraged to serve as resource persons, and be excused from exercises they have performed previously. No one can exhaust the possibilities for continued study of any problem, even in a lifetime of work. To assume that children cannot profit from continued study of a topic they have "covered" in a unit of work during the previous year is unrealistic. The building and maintenance of interest in the topic is apt to present the teacher with a genuine challenge, however, and for this reason the recommendation is made that units selected should not be those that children have had during the preceding year.

3. Avoid, if possible, selecting a unit topic that some of the children will study the succeeding year, for the reasons discussed in the preceding paragraph. When this is unavoidable, begin building a readiness for the following year's work by frequently pointing out interesting leads for additional study the children may pursue the next time the topic is studied.

4. If the social studies curriculum is rigid to the extent that certain elements of subject matter *must* be taught in specified grades, teach the two groups separately from time to time during the year between the units that are taught to the class as a whole. The topics should be organized logically and taught as topics rather than as pages in the textbooks. Emphasis should be placed on those key ideas believed to be so critical that they could not be omitted. Of course, the teacher will observe the same principles of good teaching during these times as he does in regular unit teaching: individualizing instruction, building interest, utilizing many resources.

5. Recognize that social studies units can be just as interesting, vital, worthwhile, and exciting for the children in a combination grade as in a single grade. Such an arrangement need not militate against the quality of instruction or the effectiveness of the social studies. It will, however, require even more careful planning in order to ensure a well-balanced, continuous program than in the case of single-grade classrooms.

Some elementary schools utilize a nongraded system of organization. The nongraded concept is an attempt to facilitate individualization of instruction and to discourage the application of a single standard of attainment to all children (that is, to get all children "up to grade standard").[5] In nongraded classrooms, grade designations are disregarded and pupils are placed where, in the judgment of the professional staff, individual children can make the most satisfactory prog-

5. John I. Goodlad and Robert H. Anderson, *The Nongraded Elementary School*, 2nd ed., New York: Harcourt, Brace and World, 1963.

ress. Depending on the policy used in a school district, such classes may consist of children who are all approximately the same age, or the age-range may vary as much as three to four years.

In general, the same guidelines discussed in connection with multi-grade classes should be applied in planning social studies programs for nongraded classes. Where entire elementary schools are ungraded, unit topics may be designated that correspond roughly to those studied by pupils in graded rooms. But the values of the nongraded arrangement are lost if teachers continue to teach pupils according to grade-level content and expectations. The basic principle to be applied is that the teacher perceive his class as a group of, say, nine-, ten-, and eleven-year-old children rather than as fourth-, fifth-, and sixth-graders. In this setting a social studies topic is selected in accordance with the local curriculum and is studied by the total class. Pupil differences in performance, for whatever reason, are accommodated by the teacher in making adjustments in the instructional program. The types of adjustments to be made are discussed in detail in Chapter 5.

Departmentalized Programs and Team Teaching: The Middle School

Most of the procedures discussed in this text can be applied to self-contained classrooms, where one teacher is responsible for the total instructional program for a grade, or equally well to other organizational arrangements such as platoon classes, a variation of departmentalization, or to team teaching. An extended discussion of the merits and limitations of various organizational plans is beyond the scope of this text. But because middle- and upper-grade teachers may find themselves in either semidepartmental programs or in team-teaching situations, they need to be familiar with these patterns. Organizational arrangements other than the self-contained classroom are rarely utilized in the primary grades.

Departmentalized teaching situations are common at the secondary school level and are familiar to most college students. Under this arrangement the teacher becomes something of a specialist in the subject he is teaching. His assignment may be confined to a single subject, such as social studies, but the usual arrangement is to have him responsible for two or even three subjects. Thus, one might teach social studies and language arts to three fifth-grade classes each day. Another teacher would have the same pupils for arithmetic and science, another would teach them music, and so on. This means that a teacher may be responsible for instructing ninety or more pupils each day. Because of the large number of pupil contacts, it takes more effort for him to get to know the pupils individually than it would if he had only one classroom of pupils. Instructional arrangements of this type are increasing because of the growing popularity of the "middle school." The middle school is an organizational arrangement that usually includes grades five through eight and that eliminates the junior high school.

If good instruction is to prevail in departmentalized situations or in platoon classes, the teacher will be doing precisely the same things other elementary teachers do in social studies teaching: motivating pupils, individualizing instruction, using a variety of activities and resources, developing units of study, planning with pupils, and diagnosing learners' needs and difficulties. The fact that the teacher is a specialist in the subject he is teaching *in no way* changes the pupils— they have the same learning strengths or limitations no matter what organizational scheme is used by the school. The essential point here is that appropriate teaching strategies and educationally sound procedures have to be followed whatever the organizational arrangement. Departmental or platoon plans can easily fall into the trap of using teaching styles designed for high school and college instruction. They are not satisfactory methods for elementary school pupils and do not work especially well even at the more advanced levels.

Team teaching has been applied more widely in secondary than elementary schools, although recent literature reflects a fair number of articles dealing with team teaching in elementary schools. Team-teaching plans vary somewhat, but teaching teams usually consist of teachers and such subfaculty as aides and intern teachers. One teacher is designated as the team leader. He gets the team together for planning meetings at least weekly, at which time decisions are made concerning grouping, curriculum, teaching responsibilities, and so on. Through the use of aides and intern teachers, time is available to the regular teachers for planning, supervision, and directing the study of individual pupils. Central to the team-teaching idea are the better use of the unique strengths of particular teachers because they are assigned to tasks they do best or to subjects in which they have special competence; flexible grouping arrangements—large groups, small groups, and individual study groups; and the release of teachers from noninstructional duties because aides and interns are available for those duties.

It is not possible to generalize about the quality of social studies instruction under team teaching except to say that it depends on the extent of careful planning by the team and the extent to which sound principles of social studies education are implemented. Competent teachers who do careful planning as a teaching team and who are enthusiastic about the idea of team teaching will present pupils with exciting programs in social studies. But if team teaching becomes a series of lectures to large groups in what Professor Gross has referred to as "take-turns teaching," [6] the program cannot be defended as good social studies education. The values of team teaching apparently fall outside improved pupil achievement, for there is no evidence that team teaching produces demonstrably superior pupil achievement than other teaching arrangements. Neither is there evidence that departmental or platoon organizational arrangements per se result in improved pupil performance in achievement even though it is commonly believed that they do.[7]

Teaching Procedures Related to Unit Development

The unit as a plan of organizing for instruction in the social studies has been presented and developed in this chapter. This organization has several dimensions—the learnings to be achieved, the subject matter and skills to be presented, the activities to be performed, the learning resources to be used, and the deployment of pupils. The unit is really a way of thinking about planning rather than a formal blueprint to be followed. In fact, instruction suffers when unit procedures are always the same. Imaginative use of units requires variation in approach and emphasis; otherwise units will have a sameness about them that can be as boring as a textbook approach.

The unit as a way of thinking about planning only provides an organizational structure that can facilitate good teaching. Among the teaching procedures explained in this chapter are pupil involvement in planning, the practical use of skills, committee and group work, research, reporting, discussing, and individualization of instruction. But no organizational plan can, in and of itself, ensure good teaching. Whether a teacher teaches well or poorly depends on how well he has mastered the competencies identified in Figure 12 and on his willingness to use them in a creative way in his classroom.

Discussion Questions and Suggested Activities

1. As a continuing project, begin the development of a resource unit, using the outline given in this chapter. You may wish to continue utilizing the topic chosen for Question 1 of Chapter 1. Begin a collection of pictures, charts, free and inexpensive material, pamphlets, poems, and activities that will be helpful to you in teaching such a unit to children.

6. Richard E. Gross, Professor of Education, Stanford University, in an address delivered to the Washington State Council for the Social Studies, at Yakima, Washington, May 1, 1965.

7. Robert L. Ebel, *The Encyclopedia of Educational Research*, 4th ed., New York: The Macmillan Company, 1969, pp. 560–564.

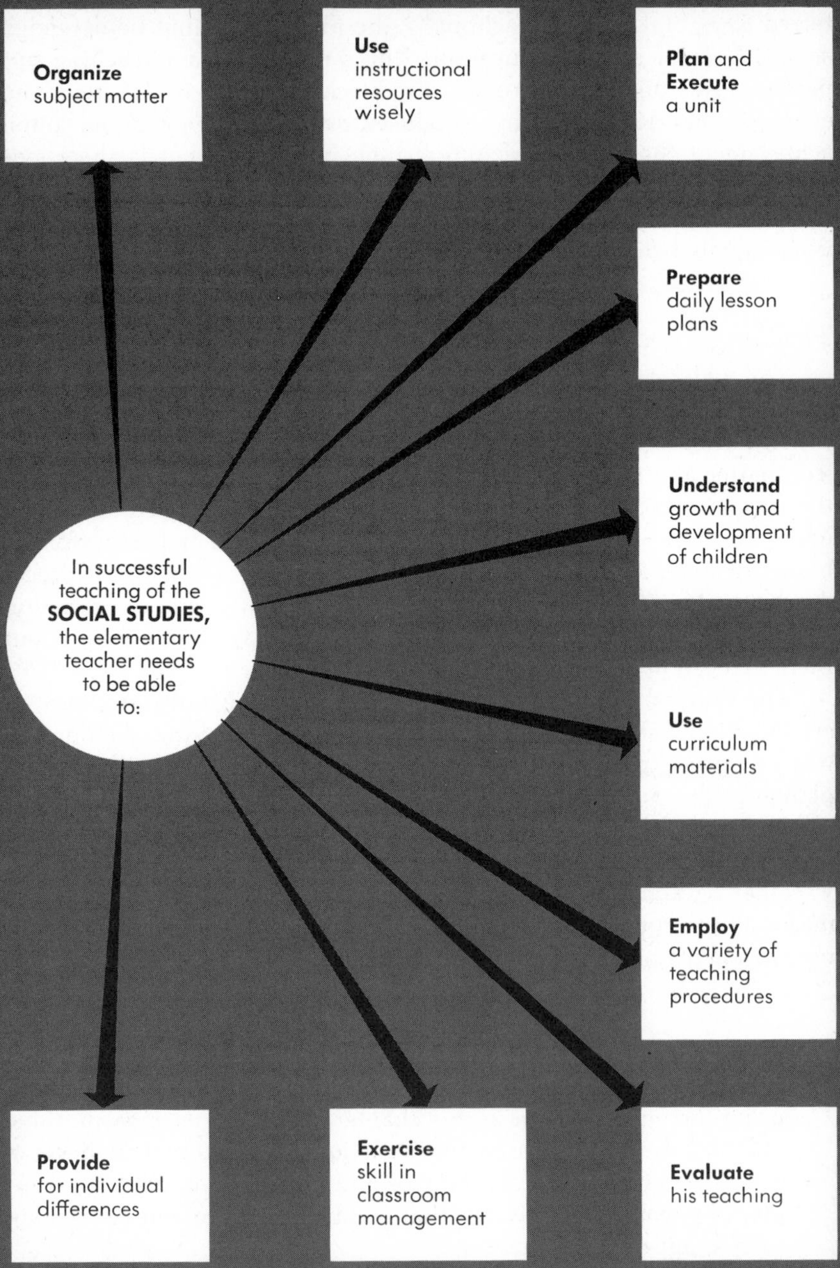

Organize subject matter

Use instructional resources wisely

Plan and **Execute** a unit

Prepare daily lesson plans

Understand growth and development of children

Use curriculum materials

Employ a variety of teaching procedures

In successful teaching of the **SOCIAL STUDIES,** the elementary teacher needs to be able to:

Provide for individual differences

Exercise skill in classroom management

Evaluate his teaching

Figure 12. Teacher competencies related to elementary social studies. Suggest sample behaviors to indicate satisfactory performance of these competencies.

2. Develop the content of your resource unit around main ideas and related ideas as is explained in this chapter. Insert one main idea and its related ideas on a chart such as the one shown on page 84. Develop plans for teaching the idea by completing the remainder of the chart.
3. Plan and prepare a bulletin board display, showing how it might be used at some point in the development of your resource unit.
4. Develop a complete daily lesson plan, just as you would teach it, using the form suggested on page 104. Utilize content and materials from your resource unit.
5. Select a social studies textbook for a grade level of your choice and read selected portions of it, noting especially references to quantitative concepts and the use of numbers. Does this suggest a need for teaching quantitative relationships during the course of a social studies unit? Are people from different cultures and races represented in the textbook? Are the case studies and biographies of people only of historical and political figures, or do they also include examples of cultural leaders?
6. Find a social studies textbook or a resource unit that has prepared unit tests. Do the tests measure skills and attitudes as well as subject-matter content? What pupil thinking processes do the questions require?
7. The text describes teacher-guided pupil planning as an attitude on the part of the teacher. Do you believe certain statements the teacher makes tend to solicit certain types of responses and feelings from children? Test your beliefs by observing teachers at work and by recording the statements of the teacher. Teachers' statements might be categorized as (1) positive statements, (2) negative statements, and (3) neither or as (1) those indicating democratic attitudes toward children, (2) those indicating autocratic attitudes toward children, and (3) neither. How does the classroom climate of a teacher who consistently makes a greater number of positive statements indicating democratic attitudes toward children differ from one who makes a preponderance of negative statements indicating autocratic attitudes toward children? Which one is likely to be more successful with teacher-guided pupil planning?
8. Do you think it wise to designate specific amounts of time for each phase of the daily social studies period, such as twenty minutes for readiness, twenty minutes for work activities, and twenty minutes for summary and evaluation? What advantages and limitations can you identify in such a plan?

9. What advantages might there be to having children from more than one grade in the same classroom? Can you cite any limitations of this type of classroom organization?
10. Visit a social studies class several times during a unit of instruction in order to observe the initiatory, developmental, and culminating activities employed by teacher and pupils.
11. Research shows that children are likely to reflect the attitudes of status adults with whom they associate. What implications does this research have for the elementary school social studies teacher?

Selected References

Allen, Rodney F., John U. Fleckenstein, and Peter M. Lyon. *Inquiry in the Social Studies*, Social Studies Readings, No. 2. Washington, D.C.: National Council for the Social Studies, 1968.

Bauer, Nancy W. "Guaranteeing the Values Component in Elementary School Social Studies," *Social Education*, XXX, No. 1 (January, 1967), pp. 43–47.

Carpenter, Helen M., ed. *Skill Development in Social Studies*, 33rd Yearbook. Washington, D.C.: National Council for the Social Studies, 1963.

Clements, H. Millard, William R. Fielder, and B. Robert Tabachnick. *Social Study: Inquiry in Elementary Classrooms*. Indianapolis: The Bobbs-Merrill Co., Inc., 1966.

Crabtree, Charlotte. "Inquiry Approaches to Learning Concepts and Generalizations in the Social Studies," *Social Education*, XXX, No. 6 (October, 1966), pp. 407–411.

Dunfee, Maxine and Helen Sagl. *Social Studies Through Problem Solving*. New York: Holt, Rinehart and Winston, Inc., 1966.

Edgerton, S. G. "Learning by Induction," *Social Education*, XXXI, No. 5 (May, 1967), pp. 373–382+.

Estvan, Frank J. *Social Studies in a Changing World*. New York: Harcourt, Brace & World, Inc., 1968.

Ezer, Melvin. "Values Teaching in the Middle and Upper Grades: A Rationale for Teaching but Not Transmitting Values," *Social Education*, XXXI, No. 1 (January, 1967), pp. 39–40+.

Fair, Jean, and Fannie R. Shaftel, eds. *Effective Thinking in the Social Studies*, 37th Yearbook. Washington, D.C.: National Council for the Social Studies, 1967.

Fancett, Verna S., et al. *Social Science.Concepts and the Classroom*. Syracuse, N.Y.: Syracuse University Press, 1968.

Finkel, N., and R. Stein. "Social Studies Unit—A Modified Approach," *The Social Studies*, 58 (November, 1967), pp. 265–269.

Fraenkel, Jack. "Value Education in the Social Studies," *Phi Delta Kappan*, L, No. 8 (April, 1969), pp. 457–461.

Fraser, Dorothy McClure, ed. *Social Studies Curriculum Development: Prospects and Problems*, 39th Yearbook. Washington, D.C.: National Council for the Social Studies, 1969 (especially Chaps. 3, 4, and 5).

Goldmark, Bernice. *Social Studies: A Method of Inquiry*. Belmont, Calif.: Wadsworth Publishing Company, Inc., 1968.

Hanna, Lavone, Neva Hagaman, and Gladys Potter. *Unit Teaching in the Elementary School*, rev. ed. New York: Holt, Rinehart & Winston, Inc., 1963.

Jarolimek, John, and Huber M. Walsh. *Readings for Social Studies in Elementary Education*. New York: The Macmillan Company, 1969.

Jenkin, Gladys G., Helen S. Schacter, and William W. Bauer. *These Are Your Children*, 3rd ed. Chicago: Scott, Foresman and Company, 1966.

Joyce, Bruce R. *Strategies for Elementary Social Science Education*. Chicago: Science Research Associates, Inc., 1965.

Kaltsounis, Theodore. *Teaching Elementary Social Studies*. West Nyack, N.Y.: Parker Publishing Company, Inc., 1969.

Lindberg, James B. "Developing Problem-Solving Skills," *Social Education*, XXX, No. 8 (December, 1966), pp. 645–648.

Mager, Robert F. *Preparing Instructional Objectives*. Palo Alto, Calif.: Fearon Publishers, 1962.

McLendon, Jonathon C., William W. Joyce, and John R. Lee. *Readings on Elementary Social Studies: Emerging Changes*, 2nd ed. Boston: Allyn & Bacon, Inc., 1970.

Michaelis, John U. *Social Studies for Children in a Democracy*, 4th ed. Englewood Cliffs, N.J.: Prentice-Hall, Inc., 1968.

Mowry, C. I. "Teaching Values Through Today's News," *The Instructor*, 77 (March, 1968), pp. 62+.

Polos, Nicholas C. *The Dynamics of Team Teaching*. Dubuque, Iowa: William Brown Company, 1965.

Preston, Ralph C. *Teaching Social Studies in the Elementary School*, 3rd ed. New York: Holt, Rinehart & Winston, Inc., 1968.

Raths, Louis E., Merrill Harmin, and Sidney B. Simon. *Values and Teaching: Working with Values in the Classroom*. Columbus, Ohio: Charles E. Merrill Books, Inc., 1966.

Rogers, Vincent R. "How to Use Inquiry," *The Instructor*, No. 78 (March, 1969), pp. 93–94.

Sanders, Norris M. *Classroom Questions: What Kinds?* New York: Harper and Row, Publishers, Inc., 1966.

Servey, Richard E. *Social Studies Instruction in the Elementary School.* San Francisco: Chandler Publishing Company, 1967.

Taba, Hilda. *Teachers' Handbook for Elementary Social Studies,* Palo Alto, Calif.: Addison-Wesley, 1967.

"The Elementary School: Focus on Skills," *Social Education, XXXI,* No. 3 (March, 1967), pp. 34–48. A collection of articles on skills in elementary school social studies.

Wolfson, Bernice J. "Values and the Primary School Teacher," *Social Education, XXXI,* No. 1 (January, 1967), pp. 37–38+.

Womack, James G. *Discovering the Structure of Social Studies.* New York: Benziger Brothers, 1966.

Selecting and Using Learning Resources

A generous supply of learning resources and aids will do much to ensure a good program of social studies for boys and girls. If nothing more is provided than a basic textbook, a set of encyclopedias, a handful of additional references, and some audio-visual materials to be shared with other rooms, it becomes easy for the teacher to fall victim to textbook teaching, ignoring individual differences in children and making social studies teaching dull, uninteresting, and largely ineffectual. But a large amount of materials will not in and of itself assure good teaching. This can be achieved only when instructional resources are used skillfully by an inspired and creative teacher.

A major deterrent to good social

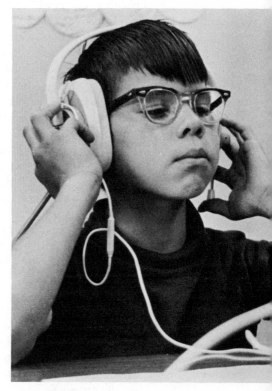

4

studies teaching in the past has been the paucity of instructional resources and aids available to the teacher for use with his class. Not only did the teacher have to be skillful in using resources, he also had to be creative in locating, obtaining, and even making them himself. Perhaps teachers will always construct and improvise some of their own instructional resources to fit unique and particular situations. But the problem of the lack of instructional resources is changing rapidly in the 1970's primarily because of the federal financial support made available to public schools for these purposes. Instructional resources in great quantities are being placed in schools at an ever increasing rate. The teacher of today who accepts a position in a school district of average or even modest means, will find a supply of instructional resources that would have been found only in the best school districts even as recently as a decade ago. The teacher's problem today, then, is not the lack of materials but how to make the best instructional use of those available to him.

Learning materials and resources for the social studies can be grouped into two categories: (1) reading materials and resources (textbooks, encyclopedias, references, magazines, pamphlets, newspaper clippings, travel folders, classroom periodicals, and similar printed material) and (2) nonreading materials and resources (pictures, films, filmstrips, recordings, field trips, maps, globes, and community resources of all types). Together they provide the foundation of research or information-getting activities and are central elements of a good social studies program. Discussions, summaries, constructions, dramatics, writing, and reporting are quite meaningless unless they have been preceded by some type of research activity. The effectiveness of social studies activities, therefore, is related directly to the teacher's ability to select and use instructional materials wisely.

In the social studies as in any other area of the school curriculum, sound principles must be applied in the selection and use of a particular learning resource. These have been treated extensively in the educational literature and, for our purposes, can be summarized briefly as follows:

1. In the selection of any instructional resource, the goals of learning should be uppermost in the mind of the teacher. The particular resource or material selected should be the one that will move the children in the direction of those goals most effectively. In short, instructional aids, materials, and resources are used to achieve specific purposes.

2. The greater the number of sensory perceptions made possible through the use of a resource, the greater is the likelihood that it will be effective. A trip to the bakery where the young child can

see and hear the production process as well as smell, touch, and taste the newly baked bread is likely to be more effective than reading about the bakery in the classroom.

3. Instructional materials must be suited to the developmental level of the child. Younger children need many more concrete and firsthand experiences than older children because they are not able to profit from vicarious experiences to the same extent as older children. Primary-grade children, for example, might make and use a layout on the classroom floor that represents the schoolyard or the immediate neighborhood, whereas middle- and upper-grade children are capable of using conventional wall maps.

4. The selection and use of instructional materials should take into full account the wide range of intellectual and achievement differences in children within the classroom. In the case of reading material, there needs to be a wide range in the reading difficulty of the material as well as in the difficulty of the content presented. The types of materials and resources available should cover the full range of abstraction from those that involve direct, concrete, firsthand experiences to those that are completely abstract.

5. Instructional materials need to be carefully evaluated before, during, and after they have been used. It is not a good policy to use any and all materials simply because they are available. The quality of the material or resource should be a primary consideration in deciding on its use. Maps that are out of date, films that are of poor quality, pictures that are inaccurate, or field trips that are poorly guided, for example, might better not be used at all.

6. The maximum value of any instructional resource requires skillful use on the part of the teacher. No instructional material is entirely self-teaching—all of them require a teacher to set the stage for learning to take place. A first-rate textbook in the hands of an unimaginative teacher can be devastating to the social studies program. The same book used by another teacher can become one of the most valuable resources available to the class. Materials of instruction can be no better than the teachers who use them.

Reading Materials

TEXTBOOKS

Educators agree that if properly used, the textbook is a valuable aid to learning. On the other hand, everyone familiar with school practice recognizes that the misuse of textbooks is fairly common. Attention is called particularly to the malpractice of expecting children who are known to vary markedly in reading and intellectual ability to use identical textbooks for identical purposes. A weekend visitor to middle-grade classrooms is likely to find in the desks of almost all the children the same basic textbook in social studies. This indicates that school leaders feel (1) that the use of a basic textbook is essential to the social studies program, (2) that teachers cannot teach social studies without a basic text, (3) more secure that specified curriculum content will be "covered" when a basic book is being used, (4) that a textbook is adequate, making additional materials less necessary, or (5) that the teacher and pupils themselves can secure additional resources. In some areas, schools must provide each schoolchild with the same basic textbook because of local school policy or state law. Basic textbooks in the social studies are likely to be widely used for years to come; thus the teacher should learn how to make maximum use of them.

Through the years, social studies textbooks have gone through an evolutionary process paralleling the changes that have occurred in teaching procedures. The authors of children's textbooks have not been unmindful of changes that have taken place in curriculum and teaching methods and have developed textbooks consistent with these changes. An examination of textbooks in social studies will show less evidence of detailed and isolated facts and a greater emphasis on fundamental information in the form of key ideas, movements, trends, and developments than in previous texts. Books of today are organized on a unit basis with an attempt to bring related materials together around a series of carefully selected, broad topics.

In addition to the improvements in the organization and presentation of material, social studies textbooks have improved in other ways. Books of today are attractive, inviting, a pleasure to look at and read. There is better use of maps and visual materials; and some social studies textbooks for elementary grades boast of at least one illustration on every page, many of the illustrations in color. There is a trend toward multiple authorship, with at least one author a specialist in elementary education. This has served to retain high scholarly accuracy as well as to refine and improve the format and reading level of the books. Textbooks of today are better suited to the capabilities of the children for whom they are intended than in any previous time. Since 1960, social studies books dealing with the United States have given greater attention to the variety of racial and ethnic groups composing American society. These many changes have produced social studies textbooks that bear little resemblance to the dull, drab, and uninteresting "geographies" of yesteryear.

The legitimate use of basic textbooks may take a variety of forms, but their use is predicated on the assumption that the teacher is fully aware of the following characteristics of all social studies textbooks:

1. Although social studies textbooks are more carefully graded for reading difficulty than ever before, they are still graded for the average reader. The teacher may anticipate that some children will not be able to read them with comprehension while others will find them something less than a challenge to read. There is no single book to adequately meet the reading needs of all children in a class of thirty to thirty-five pupils.
2. Textbooks are a highly condensed and factual presentation and are written with the thought that teachers will supplement and enrich the textbook presentation through the use of other materials. The better textbooks suggest materials that may be used in this respect in the study guides at the ends of chapters or units.
3. Textbooks are written to be used as valuable source books and are not intended to become the social studies curriculum. Teachers who feel they must "cover" the book or feel that all children must master all the facts presented in the text seem not to understand the textbook-curriculum relationship.
4. Textbook authors assume that the teacher will guide and direct the children in their use of the book. Textbooks are not meant to be entirely self-instructing, and if children use them without guidance from the teacher, much of their value may be lost. This is especially true of accompanying visual material in the form of pictures, maps, charts, cartoons, graphs, and study helps.
5. Textbooks can be used in a great variety of ways, and individual children may make different uses of the same book. For one child it may constitute a reading resource, for another child the illustrations may be more valuable, for a third child the map materials may be needed, and for a fourth child it may be a source of ideas for additional study. Similarly, different teachers may choose to make different uses of the same book, depending on their skill, experience, or method of teaching. In short, textbooks can and should be used differently by individual children and individual teachers.

Assuming that the teacher will keep clearly in mind the five characteristics discussed here, the basic textbook can be a useful tool in teaching social studies. Four of the most common uses are for (1) exploratory reading, (2) securing facts related to the study, (3) map, chart, graph, or picture study, and (4) summarization of learning.

Exploratory Reading. The textbook can be used as a point of departure in the early stages of a new study to help the children to find out "what it's all about" and to establish a common background of basic information for all pupils. Using the textbook in this fashion can help introduce the pupils to some of the key ideas of the unit, acquaint them with vocabulary, help them learn enough about the topic to be able to proceed intelligently with further teacher-pupil planning of other activities including other reading activities. When used in this manner the teacher should

1. Build readiness for the material to be read by a proper introduction of the content through the use of pictures, maps, the globe, reference to current affairs, a community problem, a short explanation, a historical event, a geographical phenomenon, or other similar and appropriate circumstance. Readiness for reading the basic textbook should be placed within the context of general readiness for the unit, which is accomplished through a series of introductory or initiatory activities.

2. Identify for the children some of the purposes for which they are to read the material. These should be clearly understood before the reading is undertaken and perhaps written on the chalkboard. When children are instructed to "read to find out . . .," the reading is likely to be much more effective than if they are simply told to "read pages 55 to 60 in the book." In exploratory reading the purposes should be general rather than detailed and highly specific.

3. Anticipate vocabulary difficulties children may encounter and develop the meaning of key new words with them prior to the reading. Consideration of a new topic commonly presents new words, and without an understanding of the new words or concepts the material lacks meaning for the reader.

4. Call attention to important pictures, illustrations, maps, or charts included in the material. This is especially necessary when some element of an illustration is highly critical to the understanding of the text but might be overlooked by the child.

5. Have some type of follow-up to the reading performed by the children individually. This logically would include an activity dealing with the purposes established for the reading.

6. Take the children who are extremely low in reading ability aside in a small group and assist them with the material. For this directed-study situation the teacher should choose *selected, short passages* for consideration along with the visual material presented in the text. An "around the circle" oral reading approach should not be used under any circumstances. Instead, the teacher can call their attention to a passage, a picture caption, a picture, a chart, or a map or diagram; discuss it with them; and ask them to see if they can find out various facts or sense implications from the material presented in the text. Just as an attorney assists the layman to read and interpret a complex legal document, the teacher can

and must assist the slow reader to read and interpret materials he might not otherwise be able to read. Unless the teacher can give this close supervision and help to the children of low reading ability and actually direct their study of the material, they should not be expected to read it at all. Other more simple material should be found for them, or the teacher should rewrite certain passages at a level they are capable of handling.

7. Provide additional, more difficult books to which the more skillful readers can turn for extended exploratory reading when they have completed the text. These could be other textbooks, encyclopedias, magazines, or supplementary books.

Securing Facts Related to the Study. When the unit is underway, it is often necessary to have pupils obtain factual information related to the topic being studied. The textbook can serve as an excellent source of such information and represents a second good use of it. When the text is used in this manner, the teacher should

1. Help children identify precisely what factual information is wanted. This can take the form of finding answers to specific questions such as: "What pieces of furniture might one find in a pioneer home?" "What steps are involved in getting a letter from the sender to the receiver?" "How does geography affect the way people live in Mexico?" "What hardships were encountered by a group of early settlers in Wisconsin?" "What crops are grown in the southeastern section of the United States?" When used on a class basis, the factual material to be obtained can be decided on by the teacher, by the pupils, or by both.
2. Teach children how to use the index, table of contents, glossary, and list of illustrations to help them develop independence in locating information in the text.
3. Have children consult other sources to confirm factual information presented in the text. This procedure helps overcome the feeling on the part of children that the textbook is a sufficient source book on any topic.

Map, Chart, Graph, or Picture Study. Modern textbooks provide an abundance of visual materials that can be used profitably by the teacher in short directed-study situations. In map study, for example, every child will have before him a reasonably well-produced map he can use during a lesson on map reading or interpretation. In the study of a chart the child can follow along in his book as the teacher explains its make-up and meaning. If children are asked to point to the elements being discussed, the teacher can tell at a glance which children are

**SELECTING AND USING
LEARNING RESOURCES**

"with" the class and which ones are not. Likewise, pictures can be used more effectively when each child has one in his hands than would be possible by passing a single print around the classroom or posting one on the bulletin board. Textbooks are, therefore, *more* than reading books and should be used in ways other than as readers.

Summarization of Learning. Textbooks can be used profitably near the conclusion of a subtopic of a study to summarize and pull together learning that has taken place through other activities. The text is presented to the children at a time when they have already built a background of information related to the topic. They are familiar with the vocabulary and concepts and are psychologically ready to take full advantage of the factual presentation of the text. The textbook, therefore, not only may serve as a point of departure for a study but also may be a frequent port of call and a point of return. When the text is used for the purpose of summarization, the teacher should

1. Establish readiness with the children by discussing material previously studied and establish definite purposes for reading the text. This, again, should take the form of "reading to find out. . . ." Purposes for this use of the text should be detailed and specific as contrasted with the general purposes discussed in connection with exploratory reading.
2. Clarify any vocabulary difficulties the children may encounter.
3. Follow the same procedure with slower and more rapid readers as was explained in the section dealing with exploratory reading.
4. Have definite follow-up activities planned that will allow the children to apply information obtained in the reading.
5. Allow for a thorough discussion of the major ideas presented. These should be summarized in writing and perhaps placed on the chalkboard or in the individual child's notebook or folder.

SELECTION OF TEXTBOOKS

Careful thought should be given to the selection of textbooks because the purchase of books ordinarily means that the school is committed to using them for a period of three to five years. With the many demands on school budgets and the limited resources that are often available, a good selection is imperative. Teachers or textbook selection committees need to establish criteria that can be applied to several sets of books to assist them in making a sound judgment concerning the one that best suits the needs of the particular school. Book company representatives can be helpful in pointing out the various strong features of the series published by the company they represent, but the selection should, of course, be made on some basis other than the charm of individual representatives.

There are many good social studies textbooks today. Some are better suited for certain purposes than others. Some more accurately reflect current curriculum development than others do. Those who are charged with the responsibility of making the selection should develop their own criteria for evaluating textbooks in social studies, but they will probably want to look critically at the following points:

1. *Authorship*—to ensure scholarly accuracy as well as suitability for use with elementary school children in terms of interest and appeal, reading gradation, and curricular consideration. How is the author identified with elementary social studies?
2. *Treatment of Content*—to ensure adequate treatment of important concepts in sufficient depth as opposed to highly descriptive factual accounts or storybook approaches to significant content. Does the book focus on relevant, key concepts?
3. *Format and General Appearance*—to ensure an interesting and appealing book, proper size, good-quality binding, suitable type size. Are illustrations functional or simply decorative?
4. *Organization*—to ensure its harmony with the existing curricular pattern and that it meets the needs of the instructional program within which it will be used. Is the book organized in a way to encourage pupil inquiry?
5. *Visual Materials*—to ensure colorful, accurate illustrations of sufficient number and size. Are these related to the text or included to enhance the attractiveness of the book?
6. *Instructional Aids*—to ensure their being an integral part of the text itself and of such nature as to be genuinely helpful to the teacher. Do study aids help explain and extend meaning of important ideas?

ENCYCLOPEDIAS

In the middle and upper grades, all classrooms should have at least one and preferably two sets of encyclopedias suitable for children. Even in the primary grades an encyclopedia can be used to good advantage from time to time, and many schools are placing them in first, second, and third grades. Much of what was said in connection with the improvement of textbooks could also be said concerning the encyclopedias. Greater use of colored illustrations is immediately apparent, and equally important has been the general downgrading in reading difficulty. The person or persons making a selection of an encyclopedia should by all means ascertain the reading level at which the material is graded before a final selection is made. Although several years old, the following criteria suggested by Sentman are still helpful in selecting reference works for schools:

1. Does the encyclopedia have enough "muscle" to stand up under heavy use, hundreds of times more use than it would get in the home? Is it sturdily bound? Is the paper tough and of good quality?
2. Does its content meet your curriculum requirements?
3. Is the arrangement of subject-matter well suited to your instruction program?
4. Is the encyclopedia well printed and easy to read?
5. Are the pictures graphic, informative and sufficiently numerous?
6. Is the set kept up to date? Most school encyclopedias have a program of continuous revision. You can form a general idea of the extent and effectiveness of revision by looking up a subject, particularly in science, in which there have been fairly recent developments or discoveries.
7. Does the encyclopedia bear the imprint of a reputable publisher?
8. Does the work stress educationally significant concepts and subjects?
9. Do the children like the set? [1]

The value of an encyclopedia lies in the easy, quick manner in which factual material can be obtained on a multitude of topics. It is, like the textbook, an important source of information and one that will be referred to many times in the course of social studies units. When encyclopedias are available in the primary grades, the teacher will find the pictures and illustrations helpful in social studies instruction. Selected short portions of content may be read to the children from time to time, and some children at these early levels will be able to read portions of the encyclopedia independently. Perhaps the chief value of an encyclopedia in the primary grades is the contribution it can make to building positive attitudes toward the use of reference materials. Children seek new information enthusiastically and enjoy nothing better than an opportunity for "Let's find out!" They learn fairly early that in the encyclopedia one can find answers to many questions on many topics. In this sense, early contact with this reference serves as a readiness for its more organized use at the upper levels. In the middle and upper grades the encyclopedia is a constant source of factual information throughout the social studies units. It must be remembered, however, that the volumes do not have locked within them the sum total of all human knowledge, and at best the articles are highly condensed presentations. This suggests that there is need for additional references—ones that may give interesting sidelights on the problems not ordinarily included in encyclopedia cover-

1. E. E. Sentman, "Encyclopedias in the Elementary School," *Instructional Materials for Elementary Schools*, 35th Yearbook, Washington, D.C.: National Elementary Principals, 1956, p. 48. A more complete discussion of criteria for selecting encyclopedias may be found in the following: S. Padraig Walse, *General Encyclopedias in Print 1968, A Comparative Analysis*, New York: R. R. Bowker Company.

age. Children must be taught the use of encyclopedias as well as other references.

With the rapidity with which the affairs of the world change, there is need to replace the encyclopedia frequently. After the set becomes five years old it should be replaced with an up-to-date one. Most sets provide yearly supplements that include changes and new knowledge, but after a five-year period some articles need complete revision. This is additional evidence that children should not regard the encyclopedia as a final and fixed source of truth.

SUPPLEMENTARY REFERENCES

In addition to textbooks and encyclopedias there is need for an abundance of supplementary books. Some of these may be other textbooks, although the need is not so much for additional textbooks as it is for nontext material on a variety of topics. In recent years we have seen the publication of many books on a wide variety of subjects for elementary school children. Books about Indians, airplanes, the United Nations, biographies of famous Americans, the farm, factory, life in other lands, and communities at work are rapidly becoming available in greater numbers. Many contemporary children's books have exceptional art work and maintain high standards of literary quality.

Literary works useful for social studies instruction may be classified as (1) *informative accounts*—works that simply convey specific information in literary form on topics studied, such as books about trucks, trains, countries, printing, communication, homes around the world; (2) *informative fiction*—reconstruction of historical events that are built around a fictionalized plot or story; (3) *biographies*; (4) *nonfiction history*; (5) *poems*; (6) *locally produced materials*—consisting possibly of works falling in any of the preceding five categories.

Literature and literary materials should play an important part in social studies instruction because they convey so well the affective dimension of human experience. The realism that is achieved through vivid portrayals in works of literature stirs the imagination of the young reader and helps develop for him a feeling for and identification with the topic being studied. The relationship between literature and some of the subjects included in the social studies—particularly history—has been noted by numerous writers. This is reflected in Horn's statement that "of all the subjects not traditionally included under the social studies, none is more intimately affiliated with them than literature." [2] Some of the great works of literature are also considered important historical documents, and the reverse is also true.

2. Ernest Horn, *Methods of Instruction in the Social Studies*, New York: Charles Scribner's Sons, 1937, p. 265.

One reason that literary materials are so important is that they provide the rich detail that is impossible to get in a well-designed text or an encyclopedia. A textbook, for example, might handle the Bird Woman, Sacagawea, in a single paragraph because space is also required to tell the rest of the story of the development of the United States. However, the child can learn much about this interesting Indian woman by reading one of the several children's biographies of her life. Here he can get a vivid word picture of the time in which she lived. Such supporting details add richness and meaning to his understanding of the historical period studied. The teacher may acquaint himself with titles of books of this type from the following sources:

1. Huus, Helen. *Children's Books to Enrich the Social Studies for the Elementary Grades,* Bulletin 32, rev. ed. Washington, D.C.: National Council for the Social Studies, 1966.
2. Eakin, Mary K., and Eleanor Merritt. *Subject Index to Books for the Primary Grades,* 3rd ed. Chicago: American Library Association, 1967.
3. Eakin, Mary K. *Subject Index to Books for the Intermediate Grades,* 3rd ed. Chicago: American Library Association, 1963.
4. Bagshaw, Marguerite. *Books for Boys and Girls,* 4th ed. Toronto: Ryerson Press, 1966.
5. Solomon, Doris, ed. *Best Books for Children,* 1969 ed. New York: R. R. Bowker Company. Published annually.
6. Sutherland, Zena. *History in Children's Books.* Brooklawn, N.J.: McKinley Publishing Company, 1967.
7. Jackson, Miles M., Jr. *A Bibliography of Negro History and Culture for Young Readers,* Pittsburgh, Pa.: University of Pittsburgh Press, 1968.
8. *Bibliography of Books for Children.* Washington, D.C.: Association for Childhood Education International, 1968.
9. *Basic Book Collection for Elementary Grades,* 7th ed. Chicago: American Library Association, 1960.
10. *Children's Catalog,* 11th ed. New York: H. W. Wilson Company, 1966.
11. Bibliographies in resource units, teaching guides, curriculum guides, and similar publications.
12. Catalogues and listings of titles by publishers.
13. Lists of supplementary readings suggested in basic textbooks.
14. Exhibits at conventions, book fairs, and local libraries.
15. Listings and/or reviews of children's books on social studies topics in various professional journals such as *Social Education, Today's Education, Elementary English, Instructor, Grade Teacher, English Journal,* and *The Horn Book Magazine.*

For factual information there is need, too, for atlases, the *World Almanac*, biographies of famous Americans, and the state legislative manuals. Many local communities and cities also publish similar information in the form of brochures, handbooks, and pamphlets. Local and state historical societies, museums, and art galleries may make available publications of this sort that are valuable for classroom work. These sources provide a storehouse of information, but children of elementary school age need a considerable amount of guidance and help from the teacher in their use.

FREE AND INEXPENSIVE MATERIALS

Free and inexpensive materials have become a valuable resource for the teacher in teaching social studies units. There is a wealth of material in the form of posters, charts, bulletins, folders, booklets, films, filmstrips, and travel folders available free on request. In addition to the free material, there is an abundance of similar material that can be obtained for less than one dollar. In past years much of the commercially prepared free and inexpensive material was of questionable value because of offensive advertising and biased presentations. Companies have recognized that if the material is to meet the needs of classroom teachers, the advertising aspects have to be kept at a minimum and the presentation kept objective and honest. Most companies that prepare free material for distribution have educational consultants of considerable competence and stature on their staffs, many of whom have been classroom teachers. They have a good understanding of the needs of children and the type of material that can be most helpful to teachers. For the most part, much of the material available today is well prepared and useful for classroom work.

Before using the material, the teacher should, of course, examine it carefully to ascertain whether or not it is suitable for use with his group. Just because the material is available and free is no assurance that it is of value. He should consider items such as these:

1. Is the material produced by a socially responsible organization?
2. Does the presence of advertising make the material unsuitable for use? A piece may or may not be rejected on this point, but it should, in any case, be considered.
3. Is the material honestly and objectively presented? Is it consistent with democratic values and ideals?
4. Is the material suitable in terms of readability, maturity of the pupils, technical qualities, and the topic under consideration?
5. Is the material up-to-date?
6. Are the sources of information given?
7. Does use of the materials carry any obligations with it?

The use of vertical file material, as it is sometimes called, presents problems of cataloguing, filing, and storage. Material that is tucked in some out-of-the-way closet, perhaps stored in a cardboard box, is usually not found when needed and, therefore is not used. The material must be carefully filed and catalogued appropriately to facilitate its availability when needed. A central collection kept in the school library is recommended in addition to smaller personal collections of individual teachers.

Because the demand for free and inexpensive material is great and the quantity usually limited, the teacher is advised to use an up-to-date listing of sources. Professional journals carry listings in almost every issue. In addition, there are compilations of sources of free and inexpensive material that can be purchased. The following are some of the better-known compilations, most of which are revised annually:

1. *Bibliography of Free and Inexpensive Materials for Economic Education,* 1212 Avenue of the Americas, New York, N.Y., 10036.
2. *Catalog of Free Teaching Materials.* G. S. Salisbury and R. H. Sheridan, Box 1075, Ventura, Calif.
3. *Choosing Free Materials for Use in the Schools,* American Association of School Administrators, National Education Association, 1201 16th St., N.W., Washington, D.C. 20036.
4. Educator's Progress Service, Randolph, Wisc., 53956: *Guide to Free Curriculum Materials; Educators' Guide to Free Films; Educators' Guide to Free Filmstrips; Educators' Guide to Free Social Studies Material; Educators' Guide to Free Tapes, Scripts, and Transcriptions.*
5. *Free and Inexpensive Materials on World Affairs,* L. S. Kenworthy, Bureau of Publications, Teachers College, Columbia University, New York, N.Y., 10027.
6. *Illustration Index,* Lucile E. Vance and Esther M. Tracey, 2nd ed. New York: The Scarecrow Press, Inc., 1966.
7. *Index to Illustrations,* Jessie Croft Ellis. The Faxon Company, 1966. 15 Southwest Park, Westwood, Mass. 02090.
8. Selected United States Government Publications, Superintendent of Documents, Government Printing Office, Washington, D.C.
9. *Sources of Free and Inexpensive Educational Material,* Field Enterprises, Inc., Education Division, Merchandise Mart Plaza, Chicago, Ill. 60654.
10. *Sources of Free and Inexpensive Pictures for the Classroom, Sources of Free and Inexpensive Teaching Aids,* and *Sources of*

Free Travel Posters and Geographic Aids, Bruce Miller, Box 369, Riverside, Calif.

11. *8 mm Film Guide,* Grace Ann Kohn, Comprehensive Service Corporation, 250 W. 64th St., New York, N.Y. 10023.

12. Obtain film indexes from audiovisual services of nearby colleges and universities.

The teacher should not overlook the diplomatic offices of foreign countries based in the United States as a source of free material. In most cases, the best place to direct inquiries concerning the availability of such material is the embassy of the country, Washington, D.C. Some countries (for example, Japan) have excellent packets of materials available for school use.

Nonreading Materials and Resources

The term *nonreading material* is a broad classification to indicate the materials that depend more heavily on sight and sound to convey meaning than on the interpretation of printed words. In the strictest sense, most learning materials depend on reading to some extent—charts and maps have titles and legends, filmstrips have captions, even films contain some print. For the most part, however, these learning devices use symbols other than print as the primary method of conveying meaning to the child.

Nonreading materials are important in social studies for a variety of reasons. First of all, they are an avenue of learning open to the child who does not have well-developed reading skills. A social studies program that depends exclusively on printed resources works a hardship on the slower reading or nonverbal child. The use of nonreading resources, however, should not be limited to those children who cannot read. Many of these materials present information that is difficult to obtain through reading. A film showing life in a faraway land is an experience that cannot be duplicated in any other way in the classroom. Nonreading materials are aids to learning that are intended to give meaning and enrich the learning of *all* children. We use maps, charts, and graphs because these devices are able to present information that is extremely difficult to comprehend in print. We use field trips to give children a firsthand experience with some aspects of the problem under consideration. We use films, filmstrips, and pictures to add realism and furnish the class with a common background of experience. Nonreading materials, therefore, have a great many values for the capable as well as the poor reader.

An extensive treatment of certain nonreading instructional materials is unnecessary because there are other sources that discuss this topic in depth.[3] The teacher should familiarize himself with the general nature of various nonreading materials and gain an understanding of the general principles under which they should be used. The following material is a brief summary of the manner in which some of these materials can be used in social studies units.

PICTURES, PHOTOGRAPHS, ILLUSTRATIONS

The most widely used of all visual aids are pictures, photographs, and illustrations. They are used to obtain realism, to clarify ideas, to recall the real object, and, in short, to give meaning to learning. It is well known that words cannot convey meanings as accurately, vividly, or quickly as pictures. It is this feature that makes some magazines such as *Life* popular with the public; they depend heavily on pictures and illustrations to tell their story. The teacher will build a substantial stock of carefully selected pictures, photographs, and illustrations to use when necessary to enrich meaning, for motivation, for clarifying ideas, and for summarization. Conscientious teachers are continually on the lookout for high-quality graphic material they can use in their teaching. The following is a partial list of sources of pictures, photographs, and illustrations:

Air Age Education, 100 E. 42nd St., New York, N.Y.
Arizona Highways, Phoenix, Ariz.
Arthur Barr Productions, Inc., 1029 N. Allen, Pasadena, Calif. 91104.
Association of American Railroads, Transportation Building, Washington, D.C.
Documentary Photo Aids, P.O. Box 2237, Phoenix, Ariz. 85002.
Informative Classroom Picture Publishers, 31 Ottowa, N.W., Grand Rapids, Mich.
Life, Time and Life Building, Rockefeller Center, New York, N.Y. 10020.
National Geographic Society, 16th and M Streets, N.W., Washington, D.C. 20036.
Pictures for Visual Instruction, 109 Market Place, Baltimore, Md.
Pictures-on-File, Gale Research Company, 1400 Book Tower, Detroit, Mich. 48226.

In the use of these materials it may be desirable to have the entire class view the illustration at one time. This is possible through the use

3. Edgar Dale, *Audio-Visual Methods in Teaching*, 3rd ed., New York: Dryden Press and Holt, Rinehart, and Winston, 1969; W. A. Wittich and C. F. Schuller, *Audio-Visual Materials, Their Nature and Use*, 4th ed., New York: Harper & Row, 1967; and C. W. H. Erickson, *Fundamentals of Teaching with Audiovisual Technology*, 2nd ed., New York: The Macmillan Company, 1968.

of an opaque projector. This device may also be used to enlarge maps, diagrams, and sketches on the chalkboard or on a large piece of wrapping paper. It is a fairly simple matter to project the required illustration on the material on which it is to be placed and then trace the projection. This provides a means of obtaining large diagrams, charts, graphs, and other illustrations difficult to enlarge in any other way.

What makes a picture, photograph, or illustration suitable for instructional purposes in social studies? Certainly, the most important consideration is accuracy of the portrayal. The fundamental purpose of any learning aid is to convey accurate meaning, and if this is lacking the picture, photograph, or illustration must be rejected unless, of course, it is being used to illustrate inaccuracy. Other factors that should be considered are that it be of sufficient size for the purpose it is to serve, appropriate to the age children with which it is to be used, of good artistic quality, impressive, of easy interpretation and that it have a definite center of interest not subordinated by a great many details.

FILMS

There are many 16 mm sound motion pictures that deal with social studies topics. Ordinarily, they are available on a rental basis and must be booked several months in advance of their anticipated use. The scheduling of films remains a serious problem in many places because it is often impossible to know the exact date on which a film will be needed.

Films have much to contribute to social studies teaching. In a film, the child can traverse great distances and move through centuries of time, having before him a picture of places, persons, and processes impossible to obtain in other ways. In many respects, the film has advantages over field trips because it singles out the most important aspects of a situation and eliminates the nonessentials. It is more selective in what it allows the viewer to see than is the human eye—thus having some advantage over an on-the-spot observation. It is a demanding medium and holds the attention of the learner to a greater extent than do most other learning aids. A film can telescope great lengths of time into minutes, making it possible to observe a timeless process in a single class period. Its greatest asset, of course, is that it depicts motion; and the best use can be made of films showing situations involving motion. If motion is not a factor, a good photograph, a slide, or a filmstrip may be equally effective.

In social studies, films may be appropriate at a variety of stages. They are commonly used at the beginning of a unit to build a common background of experience or to arouse interest. They may be used during the work stages to add meaning to material that is being read, or they may be used at the final stages of the study in order to summarize and reinforce ideas that have been developed. They should serve as a stimulus for discussion and further study whenever presented. The teacher, of course, would observe proper use of this material in social studies just as he would if the material were used in any other area of the curriculum. Specific reference is made here to previewing, building readiness, thinking in terms of specific learning goals, and follow-up procedures.

There are literally hundreds of sources of films throughout the nation. Many state universities and departments of education maintain a complete rental service for schools. Teachers interested in available films should seek out such local sources and request catalogues of films those centers provide. The following is a partial listing of some of the better-known sources of sound motion pictures:

Academy Films, 748 N. Seward Street, Hollywood, Calif. 90038.
American Economic Foundation, 51 E. 42nd St., New York, N.Y. 10017.
Arthur Barr Productions, Inc., 1029 N. Allen, Pasadena, Calif. 91104.
Association Films, 347 Madison Ave., New York, N.Y. 10017.
Association of American Railroads, Transportation Building, Washington, D.C.
Audio-Visual Center, Indiana University, Bloomington, Ind. 47405.
Bailey Films, Inc., 6509 DeLongpre Avenue, Los Angeles, Calif. 90028.
Canadian Travel Film Library, 111 N. Wabash, Chicago, Ill.
Contemporary Films, Inc., 267 W. 25th Street, New York, N.Y. 10025.
Coronet Films, Coronet Building, 65 E. South Water St., Chicago, Ill. 60601.
Curriculum Materials Corporation, 1319 Vine St., Philadelphia, Pa. 19107.
Encyclopaedia Britannica Films, Inc., 1150 Wilmette Ave., Wilmette, Ill. 60091.
Film Associates of California, 559 Santa Monica Blvd., Los Angeles, Calif. 90025.
Gateway Productions, Inc., 1859 Powell Street, San Francisco, Calif. 94133.
International Film Bureau, Inc., 332 South Michigan Ave., Chicago, Ill. 60604.
International Film Foundation, Inc., 475 Fifth Ave., New York, N.Y. 10017.
Jam Handy Organization, 2821 E. Grand Blvd., Detroit, Mich. 48211.
Joint Council on Economic Education, 1212 Avenue of the Americas, New York, N.Y. 10036.
McGraw-Hill Book Company, Inc., Text-Film Department, 330 W. 42nd St., New York, N.Y. 10036.

National Education Television Film Service, Audio-Visual Center, Indiana University, Bloomington, Ind. 47401.

Office of Media Services, Room 5819, Department of State, Washington, D.C. 20520.

Progressive Pictures, 6351 Thornhill Drive, Oakland, Calif. 94611.

Society for Visual Education, Inc., 1345 Diversey Parkway, Chicago, Ill. 60614.

Sterling Educational Films, Inc., 6 E. 39th St., New York, N.Y. 10016.

United Nations, Films and Television, Distribution Officer, New York, N.Y. 10017.

United World Films, Inc., Free Film Department, 445 Park Ave., New York, N.Y. 10029.

See Also:

A Guide to Films, Filmstrips, Maps and Globes, Records on Asia, Asia Society, 112 E. 64th St., New York, N.Y. 10021.

Blue Book of Audio-Visual Materials, Educational Screen, 64 East Lake St., Chicago, Ill.

Educational Film Guide, H. W. Wilson Co., 950 University Ave., New York, N.Y. 10052.

The Educational Media Index, McGraw-Hill Book Company, Inc., 330 W. 42nd Street, New York, N.Y. 10036.

Guides to Newer Educational Media: Films, Filmstrips, Phonorecords, Radio, Slides, TV, American Library Association, 50 E. Huron St., Chicago, Ill. 60611.

Modern Index and Guide to Free Educational Films from Industry, Modern Teaching Picture Service, 45 Rockefeller Plaza, New York, N.Y. 10020.

U.S. Government Films for Public Educational Use, U.S. Government Printing Office, Washington, D.C.

BASIC STEPS IN USING FILMS [4]

Prepare Yourself

Select film related to study.
Pay careful attention to recommended level of use.
Preview film for content.
Plan how it is to be used.

4. Adapted from material prepared by Audio-Visual Department, San Diego City Schools, San Diego, California. *Used by permission.*

Use film guide if available.

Save your film lesson plans from year to year to improve them.

Prepare the Classroom

Place title, new vocabulary, and main points or questions on chalkboard.

Set up equipment, thread, and check.

Check seating, screen, ventilation.

Prepare the Class

Discuss reasons for seeing film.

Use related instructional materials to motivate class.

Study unusual words.

Discuss main points to look for.

List students' questions.

Have class note teacher's questions.

Present the Film

One teacher—one class—one film.

Focus and frame.

Check sound level.

Watch for film damage.

Summarize and Follow Up

Discuss the students' and the teacher's questions.

Test occasionally.

Initiate creative follow-up activities.

Dramatize and do role playing.

Do further research.

Evaluate the results with class.

If necessary, reshow the film.

FILMSTRIPS

When motion is not essential in pictures, the filmstrip may be used as effectively as a motion picture. Filmstrips offer advantages over motion pictures in terms of cost, availability, and use. Because of their relatively low cost, schools ordinarily maintain their own filmstrip library, and they are immediately available, therefore, when needed. A good instructional feature of the filmstrip is that it is possible to discuss its content as it is being shown. If it becomes necessary to refer to a picture previously shown, the filmstrip can be turned back to the picture in question. Filmstrips are easy to catalogue and store and are simple to show. In this respect, they have many advantages over slides. The production of filmstrips for use in social studies has increased greatly in recent years, and there are now many good filmstrips available on a wide variety of social studies topics.

Filmstrips may be used to achieve a number of purposes in the social studies unit. A filmstrip on the New England States, for example, gives a clear picture of the physical features of this area and thereby assists in understanding map symbols and serves as a good readiness for map reading. It may serve to introduce children to other countries of the world, showing how people in other lands live, work, and play. Filmstrips are very useful in presenting material that follows a definite sequence—how a letter gets from sender to receiver; the steps in the production of milk; the history, growth, and development of an area; the course of soil erosion; or the steps to be followed in the event of some emergency such as a fire, drowning, an accident, or an air raid. The nature of the content of the filmstrip will determine how and when it can be used most effectively. Some may best be used at the initial stages of a unit to introduce a new topic and stimulate the children's thinking. Others are better suited for use in study and research and should be used during the work-study phase of the unit. Other filmstrips can serve best to summarize learnings and to reemphasize important ideas developed and can make their best contribution near the conclusion of a unit of study.

SLIDES

Lantern slides and photographic slides have been used in schools for several years. They may be purchased from commercial agencies or produced by the teachers and children. They have the same instructional use as pictures but have the advantage of being able to be viewed by the entire class at one time. Many teachers use their own 35 mm cameras with color film and have excellent personal collections of color transparencies. Because the filmstrip has many advantages over slides in terms of maintaining a permanent sequence, cost, and storage, there are many more filmstrips available commercially than slides. The following is a partial list of some of the better-known sources of filmstrips and slides:

Coronet Films, Coronet Building, 65 E. South Water St., Chicago, Ill. 60601.
Curriculum Films, 10 E. 40th St., New York, N.Y. 10016.
Curriculum Materials Corporation, 1319 Vine St., Philadelphia, Pa. 19107.
Educational Screen and Audiovisual Guide, 415 N. Dearborn St., Chicago, Ill. 60610.

Encyclopaedia Britannica Films, Inc., 1150 Wilmette Ave., Wilmette, Ill. 60091.

Eye-Gate House, Inc., 146-01 Archer Ave., Jamaica, N.Y. 11435.

Filmstrip House, 432 Park Ave. South, New York, N.Y. 10016.

Jam Handy Organization, 2821 E. Grand Blvd., Detroit, Mich. 48211.

Life Filmstrips, Time and Life Building, Rockefeller Center, New York, N.Y. 10020.

McGraw-Hill Book Company, Inc., Text-Film Department, 330 W. 42nd St., New York, N.Y. 10036.

The New York Times, Office of Educational Activities, Times Square, New York, N.Y. 10036.

Society for Visual Education, Inc., 1345 Diversey Parkway, Chicago, Ill. 60614.

Stanley Bowmar Company, Inc., 12 Cleveland St., Valhalla, N.Y. 10595.

Stillfilm, Inc., 171 S. Los Robles, Pasadena, Calif.

Weston Woods, Weston, Conn. 06880.

See Also:

Complete Index of Educational Filmstrips, Filmstrip Distributors, 2338 E. Johnson St., Madison, Wisc.

Filmstrip Guide, H. W. Wilson Co., 950 University Ave., New York, N.Y. 10052.

OVERHEAD PROJECTOR

One of the most valuable and most popular of the newer instructional aids is the overhead projector. This device is versatile and easy to use. With it the teacher may use a 10" x 10" prepared transparent acetate slide or may use a blank sheet of acetate and write directly on it with a grease pencil, a felt pen, or a slide marker. In using the overhead projector, the teacher faces the class while the image is being projected on a screen behind him but in full view of the class. This device can be used for some of the same purposes as a conventional chalkboard yet has some advantages over chalkboards. For example, the slides or drawings can be used repeatedly; the illuminated platform is easier to write on than is a chalkboard; there is no chalk dust with the overhead projector. Unlike the opaque projector, the overhead does not require a totally darkened room. Semidarkness is almost always satisfactory for overhead projector use, and in some cases no darkening at all is needed. It is not possible to project photographs or other non-transparent illustrations on the overhead projector. Hence, these slides are referred to as "transparencies." Because they are transparent, one transparency can be placed on top of another in the cumulative development of an idea. The use of these overlays is helpful in developing ideas that follow a sequential pattern.

Teachers often make their own transparencies for use in the social studies. Commercially prepared transparencies are also available through instructional resources outlets. These are usually advertised in journals such as *Instructor, Grade Teacher,* and *Social Education.*

Maps, Globes, Charts, Cartoons, Posters, and Graphs

Maps, globes, charts, cartoons, posters, and graphs are items used so extensively in social studies that they have been singled out for special consideration in a later chapter. They will not be considered here, therefore, and the reader is referred to Chapter 15.

Auditory Aids

In addition to visual material, the teacher will find the use of recordings and radio helpful in teaching social studies. Radio broadcasts for school use are common in many sections of the country; and, if the class is not ready for the presentation at the time of the broadcast, it may be available to them as a tape recording for a small charge. Conventional recordings dealing with various aspects of American history are available through commercial sources and can do much to make history "come alive" for children. Radio broadcasts dealing with historical material were special favorites of children until recently when they were displaced by television. Present-day recordings presenting authentic historical accounts related to topics under study have high interest appeal to youngsters. They can make a valuable contribution to social studies instruction.

The following sources will provide the teacher with helpful information concerning educational recordings:

Annotated List of Phonograph Records, Warren S. Freeman, ed., Children's Reading Service, 1078 St. John's Place, Brooklyn, N.Y.

The Children's Record Catalog, Harrison Record Catalogs, Department A, 274 Madison Ave., New York, N.Y.

Children's Record Guide, 100 Avenue of the Americas, New York, N.Y. 10013.

Educational Record Sales, 57 Chambers St., New York, N.Y. 10007.

Enrichment Records, 246 Fifth Ave., New York, N.Y. 10011. Records based on *Landmark Books.*

Folkways Records, 165 W. 46th St., New York, N.Y. 10036.

Listing of Educational Recordings and Filmstrips for More Effective Learning, Educational Services, 1730 I St., N.W., Washington, D.C.

NBC-RCA Radio Recordings, Radio City, New York, N.Y. 10001.

RCA Victor, Record Division, 155 East 24th St., New York, N.Y. 10010.

Recordings for Education: Social Studies, Columbia Records, 797 Seventh Ave., New York, N.Y. 10019.

Recordings for Elementary Schools, by Helen S. Leavitt and Warren S. Freeman, Crown Publishers, 419 Fourth Ave., New York, N.Y. 10011.

Riverside Records, 235 W. 46th Street, New York, N.Y. 10036.

Stanley Bowmar Company, Inc., 445 Park Ave., New York, N.Y. 10022.

The tape recorder is a familiar piece of equipment in many elementary classrooms. This versatile and easily operated device can be used to good advantage in several ways in the social studies. With it the teacher can record a radio broadcast any time—in the evening or on a Sunday afternoon—and play it for the class several weeks or months later at the precise time it can be of most use to the class in their social studies unit. Through the Department of Audio-Visual Instruction of the National Education Association it is possible to obtain prerecorded tapes on a variety of topics, many of them relevant to the social studies. The programs available through this source are listed in the *National Tape Recording Catalog.* The teacher may obtain a copy of any program listed in the catalog by sending a blank tape to Tapes for Teaching, National Repository, University of Colorado, Boulder, Colorado.

The tape recorder has many other uses. It can be used to record travel talks by teachers or other adults in the community who cannot visit the class in person. Or, the lecture of a classroom visitor may be recorded for replaying and study at a later time. Some teachers have had children write and record commentaries to accompany filmstrips to be shared with the remainder of the class, other classes, or classroom guests. It is possible for children to record their class discussions in order to note progress, to evaluate their work, or to use for future reference. Children record dramatic presentations, news broadcasts, or make "on-the-spot" recordings. One teacher had a group of children prepare a bulletin board display and record an explanation of the material posted that the viewer might listen to as he studied the display. These examples serve to show the many ways the tape recorder may be used in social studies teaching. With the help of a fertile imagination and the suggestions of children themselves, the teacher can find many situations where the tape recorder may be used, not as a toy or novelty but rather as a legitimate and helpful tool of instruction.

Children may wish to exchange fifteen-minute tapes with youngsters in other countries. This can be arranged through (1) Mrs. Ruth

Listening to recorded material has become an important way of obtaining needed information in social studies. (Courtesy of the Washington State Office of Public Instruction, Olympia)

Y. Terry, 834 Ruddeman Avenue, North Muskegon, Michigan or (2) World Tapes for Education, Inc., P.O. Box 15703, Dallas, Texas. Information concerning international tape exchanges can be obtained from these two sources.

TELEVISION

Research on the television viewing habits of children during out-of-school hours clearly indicates that television viewing is a well-established pastime of nearly all American schoolchildren. For example, a study published in 1963 reported that in that year children in grade two were spending an average of seventeen hours a week watching television, whereas for children in grade six the average weekly television viewing time was twenty-eight hours.[5] Studies have consistently shown that pupils view television from two to four hours each day during the week with some increase in that amount on weekends. The

5. Paul A. Witty, Paul Kinsella, and Anne Coomer, "A Summary of Yearly Studies of Televiewing—1949–1963," *Elementary English*, XL, October, 1963, pp. 590–597.

pupil in school, therefore, is well acquainted with this medium and is accustomed to viewing professionally produced programs even if the substance of such programs is not always of high quality.

Educators were quick to recognize the possibilities of television for school instruction, although to date its potential has been far from realized and exploited. The Federal Communications Commission reported that in 1964 there were eighty-eight educational television stations serving schools, thirty-six more than in 1960. In 1965, there were, additionally, at least two hundred to three hundred closed-circuit television systems installed by local public schools, school districts, colleges, and universities for direct systematic instruction and to share superior lecturing and educational resources.

Mechanically and technically, television reaches the classroom in three ways. First, there are educational television stations with open channels, allocated specifically for educational purposes. They are noncommercial stations, but their programs can be received on any television set in the community, in or out of school, providing they are within telecasting range of the station. Ordinarily, programs during the hours of the school day are related to the school curriculum, whereas after-school hours are devoted to programs of more general cultural interest. Second, there are *closed-circuit* television programs produced specifically for in-school viewing that cannot be received on sets not connected to the telecasting circuit. Third, there are programs of an educational nature that are shown on commercial television stations either for in-school or out-of-school viewing. Television programs themselves may be "live" (viewed at the time they are produced); they may be placed on television tape recordings; or they may be on kinescope, a type of film recording.

Part of the problem with the instructional use of television is the inclination to use it in precisely the same way a "live" teacher is used. This practice works to the disadvantage of television because the television set is often an inadequate substitute for the human teacher and because the unique characteristics of the television medium are lost in the process. If television has instructional value, it is because it can do something more effectively than other media or because it can do some things that other media cannot do at all. Educational television can be of tremendous assistance to the elementary teacher in enriching and vitalizing social studies providing it is used to achieve purposes the teacher himself cannot accomplish at least as well through the use of books and other conventional learning resources. Television instruction is always large-group instruction, and the same principles should be applied to its use that apply to any large group-teaching situation.

One valuable contribution television can make to social studies instruction is to motivate pupils. The television program has the total resources of the world outside the classroom to utilize in constructing programs that are highly interesting and motivating to pupils. Television can span both time and space in bringing relevant events into the classroom in capsule form. Television can visually transport pupils to the areas they are studying. What is more, it can show them details they would probably miss if they were actually there. The most eminent authorities and world leaders can be their teachers through television. The dramatic capabilities of good television production can be utilized in making a subject alive and exciting for pupils. Television, as are motion pictures, is a medium that demands one's attention. Furthermore, pupils are accustomed to turning to it for the experience of taking part vicariously in an exciting episode or identifying with interesting people. It is, therefore, a natural vehicle to use for motivating and stimulating pupils in a topic or subject under study.

A second contribution television can make is to provide information not available through other sources. Some of these possibilities were suggested in the previous paragraph. No other medium can make it possible for a child to witness the inauguration of the President taking place a thousand miles away. A visitor from India cannot visit all fourth-grade classrooms in a large city and tell the pupils interesting things about his country. But he can share his ideas with these pupils via television. A major strength of television is that it can assemble and distribute information widely and quickly. Television is not a substitute for books and other references or for the classroom teacher. It is, rather, a resource that can bring to the classroom a type of information that it alone can supply. If information can be obtained just as easily and efficiently through other means, television should probably not be used, because children do not habitually turn to television in search of information.

A third contribution of television to social studies is to clarify, elaborate, interpret, and enrich information that may be available through other sources. For example, a museum curator may be able to elaborate and clarify information concerning artifacts of early Indians who lived in the region. An authority or a traveler might be able to provide interesting details to help pupils understand why people of another culture do some particular thing the way they do. Television is an excellent medium for vitalizing knowledge because it can provide intimate, personal details that cannot be obtained on a large scale through other sources.

Television, just as any other learning resource, requires intelligent use by the teacher if it is going to contribute to social studies learning.

In some ways television use demands even more careful planning than other media because of a certain built-in element of inflexibility. For example, programs are presented at specific times on specific days and are presented in a specified sequence. This means that the classroom instructional program must be planned in accordance with the scheduled television programs if they are to be used profitably. Proper planning for television use calls for preparation by the teacher and pupils prior to the program and a satisfactory follow-up after the viewing. In most cases the value of the viewing depends almost entirely on what the class has done to prepare itself for the program and what they will do after they have watched it. The suggestions for use of films on page 133 also apply to television. Usually, educational television stations provide the teacher with a manual or a teaching guide that will be of assistance in planning for the viewing and in providing relevant follow-up activities.

Outside school, television is regarded as an entertainment rather than an educational device. This stereotype can work to the disadvantage of its good use in school. Certainly the possibilities for the misuse of educational television are real and great. But television is a newcomer to the educational scene, and in time the educational world will be more mature in its use of this medium. There can be little question that educational television is still in its infancy and that it will grow in use and effectiveness in years ahead. Television programs should not become the entire social studies curriculum—as has happened in some schools—neither should the programs be regarded as inconvenient extras included simply because they are available. Ideally used, the television program will become an integral part of the total instructional program planned in the social studies and will make its contribution in ways that are unique to it.

PROGRAMED INSTRUCTION

Automated teaching devices include such instructional materials as teaching machines, self-teaching programs, scrambled textbooks, and other self-instructing devices. They differ in principle from audiovisual aids of the conventional type because the learner is required to interact with the teaching device. That is, a stimulus is presented, the learner reacts to it, the response is corrected immediately, and the learner goes to the next step according to whether his response was correct or incorrect. The plan followed by the learner is called a program. Consequently, instruction presented in this way has come to be called programed instruction.

A few fundamental principles undergird most if not all programed instruction. The subject or skill to be taught is analyzed and broken down into small component elements. These are arranged sequentially in carefully graded steps, with the most basic elements presented first and moving to more complex relationships or variations as the learner progresses through the program. Steps or increments of difficulty are increased very gradually, thus reducing incorrect responses to a minimum and motivating the learner by strengthening him psychologically with a backlog of success responses. The emphasis on successful responses also ensures that the learner understands one operation before proceeding to the next, more complex variation of it.

One of the strengths of programed instruction is that it is highly individualized. To a large extent the speed of the learning experience is under the control of the learner himself—the fast learner can move through the program quickly, the slower learner more slowly, each taking as much time and practice as he needs. Moreover, the progress of one child does not interfere with that of another. Although the amount of programed material for teaching social studies is somewhat limited at the present time, there are some materials available on map reading, understanding various aspects of government, the Constitution, certain historical information, elementary economics, and so on. Teachers may find programed materials especially helpful in individualizing instruction and in providing a useful supplement to their own presentations.

A number of complicated philosophical, psychological, and educational issues surround the use of automated teaching material. There is no question that learning *can* be achieved through programed instruction. Neither is there any question that the use of such material is increasing rapidly. But the questions that deal with the role of the human teacher in the programed learning situation, whether programed instruction is effective with various types of learnings, and whether programed instruction is really an efficient method of instruction, are not resolved. Experimentation continues and teachers will want to follow the development of these new instruments of learning and explore every possibility for their use. Information on the latest developments in programed instruction may be obtained from The Center For Programed Instruction, Teachers College, Columbia University, New York City. The center is a nonprofit organization that is heavily involved in the research and application of programed instruction to practical classroom situations.

ROOM ENVIRONMENT

A frequently overlooked learning resource is the classroom environment itself. A well-planned and stimulating classroom arrangement can do much to arouse and sustain interest as well as to provide the child with many avenues for learning. This is especially true in the primary grades when children have not yet developed reading skills

Concepts are often best understood through firsthand experiences. (Courtesy of the Seattle Public Schools)

or backgrounds of experience that permit them to profit from vicarious experiences to the same extent as older, more mature children. The primary classroom needs a "home" corner where children can play the roles of various members of the family, set the table, do the dishes, run the vacuum cleaner, dress and undress "baby," and so on. They need large blocks and manipulative material with which they can build the post office or the railway station. They need building tools with which they can construct boats, airplanes, farm buildings, trucks, cars, and trains. They need a generous supply of art mediums—paints, easels, chalk, crayons, finger paint, clay, colored paper, paste—to allow them to express their ideas and feelings through art. A good primary-grade classroom environment will present the young child with opportunities for doing research long before he is capable of reading anything beyond his basic reading series. Similarly, in a middle- or upper-grade classroom one would expect to find many books, maps, globes, pictures, models, exhibits, children's work, tools, paints, art materials, costumes, and attractive and informative bulletin boards.

The arrangement of the room environment also helps create an atmosphere that can serve either to enhance or retard learning. On entering a classroom one should get the feeling of orderliness and flexibility in the classroom arrangement and say to oneself, "This would be an interesting place to spend five or six hours each day." Contrariwise, other classrooms create a feeling of coldness and rigidity that are foreboding even to the adult, to say nothing of children. Elementary classrooms generally, and primary-grade classrooms particularly, must be so arranged as to allow children to feel psychologically at home in them. Such classrooms provide materials that stimulate the curiosity and interest of the growing child and place him in a setting suggestive of warmth, friendliness, and security. Classrooms that are planned and arranged as if they were to be used as laboratories for learning by young children will not have the dreary institutional look about them that seems to have characterized some schools in the past.

BULLETIN BOARDS

Modern and well-designed elementary school classrooms provide generously for stationary, wall-type bulletin boards at a suitable height from the floor for children who will occupy the room. In addition, many schools provide various types of portable bulletin boards for use in classrooms. Bulletin boards can make an important contribution to social studies instruction if they are properly utilized. They may be used at the beginning of a unit to display pictures, study prints, maps, charts, or other related material for discussion and study. During the course of the unit they may be used for displaying the work of the children, preparing an exhibit, constructing a mural, displaying class-made maps, posting directions or samples of work to be done by the class or other items related to the topic under study. At the close of the unit, bulletin boards are helpful in displaying the work of the children and provide many opportunities for class sharing, discussing, and summarizing of learnings. The displays need to be changed frequently as the unit progresses and as the purpose of the bulletin board changes. In the primary grades, children can assist by suggesting some of the material to be placed on the bulletin boards, but the actual display will have to be handled almost entirely by the teacher. As children move into the middle and upper grades, they are able to assume more of the responsibility for posting material themselves.

In order for the bulletin board display to be effective, certain elements in its preparation and use should be observed by the teacher. The following are suggested:

1. Use interesting and captivating captions of one type and color. Letters for captions might be made from dark construction paper, corrugated paper, cardboard, yarn, aluminum foil, or material that has a related design such as discarded book jackets, newspaper, or woodgrain.

2. Use sound principles of design, balance, order, and color. Too much material carelessly displayed gives a cluttered effect. Adapt the display to the physical make-up of the room. Take into consideration door and window heights, other displays, lighting, and the location of the display in terms of its basic purpose. Secure an organized effect by developing continuity in the display. Anchor material squarely and securely on all four corners.

3. Change the displays frequently and use variety in the material posted. There should be a purpose for posting any material, and after it has served its purpose it should be removed.

4. Take time to discuss the material on the bulletin boards; call the attention of the children to new material posted; teach directly from the bulletin board from time to time.

5. Encourage children to bring or prepare material suitable for bulletin board display. As soon as the children are sufficiently mature, involve them in the planning and preparation of some of the displays.

6. Keep in mind that the bulletin board is an instructional resource for *children.* As such it must be appealing to them and suitable to their level of understanding. Although the teacher may be tempted to use the bulletin board as a fine way to impress his principal, his colleagues, or the parents of the good work that goes on in the room, he ought not to lose sight of the basic educative purpose of bulletin board displays.

COMMUNITY RESOURCES

It is in the local community that the child should sow the seeds of a lifetime study of human society. Here he may see firsthand the social processes that function a thousand times over in communities around the world. It is in the local community that the child is introduced to geographical concepts, to the problems of group living, to government in operation, to the production and distribution of goods and services, and to the rich historical heritage that is his. In most American communities the child can see evidence that it is possible for persons of varied backgrounds, nationalities, religious faiths, and races to live and work harmoniously together. The resources of the local community make a vital and indispensable contribution to a modern program of social studies instruction.

There are basically two ways in which the teacher may make use of the local community. One is to bring some portion of the community to the classroom; the other is to take the class out of the school to some place or person of importance in the community. As a matter of principle, it is advisable to take elementary schoolchildren into the community only for the experiences that cannot be duplicated in the classroom. For example, it is usually better to arrange to have a lady bring her photographs of early life in the community to the school and to speak to the children there than it is to take the class of thirty children to her home. On the other hand, the process involved in canning tuna fish, peas, beans, or cranberries cannot be observed in the classroom; and the children must be taken to the cannery if this process is to be observed firsthand. Teachers commonly make use of the first method of using community resources without thinking of them as community resources at all. This happens when children bring materials from home for the bulletin boards, the "market," or the "dry dock," when parents are asked to assist in any way, when books are obtained from the public library, when the local newspaper is used, or when children bring items from home to share with others in "show and tell." The personal experiences children have in the community and share with the class are likewise a common use of community resources.

If the teacher hopes to go beyond these incidental uses of community resources, some type of inventory must be made of the local community to identify various resources that can be used profitably in teaching social studies. The term *community survey* is used to describe this process, although the task need not be as formidable as the term suggests. The community survey or inventory ought not be a one-man job but should be carried on cooperatively by the entire staff on a continuing basis year after year. In larger school systems teachers are frequently given a comprehensive list of available community resources that has been prepared by a committee under the direction and leadership of a consultant.

The resources uncovered in the survey should be grouped in some logical way such as local industries, places of historical interest, governmental agencies, civic establishments, annual events (pageants, concerts, festivals, fairs), places of geographic importance, persons to interview, places of cultural significance, and similar categories. Additional information may then be listed for each of the persons, places, or establishments, including such details as when the resource is available, whom to contact to make arrangements for its use, how the resource might be used in the social studies program, what advance preparation is necessary, and, if the resource involves a field trip, whether the firm provides a guide. An example is given of a standardized form that could be used to record such information:

COMMERCE AND INDUSTRY

Place .... Montfort Packing Company

Address .... North 8th Avenue; Greeley, Colorado

Person to Contact .... Harold Adcock
Norman Peterson
Swede Swanson

Telephone Number .... 303-353-2311; Ext. 21, 22, 23

Advance Reservation Necessary .... Two days

Days Open .... Tuesday, Wednesday, Thursday

Hours .... 8:30 A.M., 10:30 A.M., or 1:30 P.M.

Tour ....

Guided .... Yes

Length .... 45 minutes

Maximum Group Size 25

Restroom Facilities .... Limited

Special Precautions .... Advance Preparation of Pupils—
Eleven years old or older

Admission Charge .... None

Materials Available for Distribution .... None

Speakers Available .... Harold Adcock

Appropriate Grade Level .... Sixth Grade

Other Significant Information or Comments:

Evaluation:

An examination of available resources and the curriculum guide will show the points at which the community resources can be used most profitably. There needs to be close coordination of the use of community resources at the school level to ensure the maintenance of good public relations and to make certain that best instructional use is made of whatever resources are available to the school.

The use of the community as a resource in social studies presents many opportunities for good teaching and learning. In most cases what the teacher and class do prior to and following the use of such a resource determines the extent to which it contributes to the attainment of desirable learning outcomes. This is especially true in the case of field trips, the use of resource visitors to the class, or conducting interviews with persons in the community. Uppermost in the mind of the teacher should be the thought that genuine educational purpose motivates the use of such resources. With this in mind, the teacher will prepare the class for the use of the resource and will also engage the class in appropriate follow-up activities after its use. Together the teacher and the pupils will identify specific things they wish to find out from the person being interviewed, from the person who speaks to them, or from their field trip.

The teacher must always select with care the persons who are invited to spend time with the class for instructional purposes. Some people should not be asked to speak to children, because they are not able to make themselves understood, they lack an understanding of children, they hold and express freely attitudes or beliefs that may be offensive to members of the group, or they fail completely to grasp the significance of their visit to the class. The teacher should plan to spend some time with the visitor sufficiently far enough in advance of the visit to brief him on the activities of the class, the purposes of his visit, and the points to be discussed and stressed. Likewise, the children must be prepared for the visitor, listing the purposes of his coming, questions they should like to ask, and general courtesies extended to classroom guests. Handled in this manner, persons from the community can make a positive contribution to the instructional program in the social studies. Those who might be used either for the purposes of interview or as classroom resource visitors might include

County agent
County commissioner
Members of the Federal Conservation Service, the Farm Bureau, the
    Izaak Walton League, local conservation groups, Future Farmers of
    America
4-H club leaders
Old inhabitants of the community
Professional persons: ministers, doctors, lawyers
Judges
Legislators
Local officials
Representatives of local industries
Travelers

Authors
Persons with special skills: weavers, pottery makers, jewelry makers
Armed forces personnel
Exchange students
Persons with interesting hobbies
Community helpers: policemen, firemen, postmen
Members of local historical society
Newspaper reporters
Members of service organizations

Whenever children are taken off the school site, the teacher must attend to a number of exceedingly important details. Adequate planning will help the teacher anticipate some of the problems that may arise in connection with the field trip and will help make the trip educationally worthwhile. Poorly planned field trips are worse than none at all, for they lack purpose, may jeopardize the safety of the children, may cause poor public relations between the school and community, and can break down learnings the teacher should have been trying to build in the classroom. Although the field trip should be pleasant for everyone including the teacher, it is first of all an educative experience, and its primary objective is not that everyone have a joyous outing. Good planning will ensure that the trip will be both an enjoyable as well as an educational experience. The following suggestions will be helpful in achieving that goal:

FIELD TRIPS

Preparing for the Trip

1. Clearly establish the purposes of the trip and make certain the children understand the purposes, too. The excursion should provide opportunities for learning that are not possible in the classroom. If educational purposes can be achieved equally well within the classroom, the field trip is unnecessary.
2. Obtain administrative permission for the field trip and make arrangements for transportation. As a matter of policy, it is better to use a public conveyance or a school bus than it is to use private automobiles. In using private cars the teacher is never sure if the driver is properly insured, is competent behind the wheel, or even has a valid operator's license.
3. Make all necessary preliminary arrangements at the place of the visit. This should include the time for the group to arrive, where

they are to go, who will guide them, and so forth. It is recommended that the teacher make the excursion himself prior to the time the children are taken. This will alert him to circumstances and situations that should be discussed with the children before leaving the classroom. Talk to the person who is to be the field trip guide so as to assure his awareness of the purposes of the field trip.

4. Study the literature on the subject. No teacher should approach a field trip unprepared. This knowledge will later be valuable in helping prepare pupils for the field trip and in initiating follow-up and study activities.

5. Obtain from each parent written permission for his child to go on the trip and do not take children who cannot or do not return signed permission slips. Although this action does not in itself absolve the teacher of responsibility or liability in the event of an accident, it indicates to the teacher that the parent knows of the field trip and approves of the child's going. Most schools have forms for this purpose that are filled out by the teacher and sent home with each child for the parent's signature.

6. Prepare the class for the field trip. "What is it that we wish to find out? What things in particular do we want to look for? What questions do we want to ask the guide?" Through careful planning and preparation the teacher helps children to be more observant and makes a genuine research activity out of the field trip. The chances are good that children will be taken to places many of them have been before. The first-grader has been to the supermarket a hundred times with his parents. Most of them have seen trains, many have been to the airport, some have been to the harbor, and all have been to a filling station. Why, then, should the school take children to such places on field trips? The answer is that different purposes exist for the field trip than for incidental visits. The children are prepared to look for things they would not otherwise see.

Prior to the trip is a good time for the class to set up standards of conduct for the trip. Through discussion, the point can be made that each of them is really a representative or ambassador of the school and that persons in the community may make judgments about the entire school based on the actions of one child. Children are quick to accept the challenge that the responsibility for a good trip rests personally with each member of the group. Time spent on this part of the preparation for the excursion will pay dividends when the trip is underway. There is nothing more embarrassing for the teacher, more damaging to school-community relations, or more devastating to the educational purposes of the field trip than a group of rude and unruly children. This oftentimes happens when the children have been inadequately prepared for the trip.

7. If the trip is to be long, make arrangements for lunchroom and restroom facilities.

8. Have an alternate plan in case the weather turns bad or something interferes.

Conducting the Trip

9. Take roll before leaving the school grounds and "count noses" frequently during the trip to make sure some of the children have not become lost or left in some restroom along the way. With young children it is a good idea to place them in pairs, because a child will know and report immediately the absence of his partner. To assist with the supervision of the children and to help ensure a safe trip, the teacher should arrange for other adults to accompany the group. Teachers can usually count on parents to assist in this way but should plan to meet with them prior to the trip and explain the purposes, standards of behavior, the route to be followed, and other important details. The adults accompanying the children must be prepared for the excursion just as are the children. One teacher handled this very well by having the children prepare a little booklet prior to the trip that included "Things We Will Remember," "This Is the Way We Will Go to the Lighthouse," "Things We Will See on the Way to the Lighthouse," "Things We Will See at the Lighthouse," as well as a map of the route to be followed. The booklets were reproduced in multiple and each child and parent going on the trip had one to use as a guide.

10. Arrive at the designated place on time and have children ready for the guide. Be sure to introduce the guide to the class. Supervise children closely during the tour to prevent accidents or injury. Before leaving, check again to make sure all children are with the group.

11. Make sure that time and an opportunity is allowed for the answering of pupil questions so that individual differences can be met on the trip.

12. Make sure each pupil can see and hear adequately. Be sure that a summarization is made before the trip is concluded.

Evaluating the Trip

13. Engage the class in appropriate follow-up activities. This should include writing a thank-you note to the firm and to the adults who accompanied the class. In the primary grades, the children dictate

Field trips should provide pupils with opportunities for learning that cannot be duplicated in the classroom. (Courtesy of the Seattle Public Schools and the Shoreline Public Schools, Seattle)

such a letter to the teacher who writes it on the chalkboard or chart. Individual children then copy the letter and one may be selected to be sent or, in some cases, they may all be sent. The teacher and children will also want to evaluate carefully the extent to which the purposes of the trip have been achieved. "Did we accomplish what we set out to do? Did we get the answers to our questions? What did we learn that we didn't know before? What are some other things we will want to find out?" Finally, the teacher and children will want to evaluate the conduct of the class in terms of the standards set up before the trip was made. It is not a good plan to pinpoint specific children who may have been unthoughtful—this can better be handled by the teacher on an individual basis with only the children involved. The teacher will, rather, want to have the children discuss whether they listened attentively, stayed in a group, observed habits of courtesy, and so on. This evaluation should always include some favorable reactions as well as ways in which the group might improve on subsequent trips. A list might be made of these suggestions for improvement to be saved for review just before the next trip is undertaken.

14. Discuss work and study projects in which pupils might engage for further study. Such projects might include construction activities, original stories, reports, dramatic plays, and diaries. Survey other resources available in the community for study.

15. Utilize opportunities to draw upon data and experiences from the field trip in other subjects taught in the classroom.

Every community has places that can be visited by classes and thereby can contribute to the enrichment of learning in the social studies. These will differ from place to place but any of the following could be used:

State historical society	Aquarium
Historical sites, monuments	Library
Flood plain, eroded areas, dam sites	Refinery
Razing of a building	Museum
Hospitals	Public health department
Weather bureau	Local stores
Warehouses	Legislative bodies in session
Airports	Art galleries
Railway station	Fire station
Assembly plants	Newspaper printing facilities
Post office	Bakery
Broadcasting or telecasting station	Observatory

Courthouse	The harbor
Factories	Police station
Farms	Zoo
Urban planning commission	Parks
Docks	Shopping centers

Selecting the Proper Instructional Aid

The quantity, quality, and accessibility of instructional materials have improved steadily through the years. Modern programs in social studies would not be possible without the requisite learning materials. With the wealth of good instructional resources available, there is little need for the teacher to depend exclusively on a single basic textbook and the classroom encyclopedia, important as these tools are.

But how is the teacher to know what particular resource to use? Every learning aid has definite, unique strength that probably cannot be duplicated through the use of another aid. It is also true that most aids to learning have limitations that may preclude their use under certain conditions. The characteristics and maturity of children will usually condition the choice of the aid to be used.

Perhaps the best course of action for the teacher is to familiarize himself with the many resources for learning now available in teaching social studies. Then, when he finds himself in a specific teaching situation with a particular group of children with definite learning goals in mind, he can select wisely the aids most appropriate to use under the given set of circumstances. There is rarely only one best way to do anything—what may be the best course of action under one set of conditions may not be under others. The teacher who is thoroughly grounded in the possibilities for good teaching presented by each of the many aids or resources and understands the principles of their application is the one who is likely to make the best judgment concerning their selection and use.

Discussion Questions and Suggested Activities

1. Select three or four textbooks that contain content on the topic of your resource unit you began in Chapter 3. Evaluate these texts in terms of the criteria presented in this chapter. What content will you use from these textbooks?
2. What ways can you think of to keep the school librarian informed of your social studies activities in order that she may be of greater help in suggesting and securing books and other materials?
3. Identify resource people that you might call upon during instruction in the unit you are building.

4. Make some transparencies or set up a book display that can be used in the unit.
5. Write for samples of free and inexpensive materials and evaluate them in terms of the standards discussed in this chapter.
6. Visit the instructional materials center and audiovisual center on your campus and examine the different resources available. Find media that can be used in your resource unit.
7. Prepare and display a bulletin board for the class and show how it might be used as an instructional aid.
8. Form a committee of your classmates and visit a place of interest in the local community. Plan how you would take a group of children to this place on a field trip. Indicate what contributions such a field trip might make to unit study, what children would see, what they might see enroute, and the specific purposes for planning such a trip. Complete the form illustrated in this chapter; ditto and pass out a copy to each of your classmates so that everyone might begin a file of potential field trip sites.
9. Evaluate the following statement by an elementary principal: "In my school I select the learning materials myself because teachers lack the time to do it; I am more up-to-date on what is available as well as its cost, and I can get newer materials into the hands of the teachers and pupils faster than if I wait for individual teachers to make the selections."
10. What advantages can you see for having numerous copies of several different social studies textbooks in a classroom rather than one common text for each pupil? Are there any limitations to the use of "multiple textbooks"?

Selected References

Anderson, Robert M., *et al.*, eds. *Instructional Resources for Teachers of the Culturally Disadvantaged and Exceptional*. Springfield, Ill.: Charles C Thomas, Publishers, 1969.

Arnsdorf, Val E. "Selecting and Using Collateral Materials in Social Studies," *The Reading Teacher*, No. 20 (April, 1967), pp. 621–625.

Audiovisual Instruction, 14, No. 4 (April, 1969). Devoted to the topic of teaching social studies with media.

Audiovisual Instruction, 14, No. 10 (December, 1969). Devoted to media and the culturally different.

Bergeson, Clarence O. "Using Learning Resources in Social Studies Skill Development," *Social Education*, XXXI, No. 3 (March, 1967), pp. 227–229.

Brown, James W., Richard B. Lewis, and Fred F. Harcleroad. *A-V*

Instruction: Media and Methods, 3rd ed. New York: McGraw-Hill Book Company, Inc., 1969.

Brown, Ralph A. and Marian. "Selecting Social Studies Textbooks: The Challenge of Choice," *Social Education,* XXXIII, No. 3 (March, 1969), pp. 314–320+.

Corey, Kenneth E. "Using Local Resources in Developing Geographic Concepts and Understanding," *Social Education,* XXX, No. 8 (December, 1966), pp. 617–619.

Dale, Edgar. *Audio-Visual Methods of Teaching,* 3rd ed. New York: Holt, Rinehart & Winston, Inc., 1969.

Erickson, Carlton W. H. *Fundamentals of Teaching with Audiovisual Technology,* 2nd ed. New York: The Macmillan Company, 1968.

Fraser, Dorothy McClure, ed. *Social Studies Curriculum Development: Prospects and Problems,* 39th Yearbook. Washington, D.C.: National Council for the Social Studies, 1969, Chap. 6.

Herman, Wayne L., Jr. *Current Research in Elementary School Social Studies.* New York: The Macmillan Company, 1969, Part VI.

Horn, Ernest. *Methods of Instruction in the Social Studies.* New York: Charles Scribner's Sons, 1937.

How To Do It Series. A practical set of pamphlets dealing with specific teaching procedures (single copy 25 cents). Washington, D.C.: National Council for the Social Studies.

Ingraham, Leonard W. "The 'Mixed Media' Menu." *Social Education,* XXXI, No. 8 (December, 1967), pp. 698–700.

Kendall, Lloyd. "Using Learning Resources in Concept Development," *Social Education,* XXX, No. 7 (November, 1966), pp. 542–544.

Menser, David. "Ideas and Objects: The Artifact Kit," *Social Education,* XXX, No. 5 (May, 1966), pp. 343–344.

Miller, Jack W. "How to Use Multiple Books," in *New Frontiers in the Social Studies: Action and Analysis, Book 2,* John S. Gibson. New York: Citation Press, 1967.

Rogers, Vincent R. "Using Source Material with Children," *Social Education,* XXIV, No. 7 (November, 1960), pp. 307–309.

Social Education. Washington, D.C.: National Council for the Social Studies. Contains components reviewing books, filmstrips, and so on. Published monthly during the school year.

Suppes, Patrick. "The Teacher and Computer-Assisted Instruction," *The NEA Journal,* 56, No. 2 (February, 1967), pp. 15–17.

Torkelson, Gerald M. "Using Learning Resources in Teaching Values," *Social Education,* XXXI, No. 1 (January, 1967), pp. 41–42+.

Torkelson, Gerald M. and Emily A. "How Mechanized Should the Classroom Be?" *The NEA Journal,* 56, No. 3 (March, 1967), pp. 28–30.

Walsh, Huber M. "Learning Resources for Individualizing Instruction," *Social Education, XXXI*, No. 5 (May, 1967), pp. 413–415.

Williams, Catherine M. *Learning from Pictures*. Washington, D.C.: Department of Audio-Visual Instruction, National Education Association, 1963.

Wittich, Walter A., and Charles F. Schuller. *Audiovisual Materials: Their Nature and Use,* 4th ed. New York: Harper and Row, Publishers, Inc., 1967.

The Individual Pupil and the Social Studies

American education continues to struggle with one of the most perplexing problems facing it: that of providing adequately for the diverse interests, talents, and abilities known to exist between and among members of class groups. Although the problem exists at all levels, it is particularly evident in the elementary school. Children must attend school because they are required to do so by law, and the opportunity for individual children to select their area of competition is not available to them. A typical elementary school presents a situation where one may find twenty-five to forty children in each class who are approximately the same chronological age but who are highly heterogeneous in other respects. It is this situation that

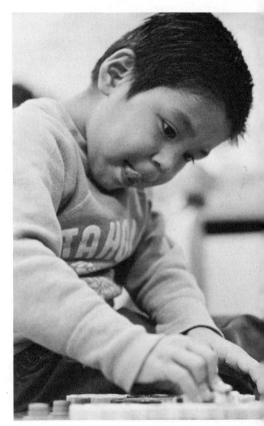

5

lies at the root of some of the most difficult instructional problems of our times.

The fact that people differ in ability has been known for centuries, but it has been only within the past fifty to seventy-five years that these differences have been subjected to serious scientific study. In recent years some progress has been made in tailoring school experiences to fit the varying needs of individual children. The concept of designing instructional programs in terms of individual differences among pupils has been accepted in principle by forward-looking educators and teachers for at least forty years. The question today is not one of whether there are to be provisions for individual differences but one of *how* the adjustments and adaptations should be made for individual pupils.

Beginning teachers frequently find it difficult to accept the fact that individual differences in children exist to the extent that they do and that these variations are actually quite desirable in terms of society's need for persons of different talents, abilities, skills, and intellectual levels. Perhaps every teacher has at some time or other said to himself, "I could teach so much more effectively if I didn't have such a range of abilities in this class." The common belief is that the teaching task can be simplified substantially if the variability of class groups is reduced. First thoughts, therefore, turn to the possibility of forming classes on the basis of the homogeneity of some trait such as reading ability or general ability.

There are two serious objections to the formation of classes in this manner. The first has to do with the social structure of the class. Parents and teachers alike tend to feel that the segregation of young children into ability groups runs contrary to some of the basic beliefs about the public elementary school as it is known in America. Moreover, this feeling has more to justify it than sentimentalism. In the elementary school the child has the opportunity to get to know and to work with children from all walks and stations of life. Rich or poor; bright or dull; black, white, red, or yellow; Protestant, Caltholic, or Jew—all sit side by side in the classroom, work together on a mural, or take their turn at bat on the playground. Few would deny that the possibilities for intergroup education and understanding in classes formed in this way are very great indeed. It is not likely that the child will ever again live as intimately for such a length of time in a group as heterogeneous with respect to talent and background as he does during the years he is in the elementary school. Many of the citizenship and socialization skills now learned through actual firsthand experiences would have to be learned through less-direct methods if children were grouped into classes on an ability basis. Added to this is the fact that ability grouping tends to pull children who would normally shoulder much leadership responsibility out of groups where they have an opportunity to exercise leadership skills and places them in situations where they have the least opportunity to assume leadership—in a class with thirty to thirty-five other children who have high leadership potential. Meanwhile, the low-ability group is deprived of the pupil leadership it requires.

The sacrificing of the social values of heterogeneous grouping might be warranted if the evidence clearly indicated that ability grouping resulted in superior achievement of pupils. However, this is far from the case. There is no evidence that one particular way of grouping pupils for instruction is demonstrably superior to others. Shane described briefly thirty-two historically interesting and educationally promising grouping plans. He concluded the review by saying, "The philosophy and ability of the able teacher are undoubtedly more important than any grouping plan however ingenious it may be, with respect to creating a good environment for teaching and learning." [1] The claims of devotees of particular grouping arrangements notwithstanding, the actual evidence from every carefully conducted experiment on the effects of grouping on pupils and their achievement suggests that there are variables other than the grouping arrangement that affect pupil achievement.

The second objection to ability grouping, therefore, is that such procedures are relatively ineffective methods of dealing with the problem of individual differences. Classes that are grouped on the basis of a single trait such as reading ability or a general trait such as mental ability remain highly variable in many other respects. This occurs because there are considerable differences in traits and abilities *within each individual child.* An examination of the achievement profiles of children will show that a child may be superior in reading ability yet be only average in arithmetic; he may be of high intelligence yet be low in musical or artistic ability. Every experienced teacher knows that the best speller, the best speaker, the best leader, or the best singer is not always to be found in the top reading group. Because differences within a single individual overlap group differences to the extent that they do, grouping on the basis of outstanding performance in one area does not assure excellence in another.

Special grouping may have a measure of justification, however, in the case of children who are at the extreme ends of the mental ability continuum—the mentally retarded and the highly gifted. The educational needs of these children are so vastly different from the re-

1. Harold G. Shane, "Grouping in the Elementary School," *Phi Delta Kappan*, 41, April, 1960, pp. 313–318.

THE INDIVIDUAL PUPIL AND THE SOCIAL STUDIES

mainder of the group as to make adequate adjustments within the regular classroom next to an impossibility. But for the great majority of children who fall between the two extremes, an attempt to solve the problem of individual differences in groups through special grouping of classes serves only to confuse the real issue. No matter what system of grouping is used, there will still be individual differences among pupils that will need to be taken into account in teaching. Therefore, curriculum adjustments to individual differences must be made in the instructional program within each classroom. In so doing, the teacher can form subgroups for instructional purposes within the classroom to meet the educational needs of individual children.

Differences That Need to Be Considered in Teaching Social Studies

The concept of individualization of instruction places the child squarely in the center of the teaching-learning process, and it is the obligation of the teacher to learn as much as possible about each child if he is to teach him effectively. Adjustments in the instructional program made for variations in individual children are made in terms of the information the teacher has about them. This information may be informal, unrecorded, and obtained without regularity or design by various teachers within a system, or it may be a complete and comprehensive record maintained by each teacher who has the child during his stay in school and accumulated from year to year. The method of obtaining the data may vary from school to school, but possession of information about the child is a necessary condition for the individualization of classroom instruction. In order to plan social studies units of instruction most effectively, the teacher must have readily available to him information on each child in at least each of the following areas: mental maturity, rate of achievement, sensory and physical status, home background, and personal and social adjustment.

DIFFERENCES IN MENTAL MATURITY

During the past half century, the research in measurement of intellectual capacity has indicated consistently and conclusively what teachers have always known on a common-sense basis, namely, that all persons do not possess equal ability to do intellectual tasks. Various individual and group tests have been devised to measure these differences somewhat objectively, making it possible to determine not only differences but also the extent of such differences. Ordinarily, results of such tests are expressed in mental ages or as a ratio between the individual's mental age and chronological age. This ratio is referred to

This child is obviously totally absorbed in what he is doing. A vital social studies program should help him sustain his interest in school. (Courtesy of the Washington State Office of Public Instruction, Olympia)

as the person's intelligence quotient or IQ. The IQ has come to be a generally accepted index of one's intellectual growth.

Basically, all mental maturity tests attempt to do the same thing. Through standardization procedures these tests establish average performances on various intellectual tasks for specific-age children who have similar cultural backgrounds and equal opportunity to learn the required tasks. With the use of carefully designed mental tests, it becomes possible to determine whether a child performs a given set of tasks equal to, below, or above the performance of other children of his chronological age. Because the tasks the child is required to do in

THE INDIVIDUAL PUPIL AND
THE SOCIAL STUDIES

the mental tests are highly correlated with tasks ordinarily associated with work in school, scores on such tests have been used as predictors of how well the child is likely to do in school.

The use of mental maturity tests has been helpful in assessing a child's ability along certain lines. They are especially useful in establishing levels of achievement expectation that are in harmony with individual children's capabilities. Intelligence tests are also helpful in determining the extent to which mental ability is a factor in poor achievement. Properly used, they are valuable to the teacher as guides in establishing realistic and reasonable standards of attainment for individual children. A study of these scores will help sensitize the teacher to the wide range of ability typically found in unselected grade groups.

There have been so many abuses made of intelligence test data in recent years that some school districts forbid the use of such tests. The risk of error in predicting and generalizing solely on the basis of measured IQ is always present and always high. It has long been known that IQ's obtained from some tests are little more than a reflection of a child's reading ability. Such tests usually only sample the child's ability to do abstract and verbal tasks and usually pay little if any attention to social intelligence, artistic and creative intelligence, as well as ability to do tasks requiring motor coordination. The conditions of similar cultural background and equal opportunity to learn on the part of the children tested are also not always met. Moreover, there is some indication that the way the teacher perceives the ability of a pupil may in itself have something to do with the expectations that are set for him and consequently with how well he performs. All in all this suggests that IQ scores must be interpreted cautiously and that much information is needed by the teacher concerning the nature of the test used and the conditions under which it was administered.

DIFFERENCES IN RATE OF ACHIEVEMENT

As has already been noted, there is a high degree of similarity between certain tasks found in mental tests and the kinds of activities usually associated with school. For this reason, higher levels of achievement are expected of children with high IQ's than of their classmates who are intellectually less capable. Although it is ordinarily true that youngsters with high measured intelligence are more successful academically, teachers are cautioned against applying this generalization rigidly. Some children consistently seem to achieve beyond a level indicated possible by intelligence tests because they are highly motivated, have developed good work habits, and are well organized and ambitious. These children are dubbed overachievers, although this is obviously a misnomer. Other children, because they lack these same qualities, seem never to perform up to expectation. A fairly common remark found on the report cards of children is that the child is not "working up to ability." It becomes clear, therefore, that there will be great differences in the rate of achievement of children in any class; some of these differences may be associated with mental ability and others may not.

There are a number of achievement tests available today that yield objective data concerning the child's achievement status. The teacher will need information of this type if he is to plan social studies units in terms of individual differences. The child's past record of achievement will also be a strong indicator of what he is likely to do in the future. These data will show a range of reading abilities in unselected grade groups of from three to four years in the primary grades to six to eight years in the upper grades. Similar ranges are found in writing skills, use of references, arithmetic, spelling, and other skills. With these data in the hands of the teacher he is better able to think in terms of suitable social studies experiences for individual pupils.

DIFFERENCES IN SENSORY-PHYSICAL STATUS

The need for information concerning the sensory-physical status of the child may seem less necessary in the development of social studies units than knowledge of the child's rate of achievement or mental maturity. Actually, the sensory and physical development of a child may contribute directly to social studies learnings—particularly to social adjustment. The obese, clumsy, awkward child has more severe personal and social adjustment problems than does the well-coordinated, agile child. The child's physical status may contribute directly to his being chosen for the games, social activities, and physical activities that children value. Folk dancing, for example, is commonly used in social studies activities—physical differences and muscular control may have a direct bearing on the child's willingness to participate in it. Teachers who are sensitive to these differences will avoid placing the child in situations that may prove embarrassing for him.

Differences in muscular coordination and physical status may also reflect themselves in the quality of the child's work. It is well known that adults tend to expect more mature behavior on the part of larger children than of smaller ones of the same age. This is true of academic growth as well as social behavior. Children who are "all thumbs" can never seem to produce written work, art work, diagrams, maps and similar products as neatly, accurately, and skillfully as other children. These differences are frequently overlooked when a single standard of acceptable work is applied.

Of course, visual, auditory, speech, and other physical handicaps of the child need to be known to the teacher and appropriate adjustments must be made. In recent years schools have shown considerable concern over the health of the schoolchild and maintain somewhat comprehensive health histories on him. Visual, auditory, and dental screenings as well as height and weight checks have become routine procedures in schools. Teachers need to avail themselves of this information in order to gain insight into the sensory-physical status of the individual children.

DIFFERENCES IN HOME BACKGROUND; THE DISADVANTAGED

Sociological and political forces in the past decade have focused the attention of the nation on the tremendous impact of the home background of a child on his success in school. The most fortunate child is the one whose home background is consistent with the teachings and value orientation of the school he attends. For him both institutions support each other. The models of conduct with which he is familiar prior to coming to school are reinforced by the school experience. Likewise, the reward system of the home and school are consistent for him. Not all children from such homes succeed in school, but the evidence is clear that their *chances* of success are much higher than for those who have not had the advantage of intellectually stimulating and culturally preparatory home experiences.

Unfortunately, there are large numbers of pupils who enter the nation's schools each year who do not find this consistency between their home life and their school life. In fact, the two environments are often in sharp conflict with one another. These children encounter role models in school that are totally and completely unfamiliar to them. Their backgrounds of experience may be so drab that they are incapable of profiting from conventionally designed educational programs. These are the children society has come to call the disadvantaged. Charles Berryman has defined educationally disadvantaged children as "those whose total life style, as influenced by social forces, results in relatively low achievement in school." [2] The number of children who are disadvantaged in some degree is larger than most persons suspect. In some specific attendance areas the number of such children may exceed 75 per cent.

The following case studies will sensitize the reader to the many forms that educational disadvantage may take. They are based on actual cases, although the locations, names, and identities of the individuals have been changed.

2. Charles Berryman, "Teaching the Educationally Disadvantaged: Some Dimensions of the Problem," *The Georgia Reporter*, Athens, Ga.: Georgia Council for the Social Sciences, Winter, 1970, p. 9.

MARY

Mary was a second-grade pupil living in a suburb of Portland. She lived with her parents and ten brothers and sisters. She had not gained even beginning first-grade reading or math skills. In addition, she was shunned by her classmates. Two physical factors partly accounted for her lack of social and scholastic success. Outwardly she was dirty. Her skin, hair, and clothing were consistently filthy. Her teeth were decaying to the extent that pieces would break off from time to time during class. These would be picked out of her mouth and shown to other children. Perhaps more damaging to her was a hearing deficiency that made ordinary classroom work impossible. The hearing loss was apparently caused by a chronic infection—an infection that could have been controlled if medication, which the family possessed, would have been administered regularly. Conferring with the parents made no change in any of these conditions.

SEAN

Sean was a second-grader living near Seattle. He was bright, interesting, and knowledgeable when conversing with adults. In school, however, he was not performing at even a readiness level. He could identify few letters of the alphabet, could barely copy his name, and was unable to do any number computation. Sean was an only child who was caught in a domestic conflict between his mother and father. Each parent would attempt to degrade the other in Sean's presence and would try to use him as a weapon against the other. Sean was aggressive toward his classmates, sometimes attacking them with scissors or a sharp pencil. In situations in which he would feel threatened or criticized, he would often become walleyed and his whole body would tremble. Sean often withdrew into a fantasy world. His parents thoughtlessly encouraged this by leaving him alone and unattended for many hours each evening.

MARK

Mark lived on an isolated farm in northern Minnesota with his parents and six siblings. They had no phone nor other modern conveniences. Mark's parents were openly antagonistic toward the school when teachers or school officials attempted to confer with them. The only cooperation received from the home was when legal action was threatened because of Mark's excessive absences. Although Mark was in the fifth grade, he was functioning at about the second-grade level.

SHARON (BLACK)

Sharon lived in a large Midwestern city. She was fourteen years old and in a special education class in a K–6 school. Sharon was the youngest of eleven children and was considered the brightest of them all. She was pleasant, quiet, and well behaved. The remedial teacher often spoke of how nice it was to have Sharon in her class. Everyone including Sharon expected that she would do and learn nothing. That is precisely what happened.

VICKI

Vicki was an unhappy and an unsuccessful third-grade pupil in a West Coast city. She was an only child living with her parents in a comfortable middle-class neighborhood. Her lack of success appeared to stem from severe emotional problems. Two manifestations of Vicki's problems were obesity and lethargy. She simply did nothing at school. Vicki's home environment included a mother who was the dominant parent and who managed the dress shop that supported the family. Her father was often intoxicated and on many occasions was gone for three to four weeks at a time. In at least one instance the mother had him arrested when he returned.

These abbreviated case studies illustrate that disadvantage and deprivation are not confined to any particular racial or ethnic group. These children come from all backgrounds. Their families present an extremely complicated picture of poverty, poor health, hostility, fear, insecurity, illiteracy, unemployment, impoverished language development, and failure. The home lives of these children do not equip them to profit from the usual instructional programs of schools, and consequently, these same youngsters, as adults, are not able to find their places as responsible and constructively contributing members of society. Many leave school as drop-outs, although many dropped psychologically out of school almost at the time they entered. Their school achievement records are described by Bloom, Davis, and Hess as follows:

> The school achievement of disadvantaged children is characterized by a cumulative-deficit phenomenon. The children begin school with certain inadequacies in language development, perceptual skills, attentional skills, and motivation. Under the usual school curriculum, the achievement pattern of deprived children is such that they fall increasingly behind their non-deprived peers in school subjects. On the aver-

age, by eighth grade these children are about three years behind grade norms in reading and arithmetic as well as in other subjects. These effects are most marked in deprived children of average and low ability. One of the consequences of this cumulative deficit is that dropping out of school is much more frequent and this in turn leads to less mobility and opportunity in the occupational sphere.[3]

Vast sums of money are now being expended to assist in the education of the youngsters who have been the victims of deprivation. Sociologists have been studying this problem and calling it to the attention of the nation for a number of years, but never has there been a large-scale national attack to match that underway at the present time. The nation has recognized that deprivation is not a problem that concerns the individual alone but is a problem of the larger society. As the national community comes to grips with this serious social problem, it can be expected that the public school system will be one important avenue through which intervention programs will be implemented.

The home background of a child is important to social studies instruction because it bears so directly on his value system, his attitudes, his social relationships, and his perception of himself as a person. The problem of deprivation is especially severe in social studies instruction because all the conflicts, prejudices, and social needs come to focus here.

The first requirement of a social studies program for disadvantaged children is an understanding and sympathetic teacher who will help them build paths of success in the direction of socially responsible behavior. Beyond personal qualities, the prospective teacher of the disadvantaged should have an understanding of the nature of the problem. There is a growing body of sociological, psychological, and educational research and literature on this subject with which the teacher should be familiar. The teaching of disadvantaged children in the past—and even today in some areas—has been guided more by folklore and myth than by research. The cause of education of these children is greatly enhanced when handled by teachers who are highly sophisticated in the sociology and psychology of cultural deprivation.

Some of the traditional ideas about the composition of conventional social studies programs need to be drastically revised in working with disadvantaged youngsters. The eminent professor of psychiatry and education Bruno Bettelheim, who has had vast experience working with disadvantaged children and their teachers, puts it this way:

3. Benjamin S. Bloom, Allison Davis, and Robert Hess, *Compensatory Education for Cultural Deprivation*, New York: Holt, Rinehart and Winston, 1965, pp. 73–74.

What it comes down to, as I tell the groups of teachers I work with, is that we must have very clearly in our minds what educational goals we have for these children. Should our goal be that these youngsters learn the important things in life: not to steal, not to hit people over the head, to be able to stand some small frustration and still go on with the task? Or should our goal be that they learn, like Lee Harvey Oswald, to read and write, no matter what? [4]

The teacher needs to think in terms of a priority of social studies learnings for these children. What do they most need to learn? What types of experiences will help them most in meeting their daily problems of living?

The following goals are being suggested as ones that deserve a high priority in working with disadvantaged pupils: (1) attainment and maintenance of an acceptable self-concept, (2) improved language facility, (3) broadened life experiences, (4) scientific orientation to healthful living, (5) opening the doors to the world of work, (6) familiarity with the legal system, (7) knowing how to use political power, (8) family life education, (9) opportunities for and experience in decision making.

Attainment and Maintenance of an Acceptable Self-concept. When one works with children who come from disadvantaged backgrounds, he is left with a strong sense that these children do not feel good about themselves. Successful people, educated people, normal people have idealized types with whom they identify. These are the "significant others" that make a difference to us. We identify with them. To some extent we model our lives after them. They represent powerful forces that propel us in our childhood, in our youth, and even to some extent in our adult lives. These role models are often absent in the case of the disadvantaged pupil. The child does not identify with anyone in particular. He is left with a feeling of utter hopelessness—of despair. No one cares. Why should they care? There is an expression, "We never had much money, but we were never poor." There is much wisdom in this because poorness is a state of mind—a feeling about one's self and one's condition rather than the physical reality of being without money. These feelings are closely related to one's total self-concept and to some extent are a part of a self-fulfilling prophecy.

Social studies instruction can assist in helping the disadvantaged child develop an improved self-concept. In the social studies the teacher can help the child build a backlog of success experiences through the use of interesting projects and activities. Role models rep-

4. Bruno Bettelheim, "Teaching the Disadvantaged," *NEA Journal,* 54, No. 6, September, 1965, p. 12.

reŝenting various racial and ethnic groups should be used to assist all children to identify with American life and culture. Traditionally, only Western European, Caucasian models were presented to American schoolchildren. Thus, many children saw little, if any, of the sub-culture of which they were a part reflected in America's story. Or, if these children were represented at all, they were represented in a negative way. There is little wonder that many children of minority groups have negative self-concepts and feelings of low personal worth.

Improved Language Facility. It is hard to know whether a low level of language usage is a cause or a result of educational disadvantage. We can say with a high degree of confidence, however, that it is almost always a characteristic of educationally disadvantaged children. The evidence is overwhelming that in disadvantaged homes there is a different pattern of language than in others. It is less elaborative, less explanatory, less descriptive, more directive. These children do not come from what Martin Deutsch has called a "verbally oriented environment." [5]

Because language and abstract thought are such closely interrelated processes, the child is likely to remain educationally disadvantaged until he masters the language at least beyond the illiterate level. This is true also because language is an important—perhaps the most important—vehicle of instruction. Even though we are stressing inquiry and discovery learning today, the fact remains that most instruction is based on the fundamental skill of language. It is extremely difficult to teach someone something without the use of language. Conversely, it is extremely difficult to learn when one has language facility arrested at a low level.

Broadened Life Experiences. In looking over case histories of educationally disadvantaged children, one often sees a pattern of limited contact beyond the immediate environment. But even in cases where the youngster has traveled a great deal—as is the case of the children of migrant workers—the experience may be limited. He may look but not see; his visual perceptions seem not to be incorporated into his experience and his psyche. Thus, he may travel a thousand miles and see nothing.

Much attention needs to be devoted to the development of perceptual skills. If it is true (1) that one learns how to learn and (2) that learning is defined as changes in behavior as a result of interacting with one's environment, then it follows (3) that one must learn how to interact with his environment, and (4) that if this process is learned, it can therefore be taught..By the time the child reaches school,

5. Martin P. Deutsch, "The Disadvantaged Child and the Learning Process," *Education in Depressed Areas*, A. Harry Passow, ed., New York: Bureau of Publications, Teachers College, Columbia University, 1963, pp. 163–179.

he may already be in need of remedial work with respect to the development of perceptual skills. It may be that he has built up his defenses to the point that prevents the type of interaction that leads to learning. It may be, too, that the school contributes to the problem rather than to its solution; that is, the child learns to "turn off" the teacher and thus further insulates himself from the opportunity to learn.

Scientific Orientation to Healthful Living.   The conditions of disadvantage are often reflected in the total make-up of a child. Many children have problems of health in varying degrees of severity. Infected tonsils, respiratory illnesses, dental caries, overweight or underweight, malnutrition, and urinary tract infections are a few of the common health problems of the disadvantaged. These conditions are relatively easily prevented or controlled when they are understood and when there is a willingness to do so. Unfortunately, those who do not have the advantages of education are often guided by superstition and fear in their approach to problems of health. Good health is so fundamental to everything else that one does that it deserves a high priority in the concerns that schools should have for pupils.

Opening the Doors to the World of Work.   Limited education usually means limited occupational choice, and one condition is fed by the other. Not only does limited education not qualify one for jobs; more important, it does not help one find out what choices there are in the world of work. A major problem among the disadvantaged is that they are unaware of the alternatives available in job opportunities.

From the earliest grades in school, the child can begin to learn about the great need for a variety of unskilled, semiskilled, or even skilled labor that does not require high-level intellectual capability. As children progress through school, the opportunity to obtain occupational information should be increased. At the upper levels they should make site visits, get firsthand information about jobs, and engage in part-time employment as an important component of the school program.

Familiarity with the Legal System.   There can be no question that our legal system does not work to the advantage of the disadvantaged. In the first place, the chances that a disadvantaged person will run afoul of the law are many times greater than the chances that an advantaged person will do the same. The disadvantaged child may have unfortunate firsthand experiences with the legal system. Thus he may learn in school that "the policeman is our friend," but outside school he learns that "policemen are pigs."

Unfortunately, the legal system is sometimes used to frustrate people and to give them the run-around. There is great resentment of our legal-judicial system by the disadvantaged and disenfranchised in this country. Plainly, the system discriminates in favor of the educated, affluent adult and against the uneducated poor and discriminates in many cases against the minor—educated or not, affluent or not.

Everyone needs to know about his rights as a citizen within the legal-judicial framework. For the disadvantaged, the rights are absolutely imperative to know.

Knowing How to Use Political Power.   Today many groups are concerned about securing political power—black power, red power, teacher power. This is a legitimate concern. People know they can achieve those goals important to themselves only if they can use what power they have in concert with other groups. Too often the school program deals with political power in an unrealistic way because it overstresses the role of the individual. Today the individual has relatively little or no power singly; it is the group that is powerful. Not one vote is delivered in an election but a whole bloc of votes; one individual does not boycott a store but the entire community does; not one person marches in a protest demonstration but hundreds do. The disadvantaged have political power if they can align themselves effectively for its use. This potential power can also be dangerous because of its attractiveness to demagogues. Thus, there is much at stake for the disadvantaged and society as a whole in the intelligent use of political power by the disadvantaged.

Family Life Education.   A disadvantaged condition—like cancer and heart disease—may not be inherited but it tends to run in families. And as with these two diseases, the earlier it is detected or the disposition noted, the more likely it is that remedial action will be effective.

The alleviation of a disadvantaged condition is more than a one-generation effort. Family life education is not going to be totally effective, to be sure, but a long-range effort that will contribute to more stable family life and better child-rearing practices will have an impact on the problem.

Educational disadvantage is characterized by a particular life style. We know that life styles are learned at home at an early age. Therefore, the inputs for change must come at that point. Family life education can serve these long-term educational goals.

Opportunities for and Experience in Decision Making.   The disadvantaged often have so little confidence in themselves that they find decision making extraordinarily difficult. Frequently those in authority are very directive in dealing with disadvantaged persons. Everyone assumes that it is necessary to be directive with the disadvantaged. Consequently, they have little opportunity to learn to make decisions for themselves. In a great many ways the school program can contribute to the education of the disadvantaged by allowing them to make up their own minds in the ordinary things that occur in school every day. Choice making is learned behavior. Successful choice making enhances the self-concept.

Along with the setting of priorities, the teacher also needs to set realistic expectancy levels for these children. Grade standards or grade norms are of no help and may actually be a detriment to improved achievement. Grades as standards of expectancy should be ignored totally, applying the "grade" concept only as a means of identifying the number of years a child has been in school. Imagine, for example, a fifth-grade class (ten-year-olds) that, as a class, is two years below grade level in reading achievement (half of them cannot write a single coherent sentence, and several of them can barely speak English at all) with a teacher who insists that they read the fifth-grade social studies text and "do fifth-grade work"! In no way can such teaching be defended, yet in one form or another, it is fairly prevalent in elementary classrooms. Very careful diagnostic procedures need to be employed by the teacher in planning instruction and setting expectancy levels for these pupils. In this way the teacher is able to establish a baseline level of achievement from which instruction can proceed and from which progress can be evaluated.

Differences in Personal and Social Adjustment

Because the social studies deal in part with social adjustment, it is necessary for the teacher to have information concerning the child's status in this area of his development. Although an appraisal may be made of a child's achievement status in a relatively objective fashion, such a degree of objectivity is not possible in the area of personal and social development. Here the teacher must rely almost entirely on subjective judgment based on observable behavior. For this purpose such devices and techniques as the behavior journal, anecdotal records, systematic observation, case studies, interest inventories, and behavior check lists are used. Collecting data of this type is a continuing process carried on throughout the school term in and out of the classroom. It often happens that a teacher can gain his most valuable insights into this aspect of the child's life by observing him on the playground, in the lunchroom, or in similar undirected situations.

Teachers may find the use of sociometric devices helpful in getting personal and social information about the child. A sociogram may take a variety of forms, the most simple being to have the child indicate the children with whom he would best like to work, those with whom he would best like to play, and those with whom he would best like to sit. These data may then be plotted in chart form to show the choices of individual children in the group. Children who are selected frequently are called *stars*, those selected only occasionally are referred to as *neglectees,* and those chosen by no other child are referred to as *iso-*

lates. Through the use of these techniques, it is possible to gain some insight into group structure and the social status of children. The results may be helpful to the teacher in improving social relationships in the group. The procedures to be followed in obtaining sociometric data are described in detail in Chapter 12.

The use of published personality scales for use with children may be of some help to the teacher in gaining an understanding of a child's behavior. The need for caution in the use and interpretation of these instruments is even greater than with mental or achievement tests. Measurement of personal and social characteristics is extremely complex because the properties to be measured are subtle and are difficult to quantify and define and because the essential conditions of measurement are more often than not impossible to meet. Because this is true, the scales available for use are not really measuring instruments but are behavior-rating scales or check lists. In addition to commercially prepared materials, the teacher may wish to develop a check list of his own in order to systematize his observations.

Providing for Individual Differences in Social Studies

Teachers everywhere are seeking new ways to deal with the problem of providing for individual differences. They are enthusiastic about newly published materials on the problem, hoping somehow that someone will come up with a new idea that will make the job easier. Unhappily, it is not likely that an easy solution to the complex problem of individual differences will be found. Basically, there are five adjustments that a teacher should make in his social studies instruction to help provide for individual differences. These are (1) adjustments in reading; (2) adjustments in classroom activities in which the children may participate; (3) adjustments in qualitative and quantitative aspects of the child's work; (4) adjustments in the level of conceptualization expected of individual children, including the formation of temporary subgroups in the class for this purpose; and (5) adjustments in the amount of supervision and guidance the teacher gives individual children.

The most important single factor in individualizing classroom instruction, however, is not to be found in various mechanical adjustments but rather in the attitude of the teacher with respect to the task of teaching children. The use of small groups and various activities and resources as well as other commonly suggested ways of adjusting instruction to individual differences will be largely mechanical and ineffectual unless there prevails in the classroom an atmosphere that is psychologically acceptable to the concept of individual differences. Historically, schools have not valued individual variation. They have

The challenge of individual differences is represented here. How can the teacher use group teaching procedures to reach individual pupils? (Courtesy of the Seattle Public Schools)

designed programs that tend to make people more *alike* than to capitalize on their differences. The whole norm concept stresses similarity —differences are called deviations. It is fairly easy to embrace human differences as a humanitarian value; it is much more difficult to accept the value of human differences in instructional settings.

ADJUSTMENTS IN READING MATERIAL

In spite of the addition of such valuable learning aids as films, filmstrips, recordings, models, and pictures, the modern social studies programs continue to depend heavily on reading. It is unfortunately true that the child who is low in reading ability is handicapped in his learning in many other areas in the school curriculum. The need for adjustment in the teaching of reading is readily seen by most elementary teachers, and the practice of subgrouping for reading instruc-

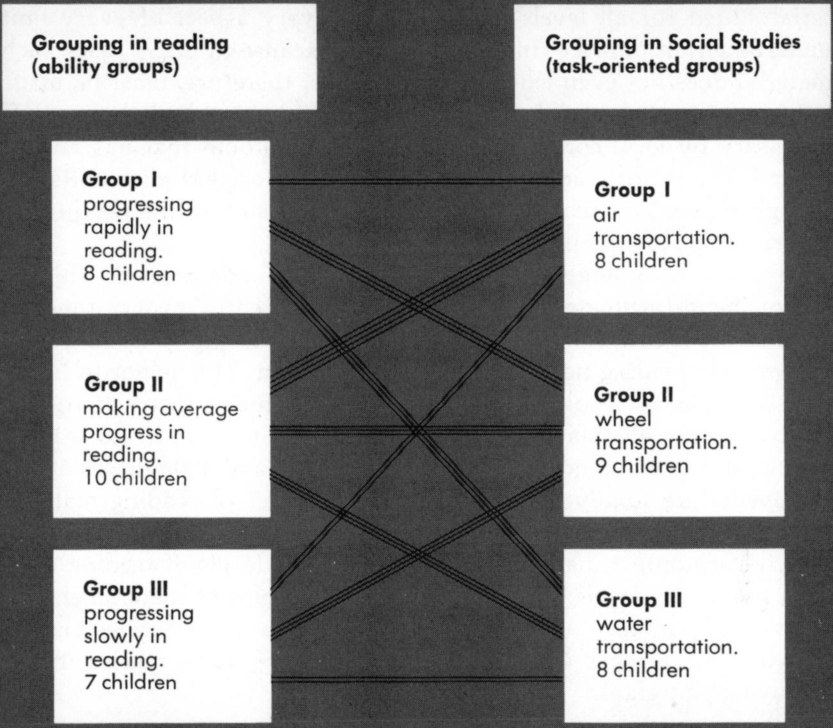

Grouping in reading (ability groups)		Grouping in Social Studies (task-oriented groups)
Group I progressing rapidly in reading. 8 children		**Group I** air transportation. 8 children
Group II making average progress in reading. 10 children		**Group II** wheel transportation. 9 children
Group III progressing slowly in reading. 7 children		**Group III** water transportation. 8 children

Figure 13. A chart showing the need for a wide range of reading material on a variety of topics in a class of 25 children. The full range of reading ability is presented in **each** of the social studies groups. This makes the need for reading materials at varying levels of difficulty imperative.

tion has become fairly common, particularly in the primary grades. Although the teacher may make adjustments in reading for the child when he is being taught basic developmental reading, a single textbook in the hands of every pupil is the rule rather than the exception in the social studies. This practice is often an indication that differences known to exist in the reading abilities of children are being ignored.

The reading problem is aggravated in social studies by the manner in which children are grouped for instructional purposes. It is not uncommon to find the complete range of reading ability represented in a group of six or seven children who are working on the same topic. This is shown in Figure 13. Ideally, the class would have reading material suited for all levels of reading on every aspect of every unit undertaken. In practice this rarely occurs because in many cases such material does not even exist. A compromise, therefore, must be made in terms of availability of material and other practical limitations made necessary by local conditions. It is a rare classroom that has an unlimited amount of reading material for use in social studies units, although elementary schools are improving markedly in the reading resources available to pupils.

The use of a single basic textbook in the hands of every child is one of the unfortunate practices that has persisted in modern times in spite of the fact that it violates every known principle of dealing with the varying reading needs of individual children. This is not to imply that the basic textbook has no place in social studies instruction; it is an extremely valuable resource and should be used. But the teacher should also understand that the basic textbook and a single set of encyclopedia are *totally* inadequate as sole sources of reading material for children in modern social studies programs. The need is for a multiplicity of nontext material representing many levels of reading difficulty and many levels of comprehension. This type of material should be available for each of the units the class studies. A brief description of what one teacher was able to do in this regard is related in the following paragraph:

> Miss Wilcox's sixth grade class was to soon begin studying a unit on the economic development of Latin American countries. In addition to the multiple copies of the three social studies textbooks and the encyclopedias already in the classroom, she found additional reading materials (books, pamphlets, magazine articles, newspaper clippings) in both her classroom and the school library. More materials, both reading and nonreading, were available from the school district's central instructional materials center and from the city library. She wrote for supplementary materials from sources listed in various guides to free and inexpensive materials. Once the unit was initiated, a number of filmstrips on the unit topic were placed in the back of the classroom where pupils, either individually or in small groups, could view and study them as time permitted. With such a wide variety of different books and other instructional aids, there were reading materials suitable for every child.

It has been said that the book is the best teaching machine ever invented. Certainly books are among the best teaching resources the school has, and there can be no substitute for them. Substandard amounts and kinds of reading materials inevitably lead to substandard instruction. In one way or another, therefore, the teacher must expand the reading resources beyond the use of a single basic text and the classroom encyclopedia. Where budgetary considerations limit the purchase of sufficient reading materials, the teacher will have to use other, more time-consuming methods of securing what is needed. The following suggestions may be of help to teachers who find an inadequate amount of reading material available for use in teaching social studies.

HOW TO SECURE READING RESOURCES FOR SOCIAL STUDIES UNITS

1. Obtain simplified texts for slower readers and obtain more difficult ones for more advanced pupils. Although it may not be possible to obtain nontextbooks, the teacher can usually get textbooks of varying levels of difficulty on a loan basis from other classrooms in the school. This material will not in and of itself be sufficient, but it is a first step in the right direction.

2. Make full use of public library facilities in the community. Many libraries have generous amounts of children's books and will allow teachers to check out several volumes at one time for use with a class. Furthermore, the children themselves can be encouraged to secure public library books dealing with various aspects of the unit. These can be brought to school and shared with others. In addition to providing more reading resources, this practice gives children valuable experience in the use of the public library.

3. Inquire about the possibility of securing books on a loan basis from some central collection such as the instructional materials center of your school district, the County Superintendent's Office, the local historical society, the County Agent's Office, or from a source at the state level. The principal, supervisor, or consultant can usually advise the teacher of the accessibility of such materials. If such persons are not available to the teacher, he can write directly to his State Department of Education or to a nearby teacher-training institution. Usually the County or City Superintendent's Office will know if such collections exist.

4. Encourage pupils to bring to school their own books that contain information on the topic under study. Children enjoy sharing books with their classmates, and this affords an excellent opportunity to give additional instruction on the care and treatment of books. Arrange for interested pupils to become members of paperback book clubs such as the Arrow Book Club.

5. Exhaust every possibility for securing free materials. Sources of free and inexpensive materials as well as a discussion of their value may be found in Chapter 4.

6. Keep a watchful eye for appropriate material in daily newspapers, adult magazines, classroom periodicals, and similar current publications that might be adapted for classroom use. Some of the more useful articles can be pasted onto uniform-sized pieces of cardboard or put inside plastic covers (pupils could write on these with grease pencils or water-soluble pens) to prevent their becoming torn and ragged. This makes filing for future use somewhat easier. Because most classroom periodicals carry the same topics for different grade levels, arrange to obtain copies for several grade levels. This will help you obtain reading materials for children of different reading abilities.

7. Do not neglect the use of poetry and literary selections in teaching social studies. Sometimes teachers concentrate on obtaining materials of a factual nature and overlook the possibility of using selections from children's literature that may be available in abundance. This includes stories, poetry, fiction, legends, fanciful tales, and biographies.

8. Explore the possibility of making use of the local high school library. This is usually a good source of material for the more able reader. The teacher himself may have to assume responsibility for obtaining the books, although in some cases it may be possible to make special arrangements for some children to make use of this resource on an individual basis.

9. Survey the community for any resources available on a free or loan basis. Business establishments such as dairies, food stores, the telephone company, the electric company, and automobile dealers often have material useful in social studies instruction and are usually glad to provide it free of charge.

10. Rewrite material or write original selections to suit the reading level of children. In this connection the following suggestions by Benbrook for rewriting material for retarded readers may be helpful:

    a. Determine the kind of information needed and choose an interesting topic.

    b. Determine the reading level of the potential readers and become familiar with that level.

    c. Listen to the potential readers and gauge the material to their vocabulary and language patterns.

    d. Record your purpose for writing the material. (Focus on needs, interests, and abilities of the reader.)

    e. Make detailed plans for presenting what you have to say.

    f. Use familiar, short words when possible.

    g. Clarify unfamiliar words by definition or defining context.

h. Use a mixture of moderately long and short sentences. (An average of ten words is desirable for grades three and four.)

i. Present the ideas in a straightforward manner.

j. Write as though you were talking to the readers.

k. Keep the tone of writing on the maturity level of the readers, with no trace of condescension.

l. Break up the writing into short paragraphs.

m. Present ideas in logical order and use good transition sentences between paragraphs.

n. Start without a long introduction. (Don't risk loss of interest.)

o. Use a direct expository style.

p. Keep in mind the important factors affecting readability—motivation, difficulty of concepts, relation of reader's experience to ideas presented.

q. Strive for some originality.

r. Revise and polish the writing. Read aloud to locate "wrong" words and sentences.[6]

11. Give more careful guidance in the use of the textbook when supplementary materials are not available. With slower readers particularly, it will be necessary to select only certain parts or passages, and give more attention to graphic materials and to the more specific and obvious points while reading the text.

12. Make greater use of other avenues of learning, such as audio-visual material, community resources, varied classroom activities, field trips, visitors brought to the classroom, and similar nonreading resources. For example, material too difficult for pupils to read but within their listening vocabulary can quickly and easily be tape recorded. A number of tapes of varying difficulty could be used to provide for individual differences. Remember, however, these activities are a supplement to reading and not a substitute for it.

It can be demonstrated that a teacher who finds himself in a situation almost barren of children's reading resources can, if he chooses, make an amazing number of adjustments in the reading requirements through the use of procedures of the type just described. The teacher who is willing to do more than despair under such circumstances or willing to do more than accept the lack of reading resources with quiet acquiescence, will put forth the additional effort needed to secure suitable materials for children. To be sure, it will be difficult and demanding of his time, but it can be done. In the meantime he should

6. Joyce Benbrook, "Criteria for Writing Informative Material for Retarded Readers," *Elementary School Journal*, 56, pp. 409–412.

constantly press, through the proper channels, for more favorable budgetary consideration for supplementary books. The teacher should be cautioned, however, against spending his own money for the purchase of materials for class use. This is not a good practice and is totally wrong in principle. It is his responsibility to teach the children, not to pay for the materials they use.

ADJUSTMENTS IN CLASSROOM ACTIVITIES

Traditionally, school activities have consisted chiefly of reading, writing, reciting—all of which demand well-developed verbal, linguistic, and intellectual skills and abilities. The picture of a quiet classroom with children poring over books for hours on end has become legendary. To minimize the importance of intellectual activities would be a disservice to modern school programs, but it should be immediately apparent to anyone familiar with the heterogeneity of today's school population that activities of an abstract nature are inappropriate ways of learning for many children. For this reason schools have expanded the number of ways schoolchildren can achieve learning goals.

The use of different learning activities indicates a recognition that it is possible to learn through the use of a variety of mediums and that what may constitute an effective learning vehicle for one pupil may or may not be equally effective for another. As an example, one child may find reading and research to be the best means of achieving an understanding of the operation of a dairy, whereas another will gain more through viewing a film, studying a chart, visiting the dairy, talking with someone and asking questions about the dairy, or listening to the teacher read material to the class dealing with this topic. Some children need repeated concrete, firsthand experiences; others need but a few and can gain more through reading. No two individuals learn in exactly the same way; the most appropriate means to learning appears to be a highly individual matter and is directly related to the type of learning desired.

The best program of social studies instruction would be one that used the means most appropriate for each child to achieve a given learning goal. In actual practice this is not entirely possible because of the number of children the teacher has and because of the impracticality of certain activities. Perhaps the best way for some children to learn about life in Japan would be to go to that country and live there for a year. This is so obviously out of the question that such a suggestion is not even considered as a remote possibility. Instead, a substitute learning activity is chosen: reading, viewing a film, talking to someone who has lived there, studying pictures of Japan, taking an imaginary trip, and so on. Furthermore, the possibilities for *all* children to learn about life in Japan are increased considerably if the teacher includes all the aforementioned activities in the unit dealing with this topic. The important thing for the teacher to keep constantly in mind is that the greater the variety of learning activities presented, the more likely is the possibility that all children will have the opportunity to learn. When social studies activities are limited to reading, research, and others of a verbal and abstract nature, the door to learning is slammed shut to those who find learning in this manner difficult or nearly impossible.

It was noted earlier that the best means of learning is an individual and personal matter. The method that is best for any given pupil in a specific situation depends on many factors, some of which are

1. General intelligence
2. Experience background
3. Nature and complexity of the material to be learned
4. Pupil's facility with the language and extent of his vocabulary
5. General maturity
6. Reading ability
7. Emotional stability (timidity, overaggressiveness, disinterest, irresponsibility, hyperactivity)
8. Physical disabilities (loss of hearing, orthopedically handicapped, brain damaged, partially sighted)
9. Presence or absence of motivating conditions; individual interest in the topic
10. Keenness of perceptive functions
11. Positive or negative attitudes associated with the material to be learned

Many of these factors are related to one another and must be considered together in planning social studies activities. Certain instructional procedures, such as nondirected group cooperative activities, are not attempted even with very bright children if their general level of maturity is low. Activities are planned differently for the child of average intellectual endowment if he is a good reader than if he is a poor one. In the case of children with various types of physical handicaps, the need for adjusting the learning activity to suit the child is so apparent as to hardly need discussion. The other factors are more subtle and more difficult to discern but are, in many cases, as vital to effective learning as are physical factors. A study of these factors as they relate to individual children will help the teacher plan a sufficiently varied approach to the types of learning tasks in which the class will engage. Because a given learning goal can usually be achieved in a variety of ways, it is the teacher's responsibility to select the right one for each child insofar as is practicable and feasible. The following list suggests the types of learning activities that should at one time or another be included in social studies instruction:

LEARNING ACTIVITIES FOR SOCIAL STUDIES

Research: reading, writing, interviewing, note-taking, collecting, using references, map work, reporting

Presentation: telling, announcing, describing, giving directions, reporting, demonstrating, dramatizing, pantomiming, exhibiting, relating events, illustrating

Creative experience: writing, drawing, sketching, modeling, illustrating, painting, sewing, constructing, soap carving, manipulating, dramatizing, comparing, singing, imagining

Appreciation: listening, describing, viewing, reading

Observation or listening: observing, visiting places of interest, viewing pictures or films, listening to recordings

Group cooperation: discussing, conversing, sharing, asking questions, helping one another, committee work

Experimentation: measuring, collecting, demonstrating, conducting experiments

Organization: planning, discussing, outlining, summarizing, holding meetings

Evaluation: summarizing, reviewing, asking questions, criticizing

In attempting to select the best learning activity for each child, there is one hazard to which the teacher must be alert. Children enjoy doing the things in which they excel and have a reluctance to experiment with new avenues of learning. For this reason some children may always be found participating in the same type of activity, unit after unit. In this way their experiences with a variety of learning mediums is narrowed, resulting in unfamiliarity with avenues of learning that may be better for them than some they are now using. If one child is selected to draw pictures in connection with social studies units simply because the other children feel he is the best artist, he may find himself being deprived of research, reading, dramatizing, and other valuable experiences. Similarly, the child who has facility and skill in research and reading unquestionably will profit from tasks involving creative ability, construction, experimentation, and others. The teacher will need to control the selection of learning projects carefully in order to direct children to the activities that will give each one the opportunity to experiment with the variety of ways in which it is possible to learn.

Finally, it must be emphasized that the value of an activity lies in its contribution to the child's learning. The particular learning tasks selected must point directly to social studies goals, and the child's involvement in the activity must represent progress in the direction of those goals. The fundamental criterion in the selection of any activity is, or ought to be, its usefulness in bringing the child nearer the realization of some important learning goal.

ADJUSTMENTS IN THE QUALITATIVE AND QUANTITATIVE ASPECTS OF THE CHILD'S WORK

Modern educational theory and practice are based on the principle of expecting quality and quantity of performance commensurate with the level of ability of each child. The adjustment of requiring more work of better quality from some pupils than others is a fairly common educational practice. It is the adjustment that occurs more frequently than any other in providing for individual differences. In practice it functions somewhat as follows: Certain basic assignments are made that apply to all—there are pages to read, questions to answer, words to look up, maps to draw, and other similar activities. In addition to this assignment, the children may be given the opportunity to follow their own interests in a topic; may be assigned additional committee work; may be asked to prepare a report or engage themselves in some related project. Ordinarily, the more able children are expected and required to do all the assigned work, but they can be left to their own devices when they have completed the assignment. The entire arrangement is handled on an extremely informal basis. For example, in the case of slow-working or slow-learning children there may be a tacit agreement between them and the teacher that, if they do about all that they can without wasting time, they will not be held accountable for the entire amount of assigned work.

Although the practice of varying the amount and quality of work expected from children is one way of providing for individual differences, it has many serious shortcomings. In the first place, it operates on the assumption that all children can and must do essentially the same work but that some will do more of it and do it better. The differentiation is made on the basis of *amount* and *quality* of work rather than on the *kind* of learning task required. Bright children do not necessarily need more of the same task to challenge them; more than likely they need an entirely different approach to the problem under consideration. Similarly, slower children do not always need less to do; they need a differentiation that represents a simplification of the conceptual level required. When simple adjustments are made in terms of time and amount of work required, the slow learner as well as the capable child suffers. No matter how little is required, the slow learner may not be able to complete or comprehend it regardless of the amount of time given. In the case of bright children, the material studied in the unit may already be known to them.

The informal manner under which this procedure operates in many classrooms leaves much to be desired. The arrangement always seems unfair to the brighter, more capable children. They cannot understand why they must do more work than someone else. Why does Jimmy have to answer eight questions when Nancy needs only to answer three? A procedure intended to be a challenge to them thereby is made to seem like a penalty for being able to do work quickly and well. This is the reaction one would expect from conscientious pupils and calls attention to the lack of effectiveness of this method of individualizing instruction. In operation it amounts to little more than keeping the bright children busy at something until the slower children are able to complete whatever minimal amounts of work the teacher expects of them. If and when this method is used, it must be carefully planned to avoid the difficulties previously described. Furthermore, it is recommended that it not be used singly but be combined with the method described in the following section.

ADJUSTMENTS IN THE LEVEL OF CONCEPTUALIZATION EXPECTED OF INDIVIDUAL CHILDREN

Ideas can be handled at varying levels of complexity. While studying a unit on air transportation, for example, one second-grade child is attracted by the shiny, huge machine that makes a frightening sound. The next child sees the airplane as a means of connecting people and places of the world, a device that gets people from one place to another quickly, and as an important part of the national defense system. The first child can perhaps distinguish between a small private plane and an airliner; the second identifies them as a Tri-Pacer and a Boeing 747. What is more, the second child can, in all likelihood, tell the cruising speed of each, its fuel consumption, and similar data. One would expect to find a number of adjustments in the social studies unit on air transportation appropriate to these varying levels of ability of individual children to handle ideas.

This type of adjustment requires a different approach to the problem than does the quality-amount-time method described in the previous section. The adjustment in this case is one of *kind* and represents a differentiation of the specific objectives to be achieved by pupils. Because the teacher may vary the difficulty of concepts or ideas, it would seem simple enough for him to adjust their difficulty to be appropriate for individual children. Under this arrangement the slow child will deal with the topic at an easier level while the able child will be involved in more complex aspects of it. The bright child will not be held to requirements that seem repetitious and inane to him but will find intellectual challenge in developing a depth of understanding. The less capable child will likewise not be asked to deal with ideas that are beyond his ability to comprehend.

In order to show how an application of this method of differentiating instruction can be made, there follows a short list of simple and more complex ideas associated with the city, a unit frequently found in second or third grade. Appropriate learning experiences could be developed around any one of the ideas to suit varying abilities of pupils. Combining these basic ideas with the use of a variety of activities previously discussed, the teacher could present each child with an interesting and challenging learning situation. This same procedure can be followed with any topic selected for study at any grade level.

CITY GOVERNMENT

Simple Ideas

1. The city government operates on a budget; so much money is allotted to maintain each of the different city services.
2. The city provides parks for the enjoyment of its people.
3. Some citizens of the city are elected to positions of authority. Such people are mayors, city managers, and councilmen.

4. Laws are made to make life in the city safe and orderly.

5. Government is one of the largest employers in most American cities.

Complex Ideas

1. Taxes are collected to pay for special services such as police protection and schools.

2. Demands of different groups in a city can lead to conflicts.
3. The responsibility for carrying out the laws and other decisions made by the city council or commission rests with the mayor or the city manager.
4. Industries cannot always locate where they would prefer, because of city zoning restrictions.
5. City government operates on the specialization of labor, people are employed to carry out specific tasks (that is, policemen, firemen, city planners, and so on).

6. Newspapers and radio and TV stations carry news about the city government and its activities to the citizens.

7. Needs of a city change over time; what was necessary fifty years ago might not even be present now.

8. The mayor of a large city must know his city and its problems well.

6. If people are not happy with the decisions made by their elected officials, one action they can take is to vote for other persons at the next election.

7. City planners and engineers must be able to predict and take into consideration future needs of a city as they perform their tasks.

8. Once the government makes laws or sets restrictions, it is expected that everyone will obey those decisions.

With the range of abilities being what they are in elementary classrooms, it should be apparent that whole-class instructional procedures have many limitations. The brighter pupils are either bored with the presentation or dominate the discussion, while the slower learners barely understand what the problem is all about. As a result, some teachers have turned to the practice of forming temporary subgroups within the class and plan work for these groups at varying levels of difficulty.

Small-group instruction, however, presents its problems, too. Unless the work of each group is carefully planned and directed by the teacher, children may make poor use of their time. In the past, teachers have often formed such groups on the basis of pupil interest in some aspect of the topic under study, but the results of this practice have been largely disappointing. Theoretically, each child is supposed to research a special facet of the topic and then share his findings with the rest of the group or with the class. The problem here is that the research is often poorly done and the reports uninteresting or inconsequential. In the group work itself, some pupils will remain on the fringe and not become directly involved. Or they may select for study a very narrow aspect of a topic, thus failing to gain any real understanding of the larger problem under study.

The difficulties described in the preceding paragraph can be overcome if the teacher plans carefully what each subgroup is to do and prepares study-guide material for the groups to use. Such study guides should be differentiated in difficulty, suitable to the ability of the pupils who are to use them. Pupils in one group are presented with tasks requiring careful research and elaborative thinking, while pupils in another group deal with more simple relationships. The research needed may be done by pupils on an individual basis, then presented and discussed in the subgroup or study team. After such periods of study in small groups, it may be profitable for the whole class to discuss what they have learned relating to the topic or to summarize their learnings. This is possible because all of them have studied the same topic or problem but have done so at differing levels of difficulty.

ADJUSTMENTS IN THE AMOUNT OF SUPERVISION AND GUIDANCE GIVEN BY THE TEACHER

A commonly held belief is that each child is entitled to an equal amount of the teacher's time and effort. Although this sounds as if it should be an equitable arrangement, it is contrary to practice and is not necessary or recommended. Children vary in the amount of supervision and guidance they need just as they vary in other respects. For one child, a suggestion from the teacher is enough to direct him for an hour or more of independent work. Each new idea he encounters suggests other lines of interest to him, and he identifies many possibilities for independent study. The next child needs each task outlined in detail and, when the task is completed, will be back to the teacher for more direction and help. It is a disservice to some children to have the teacher hover over them continually suggesting and directing when they can work independently. The teacher must know how he can be of greatest service to each child.

Fairly early in the school year the teacher will be able to identify the children who are well on the way to self-direction in their study habits, those who need a moderate amount of supervision and guidance, and those who will need him close at hand almost continuously. In the primary grades there will be a greater dependency relationship between the children and the teacher than at upper-grade levels because young children have not yet attained sufficient maturity to be capable of complete self-direction. But even at the early levels there will be big differences in the degree of individual responsibility manifested by children. In building study habits, the teacher must, on the one hand, remain close enough to the situation to lend direction and support yet, on the other hand, be far enough away to allow the child to experiment with independence. When five or six first-graders are operating the "store" in one corner of the classroom while the teacher is helping four or five other pupils with a mural in another part of the room, it can be expected that she will be needed in the "store" now and then to iron out minor problems. The same group of children as sixth-graders could be expected to work through the entire period without help if their goals were well defined.

Children need supervision and guidance from the teacher in a great variety of ways, and the amount and kind needed will differ from child to child and group to group. In every class there will be some who need special help with reading. These children may be taken singly or in a small group, while the remainder of the class reads independently. In this reading-study situation the teacher helps the children with word difficulties, helps the children get meaning from visual material, calls their attention to picture captions and discusses the pictures, selects certain key passages and singles those out for special teaching, reads to the children short selections of special significance, and tries to build independence in reading at the same time. Just because the teacher has obtained a variety of reading material is no guarantee that it will be used to good advantage. The teacher, through careful guidance, must help children make the best use of reading resources. This type of guidance is not limited to the primary grades but persists throughout the elementary school.

In most classes, too, there will be another group of children who can go much beyond the remainder of the class in their depth of understanding of the topics studied. With these children, the teacher points out possibilities for additional study, challenges them with provocative problems, suggests topics for additional research, helps them secure appropriate reading material, teaches them how to organize their ideas, and gives similar guidance. The teacher can be of most help to these children by suggesting, challenging, and holding them to high standards of achievement and yet expecting much of their study to be done independently.

For most children the teacher will be expected to lead the way, show them how to do what is expected and to get them started. From then on, occasional help and well-placed suggestions will be adequate. It is not uncommon to find teachers so interested in a social studies activity that they have to guard against doing the work for the pupils. This is most likely to happen in construction, processing, or dramatic activities related to the unit.

The teacher's role in guiding and supervising social studies activities may be described, therefore, as a function of individual children's needs in this respect. He should not feel disposed to supervise every activity so closely as to discourage independent habits of work. Neither should he retire to some corner of the classroom and abdicate his responsibility to offer the kind of constructive help and guidance growing children need. The teacher should be actively involved—on his feet— during the social studies period. He should move from group to group and child to child and should assist, encourage, suggest, and do whatever else is needed to help children move in the direction of desired learning goals.

INDIVIDUALIZING INSTRUCTION IN SOCIAL STUDIES [7]

Reading

Very *simple*	to	Very *difficult*
simplified texts		advanced texts
short stories		adult magazines
material rewritten by the		technical materials
teacher		biographies
short poems		more difficult supplementary
simple classroom periodicals		books

Activities

Primarily sensory-physical	to	*Primarily intellectual*

Quality-Quantity-Time Requirements

Minimal requirements of	to	*Maximum requirements of*
marginal quality		*high quality*

Complexity of Concepts

Simple, largely firsthand	to	*Complex, largely abstract and*
experiences, concrete level		*relational*

Supervision and Guidance

Close supervision and much	to	*Highly independent; long-range*
guidance, clearly defined		*goals less clearly defined by*
short-range goals		*the teacher*

This chapter has emphasized the need for taking a broad view of the entire concept of individualizing social studies instruction. Too frequently, individualizing instruction is understood to mean "doing something for the gifted" or "doing something for the slow learners." The fact of the matter is that *every* child presents the teacher with the challenge of individual differences. As we have seen, children differ not only in their potential for learning but also in their desire to learn, their readiness for learning, their interest in learning, and in the manner in which each learns most efficiently. The teacher who accepts

7. Adequate provision for individual differences calls for adjustments in each of these five areas. This list underscores the need for providing for the full range of abilities found in elementary school classrooms.

this broader concept of individual differences will take into account not only the child's IQ but also the other factors that influence the child's growth in social studies learnings. This will ensure that some adjustments will be made in the program for the unique needs of every child irrespective of his mental ability per se. But because the problem of providing for slow-learning children and gifted children is a matter of special concern to many teachers, the following specific suggestions are made with regard to those two groups:

IN TEACHING SLOW-LEARNING CHILDREN

1. Provide generously for experiences of a concrete, firsthand nature. These children learn best by handling, manipulating, sensing, feeling, and doing, and they learn least well by reading, analyzing, generalizing, and finding new solutions to problems.
2. Learning tasks must be specific and simple; learning goals must be definite, clear-cut, and short-ranged. They must know precisely what to do and how to do it. Use detailed study-guide material.
3. Learning experiences should be presented in one small step at a time with complete mastery of each step before advancement to the next.
4. Recognize that lessons should be short in duration due to the brevity of the attention span of many slow learners.
5. Expect them to show less initiative and less ability to plan for themselves than average or gifted children. They are also less able to evaluate their own work, making close supervision and direction by the teacher imperative.
6. Reduce their load of abstract and verbal materials to a level they are able to handle. Work in references, if used at all, must be specific; reading and research must be held to a minimum.
7. Recognize that it will be difficult for them to sense relationships, to make generalizations, or to do inferential thinking. They are more skillful in dealing with who, what, and where questions than they are with why type questions.
8. Expect less creativity and more patterned work from them.
9. When teaching crucial items such as those of health, safety, laws or conventions of society, or simple elements of social studies skills, plan to provide for much practice and repetition of the material to be learned.
10. Set realistic levels of expectation for them. Plan in terms of their most pressing needs with a view toward their future life as happy

and productive members of society. Try to visualize what the child is likely to be doing a score of years in the future.

11. Above all, maintain a patient and encouraging attitude toward them. Help them establish security and status in the classroom. Provide for them what is the birthright of every educable American child—a degree of success in the elementary school.

IN TEACHING GIFTED CHILDREN

1. Provide a generous amount of challenging reading material that will allow them to read for informational purposes.
2. Plan learning activities that call for problem solving, making logical associations, making logical deductions, and making generalizations.
3. Give them many opportunities for the planning aspects of their own work; allow for a considerable amount of individual initiative, commensurate with their degree of maturity.
4. Provide for individual study and research. This should include use of the library, references, note keeping, outlining, summarizing, and reporting.
5. Expect and encourage much originality in self-expression—in discussions, dramatizations, projects, and activities.
6. Give them many opportunities for leadership responsibilities.
7. Recognize that they have less need for *extended* firsthand and concrete experiences than do slow-learning or average-learning children, because they are able to work with abstractions more easily, see associations and relationships more quickly, and have quick reaction time.
8. Encourage these pupils to develop self-evaluative skills; these children are generally capable of effectively evaluating their own work.
9. Provide opportunities for gifted children to use their talents in helping slower-learning children on a tutorial basis. In some schools children of the intermediate grades with high intellectual abilities also work with primary-grade children.
10. Remember that gifted children have many of the common needs of all children. Although it is true that they are ordinarily accelerated in other aspects of their development as well, their physical growth, muscular coordination, social development, and emotional stability cannot be equated with their rate of growth in mental development.
11. The complete acceptance by the teacher of the high intellectual

abilities of gifted children is essential to planning an effective program for them. The teacher who sees the gifted child as a threat to his own status becomes defensive in his relationships with him and is unable to work with him satisfactorily. If the teacher takes a position of guiding, encouraging, helping, suggesting, and leading rather than of directing, telling, criticizing, and answering all questions, his task will be easier.

Discussion Questions and Suggested Activities

1. Obtain the mental ages and chronological ages for all children in a grade of your choice. Rank them from high to low on the basis of *mental* age and place their names in that order from left to right along the bottom of a sheet of paper. On the left side of the same sheet draw an age scale perpendicular to the horizontal line on which you have placed the children's names. Plot the mental ages for all children with one color and the chronological ages with another color. You should now have two curves, one representing mental ages for the class and the other representing the chronological ages. At what point does the mental age line cross the chronological age line? Which of the two is more nearly the same for all children? How can you identify children who have repeated grades? Why does a chart of this type deserve serious study?

2. What are some of the factors that might account for a pupil of above-average ability achieving at a mediocre or below-average rate? What factors might account for a pupil of below-average ability achieving at an above-average rate?

3. Select a short article related to the social studies topic of your resource unit (Chapter 3) and rewrite it to suit the reading level of slower-reading children using the suggestions offered by Benbrook listed in this chapter. What guidelines would you apply in rewriting simpler reading materials for use with the academically talented?

4. Observe an elementary school classroom during several social studies periods. What methods of individualizing instruction were used most frequently? Which methods were the most effective?

5. List ten to fifteen simple ideas associated with the topic of your resource unit and ten to fifteen ideas that are more complex and difficult.

6. Evaluate the following statement made by a teacher: "I never look at the folders and records of my children in the fall until I have had a chance to get to know them. I want everyone to have a

fresh start in my room. If I saw their records and histories, I would become prejudiced against some before I have had a chance to know them and they to know me."

7. Do you believe that certain classroom activities carry with them more prestige than others? What teaching procedures might the teacher use to combat the idea that construction and art activities are performed by dull children whereas research and intellectual activities are reserved for bright children?

8. Miss Smith was annoyed because several pupils in her class could not do "fifth-grade work." However, she continued to teach "fifth-grade work" and at the end of the year retained two children because they could not do "sixth-grade work." What basic principles of individual differences does Miss Smith seem not to understand?

9. Do you feel that there are certain elements of subject matter that all pupils should master irrespective of their abilities? If so, designate what some of those elements should be and defend your point of view.

10. Many disadvantaged children exhibit extreme language deficiencies. Should the classroom teacher attempt to change the language of the disadvantaged child? How might the social studies teacher "build on" or improve expressive skills of disadvantaged children?

Selected References

Association for Supervision and Curriculum Development, *Human Variability and Learning*. Washington, D.C.: The Association, 1961.

Bloom, Benjamin S., Allison Davis, and Robert Hess. *Compensatory Education for Cultural Deprivation*. New York: Holt, Rinehart & Winston, Inc., 1965.

Chase, W. Linwood. "Individual Differences in Classroom Learning," *Social Studies in the Elementary School*, 56th Yearbook, National Society for the Study of Education. Chicago: University of Chicago Press, 1957.

Crow, L. D., W. I. Murray, and H. H. Smythe. *Educating the Culturally Disadvantaged Child*. New York: David McKay Company, Inc., 1966.

Elkins, Deborah. "Instructional Guidelines for Teachers of the Disadvantaged," *The Teachers College Record*, 70, No. 7 (April, 1969), pp. 593–615.

Frazier, Alexander. "Individualized Instruction," *Educational Leadership*, 25, No. 7 (April, 1968), pp. 616–624.

Frazier, Alexander, *et al.*, eds. *Educating the Children of the Poor.*

Washington, D.C.: Association for Supervision and Curriculum Development, 1968.

Gagne, Robert M. *Learning and Individual Differences.* Columbus, Ohio: Charles E. Merrill Books, Inc., 1967.

Groeschell, R. "Curriculum Provisions for Individual Differences," *Social Education, XXXI,* No. 5 (May, 1967), pp. 416–418.

Higgins, John M. "Social Studies for the Other Third," *The Social Studies,* No. 59 (February, 1968), pp. 51–54.

Hunter, Madeline. "Tailor Your Teaching to Individualized Instruction," *Instructor, LXXIX,* No. 7 (March, 1970), pp. 53–63.

Jarolimek, John. "The Taxonomy: Guide to Differentiated Instruction," *Social Education, XXVI,* No. 8 (December, 1962), pp. 445–447.

Jarolimek, John, and Huber M. Walsh. *Readings for Social Studies in Elementary Education,* 2nd ed. New York: The Macmillan Company, 1969.

Lee, John R., and Jonathon C. McLendon. *Readings on Elementary Social Studies: Prologue to Change.* Boston: Allyn & Bacon, Inc., 1965.

Leeper, Robert R. *Humanizing Education: The Person in the Process.* Washington, D.C.: Association for Supervision and Curriculum Development, 1967.

Passow, A. Harry, Miriam Goldberg, and Abraham J. Tannenbaum. *Education of the Disadvantaged.* New York: Holt, Rinehart & Winston, Inc., 1967.

Rogers, Vincent R. "Individualization Plus," *Instructor,* No. 78 (January, 1969), pp. 88–89+.

Rogers, Vincent R. "Nongraded Social Studies," *Instructor,* No. 78 (May, 1969), pp. 73–74+.

Sand, Ole, and Bruce Joyce. "Planning for Children of Varying Ability," *Social Studies in Elementary Schools,* 32nd Yearbook. Washington, D.C.: National Council for the Social Studies, 1962.

"The Elementary School: Focus on Individualizing Instruction," *Social Education, XXXIII,* No. 5 (May, 1969), pp. 534–550.

"The Elementary School: Focus on Minority Groups," *Social Education, XXXIII,* No. 4 (April, 1969), pp. 429–446.

"The Elementary School: Focus on the Culturally Different," *Social Education, XXXIII,* No. 1 (January, 1969), pp. 61–82.

"The Elementary School: Focus on Urban Education," *Social Education, XXXIII,* No. 6 (October, 1969), pp. 699–712.

Thomas, George I., and Joseph Crescimbeni. *Individualizing Instruction in the Elementary School.* New York: Random House, 1967.

Thomas, John I. "Individualizing Instruction in the Social Studies," *The Social Studies,* No. 60 (February, 1969), pp. 71–76.

Geographical Elements in the Social Studies

Geography has traditionally occupied and continues to occupy a position of central importance as one of the subjects comprising the social studies curriculum of the elementary school. Social studies units and topics have a place in space, and geography is concerned with the character of those places. The nature of an area and the way it relates to other areas are tremendously significant in understanding human occupance and man's use of the earth.

Geography teaching has suffered some because of the persistence of traditional and stereotyped notions about the nature of geography. School geography has been dominated by a preoccupation with describing and naming various features of the physical environment:

locating rivers; naming mountains; learning places, products, capes, and bays. Such descriptive teaching allows little if any opportunity to approach geographic concepts in a thoughtful and reflective manner. Because such exercises often do not contribute to the understanding of social or natural phenomena, it is not likely that geography so taught will seem relevant to young learners. The status of geography teaching in American schools has been a matter of some concern to professional geographers and geography educators. It is not surprising, therefore, that in the current curriculum-reform movement, they were among the first of the social scientists to seek to improve the teaching of their discipline in the elementary and secondary schools.

Geography is by definition a science that is concerned with the study and description of the earth. Traditionally, this has meant physical geography, with studies focusing on the unequal distribution of such phenomena as water, minerals, climate, productive land, vegetation, land forms, and so on. Undoubtedly, man's intense interest in the world in which he lives and his desire to find out what lies beyond his immediate surroundings gave rise to the development of the science of geography. As early man began to move from one place to another on the earth, he began to notice that one place differed from another, and he began to make observations of these differences in the places he visited. In time these observations were systematically recorded and were gradually brought together into the discipline of geography. Geographic knowledge became extremely useful, and indeed essential, for travelers, explorers, military leaders, and those engaged in trade and commerce.

As man found his way into all parts of the world, his knowledge of the physical geography of the earth greatly increased. All parts of the world were explored in a gross way and were to some extent described and mapped. Then the emphasis in geography began to shift from simply describing phenomena to explaining the differences that were found from one place to another. In addition, the relationships between the physiographic and biotic elements within those areas were beginning to be explored. The study of the uniqueness of a particular area—the study of the factors that make an area different from any other area of the earth—is embodied in the concept of *areal differentiation*. Also, man began to explore ways that one part or area of the world related to another, that is, the links and bonds, either natural or man-made, that develop between places. Such studies concern themselves with the concept of *spatial interaction*. These two concepts—areal differentiation and spatial interaction—are central to the understanding of the concerns and approaches of modern geography. Although there are other important concepts in geography, these two serve as the backbone of modern programs of geographic education at all levels.

The Place of Geography in Social Studies

Geographic education in the elementary school takes place within the framework of the broader social studies curriculum. Geography can be taught as a part of social studies units of the interdisciplinary type, it can be handled as a separate subject, or it can be a part of a multidisciplinary program. Whatever the curricular organization, good geographic teaching can come about only when the instructional program is planned to achieve certain understandings and skills important to this field. Incidental teaching of geography, largely unplanned, as it happens to relate to topics under study usually means poor teaching and misplaced emphasis. Often this means learning a few geographic facts that are not tied to basic concepts. This is not to minimize the importance of geographical facts, for such knowledge is not only desirable but essential. But facts must be placed in an organizational framework if they are to be meaningful, and this rarely happens without careful planning. Modern programs in geographic education are broad in scope, with the emphasis on a few key ideas or basic concepts supported by a knowledge of significant geographic facts needed to understand major ideas. In addition, modern geography teaching places a heavy emphasis on people and the manner in which they handle the phenomena of the earth as they meet their problems of living with each other on this planet.

Many objectives could be stated for geography teaching, but the dominant ones are (1) those that seek to develop the child's insight and understanding of the problems of man that are activated by man's interaction with his natural surroundings and (2) those that have to do with learning the methods of perceiving and studying problems from a geographic point of view. That geography can and should be used as an instrument to gain insight into the relationship of man to the earth has been noted by numerous authors. The human aspects of geography are evident in much of the writing of geographers and geography educators. Hartshorne, for example, writes, "The relations between the world of man and the non-human world are of the greatest concern in geography." [1] Morris identifies three important questions to be answered in the study of geography at any level: "(1) Where is the item or place being discussed located? (2) Why is it there and why is it as it is? (3) What is its *relationship to man?*" [2]

Geography instruction would be both more interesting and meaningful for elementary school pupils if this people orientation were maintained. Geography teaching can capitalize on the natural interest and curiosity that children have about people. Pupils can become fa-

1. Richard Hartshorne, *Perspective on the Nature of Geography*, Chicago: Rand McNally, 1959, p. 48.
2. John W. Morris, "Geography—Separate Course or Integrated," *Journal of Geography*, 54, No. 5, May, 1965, p. 203.

miliar with the characteristic types of adjustments man has made in various regions of the world. They can learn how people in different geographic settings interact with their natural and cultural environments. Naturally, care must be taken not to stress incorrect concepts such as teaching that geography causes people to live the way they do or that geography consists only of the relationship between the physical environment and man. The point here is that it is possible to develop programs in geography at the elementary school level that are soundly based conceptually and that, at the same time, are people oriented as opposed to place-thing oriented.

The possibility of organizing geographic instruction around central concepts of the discipline is receiving much attention today. The following basic concepts were derived from the current spate of redefinitions for geography:

1. *Spatial distribution*—The distribution and arrangement in the modern world of such geographic phenomena as people, physical features, natural resources, economic activities, sociocultural patterns, and political systems as they are attributable to valid causal connections
2. *Areal coherence*—Areal associations and variations of geographic phenomena as they reflect the process/processes of cause-and-effect relationships. Thus, order and reason are observed in sets of geographic elements that coexist in an area
3. *Regional concept*—"The face of the earth . . . marked off into areas that are homogeneous in terms of specific criteria"
4. *Location theory*—The attributes of place, the mode for establishing position, the significance of relative position (the situation), all of which impart uniqueness and personality to any given place on the face of the earth
5. *The cultural viewpoint*—The significance of a society's goals, technology, value system, social-cultural-political structure in creating a perceptual framework for understanding man's impact on the physical environment
6. *The human relationship to a natural resource*—The interpretation of the existence, value, and utility of a natural resource in terms of the cultural achievement of a society
7. *The dynamic nature of geographic analysis*—The general principle of continual change in human affairs, in the habitat features, and in their interrelations that necessitates the reappraisal of the geographic landscape at any given time
8. *The importance of time*—Intellectual insights into the nature of the human occupancy and the trends for the future revealed through cumulative knowledge of historic occupancy; the time perspective, an essential dimension of the man-land complex
9. *Spatial interaction*—The connections and movements within and between regions as zones of dynamic interaction that induce patterns of migration, trade, and transportation, or cultural diffusion

10. *Man-land relationships*—The entire man-land complex and the understanding of every aspect of this interrelationship on a world-wide system, a unifying theme in geography
11. *Global interdependence*—Increasing interdependence on a wider and more complex scale, concomitant with progress in the industrial-urban society.[3]

A number of lists of basic concepts stated in the form of main ideas or as generalizations have been prepared in recent years. Examples of these are provided on pages 209–210 of this chapter and also in the Appendix on page 514. In all cases where conceptually based programs are planned, the idea is to use these basic concepts as organizing ideas around which instruction is planned. As was explained on pages 38–42, the result is a spiral-type curriculum in which simple variations of the concept are introduced at early levels and more complex variations at later grades. The basic concepts provide the framework within which is placed a vast amount of specific, supporting detail. This principle is being applied not only to the teaching of geography but also to the other social science disciplines.

Thus, in conceptually oriented programs, learnings are spread over a span of several years. This should dispel the idea so widely held by parents and teachers alike that geography is taught only in a specific grade or grades of the elementary school. To get continuous development of important concepts and skills and to get them to a sophisticated, mature level, systematic attention needs to be given these learnings *in all grades*—including those beyond the elementary school. One reason many adults seem to have their map-reading skills and knowledge of geography arrested at about the sixth-grade level is because little systematic attention is given these learnings beyond that point in many schools. This does not mean that separate courses in geography need to be planned for all grades. However, it does mean that planned attention to the teaching and maintenance of these learnings needs to be given to them in most, if not all, of the social studies units, with especial emphasis given to geography in selected units of study. In this way geographic understandings and skills develop gradually throughout the grades of the elementary and secondary schools.

Methods of Inquiry in Geography

As more attention is given to the disciplines contributing to social studies education, there is increased interest in acquainting pupils with the methods of inquiry that characterize the various disciplines. Each field has, to some extent, its own method of study, its own peculiar data sources, its own way of collecting, summarizing and reporting

3. Midori Nishi, "Geographic Guidelines for Reconstructing the Social Studies Curriculum," *Journal of Geography,* LXV, No. 7, October, 1966, pp. 328–331.

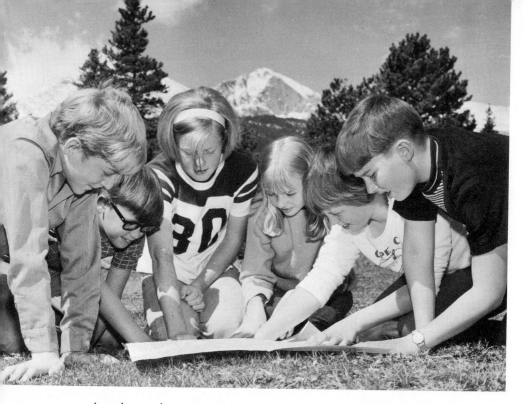

A good way to learn geography is to do so on site in the field as these pupils here are doing. (Courtesy of the Colorado State College, Greeley)

data. Similarly, each one arrives at certain types of conclusions that are identified with it as a discipline. Suppose, for example, a geographer, a historian, and a sociologist were to conduct independent studies of a large community. It is apparent that the geographer would collect, assemble, and report data that might be of no concern to the historian or the sociologist. The reverse would also obtain. In some cases they might be interested in examining the same data but for different reasons and would, thereby, draw different inferences and come to different conclusions based on the data.

The possibility of having young pupils apply some of the same techniques of study practiced by scholars in the field has produced some new and exciting dimensions to social studies education. This is not to suggest that all pupils are to become miniature social scientists or that all the instruction needs to follow this pattern. As is true with most procedures, if it is sensibly applied and not regarded with special devotion to the exclusion of other sound procedures, it can do much to stimulate good teaching and learning in the social studies.

The term *method of inquiry* has come to be widely used in education in recent years. The idea of applying methods of inquiry that are used by scholars, however, is hardly a new idea in education. In 1937, for example, Horn commented, "The student who would learn how to attack problems in the social sciences should practice the modes of thought of the social scientists themselves. If, for example, a student wishes to learn how to deal with the historian's problem, he should choose the historian's methods." [4]

What has been said thus far applies to all of the social sciences, and it is within this context that methods of inquiry will be discussed in subsequent chapters dealing with other disciplines. We turn now to geography. What are the methods of the geographer, how does he conduct his studies, and, most important, how can these be applied to elementary social studies instruction?

Whatever else geographers do, they are concerned fundamentally with place and space. Their studies have a locus in some place in space. This leads geographers to be concerned with regions. The *region* is a construct that is defined by the geographer in a specific way. In discussing the regional concept, for example, James writes,

> The regional concept holds that the face of the earth can be marked off into areas of distinctive character that are homogeneous in terms of specific criteria. Since no two points on the face of the earth are identical, no area, even a small one, can be entirely uniform and homogeneous. Even a field of corn includes much surface on which there is no corn, and there may be more ragweed plants than corn plants in the field if it is poorly tended. Yet the field is described as homogeneous in terms of a specific criterion—a cultivated crop. The region is a geographic generalization, an intellectual concept. There is no such thing as a "true region," or one that might not be further subdivided if subdivision were desirable. Regions are defined for specific purposes, and for each purpose a different regional system may be needed. Regions are judged good or bad by the degree to which they illuminate a problem: regions that have the effect of obscuring area relationships are bad regions.[5]

When the geographer has selected a region, as defined by James, for study, he begins collecting information about the area and seeks to enlarge his knowledge of it. Much of his information comes from existing sources, such as libraries, government publications, abstracts, commercial agencies, and published documents. He goes into the field and observes land forms, vegetation, land use, and economic activity. He may make surveys or do aerial reconnaissance to gather data. He

4. Ernest Horn, *Methods of Instruction in the Social Studies*, New York: Charles Scribner's Sons, 1937, p. 287.

5. Preston E. James, "Geography," *The Social Studies and the Social Sciences*, New York: Harcourt, Brace and World, 1962, p. 51.

makes much use of maps and photographs. He studies the movement of goods and people in and out of the region and relates these data to other variables such as climate and economic cycles. Through comparison and analysis he sharpens the boundaries of the region under study. Having gathered these data from a variety of sources, he begins to make an analysis of the area to detect patterns and relationships associated with certain conditions or variables in terms of the particular problem under study. Sometimes problems are studied historically to note trends, movements, and changes over time.

It is often said that maps are the constant companions of the geographer, and he must be expert in using and making many types of maps. He uses maps to record his data and his observations, as devices for studying relationships, and as a means of communicating some of his findings. The geographer often makes comparisons of maps and matches one map with another to note associations and relationships. In addition, the geographer makes much use of tables, charts, lists, and statistics, both in gathering data and in reporting findings.

This brief description of the methods of the geographer suggests some ways these methods can be applied to the teaching of geography in the elementary school: (1) use of a variety of specialized sources of data, (2) direct observation of phenomena in the field, (3) analysis of photographs, (4) map making and map reading, (5) using the regional concept and defining regions, (6) identifying associated phenomena and making conclusions and inferences from such associations.

Geography Teaching in Primary Grades

The teacher of primary-grade children can and should introduce them to geographic education in a wide variety of ways through the social studies units of the class. Grades one, two, and three are sometimes thought of in terms of developing a readiness for geographic understandings. This procedure is similar to the practice of presenting young children with a variety of number experiences before introducing them to formal mathematics. Where this procedure is followed, the child's learning of geographic materials is enhanced, because his teachers have helped him lay a sound groundwork for more structured and formal experiences with geographic understandings that will follow at advanced levels.

The primary-grade program, however, should be more than experiences in readiness for geography teaching that will occur later. It should be perceived as a part of a continuous program of geographic education that begins in grade one and extends throughout the elementary school and beyond. The primary-grade teacher will, therefore, not depend entirely on incidental and chance opportunities to bring some geography instruction into the curriculum but will deliberately plan experiences for the children in their social studies units that will bring them in direct contact with geographical concepts. This is done not only as a readiness procedure for work to come later in the grades but also to help the children gain an elementary, but genuine, knowledge of geographic concepts appropriate to their level of maturity. Examples of the types of elementary geographic learnings suitable for use with children in primary grades follow:

1. We go in a direction no matter where we go.
2. Many people make their living by taking care of the resources that are important to an area.
3. There are different kinds of maps, each having a specific purpose.
4. People adapt themselves to conditions in the environment.
5. Transportation plays an important part in the distribution of food.
6. The globe is a very small model of the earth on which we live.
7. People earn their living doing many different kinds of jobs.
8. Things can be located at specific spots on the earth's surface.
9. Nature changes the character of the earth.
10. The rotation of the earth produces night and day.
11. Communities change with the passage of time.
12. Some people live in cities in order to be close to their jobs.
13. People as well as animals change their ways of living at different times of the year.
14. Man uses natural resources to satisfy his needs.
15. Weather plays an important role in the lives of all living things.
16. People need plants and animals for food.
17. The same land can be used for many different purposes.
18. Cities are often located near sources of power.
19. No two places are exactly alike: each place looks somewhat different from other places.
20. Every day we use things that have come from all over the world.

The primary-grade teacher will have no difficulty finding ways to include geographical elements in social studies units. Children have a natural curiosity concerning the world about them and have endless questions to which they are seeking answers. Much of the early geography teaching centers about the local community. It is in the local community that the primary-grade child may experience and observe firsthand various land and water forms—lakes, creeks, islands, gullies, slopes. The teacher encourages children to explore the various forms of native plant and animal life and observe the characteristic changes of these with changing seasons of the year. With some help from the teacher, the children can find answers to questions such as these:

"What do animals do to prepare for winter?" "What would happen to them if they did not make these preparations?" "What things do we do to prepare for winter?" "Why is the creek dry at this time of the year?" "Why can't we grow bananas in our back yard?" First-graders discussing problems of this type are getting their first lessons in the relationship of man to his environment.

The opportunities for children to explore geographically in and around the school site are almost limitless. A primary-grade teacher takes her class to a nearby basement excavation for a new home. The children observe the various layers of soil and the teacher calls their attention to the many roots found in the fertile topsoil. The class is able to obtain samples of the various strata of soil to take back to their classroom for an experiment in seeing how well plants grow in the various layers—an early beginning in the appreciation and understanding of the value of soil conservation. The presence of earth-moving equipment suggests that man is not completely at the mercy of natural phenomena but that he can, within certain limits, do things to modify his environment. Sometimes these modifications are helpful; other times they are destructive and harmful. The imaginative teacher can plan similar experiences in purposeful exploration in connection with soil, water, water bodies, minerals, rocks, local vegetation, surface features, and occupations of parents. Experiences of this type provide an opportunity to learn and apply an important method of study used by geographers: careful observation of phenomena.

Weather and climate present another area of exploration for young children. The child has frequently heard his parents and other adults discuss weather conditions, and many children have viewed weather forecasts on television. The frequency of reference to weather in adult conversations indicates the degree to which weather and climatic conditions have an effect on the lives of people. In primary-grade classrooms, children will want to have their own charts on which they can record various weather data observed each day. The teacher reads the daily temperature, or the children report the official daily temperature that they have heard over an early morning radio broadcast. These temperatures can be shown graphically, thereby applying knowledge of numbers and graphs in a functional setting. Over a period of several weeks or months the graph will show the changes occurring with reference to temperatures and seasons of the year. Children can also record data dealing with wind velocities, cloud formations, precipitation, and similar subjects. They can also make their own predictions based on the data they have collected. Sensitivity to weather changes will again call attention to the changes in native plant and animal life as well as to the adaptations people make to changing seasons. Here the teacher can apply another technique of the geographer: recording data and using simple charts.

Earlier in this chapter a reference was made to the numerous questions children have about the world and its people, and this suggests another possibility for much good geography teaching. In many cases the teacher may use the effective "Let's find out" method in dealing with children's questions. If children find the classroom to be a place where they may ask questions and find answers to their questions, the teacher is likely to have children asking, "Where do the spices come from that Mother has on her spice shelf?" "Where does the grocer get the fruit he sells?" "What is in the freight cars that rumble through the station?" "Where do they go?" "Why was the town located here?" "Why do the leaves fall in autumn?" "Why are days shorter in winter than in summer?" "Do people in China have to stand upside down?" "Why don't they fall off the earth?" The teacher can use these questions for a substantial amount of geography teaching. The answers to some they will find out together, others will be answered in stories the teacher reads to the class, and still others she explains simply and forthrightly in language at the pupils' level of understanding. Complex explanations are neither desirable nor necessary with children in the primary grades. What is needed are accurate but simple explanations to satisfy the child's curiosity. In this case a third method of the geographer is stressed: the inductive approach to the study of problems.

A number of opportunities for geography teaching may grow out of the reading and language program of the class. In the basic reading series one will find many stories and selections with a geographical setting. The children read about the family that took a weekend trip to the lake or spent a summer in the mountains. They read about the antics of the monkeys in the zoo and wonder about their natural habitat. Brief explanations and discussions of accompanying geographical elements are helpful in gaining a better understanding of the meaning of the story. Primary-grade teachers spend much time reading to children, and many of these stories present opportunities for geography education. These situations, plus the selections the children read in their classroom newspaper and the current affairs that children report, present many opportunities not only for language development but also for developing geographical concepts.

Geography Teaching in the Middle and Upper Grades

With the good beginnings the child has made in understanding geographic concepts in the primary grades, he is ready to move into the more formal approach to geography education characteristic of the

This excited youngster is showing his teacher where his home town is on a map of the United States. It was the first time he had seen his city on a map. (Courtesy of the Washington State Office of Public Instruction, Olympia)

middle grades. In the middle and upper grades the child is not handicapped in dealing with geographical concepts because of immaturity, vocabulary limitations, reading ability, and experience background *to the extent* that he was in the primary grades. The teacher need not depend entirely on firsthand experiences of the children for geography teaching but may enrich and extend his teaching through the use of printed material, maps, globes, charts, pictorial material, graphs and similar abstract learning aids. More systematic use can be made of the methods of geographic study in the middle and upper grades. Naturally, the child should not be thrust into such material abruptly in grade four. Rather, the progression from the informal program of the primary grades to the more structured program of the middle grades should represent a gradual transition. Although the middle-grade child is capable of handling much abstract material and, thus, does a considerable amount of experiencing vicariously, there will still be a need for many firsthand experiences as well.

Children in the middle and upper grades can delve more deeply into the relationships between the earth and the activities of man than they could in the primary grades. They learn that people the world over attempt to satisfy their basic needs in ways that are influenced by their environment, their past experiences, and present resources. Even though the methods various people use to meet these needs in specific regions of the world may seem strange to us, they are not unusual for those who inhabit that region. Although children will *not* be taught that geographic conditions determine how people live, they should learn that geography sets certain limits on the choices available to them. (For example, people in the Arctic are probably not going to find it profitable to grow oranges and bananas no matter what their level of technological or cultural development.) In this connection, children learn that historical and cultural items as well as natural ones have significance in the development of geographic relationships. A few examples of some of the key geographical ideas that should be stressed in the middle and upper grades are

1. Places on the earth have a distinctiveness about them that differentiates them from all other places.
2. Man uses his physical environment in terms of his cultural values, perceptions, and level of technology.
3. A nation's use of its geography depends on its political and economic objectives.
4. Physical and human changes in one part of the world affect people's lives in other parts of the world.
5. Relationships between cultural areas tend to expand with increased technological development.
6. Conflicts between nations often arise because of geographic factors.
7. An area may be kept together through a pattern of circulation binding the area to a central place.
8. The relationship between agricultural resources and man is less direct in highly urbanized societies than it is in other areas.
9. Areas of the earth develop bonds, interconnections, and relations with other areas.

10. The wasteful exploitation and pollution of natural and human resources poses serious problems for the welfare of the earth's rapidly growing population of human beings.

The direct experiences that the child has had in the local community help him to relate himself and his community to the world's
communities. In the study of various regions of the world, the child
will follow somewhat the same pattern of exploration and problem
solving as in the primary grades. In planning the study of the life of
a people in a specific region, such factors as these will be included, although not necessarily in this sequence: the surface features of the
region; the plant and animal life characteristic of the region; and the
relationship of this life to the climatic and weather conditions that
affect the occupations and way of life of the people of the area. From
this systematic study of communities in various natural regions of the
world, the child can discover some relationships between various geographic conditions and the activities of man. For example, he might
discover that in places where one finds very similar physical geographic conditions, people may live quite differently. The reverse could
also be true. How man uses his natural surroundings depends mainly
on cultural factors.

The study of particular communities and regions presents difficult
instructional problems, no matter what system is used in selecting
them. Too often they are treated in a superficial or romantic way. It
becomes easy to make unwarranted value judgments about the people
studied, to arrive at hasty and inaccurate generalizations, and to develop stereotyped ideas of people. The tendency has been to stress
traditional or legendary aspects of a people's culture rather than come
to grips with their way of life in modern times. A good example is
provided in our lack of understanding of Latin America. There is much
evidence that the people and their problems of this vast area are poorly
understood by citizens of the United States, yet "Latin American
Neighbors" has been in the social studies curriculum of many elementary schools for at least thirty years. The need for accurate information and a proper instructional emphasis is essential if valid
understandings are to develop.

Units in the primary grades have stressed the study of the local
community, and this background should serve as a basis for community studies throughout the world. The natural regions in which the
communities are located should be sufficiently different from one another to help the child learn the characteristic adjustments man makes
under varying conditions. These then may be compared with life in his
own community, stressing the similarities that exist between people.

Such a study should, of course, include historical and cultural elements as a natural part of geographic study.

At the beginning of the study of a community or a region, it is helpful to make an overview of the continent on which the region is located. This helps the child place the area properly in its larger geographical setting. Oftentimes, at the beginning of such units, the teacher will use a globe and a series of wall maps. Beginning with the globe, he will focus attention on the continent on which the study is to be made. He will point out its location in terms of other known places on the earth. Then he can move to a wall map of the continent and point out the particular area to be studied. This can be followed with a brief study of the geographical features of the continent in terms of their relationship to the particular area to be studied in greater detail. Such a spot location of places will make it easier for the pupil to visualize the types of interrelationships and associations that are possible for a given area.

Intensive continental studies are usually not well suited for elementary school grades because the natural, cultural, and historical backgrounds of various sections are generally so diverse that it is difficult to select a unifying set of concepts for the study. Consequently, pupils often learn a number of facts regarding natural items but fail to relate these to the people who inhabit the area. It is ordinarily better to select specific communities in representative regions of the world and study those intensively. Rather than select a continent for study in the fourth grade, the teacher, for example, might better select a Scandinavian community for one unit, a Mediterranean community for another, a Latin American community for another, a Middle Eastern community, an Oriental community, an island community, and a Southeast Asian community that has a typical Western civilization cultural orientation. These communities are sufficiently different from one another to show how man solves his problems of living under a variety of natural conditions. Running through the entire study should be a central theme to help the child understand that the common needs and problems of people wherever they are found are basically similar yet differ in specific respects because of differing circumstances. People everywhere satisfy their basic needs and solve their problems within the context of their historical and cultural backgrounds as well as in relationship to their natural environment. (See Figure 14.)

Some elementary school teachers cling to the concept of environmental determinism, although geographers rejected it years ago as an explanation of differing ways of living. Geographic conditions should be taught as factors that relate to, condition, or affect ways of living but do not *cause* them. If geographic conditions caused people to live

GEOGRAPHICAL ELEMENTS IN
THE SOCIAL STUDIES

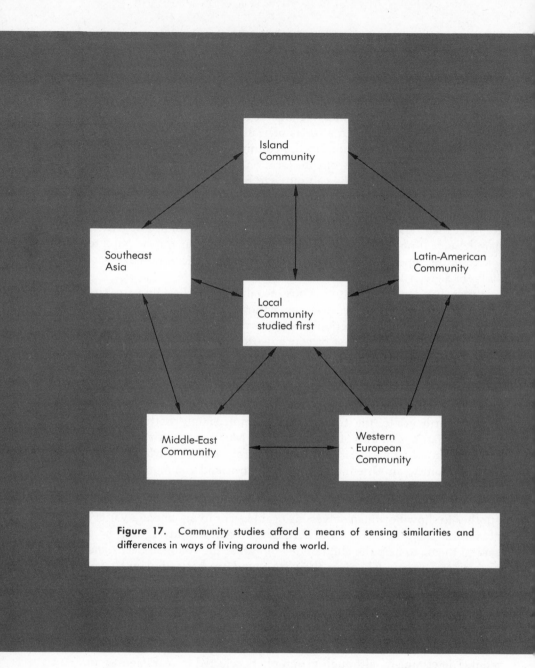

Figure 17. Community studies afford a means of sensing similarities and differences in ways of living around the world.

the way they do, everyone in a given area of the world would live the same way; and, of course, this is not the case. For example, some of the people of the world who inhabit the deserts live in tents, tend sheep, and live nomadic lives; others who live in desert areas have air-conditioned ranch-style homes, work in comfortable office buildings, and drive modern automobiles.

The teaching of the earth's climatic zones also persists even though this concept, too, has been discarded by geographers. Traditionally, children were taught that the earth had climatic belts known as the Frigid, Temperate, and Torrid zones that surrounded the earth at certain latitudes. The implication in this is that these areas are homogenous with respect to climatic conditions. This conclusion is in error, because there are places in the so-called Torrid Zone that have snow the year around; places in the so-called Temperate Zone that have winter temperatures as low as 40° below zero; and places in the Frigid Zone that record fairly mild temperatures even in the winter months. These zonal designations with respect to climate should *not* be taught. The terms *low latitudes, middle latitudes,* and *high latitudes* are acceptable in referring to these parts of the world because they do not imply that a specific climatic condition prevails throughout the area so designated. Climate should not be explained entirely in terms of latitude.

In the study of ways of living around the world, usually at the fourth grade, many programs focus on primitive societies because these people relate so directly to their surroundings in meeting their basic needs of food, clothing, and shelter. They make their homes and clothing from materials close at hand, and these necessities are usually entirely functional. All food is grown, gathered, or hunted. Where there is trading or other contact with the outside world, ways of living begin to change. Even under primitive conditions, however, the people have their moments of happiness and pleasure as well as periods of sorrow and disappointment. Much of value can come from studies of this type, but the teacher needs to be careful not to develop the idea that just because these people meet their basic needs in simple ways, their social organization is easy to understand. Often the customs, mores, and taboos of primitive cultures are exceedingly complex. When studies of primitive peoples (Indians, Eskimos, jungle people, desert people) are undertaken, the units should be used to demonstrate specific points: man can live under a variety of geographical conditions; primitive people have less need for the great variety of resources needed by industrial societies; certain human qualities are apparent in all people no matter how they live; people do not need great material wealth in order to be happy; primitive people spend a disproportionate amount of time seeking basic needs; ways of living change when people meet others from a more advanced culture; and so on.

In the fourth grade, one also finds the study of home states to be fairly common. Many of the states are sufficiently diverse in geography to allow parallels to be drawn with similar places around the world.

If the state has plains, for example, pupils might find out where else in the world one finds plains and how the people there make use of them. Or the state might have mountains, or deserts, or good harbors —any of these and many more can be used to teach geographical concepts to children on a broad basis.

The same principles hold true in the fifth-grade social studies curriculum, which in many schools deals with communities or sections of the United States, its history, and the movement of people from one section to another within it. In the consideration of historical developments, life in early America, or contemporary life in various communities of the United States, the teacher should relate geographical factors to the study of such units. What did the geography of the region have to do with the way people lived and how they made their living? Why did large cities grow where they did? Why did the people moving west follow certain routes? How were people able to make use of the resources they found? All these questions relate to geography, and geographical understanding should be used to help explain them.

In the upper grades, many social studies units provide the opportunity for relating man's activities to his environment. As a result of their studies, children should learn how such social functions as making a living, producing goods, building homes, making clothing, transporting goods, and communicating ideas relate to the specific region in which people live. It is also in these grades that children should develop considerable skill in the use of the tools of geography—charts, graphs, source books, and most particularly, maps and globes. These are indispensable in the serious study of geographical elements in the social studies.

In the middle and upper grades, some attention should be given to the historical dimension of geography. For example, in studying the location of cities, teachers frequently have pupils explain why the particular place is a good location for a city. What is often overlooked in such an exercise is that the choice was made a hundred or two hundred or even more years ago. *At that time* in terms of the technology of the period, the site may have been a good one, but in terms of present-day technology it may be a bad site. If the choice of a place for a city were made today, perhaps it would be located somewhere else. Ghost towns are good examples of poor site selection for permanent settlement. The same applies to many other man-made features. Roads today were formerly cow paths and horse trails or old logging roads. Industrial centers grew up in places easily accessible to employees who walked to work or who rode trolleys. Downtown shopping centers were established before automobile parking became a problem. Very profitable and interesting studies can be made of areas as they were in early days: land division and use, the pattern of transportation, the location of processing and manufacturing facilities, the location and distribution of markets, and interactions with surrounding areas can be noted. The study then shifts to an examination and analysis of these factors in the same area as they are today, thereby gaining an understanding and appreciation of the problems related to area growth and change.

In this connection, too, geographic thinking can be stimulated through the consideration of hypothetical propositions. For example, a fifth-grade class might consider the following proposition: Suppose instead of being located in northern Minnesota, the large iron deposits of the Mesabi had been discovered in southern Missouri. What effect might this have had on the location of northern cities? Would the major transportation systems and routes of the area be the same as they are today? Would major industrial and manufacturing centers be located where they are today? Teachers can easily devise problems of this type from time to time by selecting a situation and shifting a critical variable. Pupils cannot arrive at final answers to such problems, but they can speculate on possible solutions and can demonstrate their ability to apply their geographic knowledge. Hypothetical propositions, if well selected, provide good ways for a teacher to evaluate a pupil's understanding of important concepts and his ability to transfer such knowledge to other situations.

Discussion Questions and Suggested Activities

1. Identify some geographic generalizations appropriate for the unit that you are developing. What main ideas will you incorporate in teaching each generalization?
2. Develop several learning experiences for each of the generalizations listed in your answer to Question 1.
3. Select some of the books and stories that are favorites of children in the lower grades and identify ways in which these present opportunities for teaching geographic concepts.
4. Use a map of your city or state to illustrate the distribution of some phenomenon over space. For example, using the yellow pages of the city telephone directory, find the geographic locations of all elementary schools in the city. Put a symbol for a school at each location. Describe the pattern of the spatial distribution. How would you adapt this activity for use with elementary school children?
5. Develop a list of geographical terms and prepare charts or posters to portray their meaning.
6. Obtain a basic textbook in social studies for upper grades and

select at random ten pages for study and analysis. Write down all places referred to in these ten pages that could be located by referring to a wall map. Do you find that the authors have children doing a lot of "intellectual traveling"? Do you think a child can meaningfully go from New York to London to Tokyo in a single paragraph? What instructional problems does this present?

7. Make a study of news releases of AP and UPI by dateline. Discounting disasters and once-in-a-lifetime occurrences, what places do you find in the news most frequently? Should this be used in determining what places children should learn to locate? Do you find the capital cities of the fifty states mentioned frequently?

8. There has been a growing trend toward the inclusion of concepts and generalizations for urban geography in the elementary school social studies program. What are some factors that may have created this recent emphasis?

9. What advantages do you see for using selected "depth studies" at each grade level rather than for studying all countries of the world at some time in the elementary school social studies program? What limitations might this practice have?

10. Do you think that special geography textbooks are needed for middle-grade classes? What specific things might a teacher do to build his own background of geographic understandings?

Selected References

Bacon, Phillip, ed. *Focus on Geography: New Concepts and Teaching Strategies,* 40th Yearbook. Washington, D.C.: National Council for the Social Studies, 1970.

Broek, Jan O. M., and John W. Webb. *A Geography of Mankind.* New York: McGraw-Hill Book Company, Inc., 1968.

Cohen, Saul B., ed. *Problems and Trends in American Geography.* New York: Basic Books, 1969.

Conroy, William B. "The Misuse of Geography," *Journal of Geography,* LXV, No. 3 (March, 1966), pp. 109–113.

Gabler, Robert E., ed. *A Handbook for Geography Teachers.* Geographic Education Series No. 6. Chicago, Ill.: National Council for Geographic Education, 1966.

Hanna, Paul R., et al. *Geography in the Teaching of Social Studies: Concepts and Skills.* Boston: Houghton Mifflin Company, 1966.

High, James. "Teaching Conservation in Geography," *The Social Studies,* No. 59 (February, 1968), pp. 55–62.

James, Preston, ed. *New Viewpoints in Geography,* 29th Yearbook. Washington, D.C.: National Council for the Social Studies, 1959.

Journal of Geography, LXVI, No. 5 (May, 1967). This issue focuses on the use of media in geography.

Journal of Geography, LXIX, No. 5 (May, 1970). This issue contains a series of articles dealing with the topic of environmental education.

Morris, John W., ed. *Methods of Geographic Instruction*. Waltham, Mass.: Blaisdell Publishing Co., 1968.

Murphy, Raymond E. *The American City: An Urban Geography*. New York: McGraw-Hill Book Company, Inc., 1966.

National Council for Geographic Education. *Geography and Educational Media*, Topics in Geography Number 3. Chicago, Ill.: The Council, 1967.

Nishi, Midori. "Geographic Guidelines for Reconstructing the Social Studies Curriculum," *Journal of Geography*, LXV, No. 7 (October, 1966), pp. 328–331.

McAulay, J. D. "Geographic Understandings of the Primary Child," *Journal of Geography*, LXV, No. 4 (April, 1966), pp. 170–176.

Michaelis, John U., and A. Montgomery Johnston. *The Social Sciences: Foundations of the Social Studies*. Boston: Allyn & Bacon, Inc., 1965.

Muessig, Raymond H., and Vincent R. Rogers. *Social Science Seminar Series* (volume on geography). Columbus, Ohio: Charles E. Merrill Books, Inc., 1965.

Rushdoony, Haig A. "Population Growth and the Six Year Old," *Journal of Geography*, LXVII, No. 6 (September, 1968), pp. 367–373.

Scarfe, Neville V. *Geography in School*, Geographic Education Series No. 5. Chicago: National Council for Geographic Education, 1965.

Social Education, XXX, No. 8 (December, 1966). This issue is devoted to geography.

"The Elementary School: Focus on Geography," *Social Education*, XXXI, No. 7 (November, 1967), pp. 609–624.

Warman, Henry J. "Geography in the Elementary Schools of the United States," *Journal of Geography*, LXVII, No. 5 (May, 1968), pp. 262–273.

Historical Elements in the Social Studies

The eminent historian Henry Steele Commager conveys some of the excitement that can accompany the study of history, a subject with a long tradition as an important part of the elementary school curriculum, as follows: ". . . no other subject, it is safe to say, can be relied upon more confidently to catch the imagination of the young. No other offers such continuous drama; no other presents such a spectacle of greatness. If there is any value in history, our first task must surely be to catch the interest of the young. . . ." [1]

Perhaps the statement is more a reflection of what is potentially possible in

1. Henry Steele Commager, "Why History," *American Education*, Washington, D.C.: Office of Education, June, 1965.

7

the teaching of history than what actually occurs in a vast number of classrooms. Pupil dislike of history has been well documented in studies investigating preferences for school subjects. One would not need to look far for the reasons leading to such attitudes. Instead of being a "continuous drama" and "a spectacle of greatness," for many pupils history has meant names, dates, places, battles, and past political facts that had to be memorized. Also, the nature of history is such that it is easy for the child to separate himself from the topic or period studied to the extent that he is not able to relate himself to it. Consequently, it does not seem vital or important to him. Historical material per se is neither interesting nor uninteresting; it is the manner in which it is presented and taught that gives it one or the other of these values. The pupil who encounters a teacher who can give historical study the qualities described by Dr. Commager frequently develops a lifelong interest in it.

Children often become utterly and completely confused about the relationship of events, people, movements, and developments to one another, possibly because the historical story, as presented, is not complete enough to make sense to them. Imagine how confusing and uninteresting one would find a novel if he read the first two chapters, then skipped to chapter fourteen, then went back to chapter eight, then read the final chapter, and last, read chapter eighteen. Perhaps such a reader would be no less confused about the events in the story than are many schoolchildren when they complete a series of units dealing with United States history. To confirm this, the reader should interview a few children in the upper elementary school grades and ask them to tell him the story of America, beginning with Columbus.

In the current curriculum-reform movement, history has not received the same intensity of study as has geography, economics, and anthropology. Nonetheless, historians and social studies educators are promoting the improvement of history teaching through curriculum development in local school districts, through local and state social studies councils, and through inservice workshops and institutes. The examination of the role of history and the teaching of that subject has also been an important part of some of the national curriculum revision projects, even though the central concern of the project may not have been history specifically. Whether taught as a separate subject or as part of an interdisciplinary approach to social studies, history occupies a position of importance in the curriculum. It provides the time dimension in the study of topics. Thus, most units studied, whether they are history per se or are based in one of the other disciplines, will have historical elements and concepts associated with them.

Major Purposes of Historical Study

Many educators feel that history can and should contribute directly to attaining the broad goal of good citizenship. For this reason many states have legislative requirements concerning the teaching of state and national history. A knowledge of history supported by actual experiences in the practice of responsible citizenship in the school and classroom unquestionably contributes to strengthening of loyalties and helps children identify with their rich historical background. Persons develop love of country, loyalty, and fidelity through a knowledge, appreciation, and understanding of the struggles of the people who contributed to the building of this great and powerful nation. History teaching is valuable in this respect if it provides opportunities for the child to identify himself as a person with the historical past. The historical experiences of the nation then become part of the heritage of individual children and, thus, the common cultural background of the citizenry.

History teaching has traditionally been justified on the basis of helping persons understand the present in terms of the past. Presumably we study the past, learn of the successes and failures of man in the past, and plan for the future accordingly. Individuals do this in their personal lives. They refer to past experiences, generalize from them, and plan intelligently for their future. Although this holds true for individuals, it unfortunately does not work well where societies and large groups of persons are involved. It can be argued that history teaches that man has *not* learned the lessons of history well, because he continues to make many of the same mistakes over and over again. It shows, for example, that wars are not satisfactory methods of settling international disputes, yet the nations of the world now find themselves in the greatest arms race the world has yet known.

Knowledge of history does not lend itself to the practical solution of everyday problems *in the same way* as does a knowledge of spelling words, or skills in reading or mathematics. Because little direct relationship between a knowledge of history and daily problems of living exists, it cannot and should not be thought of as an entirely practical subject. In this sense, history resembles literature, art, and music in that its contribution may lie along cultural lines rather than along strictly practical ones. Although the child will not apply his knowledge of history directly to the solution of the many complex problems of man in the twentieth century, it will give him an insight, appreciation, and understanding of these problems that he otherwise would not have.

History teaching also has value because it helps children learn the

The study of history should provide pupils with an opportunity to identify with their own family heritage. (Courtesy of the Washington State Office of Public Instruction, Olympia)

inevitability of change. The record of man's tenure on earth is a succession of changes, some representing progress and others not. The necessity of learning to adapt to changing conditions will be a lesson the child of today will have to learn fairly early in life. The changes that occur within the period of a single lifetime are becoming almost more than the human organism can withstand. But despite these changes, people still spend much of their time dealing with the fundamental problems of securing food, clothing, shelter, of protecting their young, and of seeking a measure of personal happiness and contentment. The attitudes of smugness and provincialism bred by a reluctance to accept the inevitability of change can be countered through the good teaching of historical material.

Although history is ordinarily thought of as a record of times past, it is in the true sense a living record. History is not made by historians —they only record and interpret it. History is made out of the everyday affairs of living people; and children should learn that they, too, are living during a history-making period. An appreciation of this fact of history helps the child understand one of the major purposes of historical study—to understand the variety of factors that lead to historical events. Points of major historical significance generally identified by a single date have a *spread of effect* that extends prior to the point and subsequent to it. In order to understand the Korean incident, for example, one must go back to the events subsequent to World War II. To have some grasp of World War II, one must go back to World War I and understand the series of events that led to December 7, 1941. History is a continuous story of man's activities; it cannot be severed into discrete parts separated only by dates. History is being made and written continuously.

Finally, history deserves serious study within the social studies because it is the record of human relationships. If the social studies concern themselves with human relationship as they purportedly do, then surely the past record of mankind merits careful consideration. Here the child can gain some understanding of the hopes and aspirations of mankind through the ages as well as a knowledge of his achievements and failures in the area of human relationships. It gives the child a perspective and depth to his understanding of people that is perhaps not attained in other ways.

Because the question "Why study history?" is raised so frequently, it may be helpful to note how historians themselves answer this question. Two historians will be cited here. According to one historian, the goals of studying the past are these:

1. To increase understanding of human behavior and of the human situation
2. To realize the past with empathy, to experience it in a fashion which makes it come alive
3. To experience the past in its own terms, rather than in the terms of the present
4. To increase understanding through use of the methods and outlooks both of disciplines in the field of the humanities and also in the field of the social or behavioral sciences
5. To develop broad understanding and mental discipline, avoiding an exclusive and narrow focus upon attempts to find solutions for specific problems of the moment [2]

Another historian addressing himself to "Why History?" responds in part as follows:

History is useful in the sense that art is useful—or music or poetry or flowers; perhaps even in the sense that religion and philosophy are useful. . . . The first and perhaps the richest pleasure of history is

2. Thomas J. Pressly, "The Structure of History," *The College of Education Record*, 32, No. 1, November, 1965, Seattle: University of Washington, p. 20.

that it adds new dimensions to life itself by enormously extending our perspective and enlarging our experience. . . . This immense enlargement of experience carries with it a second pleasure or reward, for it means that history provides us with great companions. . . . A third and familiar pleasure of history is the experience of identifying the present with the past and thus adding a new dimension to places. . . . There is another and perhaps a deeper value in history, for it is the memory of man, and it is therefore the way man knows himself.[3]

Methods of Inquiry in History

Historians focus their studies primarily on events. Specific events of the past are selected for study, and relevant traces of these events are gathered and evaluated. From these data, historians are then able to make certain deductions and inferences concerning the event. In so doing they attempt to gain a more complete knowledge of the past by reconstructing it on the basis of traces and evidences that are available. It should be clear that historians can never record and interpret all the events of the past, nor can they gather all the data that may be relevant to an event. To some extent the historian always bases his conclusions on limited information. Consequently, historical events are interpreted and subsequently reinterpreted as additional data are uncovered by historical research. The historian may accept certain conclusions—at least tentatively—but he continues to search for confirmatory traces and new sources of data that may help him gain a more complete understanding of past events.

Part of the historical method, therefore, involves assembling traces of events. The traces not only include a vast array of material objects —coins, tools, diaries, papers—but also beliefs, legends, tales, customs, folklore, and so on. Written traces, of course, are widely used and include various types of private and/or official documents, letters, records, annals, and chronicles. Much material relevant to the historian's work can be found in libraries and museums. Historians often visit sites of historical events in order to search for original traces. The historian, therefore, needs to have the skills that are essential to the identification and searching out of such traces—observation, analysis, reference use, note taking, interviewing, classifying, recall of bibliographical sources, and use of tables, charts, and maps.

Gathering traces of events is only one concern of the historian. In addition, he must evaluate the traces for their relevance, genuineness, and authenticity. The historian is something of a skeptic, but he must be one with integrity. He cannot arbitrarily accept some traces and reject or ignore others that may be equally relevant and valid. Bias is

3. Commager, *op. cit.*

brought into the historical record of the event when traces are not subjected adequately to the canons of historical criticism. This accounts in part for different versions of identical historical events.

Finally, the historian must prepare conclusions based on his data. This usually takes the form of a narrative. In this account he analyzes and synthesizes his findings, which can then be compared with other narratives of the same event. In constructing his narrative the historian exercises his judgment, applying principles of logic based on the evidence he has collected. Historical accounts are always subject to the limitations of the historian's ability to analyze and synthesize his findings adequately, completely, or accurately.

Elementary school pupils are not being prepared to become historians, but there is much in the historical method that can be of value to them as citizens. Knowing something about the methods of the historian can help them better understand and appreciate the nature of historical accounts. Certainly it should engender in them a wholesome respect for the truth in the recording of human events. It should also help them appreciate the reasons for the reinterpretation of historical events.

Pupils can apply some of the historian's methods of study to their own studies. For example, the local community and state provide excellent laboratories for the examination of primary source materials. They can examine firsthand some of the same traces of events that are used by historians in studying local events. They can visit museums and historical sites and can examine original documents. They may propose their own hypotheses, simply stated, and test them. For example, a fourth-grade class might hypothesize that a local Indian tribe left one area and moved to another because of the coming of white settlers. Through research on the problem—consulting local museum resources—they discover that the Indians had left the region and moved elsewhere prior to the coming of the white settlers. The move was made not because of the intrusion of outsiders but because of more favorable food resources in the new location. This represents only one of a great many possibilities for young pupils to assemble evidence and come to possible conclusions based on the data.

Middle- and upper-grade pupils can also profit by considering the nature of historical evidence and how they know something to be historically true. How can they verify that an event actually did occur? If they rely on secondary sources only—which is usually the case—could they validate the accuracy of the account if they had to do so? Where would they search for evidence and what kind of evidence would they be willing to accept? Considerations of this kind remind the pupil of his very heavy reliance on the research, interpretation, and word of someone else in the use of historical material. Experiences of this type should make him less rigid in his acceptance of a single interpretation of historical events. Even though this may not be of immediate use to him as an elementary school pupil, it does sow the seeds of a healthy skepticism—the first rung of the ladder leading to critical and reflective thinking about social issues and events.

Selecting Historical Elements for Social Studies Units

The teaching of history in modern elementary programs occurs within the various social studies units of the grades, and historical elements contribute substantially to such units. The emphasis in modern programs is on understanding the past, the people who lived during those times, their problems, ways of living, and their struggles to meet basic needs. History taught in this manner helps the child develop a better understanding and appreciation of man's growth through the years—not only along political lines but in all phases of his activities —that contribute to a richer and more abundant way of life. This would include growth of the arts, sciences, literature, humanitarian movements, and other cultural aspects of man's life.

The teacher's task in teaching historical elements is twofold: he must first select *what* to teach, and then he must decide *how* to teach what is selected in a way that is meaningful to young children. Some historical concepts, trends, ideas, or movements, because of their complexity or remoteness, are inappropriate and could not be grasped by young children no matter how they were presented. The teacher will want to be off to a good start by making sure that what is selected for study is within the comprehension abilities of the pupils.

If we bear in mind the limitations just cited, the following represent *samples* of major generalizations from the field of history that have been used as organizing ideas in developing programs in historical study:

1. The history of a country has a definite bearing on the culture, traditions, beliefs, attitudes, and ways of living of its people.
2. Although people in different cultures do not always agree on what constitutes progress, the history of the world is a record of many steps made toward common goals.
3. The affairs of human societies have historical antecedents and consequences; events of the past influence those of the present.
4. Human societies have undergone and are undergoing continual, although perhaps gradual, changes in response to various forces, but not all change is progress.
5. People are influenced by values, ideals, and inherited institutions as well as by their environment.

6. The methods of rational inquiry have increased man's knowledge of the world and have greatly accelerated the accumulation of new knowledge.
7. Man's struggle for freedom and human dignity has occupied a relatively brief period of time as compared with the total span of his existence.
8. In the contemporary world, historical events have a significance that reaches far beyond the time and place of their origins.
9. Many causes of historical events are complex in nature.
10. Guidelines for understanding thought and action in contemporary affairs can be derived from the historical backgrounds of society.
11. "Facts" are susceptible to varying interpretations depending on the point of view of the historian or the student of history.

The following list suggests types of topics and experiences dealing with historical elements that can be planned at various grade levels. This list should not be construed as being complete, neither should it be considered as a course of study for the grades—experiences or topics suggested for one grade level may be appropriate for a higher or lower grade as well. The suggestions may be of help to the teacher in selecting historical elements for study as well as in planning experiences for children at various ages:

KINDERGARTEN, GRADE ONE, AND GRADE TWO

1. Listening to stories of the origin of special days
2. Simple dramatics, music, or art activities associated with holidays
3. Talking about bulletin boards prepared in connection with holidays and festivals such as Columbus Day, Thanksgiving Day, Lincoln's and Washington's birthdays, Veteran's Day, Memorial Day or Arbor Day
4. Learning to respect the symbols that represent our country, such as the flag or the Pledge of Allegiance
5. Observing change in the community environment, such as the demolition of old buildings and the construction of new roads, homes, and offices; and looking at pictures of homes in olden days
6. Listening to a resource person tell about a patriotic holiday in child-like terms
7. Enjoying stories, poems, or songs about heroes, past and present, or about others who have contributed to our cultural heritage
8. Learning the origin of local holidays and festivals

9. Attending assembly programs of historical significance, such as a dramatization by older children, a pageant, or a film presentation
10. Discussing family customs and traditions

GRADE THREE

1. Becoming acquainted with the historical significance of the name of the school; learning about the history of the school; learning about early school days
2. Learning about pioneer life in early settlements, their food, clothing, shelter, recreation
3. Studying local community history: learning how the community was first settled and why it was located where it was; finding out about local disasters such as fires, floods, earthquakes; studying the history of local parks, how they were named and why they are located where they are; becoming acquainted with local historic buildings and spots as well as learning about famous local historical figures; learning about early churches in the community
4. Learning about the background of local festivals and "days" such as the Mummer's Festival in Philadelphia, the Camellia Festival in Sacramento, Kolachy Day in Montgomery, Minnesota, the Tulip Festival in Holland, Michigan, or the Cinco de Mayo celebrations of the Southwest
5. Studying transportation of pioneers: how they traveled, routes they followed, problems they encountered, how they met enroute their basic needs of food, clothing, and shelter
6. Learning of early Indian life and its contribution to our culture
7. Learning of the various national groups that settled in the local area and of their contributions to the modern community
8. Learning about the lives of famous men in connection with units in the social studies, such as Pasteur in connection with a dairy unit, Bell and Edison in a unit on communication, or Fulton in a unit on transportation
9. Studying how messages were sent in early times, such as cave drawings, Indian smoke signals, drum beats, pony express, stagecoach, and others

GRADE FOUR

1. Learning of the contribution of people from various countries to American life—the Spanish in the Southwest, the English and Dutch on the Atlantic Coast, the Scandinavians in the upper Midwest, and so on

2. Studying the history of the home state: the people who came to the home state (when, how, and why they came); how early settlers in the state earned a living; the founders of local city and state; the origin of the names of places in the community and state; the part the home state played in the founding of the nation; the places of historical interest in the state; and famous inventors, scientists, and discoverers from the home state

3. Learning how communication and transportation services in the community, state, and typical regions of the world have grown and developed

4. Studying the history of national parks

5. Learning how early settlers met their basic needs—food, clothing, and shelter. How children of early settlers learned to read and write. Pioneer entertainment, early health measures, religious customs, modes of dress, family life, and so forth

6. Learning how home and family life has changed, reasons for the change, effect of power machines on living, how people have changed their environment

7. Gaining a knowledge of early Indian life in the local area

8. Learning about the development of local and state government at an elementary level: why the capital is located where it is; famous statesmen from the home state

9. Various historical elements related to units of study such as the history of aviation, weather forecasting, farming practices, health measures, inventions, the number system, money, or sports

GRADE FIVE

1. Learning of the beginnings of the United States: explorers and land claims; expansion of settlements, troubles with the Indians; routes of early explorers; settlement of the United States; formation of colonies along the coast

2. Studying differences in ways of living in pioneer days and now. Learning colonial games, songs, dances. Noting changes in meeting basic needs. Comparing family life today with life in colonial times and life on the frontier. Learning the effect of inventions and discoveries for ways of living

3. Learning the history of different kinds of work in various sections of the country; learning of the different groups that settled in parts of the country; becoming acquainted with simple ideas related to sectionalism and controversy; understanding reasons for differences

4. Becoming familiar with the cultural growth of the nation; learning of America's famous writers, poets, artists, musicians, and actors through their works; learning of the folklore, art, music, dramatics, and dances of various regions of the United States from colonial times to the present
5. Knowing something of the men and women who have made America great—statesmen, leaders, inventors, scientists, explorers, frontiersmen, soldiers, heroes, persons associated with the growth of transportation, communication, the arts, science, education, religion, conservation, and human welfare
6. Learning of the great documents of freedom; knowing that the Constitution guarantees our freedom; appreciating that freedom is secured at great cost and sacrifice
7. Learning of the extension of the privileges of democracy to more and more persons; studying the development of state and national agencies for health, safety, and protection of citizens
8. Studying the growth of the nation with emphasis on ways of living in colonial times, the birth of the nation, the Westward movement, War Between the States, and so forth
9. Various historical elements related to units of study, such as those listed in Entry 9 under grade four

GRADE SIX

1. Learning how people of long ago have enriched life today; studying progress in science and medicine; learning the effects of inventions and discoveries on ways of living; growth of the arts; struggles of countries for freedom
2. Studying the cultural impact of early settlements—the Indian and Spanish influence in Latin America, or the French and English influence in Canada; learning the role that Old World events played in the discovery of the New World
3. Studying the history of trade and commerce; learning how world systems of transportation and communication developed; learning how man has overcome physical barriers
4. Learning about the history of countries studied in social studies units —the ancient civilizations of Mexico, Egypt, the Orient, or Central America; learning about famous men and women of the countries studied, past and present, as well as the history of the country's customs, its early inhabitants, its races, and national heroes
5. Studying how early man struggled to solve his problems of living; learning of the migration of peoples and the reason for such movements

GRADE SEVEN

1. Studying the historical development of the home state; similar to suggestions listed under grade four, but at a more complex level
2. Learning that present-day civilization is built on the contributions of others—contributions of past civilizations
3. Learning that men lived in groups very early in recorded history; studying the emergence of modern nations
4. Discovering present-day problems that have had their origins in Old World conflicts and struggles, such as trade problems, immigration, language barriers
5. Learning of the traditions that affect family life—ancestral ties, religious beliefs, attitudes; studying the history of one's own family—its migration and settlement in this country
6. Learning how history and customs affect the lives of people living in the country in modern times
7. Studying historical elements associated with regular units of study, such as evolution of various forms of government, growth of concern for the individual, history of trade, commerce, conservation, money, and so on

GRADE EIGHT

Historical elements in the eighth grade almost universally deal with the growth and development of the United States as a nation. The program of instruction might include such things as

1. Exploration, settlement, and expansion of the United States
2. Change from rural to industrial economy and its accompanying effect on life
3. Outstanding leaders of the United States in politics, statesmanship, science, the arts, industry, labor, medicine, and human welfare
4. Growth of the United States from a small rural nation to a major world power
5. Growth of democracy in the United States
6. Rise in the standard of living
7. The growth and development of business and industry
8. Growth of the United States along cultural lines
9. Increase in the interest of the government in the welfare and protection of all citizens
10. Historical development of such social functions as transportation, communication, distribution, recreation, education, conservation, religious expression, and consumption in the United States
11. History of specific ethnic minority groups
12. Effects of settlement on environment

HISTORICAL ELEMENTS IN
THE SOCIAL STUDIES

Procedures in Teaching Historical Elements

The spark that vitalizes history and makes it a "continuous drama" and "a spectacle of greatness" for children must be struck by the classroom teacher. Most elementary teachers are not historians, but they must approach their teaching with the enthusiasm and scientific point of view of the historian. To do this, the teacher will find a good background of historical information helpful in giving him confidence, and an energetic approach to the teaching task will reflect itself in the enthusiastic reactions of the children.

Early contact with historical material should be interesting, enjoyable, and satisfying for the child. Exciting experiences with history at an early age will help keep the child receptive to subsequent contacts he has with it. Chase has expertly put his finger on what history should mean to boys and girls when he says,

> To a ten-year-old, history can be tramping the wilderness with Daniel Boone, raising the flag with the Marines at Iwo Jima, living with seventy-five others 'tween decks on the *Mayflower* in the long voyage across the Atlantic, riding with Paul Revere through the night to Concord town, and floating down the Mississippi with Père Marquette. It can be an Indian watching the *Santa Maria* and her sister ships drop anchor, climbing the heights of Darien with Balboa, surveying with Washington in virgin territory, imprisonment by Indians with Captain John Smith, and traveling under the North Pole in a nuclear-powered submarine. It can be seeing new homes rise one by one in Jamestown, tasting buffalo meat on the trek by covered wagon across the western plains, smelling exploding gunpowder in many a French and Indian battle, feeling cold water rise to one's armpits in Arnold's march to Quebec, and hearing the great peal of the Liberty Bell on that first Fourth of July.[4]

People have difficulty understanding history because they seem not to be able to identify themselves with the past. This is especially true of young children. Historical figures such as Washington, Lincoln, and Franklin are so far removed from the child that he is likely to think of them in much the same way he thinks of storybook characters or as he thinks of fairies, angels, or the Deity. The child has difficulty casting historical personages in the role of human beings who once lived and faced many of the same problems people living today must face. It is because one identifies with the past that he experiences an inward feeling of excitement when he views original historical documents such as the Constitution or the Declaration of Independence. Such experiences

4. W. Linwood Chase, "American History in the Middle Grades," *Interpreting and Teaching American History*, 31st Yearbook, Washington, D.C.: National Council for the Social Studies, 1961, p. 342.

just for a moment tend to link one with the past and give some means of associating oneself with it. A good social studies program in the elementary school will help the child build these bridges or links with the past through a series of planned experiences. The following are only a few examples of activities that may be helpful for this purpose.

Opportunity to Examine and Handle Objects of Historical Significance

Children are intensely interested in objects of historical significance, particularly if they can examine them closely and handle them. Items out of the past that will be helpful in teaching are such things as these: newspapers, letters written during the Civil War or the Gold Rush, a canteen used by a soldier in an early war, a slave contract, a family Bible, deeds, photographs, church membership rolls, school records, a hymnal, and branding irons. Children, themselves, may bring items of this type to school to share with their classmates. Such objects may have some monetary value and a considerable sentimental value and must be handled accordingly. If a particular item is highly valued, it is best for the adult owner to bring it to the school to show the children and tell them of its significance. Occasionally, in the collection of historical realia, some child will bring old firearms to school. These may be extremely dangerous and, if brought at all, must be handled with utmost caution.

Some teachers like to start their social studies units by allowing children to examine objects of this type that are displayed around the room. Then the children are brought together for a discussion of what they observed. Discussion will be stimulated by such questions as these: "What do you suppose this object is? How was it used? Do we still use it today? Why did it have to be made of iron? How do you suppose this object was kept through the years? How old is it? Where was your family when this article was made?" The discussion will give rise to many questions that the children have. These will serve to give the pupils purposes for finding out more about the topic under study.

In addition to historical realia that can be brought to the classroom or to those that may be in a school museum, the teacher should look into the permanent museum resources of the community. Most larger communities maintain museum exhibits of historical materials significant to the local community and state. School groups are always welcome to make visits to local museums and are frequently taken on guided tours through the exhibits. Some museums change their displays from time to time and will on request gladly furnish schools with information concerning current exhibits. These resources present valuable opportunities for the teaching of historical elements and need to be used extensively.

Photographs often provide interesting and informative sources of data for historical study. (Courtesy of the *Northshore Citizen*, Bothell, Washington)

A modern museum is a learning resource, and pupils will find a visit there more profitable for them if they are prepared to use it. The best use of the museum can usually be made by pupils after they have had an opportunity to develop an understanding of the material on display. This means that visits will be made after the pupils have been able to explore ideas and concepts in the classroom through reading, study, and discussion rather than at the very beginning of a unit of study. They will then be ready for the clarification of ideas: they can ask intelligent questions and can enrich their understanding through the museum visit. In taking pupils to a museum, teachers will want to ready the class beforehand by identifying a few relevant questions concerning items to be observed.

Many museums in the country have assembled artifacts, pictures, and other items of interest into kits that are available to schools on a rental basis. The materials provide the teacher with an excellent opportunity to apply some of the methods of study of the historian discussed earlier in this chapter. Study kits ordinarily have a teacher's guide providing background information for the teacher as well as providing practical suggestions concerning the use of the material.

Opportunity to Talk with Older People of the Community

This procedure presents another excellent means of helping the child establish contact with the past. Children are fascinated when old-timers talk of their exciting experiences in the early community. They are surprised and electrified by the thought that the person now speaking to them served with General Eisenhower or shook President Kennedy's hand. These experiences make real people out of historical figures and remove them from the realm of myth and unreality. Interviewing persons who have had firsthand experience with an event under study is a technique often used by historians.

Almost every community has one or more persons who has devoted a substantial amount of time to the study of local history as a hobby. These individuals are excellent resources for the classroom teacher, not only in their personally speaking to the pupils but in directing the teacher's attention to other resources that might otherwise be overlooked. To catch some of the enthusiasm and interest such persons ordinarily have for history is, in itself, a valuable experience for both the teacher and the pupils.

Use of Historical Films and Recordings

There are a number of films and recordings dealing with historical incidents and personalities that can help the child place himself in the setting of the historical period under study. These may be biographical sketches of persons or an authentically portrayed reproduction of a historical incident. The reader is referred to pages 132 and 137 for sources of such films and recordings. School of the Air broadcasts commonly include programs of this type and may be available to the teacher on tape recordings for use when needed. Through these mediums the child can at least for the moment identify himself so strongly with the portrayal that he shares the anxieties, fears, joys, and disappointments of the historical figures. The popularity of this type of program in television and commercial movies attests to its appeal to

This is a good example of the application of knowledge. This exercise is also a good illustration of how geographical and historical studies can be combined. (Courtesy of the Seattle Public Schools)

children. Schools should not fail to use these excellent mediums to teach historical concepts.

READING MATERIALS

Well-written, vivid books and stories of historical nature have great value in helping children identify with the past. Children do this when they become "lost in a book." In the vivid accounts of the adventures of early explorers, the child relives the perils, dangers, and excitement of Lewis and Clark, the disappointments and trials of Abe Lincoln, the hazards of a trip across the Western plains, or the rugged winters of Wisconsin. *Makers of America Books, Signature Books, The Life Stories of Great People,* and *Landmark Books* are good examples of the high-quality material now available for this purpose. As a first step in the improvement of teaching historical elements, the school should build up its library in the field of national, state, and local history with interesting books, magazines, newspapers, documents, and photographs. Local and state historical societies are usually willing and able to furnish help in the way of suggesting book titles and, in some cases, providing the material itself at a reasonable cost. It is significant to note that studies have shown history to be one of the least liked subjects in school, and yet some of the best-selling books of our times have had historical settings. Adults as well as children enjoy reading historical material. It is unfortunate that teaching procedures have not capitalized on the basic interest people seem to have in their past.

UTILIZING INTERESTING PROJECTS AS A PART
OF THE INSTRUCTIONAL PROGRAM

In addition to the learning activities planned specifically to help the child build psychological bridges with the past, the teaching of historical elements in the elementary school can be enlivened and made more meaningful through the use of a variety of other activities. The following are examples of only a few that have been used successfully by elementary teachers:

1. *Collect and exhibit* old photographs that show the history of the community.
2. *Collect and try* pioneer recipes, learn folk dances, investigate local cultural contributions of various nationality groups.
3. *Write items* of local history for the school paper or for the local newspaper.
4. *Write biographical sketches* of early settlers in the community.
5. *Investigate the history* of some important old buildings in the community.
6. *Trace the history* of some local industry such as mining, manufacturing, or lumbering.
7. *Make models* or sketches of oxcarts, prairie schooners, canoes, spinning wheels, or other pioneer equipment.
8. *Collect and use* primary data sources.
9. *Interview old-timers* of the community.
10. *Paint a mural* of some aspect of the history of the local community or state.
11. *Write and present* a pageant telling the story of some aspect of local, state, or national history.
12. *Collect songs* of various periods of history and present a costumed recital of them.
13. *Make a model* of the town as it looked fifty, seventy-five, or one hundred years ago, or a diorama of life in the town at some such time.
14. *Make a topographical or relief map* of the local area indicating points of historical significance.
15. *Use historical setting* for creative dramatics activities.
16. *Make pictorial time lines* tracing periods of national, state, or local history.

17. *Prepare bulletin boards* and other exhibits having a historical theme.
18. *Write, plan, and prepare short plays* or presentations in connection with holiday observances.

ORGANIZING LOCAL CHAPTERS OR CLUBS THAT ARE AFFILIATED
WITH STATE HISTORICAL SOCIETIES

Many state historical societies have junior memberships and encourage school-age children to establish junior historian clubs in their classrooms. The parent organization provides many suggestions, a history magazine prepared for children, and other instructional material the class will find interesting. A letter of inquiry to the state historical society will bring information relative to the nature of such organizations in the various states.

Holiday Observances

Some of the most satisfying and long-remembered experiences children have in the elementary school are those associated with the observance of holidays. Some of these are out-and-out "fun" days, such as Halloween and Saint Valentine's Day; others, such as Christmas and Easter, have religious implications, whereas others have historical significance. Many schools and states require observance of holidays such as Columbus Day, Washington's and Lincoln's birthdays, Thanksgiving Day, Veteran's Day, Memorial Day, and other days of import to the local community and to the state. Although school programs in connection with the observance of such historical holidays have frequently been guided more by fancy than by historical fact, these situations, nonetheless, do present excellent opportunities to do some good teaching of historical material.

The basic considerations in teaching historical concepts in connection with holidays ought to be accuracy and authenticity. The use of stories, dramatizations, and other activities that exaggerate and extol the virtues of certain national heroes beyond truth is a questionable teaching procedure. This leads children to believe that such figures were some special type of "Supermen" rather than human beings just as are the great men of our time. Furthermore, the child may believe that the great leaders of contemporary America are less capable than those of early America. This type of thinking is unrealistic. Many of the stories surrounding the birth of the nation, the lives of Washington and Betsy Ross as well as the lives of other pioneering Americans are totally inaccurate and entirely fanciful. Others fall into the categories of folk tales and legends and may, of course, be used with elementary school children providing they are taught as folk tales and legends and not as historical fact. Even the well-known cherry tree story of Washington might be used with young children, not as an account of historical fact but as a legend that represents Washington as a man having the qualities of honesty and truthfulness. But the teacher should always separate and point out the elements that are fiction from those that are fact.

The chief contribution holiday observances can make to the education of the young child is to acquaint him with his rich cultural heritage and help him grow in his appreciation of it. With this in mind, the teacher can plan a short unit relative to the holiday, keeping the content simple but truthful. Commonly, such short units have as their culminating activity a dramatization that is shared with another room. These activities have value insofar as they are accurate portrayals and insofar as the emphasis is on the basic learnings involved rather than on putting on a good show. If the teacher does not plan to devote more than a class period or two to such an observance, the reading of an appropriate story or poem, followed by discussion, can be a profitable experience for the class. Following the reading of a story, poem, or short play, the children can participate in a suitable follow-up activity such as drawing, painting, singing a related song, writing an original poem or story, or listening to a recording, or they can use the story for creative dramatics. This is also an appropriate time to view a film dealing with some aspect of history related to the holiday or to listen to a recorded dramatization of a historical event. In this same connection the teacher may discuss with the class the significance of a classroom picture or a symbol such as the flag, the Declaration of Independence, the Constitution, or the national anthem. The amount of time spent on activities of this type ought always to be weighed against their value as educational experiences. There seems little justification in spending the entire month of December preparing for the Christmas pageant or spending the entire month of February celebrating George Washington's birthday.

Helping Children Understand Time Concepts

The teaching of historical material to elementary-age pupils must take into account the problems they encounter in dealing with time concepts. The young child in the primary grades deals almost entirely in the here-and-now. His birthdays seem a long way off; Christmas seems never to come; his mother and father are "old" people. He is interested in what will happen this afternoon, tomorrow, or today after recess. Anyone who has traveled with young children knows how endless the time seems to them and knows how frequently they ask, "Aren't we there yet? How many more towns?"

The development of time concepts is a gradual growth process extending over a period of several years. The understanding of time in the historical sense represents a fairly mature level of dealing with time and, therefore, is not expected of young children. The development of time concepts for children in the elementary school should begin with time situations that are within the realm of experience of the child. Children should be given help in learning to read clock time and in understanding references to the parts of the day, days of the week, months, seasons, and the year. Even though primary-grade children make statements about things that happened "a hundred years ago," they have little comprehension of the real meaning of the expression and simply use it as an indefinite reference to something that happened in what seems to them a long time ago.

The placing of related events in chronological order requires considerable maturity and, except for the events within the child's own experience, should not be expected of children below fifth or sixth grade. The use of time lines in the upper grades may be helpful in teaching the extent of time separating one historical event from another. They must, of course, be accurately drawn and are more effective if events are represented pictorially. Research on this problem seems to indicate that below sixth grade the use of time lines is questionable.

Through the years a number of investigators have studied problems relating to children's ability to understand time concepts and the development of a sense of time and chronology in children.[5] In a recent publication, Penix reviews several such studies and concludes that there is increasing evidence to suggest that

> (1) although there is a steady growth with age in the ability to understand time concepts, this understanding varies considerably with the individual child and occurs with some children at a much earlier age than has heretofore been believed; and (2) planned instruction relating to time concepts reduces difficulties and increases understanding. Strongly implied here are revision of the curriculum to provide for

5. See Val E. Arnsdorf, "An Investigation of the Teaching of Chronology in the Sixth Grade," Journal of Experimental Education, XXIX, 1961, pp. 307–313; Muriel Farrell, "Understanding the Time Relations of Five-, Six-, and Seven-Year-Old Children of High IQ," Journal of Educational Research, 46, April, 1953, pp. 587–594; Kopple C. Friedman, "The Growth of Time Concepts," Social Education, 8, January, 1944, p. 30; O. L. Davis, Jr., "Children Can Learn Complex Concepts," Educational Leadership, 17, December, 1959, pp. 170–175; R. Lovell and A. Slater, "The Growth of the Concept of Time: A Comparative Study," Journal of Child Psychology and Psychiatry and Allied Disciplines, I, 1960, pp. 179–190; J. D. McAulay, "What Understandings Do Second Grade Children Have of Time Relationships?" Journal of Educational Research, LIV, 1961, pp. 312–314; Doris V. Springer, "Development in Young Children of an Understanding of Time and the Clock," Journal of Genetic Psychology, 80, March, 1952, p. 95.

flexibility rather than the fixed introduction of time concepts at stated grade levels, experimentation with methods which utilize both in-school and out-of-school time experiences of children, and more intensive investigation of the levels of understanding of time concepts and the ways in which such understandings develop.[6]

Teachers in the upper grades who teach units dealing with aspects of American history should devote a sufficient amount of instruction to clarification of time concepts, particularly the time separating one historical event from another. Textbooks may be confusing to the child in this respect, because the long periods of discovery, exploration, and settlement of the New World may be condensed in the first fifty to seventy-five pages of the text. The remainder of the book deals with the time since the American Revolution. The child inadvertently regards the book itself as something of a time line and assumes the earlier period to be much shorter than it actually is. Much confusion results in the minds of the children; many have the original settlers of Jamestown and Massachusetts doing battle against the British at Lexington and Concord. History teaching would unquestionably be more intelligible to youngsters if a greater teaching effort were directed toward clarifying time concepts commensurate with the developmental level of the child.

Discussion Questions and Suggested Activities

1. Select the historical elements and generalizations suitable for study in the resource unit you are developing (Chapter 3). Do you believe it is possible to teach these learnings in a meaningful way?
2. What reasons can you give for the general unpopularity of history as a school subject? What are some ways in which teachers can make the study of the past interesting and challenging? What historical studies do you most vividly remember from your elementary school experience?
3. What are some ways maps and globes can be used in teaching historical materials? Construct a map that might be used with middle- or upper-graders portraying something of historical significance.
4. Rather than attempting to cover all possible elements of historical study for a unit, the "post-holing" approach of selecting fewer more important elements and studying them in depth is frequently utilized. A fifth-grade class is studying a unit entitled "European Explorers of the New World." Use the "post-holing" approach to

6. Findlay C. Penix, "Teaching Social Studies in Elementary Schools," *New Challenges in the Social Studies*, Byron G. Massialas and Frederick R. Smith, eds., Belmont, Calif.: Wadsworth, 1965, p. 72.

determine specific examples for study during such a unit. What factors did you take into consideration in the selection of this content?

5. Plan a legitimate holiday observance for a grade in which you have a special interest. Identify any popular misconceptions that might surround this holiday. How will you correct these misconceptions?

6. How can biographical materials be of use in teaching historical elements? Go to the curriculum library on your campus and examine some of the widely used biographies of famous Americans published for use by elementary school children. Also locate and examine available materials concerning the history of various minority groups of America.

7. Develop a list of the sources of historical information that can be obtained from local businesses and civic and historical organizations. What local sites could be utilized in the historical study of your community? What principles would you use in selecting appropriate historical information and sites?

8. Develop and present to the class one or more of the activities suggested on pages 236–238 of the text.

9. Collect a series of pictures depicting various incidents in the life of a famous person or phases in the development of some activity such as transportation. How could you use these pictures in developing knowledge of time sequence?

10. What are some of the uses and variations of time lines? Construct one type of time line and demonstrate to your class how it could be used in clarifying some time concept for children.

11. Develop a role-playing situation concerning a historical event. How will this experience help pupils realize the past with empathy?

Selected References

Alilunas, Leo J. "The Problem of Children's Historical Mindedness," *The Social Studies*, No. 56 (December, 1965), pp. 251–254.

Banks, James A. *Teaching the Black Experience: Methods and Materials.* Belmont, Calif.: Fearon Publishers, 1970.

Banks, James A. "Utilizing Historical Method in Social Studies," *Instructor*, LXXVII, No. 5 (January, 1968), pp. 104–105.

Brown, Ralph A., and William G. Tyrrell. *How to Use Local History*, rev. ed., How to Do It Series, No. 3. Washington, D.C.: National Council for the Social Studies, 1966.

Burston, W. H., and D. Thompson. *Studies in the Nature and Teaching of History.* New York: Humanities Press, 1967.

Cartwright, William H., and Richard L. Watson, eds. *Interpreting and Teaching American History*, 31st Yearbook. Washington, D.C.: National Council for the Social Studies, 1961. Chap. 19: W. Linwood Chase, "American History in the Middle Grades"; Chap. 20: I. James Quillen, "American History in the Upper Grades and Junior High School"; Chap. 22: John W. Morris, "Use of Geography in Teaching American History"; Chap. 24: William G. Tyrrell, "Local Resources for Teaching American History."

Clements, H. Millard. "Social Study: A Focus on History," *Elementary School Journal, 66*, No. 2 (November, 1965), pp. 55–62.

Clements, H. Millard, William R. Fielder, and B. Robert Tabachnick. *Social Study: Inquiry in Elementary Classrooms*. Indianapolis: The Bobbs-Merrill Co., Inc., 1966.

Commager, Henry Steele. *The Nature and the Study of History*. Columbus, Ohio: Charles E. Merrill Books, Inc., 1965.

Davis, O. L., Jr. "Learning About Time Zones in Grades Four, Five and Six," *Journal of Experimental Education, XXXI* (1965), pp. 407–412.

Douglass, Malcolm P. *Social Studies: From Theory to Practice in Elementary Education*. Philadelphia: J. B. Lippincott Company, 1967.

Estvan, Frank J. *Social Studies in a Changing World: Curriculum and Instruction*. New York: Harcourt, Brace & World, Inc., 1968.

Ezegelyan, Alice. "Introducing the Time Line in Social Studies," *Grade Teacher, 87*, No. 4 (December, 1969), pp. 76–77+.

Friedman, Kopple C. *How to Develop Time and Chronological Concepts*, How to Do It Series, No. 22. Washington, D.C.: National Council for the Social Studies, 1964.

Goldmark, Bernice, and Morris Schmeider. "Not 'History' but 'Historiography'," *Social Education, XXXI*, No. 3 (March, 1967), pp. 201–204.

Johnson, Henry. *Teaching of History*, rev. ed. New York: The Macmillan Company, 1940.

Krug, Mark M. *History and the Social Sciences*. Waltham, Mass.: Blaisdell Publishing Co., 1967.

Michaelis, John U., and A. Montgomery Johnston. *The Social Sciences: Foundations of the Social Studies*. Boston: Allyn & Bacon, Inc., 1965.

Morrissett, Irving, ed. *Concepts and Structure in the New Social Science Curricula*. New York: Holt, Rinehart & Winston, Inc., 1967.

Muessig, Raymond H., and Vincent R. Rogers, eds. *Social Science Seminar Series* (volume on history). Columbus, Ohio: Charles E. Merrill Books, Inc., 1965.

Nugent, Walter T. K. *Creative History: An Introduction to Historical Study.* Philadelphia: J. B. Lippincott Company, 1967.

Preston, Ralph C. *Teaching Social Studies in the Elementary School,* rev. ed. New York: Holt, Rinehart & Winston, Inc., 1968.

Roose, G. E. "Local History Can Enliven Social Science Concepts," *Elementary School Journal,* No. 69 (April, 1969), pp. 346–351.

Schultz, Mindella. "The Place of History in the Social Studies Program," *Social Education, XXXII,* No. 8 (December, 1968), pp. 794–797.

Sellers, Charles G. "Is History on the Way Out of Schools and Do Historians Care?" *Social Education, XXXIII,* No. 5 (May, 1969), pp. 509–515.

"The Elementary School: Focus on History," *Social Education, XXXII,* No. 5 (May, 1968), pp. 454–468. A collection of articles discussing the teaching of history in the elementary school.

Strayer, Joseph R. "History," *The Social Studies and the Social Sciences.* New York: Harcourt, Brace & World, Inc., 1962.

Elements from the Complementary Social Sciences

Through the years, the two subjects history and geography have been prime contributors of content to elementary social studies programs. Great faith has been placed in these subjects as vehicles for achieving the goals of the social studies. Along with them, civics was usually included at the upper-grade or junior high school levels. In recent years, and especially within the past decade, increasing use has been made of concepts from a broader range of the social sciences. Interesting and exciting social studies programs are being planned that incorporate concepts from economics, anthropology, sociology, political science, and, to a lesser extent, psychology, social psychology, and philosophy. It is not accurate to say that these disciplines

8

have displaced history and geography in the social studies program or that their inclusion has reduced the importance of the more traditional subjects. The attention given the newer disciplines simply indicates that there is a growing awareness that they have an important contribution to make in the quest for a better understanding of man, society, and human institutions. As such it is appropriate to refer to them as *complementary* social sciences. Basic concepts from these disciplines constitute a vital, necessary, and integral component of a modern approach to social studies education.

Although the importance of these disciplines vis-à-vis the elementary social studies curriculum is generally conceded, there is less agreement as to exactly how they are to be built into programs. A number of experimental and developmental projects have tried possible patterns and designs that include these disciplines. In some cases, the discipline provides the central organizing format for the units. Some of the programs in economic education have done this. In others, the approach to units has been cross-disciplinary, with systematic treatment of important concepts from several of the social sciences. More commonly, programs have retained history and geography as organizing frameworks (or *integrating disciplines*) and have incorporated related concepts from supporting disciplines in such units. It is not possible to say which of these organizational formats is best, because good programs have been developed using several different plans. The teacher's willingness to incorporate ideas from these disciplines, his knowledge of the possibilities they present for social studies instruction, and his imaginative approach to teaching are probably more important to the conduct of good instruction in these disciplines than is the particular organizational scheme followed.

Units and topics that focus on basic concepts from the complementary social sciences are often interesting and attractive to young pupils. Perhaps this is because they stress people and the behavior of people, as opposed to things and places. The children see people doing things: making a living, hunting, gathering food, governing themselves, and so on. These basic activities of man represent the way knowledge is organized in the social sciences and constitute the hard core of social studies education. As pupils make careful studies of the people of the world, whether they are people in the local community or those of a far-off land, they see them engaging in certain basic social activities:

1. *Economic* activities—producing, distributing, transporting, consuming, protecting and utilizing resources
2. *Political* activities—governing, regulating the conduct of individuals and groups, protecting individuals and groups

3. *Religious* activities—relating man to the universe, developing ethics and values, conducting affairs individually and collectively in terms of certain basic beliefs
4. *Educational* activities—teaching the language, preparing and teaching the young for life in the culture
5. *Recreational* activities—engaging in play
6. *Family* activities—bearing young, caring for children, defining roles of the sexes, governing sex activities

Some familiarity with these basic human activities is a necessary part of the general education of citizens, and the concepts and ideas from the complementary social sciences can be used to further an understanding of them. They deal with ideas that are practical and useful —ideas about government, community institutions, basic beliefs, family life, using resources, producing and consuming, and how people earn a living. These learnings are, therefore, well suited for the general education program of the elementary school.

The increased attention to the disciplines, although in itself a desirable development, nevertheless necessitates a few words of caution to the teacher. The greater attention that is now given to substantive content in no way lessens the need for the teacher to be concerned about the learning needs of individual pupils. If anything, it increases his responsibility to make sure that social studies instruction makes sense and is relevant to individual pupils. As was noted earlier, most elementary school classrooms would benefit by more, rather than less, attention to individual learners and their needs. Even though the idea of studying these disciplines as the scholars study them has merit if sensibly applied, the teacher must recognize also that many pupils are not potential scholars and have little inclination toward scholarship.

Along with the disciplines has come their technical vocabulary, and the teacher must guard against assuming that the child understands a concept simply because he has a fluency with the verbal symbol used to represent it. If a child is able to use the terms *consumer, producer,* and *standard of living,* this does not necessarily mean that he understands the concepts; nor does it mean that he understands economics —even if he uses the terms correctly. The use of precise and technical language needs to be encouraged, of course, when this can be done appropriately and with understanding. Perhaps there is no greater deterrent to clear thinking in the social studies than the inadequate and imprecise use of terms and words. The technical language of the social sciences should not, however, be allowed to be used as status-symbol jargon that children parrot without understanding. This would encourage them and their teacher to believe that verbalism is a substitute for knowledge, thereby compounding the deception.

Economic Education—Economics

Of all of the newer social sciences that are gaining a place in the social studies program, none has received more attention or been promoted with more enthusiasm than has economics. In one form or another, economic education has been a part of the American school curriculum for a great many years. A good example of a statement of such concern in modern times was one by the Educational Policies Commission in 1937 when it proposed "economic efficiency" as one of the four broad purposes of American education. But following World War II the feeling became widespread among educators and laymen alike that citizens needed greater knowledge of economic realities than they had if they were to make wise decisions individually and as a society in dealing with economic problems. Thus, in 1948, the Joint Council on Economic Education, representing business, labor, education, agriculture, and other groups, was organized. The council, with affiliated local and state councils, has actively promoted economic education in the schools ever since. The council is in the process of developing a sequential program in economic education entitled "The Developmental Economic Education Program" (DEEP).

In 1960, the American Economic Association named a National Task Force on Economic Education that addressed itself to economic education in the schools in its report issued in 1961. This report was widely publicized throughout the country and did much to call the attention of the schools and the nation to what the Task Force believed to be essential background knowledge for citizens—economic understanding. The Report dealt mainly with economic education in the secondary schools and only incidentally with the elementary school. Nonetheless, its impact was felt in elementary school social studies planning.

Two other projects in recent years have been particularly influential in stimulating interest in economic education in elementary schools. One of these was the Elkhart, Indiana, Experiment on Economic Education, which worked at developing an economics-oriented social studies program throughout the grades. Dr. Lawrence Senesh, an economist then at Purdue University but now at the University of Colorado, Boulder, was its director. The other project is the Elementary School Economics Program, based in the Department of Industrial Relations at the University of Chicago and directed by William D. Rader. This latter project has focused on economic education in the middle elementary school grades. Materials for classroom use are being developed by both of these projects.

Learning resources and teaching materials for economic education in elementary schools are becoming available in increasing quantities.

Perhaps the best source of such learning resources is the Joint Council on Economic Education, 2 West 46th Street, New York City, 10036. From this source, the teacher can secure sample units, scope and sequence charts, background information, and other teaching materials, as well as information concerning other sources of aids for teaching economic concepts.

ECONOMICS

Economics is the study of the production, distribution, exchange, and consumption of goods and services that people need or want. In a modern, industrialized society such as ours, with its materialistic emphasis, wants and needs are very great. Moreover, the processes involved in the production, distribution, exchange, and consumption form an interrelated web of relationships. So directly are individuals enmeshed in it that almost everything they do is, in one way or another, related to our economic system. Economic education concerns itself with helping pupils achieve an understanding of some of the basic relationships between our economic system and our way of life, thereby enabling them to make informed decisions on economic matters as citizens.

These samples represent major generalizations from economics that have been used as organizing ideas in developing programs in economic education:

1. The wants of man are unlimited, whereas resources that man needs to fulfill his wants are scarce; hence, societies and individuals have to make choices as to which needs are to be met and which are to be sacrificed.
2. Economic stability is one goal toward which all parts of an economy strive—that is, to moderate the upswings and downswings in the economy.
3. The interdependence of peoples of the world makes exchange and trade a necessity in the modern world.
4. Economic systems are usually mixed with both public and private ownership and with decisions made both by the government and by individual members of society.
5. Increased specialization in production has led to interdependence among individuals, communities, states, and nations.
6. Competition among producers largely determines how things will be produced in a private enterprise economy; the producer will try to make the most efficient use of resources in order to compete with other producers.
7. In the complex, modern industrialized society of today, government plays an important role in the economic life of society.

8. Most modern societies perceive economic welfare as a desired goal for their members; universally, poverty is devalued as a human condition.
9. Most economic systems are in the process of continual change.
10. Different groups of a society are affected differently by economic changes; nevertheless, all groups are affected because of interdependence.
11. The economy of a country (or region) is related to available resources, investment capital, and the educational development of its people.

The elementary school program of instruction should be built around basic economic concepts (such as production, distribution, exchange, and consumption) that are related to one or more of the generalizations listed. Each of these fundamental concepts can be developed with pupils in many of the unit studies undertaken. There may be times, however, when particular units are selected because they have special usefulness in developing specific economic concepts. Units on The Market in the primary grades are of this type and ordinarily focus on the distribution of needed goods.

PRODUCTION

Our high standard of living is quite directly related to our ability to maintain high production consistent with consumer needs and buying power. This is a basic concept in understanding our economic system. High production means jobs for workers. Continued employment provides workers with money to buy goods and services or to save and invest, resulting in an increased need for goods and expanding economic growth. Thus, in the production process, there are three basic components that lend themselves to study: *resources, capital,* and *labor.*

The following are a few *examples* of the types of learnings dealing with *production* that might be included in units at the first- and fourth-grade levels:

THE FARM—GRADE 1

Farms are the source of most of our food.

Good soil is needed for good crops.

The amount of goods the farmer can produce is influenced by a number of factors, one being the weather.

Farmers use machines made by other workers.

Farmers need much money for land, machinery, and buildings.

Machines reduce the number of workers needed to run a farm.

Good prices for farm products mean that the farmer can buy other things.

Not all farmers produce the same foods.

Good farmers try to increase the amount of food they produce.

The farmer owns his own land or rents from someone else who owns it.

Methods of farming and the amount of food the farmer can produce change as farmers learn new ways of growing crops.

Farms are becoming larger so that the farmer can produce more food with less cost.

Some people produce goods while others produce services.

Everyone is a consumer but not everyone is a producer.

THE HOME STATE—GRADE 4

Natural resources are soil, water, forests, minerals, wildlife, and places of natural beauty.

People use resources of a state to make their living.

Some states are more favored with resources than are others.

The number of people a state can support depends on its resources and how well they are developed.

State conservation departments are organized to protect the resources of the states.

People develop more efficient ways of using their resources in order to increase the amount of goods and services they can produce.

States encourage business to invest money in their states.

State laws protect resources and control their use.

States regulate conditions of labor, such as safety, working conditions, wages and hours.

States protect consumers in the production processes.

Man has learned to use the resources of nature for power to do work.

Through the use of power to do work, man is able to produce much more than he could using only human power or animal power.

DISTRIBUTION

In earlier times, distribution of goods was less complicated than it is today because the demand for goods was less than it is now, and because producers and consumers were closer to each other.[1] In an agrarian society, consumers often dealt directly with producers. The craftsman not only made a product but maintained his own store where his goods were sold. Today all this is different. Our needs are

1. In economics, the concept *distribution* can apply to the distribution of income or wealth or, more commonly, to the processes related to the getting of goods from producers to consumers. The latter meaning of the term is the one developed here.

such that we draw on the resources and products of the entire world. Consumers and producers are widely separated by a great number of middlemen in the way of shippers, handlers, wholesalers, retailers, and others. Behind the can of beans at the supermarket stands a multitude of workers who were responsible for getting the product within easy reach of the consumer. In the process of distribution are involved such concepts as *packaging, advertising, shipping, storing, wholesaling,* and *retailing.*

The following are a few *examples* of the types of learnings dealing with *distribution* that might be included in units at the second- and fifth-grade levels:

THE NEIGHBORHOOD SHOPPING CENTER—GRADE 2

Almost every service and all goods needed for living are available to us at local shopping centers.

Goods from all over the United States and from many parts of the world are found in the shopping center.

Many people make their living by getting goods from the producer to the consumer.

Retailers get the goods they sell from wholesale houses.

After the goods get to the store, they are arranged in sections or departments.

Everyone who handles the goods in getting them to us deserves to, and does, get paid for his work.

Advertising tells us about products that we might want to buy.

Small stores plan for trade in just their neighborhood; large shopping centers plan to serve customers from outside the neighborhood also.

Goods are brought to the store by ships, planes, railroads, and trucks.

The cost of bringing goods to the store is included in the price of the article.

There are many steps between the production of goods and their placement on the store shelves.

The retail store can buy its goods cheaper than the consumer because it buys in large quantities.

The more people who handle the goods, the higher will be the cost to us.

It is easier for us to go to the store to buy things than it would be for us to deal directly with the producer.

Shopping centers are located where they can get the most business.

Some goods must be brought to the shopping center frequently and in small quantities; other goods can be brought in large quantities less frequently.

Goods often have attractive labels so they will be easier to sell.

Labels tell who made the goods; and in the case of packaged goods, they give the contents and weight.

Prices for the same goods are not always the same in all stores.

Some stores give better service to customers than others.

Stores have big expenses in heating, lighting, paying help, and paying for their furnishings.

In order to sell their goods, stores advertise their merchandise.

MACHINES CHANGE WAYS OF LIVING—GRADE 5

Much of the goods we use must be processed before it is possible for us to use them.

Factories produce goods in great quantities, and they are stored until they are sold.

Men have developed ways of keeping perishable foods for long periods of time.

Modern equipment and rapid transportation make it possible to get goods to us from faraway places.

We need a wide variety of goods available so we can exercise choice in our buying.

Advertising has both beneficial and detrimental aspects.

All costs of distribution, including advertising, are included in the cost of items to buyers.

Modern methods of transportation make it possible to locate factories in places with conditions favorable to industry.

Small, light-weight goods can profitably be shipped farther than large, heavy ones.

Factories manufacturing large, heavy goods try to locate near their markets.

Certain places grew up as distributing and trading centers because of their strategic locations.

A tremendous volume of goods must come into a large city each day to take care of the needs of its people.

Much of the handling, packaging, and shipping processes formerly done by hand are now done by machines.

Scarce goods, or goods that must be shipped a long way, usually command higher prices.

Trade with foreign countries helps us get goods we do not make ourselves or that we do not make as well or as cheaply as they do.

Machines make it possible to do more work in less time, giving man more free time.

EXCHANGE

Some differentiation of labor is an old social phenomenon and is found in all societies, including preliterate ones. With the growth of the industrial society, however, a high level of specialization in the work people do has developed. Instead of everyone making his own shoes, furniture, clothing, and other necessities for living, particular persons specialize in the making of some goods and do not concern themselves with the making of others. This means that if everyone is to get the things he needs or wants, these specialized workers must exchange their goods or services. Originally, this took the form of barter (exchanging goods for other goods). Gradually men developed mediums of exchange, such as money, which is used almost universally today. The process of exchange deals with such concepts as *division of labor, specialization,* and *mediums of exchange.*

The following are a few *examples* of the types of learnings dealing with *exchange* that might be included in units at the third- and seventh-grade levels:

MONEY—GRADE 3

Money helps us measure and compare the value of goods and services.

People earn money by the work they do for a living.

Money comes in different denominations; it is necessary to know how to count money correctly.

What we buy must be determined by the amount of money we have to spend.

Saving money is a way of providing for future needs and wants.

Goods that cost the same amount of money may vary in quality.

People usually give first priority in buying to necessities rather than to luxuries.

People cannot always afford to buy the things they desire.

Communities and governments have need for money; this is obtained through taxes.

Not everyone has the same amount of money to spend for things.

In early times, people traded with one another rather than used money.

Many systems of money have been used by man; each country has its own money system.

Money used in the United States can be made only by the government of the United States; places where money is made are called mints.

Money itself has no value; its power to buy things is what makes it valuable.

There are many things that money cannot buy.

Banks provide a safe place to keep money; they also provide many services to people in a community.

Not everyone does the same kind of work for a living.

We depend on others for most of the goods and services we need.

People are willing to pay a fair price for goods that are well made or for good service.

Banks use people's savings to loan to other people and then pay people for the use of their savings.

Money can be in the form of currency and coin or checkbook money.

Checks are a way of paying out money from a bank account.

People use credit cards instead of money to buy some things; this way they can pay for their purchases later.

WORLD TRADE—GRADE 7

Industries of the United States need raw materials from many parts of the world.

Places that specialize in some product can usually make it of better quality and more cheaply than other places.

Many geographical discoveries were the result of man's seeking new trade routes.

A market may be local, regional, national, or worldwide.

International trade takes place because people in one country need and want what people in another country produce.

The interdependence of peoples of the world makes exchange and trade a necessity in the modern world.

The only communities that are self-sufficient are extremely primitive and backward ones.

Because we produce more goods than we can use, we need to have foreign markets for our goods if we are to maintain a high level of employment.

Good systems of transportation are needed to handle the exchange of goods.

The business of exchanging and trading goods provides work for many thousands of the world's people.

The flow of trade must be two ways: a nation must be able to sell its own goods (exports) in order to pay for those it buys from other nations (imports).

Sometimes countries place barriers to trade called tariffs.

Several countries of the world have formed trade unions in order to develop better trade relations among themselves.

Greater travel has increased peoples' wants and desires for things from other parts of the world.

> Wherever one goes in the world, he will see goods that bear the label "Made in the U.S.A."

CONSUMPTION

Such callous disregard for consumers as is apparent in the "then let them eat cake" response to the public's need for food, which is alleged to have been made by Marie Antoinette in the eighteenth century, is not sanctioned under our economic system at the present time. In general, the economic policy of the United States is that those who contribute to production should share in its benefits. Theoretically at least, the consumer exercises great power. Competitive producers present him with a wide variety of alternatives from which to select the things he wants or needs. It is then up to him to exercise a free choice in the things he will buy. Presumably, he weighs the alternatives carefully and selects the goods that will give him the most for his money. Items of poor quality, priced too high or of no use, are avoided; those of good quality are priced fairly and do what they are supposed to do —have high sales. On this basis, some businesses flourish and expand; others do not. Producers compete among themselves to give the consumer the best possible product at the lowest possible price.

Needless to say, decisions to buy or not to buy are not always made as objectively and as carefully as has been described here. The consumer is confused in making his decision because of conflicting advertising claims, the prestige and status values of certain commodities, and other factors affecting consumer motivation. Oftentimes persons buy things for reasons other than the actual use of the articles. Many opportunities for fraud and misrepresentation are inherent in this system; thus, some system of consumer protection is required by government or by private agencies. In general, the system has worked well for the American consumer. Consumption concerns itself with such concepts as *advertising, needs and desires of consumers, competition,* and *protective agencies,* both governmental and private.

The following are a few *examples* of the types of learnings dealing with *consumption* that might be included in units at the second- and eighth-grade levels.

WHY DO WE BUY THE THINGS WE DO?—GRADE 2

Families need to buy most of the things they must have for everyday living.

Stores advertise the things they have for sale.

Shoppers usually try to get the best buy.

Stores advertise in newspapers, on the radio, on television, and by using signs.

Some of the things we buy we really do not need, but they are fun to have and we buy them for enjoyment.

When we have money to spend, we usually spend it on the things we really need first.

Not all stores charge the same prices for the same things.

The government checks to see that the stores' scales are correct.

Advertising makes us want some things that we may not need.

We buy certain foods instead of others because they are more healthful.

Products are sold in a variety of quantities, such as by the pound, quart, gallon, yard, ounce, or dozen.

We buy some things simply because they are appealing or are what is popular at the time.

Some stores offer special services with their merchandise.

Some goods are consumed slowly whereas others are used quickly and need constant replacement.

STANDARDS OF LIVING—THEN AND NOW—GRADE 8

Buying involves choice making; one must learn to make wise choices in the things he plans to buy.

Advertising can be both helpful and harmful to the buyer.

Advertising is controlled by the government; it is against the law to make false advertising claims.

Price is not necessarily an indication of the value of an article.

Labels on articles legally must include certain information.

Most people face the problem of wanting more than they can afford to pay for.

The buyer owes it to himself to get the best buy he can.

Advertising, labeling, and packaging are done in such a way as to make the product attractive to the buyer.

Attractive labeling and packaging has nothing to do with the quality of the product inside the package.

Because our needs and wants often exceed our resources, we must plan and budget our personal financial affairs carefully.

Before making major purchases, one should get as much reliable information as necessary in order to make a wise choice.

Both the government and private agencies protect the buyer from fraud, but the buyer must also protect himself by buying carefully.

If these learnings and others like them are to be included in units, they will have to be developed in ways that are educationally and psychologically sound. Telling them to the pupils or lecturing about them is not likely to be very effective. Pupils will need to work on problems of which these learnings are a part, and in the process of study, economic understanding is developed. Economics is a dynamic and changing social science; therefore, it is better to focus instruction on basic principles rather than on specific data at this level. For example, rather than teach children what to look for in buying a pair of shoes, it is better to teach them that if one has holes in his shoes and only ten dollars to spend, he should buy shoes instead of roller skates.

Civic Education—Political Science

The problem of precisely defining the scope, concerns, and limits of political science is a difficult and technical one, and most writers in this field have their own definition of it. For purposes of the elementary school social studies curriculum, political science can be regarded as a discipline concerned with the study of government, political processes, and political decision making.

In Chapter 2 (page 30) it was noted that almost all states have legislative requirements calling for formal instruction in citizenship. Some of this is handled through content in courses that are nominally history. In the upper grades, many schools have had courses called civics comprised of instruction in the role, function, and organization of government with some attention to political processes, political institutions, and political decision making as these apply to citizenship behavior. Many of the concepts relating to instruction of this type are drawn from the discipline of political science.

There are three concepts basic to the understanding of the organization of human societies. One is that all societies have developed ways of establishing and maintaining social order; the second is that the central order-maintaining instrument has great power over the lives of individuals subjected to it; and the third is that all such systems demand and expect a loyalty to them when they are threatened by hostile opposing forces. It is apparent that if an individual human being is to function in a society as a member of it, he must conduct himself in politically appropriate ways. Not to do so might result in disastrous consequences for him. Consequently, societies provide ways of inducting the young into the political life of the society. Through this process, the child internalizes a set of values, beliefs, and attitudes consistent with the political system of the society. He learns how the system functions and eventually contributes to its perpetuation. This process of learning has come to be called political socialization. According to Kazamias and Massialas, political socialization "has the explicit purpose of molding the behavior of the young and immature into politically and socially relevant form. Or, to put it another way, political socialization is the process through which a person acquires his basic political orientation from his environment." [2]

All of this is relevant to the elementary school teacher of social studies. Recent research suggests that the values and attitudes undergirding political socialization are formed fairly early in life. A recent and frequently cited study of this problem is that of Easton and Hess. These researchers included some 12,000 elementary school children in this study and on the basis of their findings concluded that the child's political world begins to take form before he enters the elementary school and that "the truly formative years of the maturing member of a political system would seem to be those years between the ages of three and thirteen." [3] The study also found that formal instruction about government and politics had little effect on the student's political values and attitudes formed earlier. He is able to add to his fund of information and knowledge, to be sure, but his basic political orientation is well established by that time. It seems that during the years the child is in the elementary and junior high school, he is still relatively flexible in his political outlook, making these years extremely important from the standpoint of social studies instruction.

The school program, therefore, needs to begin early in helping the child develop his political orientation. Children need school experiences that familiarize them with the techniques of democratic procedures and that help them develop a sense of appreciation of the liberties enjoyed by citizens of this nation. Such appreciations and skills can scarcely be built on a foundation of ignorance. Thus, the school program is planned to help the child begin his understanding of some of the basic concepts related to our political system. Accompanying the development of these understandings, the child should be given practice in using his knowledge and skills in the regular work of the class and the school. In another source, this author has suggested six guidelines for programs in political science at the elementary and junior high school levels:

1. Provide systematic instruction which assists the pupil to gain an understanding of important concepts and ideas relevant to political science.

2. Andreas M. Kazamias and Byron G. Massialas, *Tradition and Change in Education*, Englewood Cliffs, N.J.: Prentice-Hall, 1965, p. 130.

3. David Easton and Robert Hess, "The Child's Political World," *Midwest Journal of Political Science*, 6, 1962, pp. 227–246.

2. Provide opportunities for firsthand experiences which represent simple but realistic variations of political behavior.
3. Provide pupils with opportunities to deal with ambiguous situations and problems (i.e. situations and problems in which the solutions are not clear-cut and discrete, less concern with "finding the right answer"—the opposite of those which are clearly right or wrong, or ones in which only one solution is acceptable).
4. Provide pupils with opportunities to learn and practice intellectual skills essential to political action (i.e. critical thinking; gathering, organizing and evaluating data; learning about and using data sources; analyzing problems; expressing a point of view orally or in writing; summarizing and drawing conclusions; etc.).
5. Acquaint pupils with role expectations of responsible political behavior.
6. Help pupils develop some sense of appreciation for their political heritage.[4]

Specific instances of how these principles can be applied in the various grades are given on pages 263–267.

As is the case in all the other disciplines contributing to the social studies curriculum, certain organizing ideas from political science are used to provide a focus for studies that include political science concepts. The following represent samples of major generalizations from political science that have been used as organizing ideas in developing units with a political science emphasis:

1. Every known society has some kind of authority structure that can be called its government; such a government is granted coercive power.
2. A stable government facilitates the social and economic development of a nation.
3. All societies have made policies or laws about how groups of people should live together.
4. Each society has empowered a body (that is, tribal council, city council, state assembly, parliament) to make decisions and establish social regulations for the group carrying coercive sanctions.
5. The decisions, policies, and laws that have been made for a given society reflect and are based on the values, beliefs, and traditions of that society.
6. Throughout the history of mankind, man has experimented with many different systems of government.
7. The consent of the governed is to some extent a requirement of all governments, and without it a government will eventually col-

4. John Jarolimek, "Political Science in the Elementary and Junior High School Curriculum," *Political Science in the Social Studies*, Robert E. Cleary and Donald H. Riddle, eds., 36th Yearbook, Washington, D.C.: National Council for the Social Studies, 1966.

lapse; but in a democracy, consent of the governed is clearly recognized as a fundamental prerequisite of government.

8. A democratic society depends on citizens who are intellectually and morally competent to conduct the affairs of government.

School policies in connection with studies of government, political institutions, ideals, and citizenship have never been entirely clear or consistent. Hardly any component of the school curriculum is as potentially explosive and fraught with sensitive issues and ideas. A teacher who seeks to approach political matters in a conscientious and honest way may, unfortunately, find himself the victim of attack by individuals or groups who are not in accord with his method of presentation. In another source this author has commented on the problem as follows:

> The tendency . . . is to seek approaches to the presentation of political content in so-called safe ways. This is sometimes defended on the basis that the teacher is relying only on facts rather than opinion, that objective non-controversial procedures are being employed, and that pupils are not being indoctrinated with a particular point of view. Objections to this approach are immediately raised by those who believe that such procedures make any realistic consideration of political issues impossible. Objections are also raised by those who believe that the role of the school ought to be precisely that of instructing pupils in "the American way of life." This latter point of view would have the school play a much more forceful and positive role in political socialization. Needless to say, such teachings would have to be in accordance with "the American way of life" as perceived by those who seek such an emphasis in the school program. Just how the school can instruct pupils about a political system which values a free and open consideration of issues in ways which violate these principles is not altogether clear. Indeed, it would be difficult to conceive an instructional program less consistent with the American political tradition than some which have been suggested in recent years—ones which seek to instill in children the "right" attitudes, values, and beliefs.[5]

In teaching an appreciation of the political heritage, schools commonly do something that is loosely labeled teaching patriotism. Very often they rely heavily on patriotic symbolism to stir the emotions of children. These programs are characterized by activities calling for the learning of a few emotionally charged facts, the memorization of a few memorable expressions ("Give me liberty or give me death!"), the drawing of "pretty" flags or Liberty Bells, a school essay contest on a subject that arouses strong feelings, the singing of patriotic songs, and

5. *Ibid.*

the performing of PTA programs that have patriotic themes. Such activities often get strong support from certain elements in the community because it is assumed that visible expressions of patriotism actually contribute to loyalty and fidelity to one's country.

Few would deny that there is a place for a certain amount of symbolism in school programs. The pageants, plays, creative stories, poems, and creative dramatics activities that are typically a part of good elementary school education are powerful tools in building appreciations, ideals, and values. Moreover, they are often favorite school experiences of children and are remembered for years to come. But when symbolism is used, it should be placed on a rational basis as soon as possible. For example, children not only should learn to say the Pledge of Allegiance but also should begin learning what it means and why it is recited. Unless the use of symbols is accompanied by an attempt to get children to understand their meanings—however simply this is done—the activities will be devoid of any significance insofar as enhancing the growth of good citizenship. In fact, they may even be harmful, because the young learner is likely to construe overt patriotic expressions and demonstrations as being synonymous with good citizenship. The story is told of one teacher who said to her class, "We will be democratic about it, even if I have to force you to vote!" The story is probably not true, but it demonstrates the kinds of ludicrous inconsistencies that develop in patriotic programs that lack sound basic objectives.

Perhaps the best way to teach concepts drawn from political science at the early levels is to select those that can become a part of the immediate life of the child. For example, primary-grade children can learn that when people live together they must establish and observe rules. When people have rules, they know what they can and what they cannot do. Rules are made so that everyone is treated fairly. Children can understand this because they have rules in their classroom, in their school, and in their homes. They can learn that grownups have rules, too. These are written down and are called laws. When people break the rules, or laws, they are usually punished in some way. If a person keeps on breaking the law or does something that is very harmful to another person, he is not allowed to live with the other people in the community. In this way, children learn not only that laws limit what one can do but also that they have a protective function. Through a series of such learnings, children's concepts of rules and laws, as needed for orderly living, develop. Naturally, such concepts are given increasingly greater depth as the pupils progress through the grades. For example, later in the grades, they will learn that rules and laws are not exactly alike; laws are more binding than are rules.

The following are *examples* of the types of learnings and experiences related to *civic education* that would be appropriate for grades one, two, and three.

LEARNINGS

When we live together we must have rules.

We help make rules and then we live by them.

In our country, everyone helps make rules; these are called laws.

People obey laws because the laws are good for our community or country, not because it is against the law to disobey them.

Most people obey rules and laws without being forced by policemen.

Policemen are needed because otherwise a few people would not obey the law.

Policemen work for the community and are paid by the community.

People in our country choose who their leaders are to be.

Our government does such things as build highways and parks; people pay for these through taxes.

When we choose someone for a leader, we give him certain powers.

Persons who are chosen as leaders must be fair to everyone, not just to their friends.

We cannot have our own way in everything all the time.

The flag stands for our country.

We promise to be true to our country when we say the Pledge of Allegiance.

EXPERIENCES

Participating in classroom planning under teacher guidance.

Selecting temporary room chairmen.

Serving as temporary room chairman.

Saying the Pledge of Allegiance.

Establishing room rules under teacher guidance.

Assuming minor responsibilities for classroom housekeeping.

Cooperating with school safety patrolmen.

Obeying playground rules; cooperating with playground monitors.

Serving as a representative to the school council.

Talking with police officers.

Singing patriotic songs.

Assuming leadership and followership roles in small-group work.

Volunteering for jobs that need to be done.

Listening to stories about famous Americans.

Serving as classroom host or hostess.

The program for building civic competence, therefore, begins in the primary grades with the introduction of the most elementary and fundamental concepts relating to people living and working together under a system of order that preserves individual freedom. Great stress is placed on applying the learnings as they are presented. Theoretical and complex explanations of the structure of government are inappropriate at this level. The main goals are to get children to handle themselves in responsible ways, to see the need for order in living, to govern their actions with consideration for the rights of others, and to realize that the whole realm of human activity is based on a system of rules and laws. Although children at this level are too immature to comprehend the meaning of freedom as an abstract concept, they can, nevertheless, understand it in terms of activities in which they can choose their own pupil leaders or help to establish their classroom rules.

As pupils advance to the middle grades, more can be done in direct teaching of the manner in which our system of government functions. At this level, pupils also have greater opportunity to participate in school activities that promote civic learnings. For example, they can take a more active part in the school council if there is one, they can serve as safety patrolmen or playground monitors, and they can assume greater responsibilities for affairs within their own classroom.

The exact concepts and learnings to be included in each of the three middle grades will depend on the content of the school curriculum. In the fourth grade, many schools have units on the home state. These units are filled with good possibilities to include civic learnings. Pupils can study the early beginnings of their state and learn how its government developed. The teacher will need to be careful not to make the concepts relating to state government too difficult for children of this age. Even the matter of differentiating between a city, a state, and a country, for example, may be quite difficult for some fourth-graders. Should the curriculum call for a study of communities around the world, the teacher should take note of the fact that all of them have some type of government. Pupils will learn that governments are not all like ours, and the teacher will have to guard against having children make unwarranted value judgments about other governments. The essential learning here is that all peoples have some type of government, and although we would not choose their systems for ourselves, their governments may serve the people of those particular countries very well. There may be other cases, of course, where the teacher will want to call attention to unfair actions of governments, especially those that have utter disregard for the dignity of the human being. The likelihood is great, however, that a fourth-grade class will not make a study of a community with a government of that type.

The following are *examples* of the types of learnings that would be appropriate at the fourth-grade level:

1. In our country we have several governments: the community, the state, and the government of our whole country.
2. Our country is made up of fifty states.
3. The place where the state government has its offices is the state capital.
4. The head of the state government is the governor.
5. The people of a state choose persons to make the state laws.
6. The part of the government that makes state laws is called the state legislature.
7. In our country, people think about the feelings of others.
8. People everywhere have governments; some of these are different from ours.
9. We believe that people should have the right to choose the kind of government they want.
10. Our government is based on fair play and on doing what is right.
11. People who violate the rules of the government are subject to punishment.
12. The capital of our country is Washington, D.C.
13. When our country was first formed, there were only thirteen states; the stripes in the flag stand for the first thirteen states.
14. Each of the stars in our country's flag stands for one of the states.
15. States have mottos and symbols such as a state flag, a bird, a tree, a flower, a song, and a seal.
16. State governments have much to do with our everyday affairs of living.
17. It is important that the best people possible be chosen for positions in the government.
18. Many times people are not paid to serve in community government.
19. Good citizens feel it is their duty to serve in government even though they are not paid for it.

Many schools in the country include in grade five, units dealing with the development of the United States. As this is handled in most schools, the emphasis is not on the political growth of the nation, nor should it be. Many schools emphasize ways of living during the period of exploration, colonization, and the westward movement. However, this does not mean that early beginnings in representative government should be ignored. Youngsters at this level can achieve substantial understanding of some of the foundations of the government of this country. They are particularly interested in and ready to learn of the lives of some of the great champions of American freedom. Pupils can

ELEMENTS FROM THE COMPLEMENTARY SOCIAL SCIENCES

learn the differences in the way Spain, France, and England ruled their colonies in the New World and relate these colonial attitudes to the kinds of governments that developed in each of the areas. They can learn how local representative government grew in the English colonies and can grasp simple concepts relating to the development of our own national government. It is easy to make such studies too technical and difficult for fifth-graders; ideas will have to be dealt with at a level suitable to the pupils.

The following are *examples* of the types of learnings that would be suitable at the fifth-grade level:

1. The major European nations in Columbus' time were ruled by kings and queens.
2. The Indians of the New World had tribal governments.
3. Many people came to the New World to gain freedom.
4. One of the early documents of government in the New World was the Mayflower Compact.
5. Early English colonies were ruled by governors.
6. The colonial assemblies were important in the growth of representative government.
7. Not all the colonies were ruled in the same way.
8. The first plan of government of the United States was based on the Articles of Confederation.
9. Representatives from the states developed a new plan of government; it is described in the Constitution.
10. Laws in our country are made by Congress.
11. The President is the head of our country's government.
12. The headquarters for our country's government is in Washington, D.C.
13. The President and members of Congress are elected by the voters.
14. New territories can become a part of the United States as states, but states cannot withdraw from the Union.
15. Changes that have been made in the Constitution are called amendments; many of them protect the rights of individual citizens.

The sixth-grade program affords opportunities for pupils to learn something of the governments of other nations, because, at this level, units often deal with countries in various parts of the world. Some schools include a study of early civilizations on the Mediterranean, and this affords an opportunity to show the beginnings of the democratic concept of government and law and how this idea found its way into our own system of government. If countries of Western Europe are studied, children can learn of the growth of freedom and that modern-day monarchies are based on democratic principles of government. They can also learn that in many nations of the world, individual citizens have little or nothing to say about the way they are governed. Units on Africa are popular in this grade and this makes it possible to show the problems of government new nations have and how the United States assists new self-governing countries.

A unit on the United Nations may be included in the sixth grade, in which case the need for lawful international relations can be developed. This will provide an opportunity for pupils to learn how and why national governments join together for the fulfillment of mutual self-interests. The concept of alliances and their purpose can be studied as it applies to the United States.

The following are *examples* of the types of learnings that would be appropriate for the sixth grade:

1. All countries have some type of government.
2. The earliest group of people was the family; from this grew larger groups such as tribes, which had leaders.
3. As people acquired more property, there was need for more laws.
4. Democracy as a system of government was developed by the Greeks.
5. Many of our ideas about government and law have come to us from the Romans.
6. Not all nations of the world allow citizens to have anything to say about how they are governed.

The program of the seventh grade depends on the sixth-seventh grade sequence followed in the school. If nations of the Western Hemisphere are studied in the sixth grade, the Eastern Hemisphere nations are usually studied in the seventh grade; or the order can be reversed. Some schools also include home-state studies in the seventh grade. Whatever pattern is followed, there will be many opportunities to include learnings relating to government in connection either with other nations or with the home state. The learnings suggested for the previous grades will give the teacher clues as to which would be appropriate for grade seven.

In most schools, grade eight deals with the development of the United States, and there is ordinarily a heavy emphasis on the growth of the government of this nation. Attention is directed to the early colonial governments, events that led to the American Revolution, and the formation of the new government. Pupils study the significance of such documents as the Declaration of Independence, the Articles of Confederation, and the Constitution. They learn of our political system and how it functions. They learn how the government of the United

States grew in power and how it relates to the private lives of citizens. When the pupil completes the eight grades, he should have a functional, citizen's knowledge of government and civic responsibility. He also should have had a great many experiences that will have given him the opportunity to learn, practice, and use democratic citizenship skills. This does not mean that he need not or cannot learn more; it means simply that he has completed the basic, introductory work in civic education that serves as the common foundation for all citizens of the United States.

Societal Education—Sociology, Social Psychology

Sociology is a relatively new and broad social science that deals with the study of the structure of society, its groups, institutions, and culture. Sociological studies often focus on the diverse societal and cultural phenomena that influence the behavior of individuals and groups. Sociology is especially concerned with social organization and the way people organize themselves into groups, subgroups, social classes, and institutions. It is difficult to draw a sharp line between the content of sociology and some of the other social sciences because their areas of concern overlap.

A considerable amount of content of the elementary school social studies is drawn from sociology. This is particularly true in the primary grades. One of the units studied in first grade is "The Family." Children learn about the structure of this basic group in our society, some of its functions, and the roles of various members. This is usually followed in the primary grades by units dealing with the neighborhood, community workers, community living, and community institutions. As children study the diversification of work that is done in a modern community, they begin to see how various groups are formed, and learn of their purposes. Later in the grades, pupils will learn that the interests of such community groups are often in conflict and that this sometimes results in disorganization and community problems. Programs that are organized in terms of social functions draw heavily from sociology for their subject matter.

These are representative samples of major generalizations from sociology that have been used as organizing ideas in developing social studies units with a sociological emphasis:

1. The family is the basic social unit in most cultures and is the source of some of the most fundamental and necessary learnings in a culture.
2. Social classes have always existed in every society, although the bases of class distinction and the degree of rigidity of the class structure have varied.

3. The trend toward urbanization within the United States as well as in the rest of the world has accentuated problems of social disorganization, interpersonal relationships, and group interaction.

4. Population growth is presenting mankind with one of the most challenging problems of modern times.

5. Every society develops a system of roles, norms, values, and sanctions to guide the behavior of individuals and groups within the society.

6. In order to meet individual and group needs, societies organize themselves into subgroups that, in time, become institutionalized; individuals are members of several such subgroups or institutions.

7. The satisfaction of social needs is a strong motivating force in the determination of individual behavior.

8. All societies develop systems of social control; conflicts often arise between individual liberty and social control in societies where both values are sought.

9. Status and prestige are relative to the values sought by a social group; behavior that is rewarded in one social group may be suppressed in another.

10. The social environment in which a person is reared and lives has a profound effect on the personal growth and development of every individual.

At some point in the grades, and perhaps at several points, pupils will have units dealing with ways of living. These units often stress sociological concepts. When primitive societies are selected, the teacher is cautioned not to assume that because the culture is simple, it will be easily understood by the pupils.

Martindale and Monachesi draw attention to the complexity of some of the so-called simple cultures when one examines their social organization. For example, in speaking of the Australian bushman, they say,

> Every tribe was a complex organization of such (totemic) clans. Taboos were observed toward the totemic animal except on special feast days. Further, marriage was exogamous to the clan and governed by a complex system of rules such that among some Australian tribes a man was permitted to marry only his mother's mother's brother's daughter's daughter—that is, his maternal second cousin. In view of these facts, to continue to think of the degree of culture in terms of its degree of complexity and organization is to conclude that our own system of social organization is incredibly crude by comparison with that of the Australian Bushman.[6]

6. Don Martindale and Elio D. Monachesi, *Elements of Sociology*, New York: Harper & Row, 1951, pp. 109–110.

Studies of various cultures should focus on fundamental and basic social processes rather than on the quaint ways used by the group to achieve them; that is, all groups have systems of communication, worship, education, government. Much of value can be learned by showing what factors tend to disrupt conventional ways of living and cause people to change to other ways. Pupils in the middle and upper grades can also learn the consequences that befall cultures that do not make necessary changes in their way of living as external conditions change.

In units on the growth of the United States in grades five and eight, as well as in home-state units in the fourth grade, pupils will want to study the cultural, religious, and racial backgrounds of the people who live there. Such a study will show that the United States has benefited from the contributions of many other peoples in the world. Often it is possible for pupils to see concrete evidences of contributions of other cultures in the life about them in things such as the names of towns, cities, bodies of water, festivals, customs, language, and famous men in our history. A knowledge of and appreciation for the contributions of other cultures to our own can be a strong force in combating harmful aspects of ethnocentrism.

Certainly a problem that will be receiving increasing attention in the social studies is that of population growth. In its simplest form, the study of population might call for the examination of the location of settlements and population centers. Which areas are densely populated? Which are more sparsely settled and why? In the upper grades, pupils can study more intensively some of the problems that develop in areas of high population density. They can trace the movements of peoples and discover why they move when and where they do. They can study population trends, birth and death rates in countries, and examine problems faced by countries with rapidly increasing numbers of people.

Social psychology and sociology concern themselves with somewhat the same social phenomena. Whereas sociology focuses on groups, social psychology studies the individual in a social situation. Social psychology is particularly concerned with the effects of group life on the behavior of individuals. Studies in social psychology deal with the problems of the individual's role in groups, the development of the self-concept, the effects of group pressure on individual behavior, attitudes, and how they are formed, leadership, followership, and the effects of social-class structure.

The field of social psychology perhaps has less to offer to the *content* of the elementary social studies than it does to the teacher in working with children. For example, much of the research on group processes has been done by social psychologists and has many implications for social studies teaching, as is discussed in Chapter 12. The manner in which group pressures operate to cause people to behave the way they do is also significant to an alert teacher. Establishing a healthful classroom emotional climate that will allow individual children to develop feelings of personal worth is, likewise, a necessary prerequisite to sound social studies instruction. Thus, in a variety of ways, social psychology makes a substantial contribution to the *methodology* of the elementary social studies.

Anthropology

Anthropology, with its several divisions, is often thought of as a unifying social science, because it is by definition the study of man. It is the total study of man and his culture and is the study of the growth of man toward civilization. Anthropology is concerned with the development of language, social institutions, religion, arts and crafts, physical and mental traits, and similarities and differences of cultures. Much of the research that has been done on the characteristics of various racial groups has been done by anthropologists. Anthropological concepts become a part of the social studies in the culture studies that are made of human societies.

Anthropological studies are often comparative. Such comparative, cross-cultural studies show the wide range of capabilities of man: modern medical practice and the primitive medicine man; affluence and poverty; humanitarian behavior and cruelty and war; urban living and rural life; life in extremely cold areas and life in hot, desert regions. Man is, therefore, a contradictory creature, highly adaptive in his behavior, capable of remarkable achievements, rational yet often acting in irrational ways. Man is, within limits, a controller and shaper of his environment, a builder of culture. He relies on his ability to think, imagine, and innovate to solve his problems of living. This characteristic results in great diversity among the people of the world in how they live, what they believe, and how they conduct their affairs. Nonetheless, people are all part of the human family; all are a part of what is called mankind and all have many common physical and social needs.

There has developed a considerable amount of interest in the exciting possibilities for social studies programs with an anthropological orientation. Perhaps this is in part because of the increased importance of the non-Western world in international affairs and the traditional interest of the anthropologists in non-Western cultures. Perhaps, too, it is because anthropology deals with concepts so fundamentally related to the shaping of the human personality, human institutions, and the evolution of man and his culture. The growing importance of

ELEMENTS FROM THE COMPLEMENTARY SOCIAL SCIENCES

anthropology in the social studies curriculum is demonstrated by the number of major curriculum-development projects relying wholly or in part on the concepts and content of anthropology.[7]

These samples represent major generalizations from anthropology that have been used as organizing ideas in developing social studies units with an anthropological orientation:

1. Every society, however primitive, has formed its own system of beliefs, knowledge, values, traditions, and skills that can be called its culture.

2. Culture is socially learned and serves as a potential guide for human behavior in any given society.

3. Although all mankind is confronted with the same psychological and physiological needs to be met, the manner in which they are met differs according to culture.

4. A society must continuously evaluate and modify its culture in order to adjust to changing conditions; failure to do so leads to social disorganization or the absorption or exploitation of the society by more aggressive and rapidly developing cultures.

5. Man's cultural adaptations result in great diversity in ways of living and allow him to be highly versatile in selecting where and how he will live.

6. The art, music, architecture, food, clothing, sports, and customs of a people help to produce a national identity.

7. All human beings, since long before the beginning of written history, have been members of the same biological species.

8. Nearly all human beings, regardless of racial or ethnic background, are capable of participating in and contributing to any culture.

9. Social functions such as communicating; producing, distributing and consuming goods and services; educating; recreating; governing; conserving resources; and expressing religious and aesthetic feelings are primary activities of all organized societies.

10. The increased and more frequent contacts of persons from various cultures made possible by modern-day transportation and communication systems are resulting in extensive cultural diffusion, cultural borrowing, and cultural exchange.

7. Three of these are Wilfred Bailey and Marion J. Rice, *Development of a Sequential Curriculum in Anthropology for Grades 1–7*, Department of Sociology and Anthropology, University of Georgia; Malcolm C. Collier, *Anthropology Curriculum Study Project* (high school), University of Chicago; Peter B. Dow, Director, *Man: A Course of Study*, Educational Development Center, Cambridge, Massachusetts.

Philosophy

Philosophy, the father of all the social sciences, influences the elementary social studies curriculum but contributes very little in actual subject-matter content. When pupils are identifying problems, stating hypotheses, gathering relevant data, testing hypotheses, and verifying their conclusions, they are applying the methodology of philosophy. This procedure usually goes under another name: problem-solving, reflective, or critical thinking. But these intellectual processes represent a search for truth, and this is the basic concern of philosophy. Social studies procedures and objectives that deal with aspects of thinking—reasoning, critical thinking, using evidence to substantiate claims—consist of elements of philosophy. In this way, philosophy is a part of the *process* of learning in the social studies.

Much of the work in social studies deals with values. As pupils study the various people of the world, the pupils wonder why those people are willing to live the way they do, why they believe the things they do, and why they do not seek a better life for themselves. They learn that people everywhere have ideas about what is good and what is bad; what is ugly and what is beautiful; what is the honorable thing to do and what is not. People govern their behavior in terms of the basic beliefs that are a part of their culture. In our materialistic society, pupils may be surprised to learn that there are people with very little of the earth's goods who lead happy lives, while others who are well equipped materially are sometimes unhappy. They learn that happiness comes, not from what one has, but from the quality of one's relations with other human beings.

Methods of Inquiry in the Complementary Social Sciences [8]

There are distinctive differences as well as common elements that characterize methods of inquiry in each of the social sciences. The unique qualities of the methodology of a discipline have to do with (1) the kinds of questions asked and the types of hypotheses tested, (2) the data each considers relevant, (3) the data sources it finds useful (4) the manner of collecting data, (5) the kinds of conclusions reached, and (6) the kinds of predictions concerning natural or social events that it is able to make with degrees of confidence. There is, of course, some amount of overlap from one discipline to another. For example,

8. The author is indebted to Mr. Irving D. Smith, graduate student at the University of Washington, for research relative to methods of inquiry in the social sciences on which portions of Chapters 6, 7, and 8 are based.

an anthropologist studying the political behavior of people in a particular culture will be working, in part at least, with data relevant to political science, sociology, geography, and history. But when he does, he deals with the data as an anthropologist rather than as a political scientist, economist, sociologist, geographer, or historian. For the elementary teacher of social studies, it is important to know enough about the parent disciplines—the social sciences—to understand the basic concerns of each and how the scholars pursue their research and studies in these fields. Some of the procedures can be adapted and applied in a simple way to social studies instruction in the elementary school.

In all the disciplines, there has been a trend toward increased use of inductive procedures and toward quantifying data. Increasing use is being made of mathematical models and the utilization of computer science. These are highly sophisticated techniques, far beyond what would be remotely practicable for elementary school pupils. Nevertheless, the developments suggest a *teaching style* that does have relevance for the elementary teacher. It suggests that more attention could profitably be given to asking questions, posing hypotheses, gathering data, testing possible solutions and hunches, and coming to conclusions. Moreover, pupils can be taught to quantify data, to classify it, to keep careful records, to chart trends on graphs, and so on. These are important skills that can and should be taught in the elementary school.

Almost without exception, modern methods of inquiry in the social sciences are stressing inductive, empirical approaches. For at least two generations, inductive procedures have been recommended for elementary school teaching under the title *problem-solving;* however, the extent to which such procedures have been applied in teaching social studies has been disappointing. Programs continue to concern themselves largely with descriptive information that the pupil is supposed to learn, operating under the mistaken assumption that one gains information first and applies it later. There can be little doubt that social studies instruction would be much improved and the studies more interesting and vital to pupils if more generous use were made of inquiry strategies. As an example, imagine a teacher holding an artifact before a middle-grade class. She asks them such questions as these:

1. What is it?
2. Who used it?
3. How was it used?
4. Where do you suppose it was used?
5. Where might it have been found?
6. What does it tell us about the people who used it?

7. Would it be used today?
8. Where could we look to find out which of our answers is most correct?

In handling pupil responses to questions such as these, the teacher does not evaluate them by saying, "Yes, that's right," or "No, I don't think so." He clarifies the statement and accepts it as a hypothesis to be tested. The statements can be written on the chalkboard, and as the class proceeds with research, incorrect propositions can be eliminated. Eventually, some sound conclusions can be based on the data collected. Compare that procedure with this one in which the teacher says,

> Boys and girls, this is a bone scraper used by the Eskimos of northern Canada in cleaning the flesh from the hides of animals. It was held in the hand like this and used with a back and forth motion. This is a crude tool used by people who are quite primitive in their development. A tool such as this one is still used by some of the far north people of North America and Asia. Now open your social studies books to page 28 and read about the Eskimo people of the Far North.

In the first case, the teacher is stimulating the pupils' thinking with provocative questions. Pupils are given the delightful experience of learning something for themselves. In the second case, the teacher is confusing telling with teaching. In the first case, pupils are involved in the finding-out process; in the second case, they are receivers only. Now, it really does not matter much whether American schoolchildren know about Eskimo skin scrapers or not. But, if such a bit of information can be used by a skillful teacher to help children build intellectual skills and thought processes, it can be used to good advantage. Note that this requirement is not met in the second case cited.

In a vast number of ways, elementary teachers can begin to acquaint pupils with some of the tools, techniques, and modes of thought of the social sciences. For example, instead of keeping a boxful of photographs or newspaper clippings of early life in the community, the class might arrange and carefully label them, thereby making a good study collection. Pupils can be taught to be more precise in the statement of questions to which they seek answers. They can learn to utilize data sources other than the conventional ones of the classroom. They can be taught to place data on maps and graphs for purposes of comparison. They can be taught to evaluate data sources and to determine the relevance of information as it applies to a problem or topic under study. If teachers are discriminating in their choice of activities and projects of this type, there is much of value that can come from them in promoting good social studies education. On the other hand, if the methods of the social scientist are utilized in an unenlightened way in teaching elementary school pupils, such procedures can serve only to confuse and frustrate children.

Discussion Questions and Suggested Activities

1. Select generalizations from the complementary social sciences that are appropriate to the resource unit you are developing (Chapter 3).
2. Study a community with which you are familiar and list five community resources that might be utilized in teaching elements of the complementary social sciences to children in a grade of your choice.
3. Examine a social studies textbook and its accompanying manual. Are concepts from the eight social sciences included? Is the textbook dominated by certain social sciences? Can you cite specific instances where the complementary social sciences could have been utilized to a greater extent?
4. What are the advantages and limitations of such organizations as the student council? Do you think the use of pupils as hall and playground monitors is a good practice? How would you organize such a procedure to avoid having pupils become informers on their schoolmates?
5. Construct a chart that will help upper-grade children understand the concept of local, state, or national government.
6. What learning experiences other than formal textbook study can contribute to children's understanding of sociology?
7. Some of the recent social studies curriculum reform projects (for example, the Georgia Anthropology Project) have developed materials centered around the complementary social sciences with the intention that these materials will become separate parts or units within the regular social studies programs—"infusions." Why do you think this approach was employed rather than attempting to incorporate the complementary social sciences into all units and learning? What are the advantages and disadvantages of this method of curriculum construction?
8. Describe problems that could be resolved by voting in a classroom and other problems that should not be so handled. Is it consistent with democratic processes to vote whether or not an answer is correct? Can you give examples of situations where it is better to arrive at classroom decisions through consensus rather than by voting?
9. What are some common political attitudes of elementary school children? (See the "Selected Readings" that follow, for information.) Report your findings to your classmates. What implications

do the findings have for the teaching of political science concepts in the elementary grades?

Selected References

Berelson, Bernard, and Gary A. Steiner. *Human Behavior: An Inventory of Scientific Findings.* New York: Harcourt, Brace & World, Inc., 1964.

Cleary, Robert E., and Donald H. Riddle, eds. *Political Science in the Social Studies,* 36th Yearbook. Washington, D.C.: National Council for the Social Studies, 1966.

Douglass, Malcolm P. *Social Studies: From Theory to Practice in Elementary Education.* Philadelphia: J. B. Lippincott Company, 1967.

Fraenkel, M. L. *Economic Education.* New York: Center for Applied Research in Education, 1965.

Francello, Joseph A. "Anthropology for Public Schools: Profits and Pitfalls," *The Social Studies,* No. 56 (December, 1965), pp. 272–275.

Greenstein, Fred I. *Children and Politics.* New Haven, Conn.: Yale University Press, 1965.

Hess, Robert D., and Judith V. Torney. *The Development of Political Attitudes in Children.* Chicago: Aldine Publishing Company, 1967.

Hunt, Elgin F. *Social Science,* 3rd ed. New York: The Macmillan Company, 1966.

Jarolimek, John, and Huber M. Walsh. *Readings for Social Studies in Elementary Education,* 2nd ed. New York: The Macmillan Company, 1969.

Joint Council on Economic Education, 2 West 46th St., New York, N.Y. Has many materials on economic education available at low cost.

Joyce, Bruce. "Social Sciencing: New Concept in the Social Studies," *Instructor,* No. 78 (October, 1968), pp. 85–92.

McLendon, Jonathon C., William W. Joyce, and John R. Lee. *Readings on Elementary Social Studies: Emerging Changes,* 2nd ed. Boston: Allyn & Bacon, Inc., 1970.

Mial, D. J. "Behavioral Science in the Classroom," *NEA Journal,* No. 57 (March, 1968), pp. 21–22.

Michaelis, John U., and A. Montgomery Johnston. *The Social Sciences: Foundations of the Social Studies.* Boston: Allyn & Bacon, Inc., 1965.

Morrissett, Irving, ed. *Concepts and Structure in the New Social Science Curricula.* New York: Holt, Rinehart & Winston, Inc., 1967.

Muessig, Raymond H., and Vincent R. Rogers, eds. *Social Science Seminar Series* (volumes on anthropology, economics, political science and sociology). Columbus, Ohio: Charles E. Merrill Books, Inc., 1965.

Preston, Ralph C. *Teaching Social Studies in the Elementary School,* 3rd ed. New York: Holt, Rinehart & Winston, Inc., 1968.

Price, Roy A. *New Viewpoints in the Social Sciences,* 28th Yearbook. Washington, D.C.: National Council for the Social Studies, 1958.

Quigley, Charles N. *Your Rights and Responsibilities as an American Citizen.* Boston: Ginn and Company, 1967.

Rogers, Vincent R., ed. *A Sourcebook for Social Studies.* New York: The Macmillan Company, 1969.

Roselle, Daniel. "Citizenship Goals for a New Age," *Social Education,* XXX, No. 6 (October, 1966), pp. 415–420.

"The Elementary School: Focus on Anthropology," *Social Education,* XXXII, No. 3 (March, 1968), pp. 245–259. A collection of articles devoted to the teaching of anthropology in the elementary school.

"The Elementary School: Focus on Economics," *Social Education,* XXXII, No. 1 (January, 1968), pp. 47–62. A series of articles discussing the role of economics in elementary school social studies programs.

Vernon, Glenn M. *Human Interaction: An Introduction to Sociology.* New York: Ronald Press Company, 1965.

Wrench, David F. *Psychology: A Social Approach.* New York: McGraw-Hill Book Company, Inc., 1969.

Current Affairs in the Social Studies

The professional literature indicates a considerable number of articles dealing with the general topic of "Current Affairs Teaching" under the headings of "Current Affairs," "Current Events," "Current Issues," "Current History," and "Contemporary Affairs." Although there is some difference in terminology, with each term implying a slightly different shade of meaning, there is general consensus among the authors of the articles that teaching current affairs in some form must be an essential part of the curriculum. Good beginnings in the elementary school are important in this respect.

The term *current affairs* is used in this chapter because it includes both events and issues and is broader in scope

9

than any of the other terms taken singly. A current *event* is simply something that is happening or has happened recently; it may be significant or it may be trivial. A current *issue* implies a degree of controversy concerning a contemporary problem that may or may not be resolved at a future time. The two terms are obviously closely related, because an event can precipitate a problem that becomes an issue. There is a place for both current events and current issues in the elementary school social studies program.

The point of view to be developed in this chapter is that the program of current affairs is a matter of importance in the school program, and as such, requires careful planning and teaching. Pupils cannot be subjected to several years of boring experiences with current affairs in school and leave school convinced that they have any responsibility to keep themselves informed on the affairs of the world. Pupils cannot have news sharing while the teacher takes roll, collects lunch money, completes plans for another lesson, or does other things about the room that draws his full attention from the news reports. The teacher could not successfully teach mathematics, reading, or spelling in this manner, and there is no reason to believe that current affairs can be taught with any degree of success in this way either. Poor teaching of current affairs is worse than none at all, for such depressing experiences subvert any natural curiosity the child might have had about current happenings.

Writing in *Social Education*, Smith summarizes the importance of current affairs in the elementary school:

> The current events program, properly carried out, stands to provide that most important link between gaining new knowledge and the application of that knowledge to something which is immediately important. Within the program, too, can be developed the process of learning how to think critically and to judge realistically how the world works. For many years, current events appear to have been thought of as a part, but essentially an unplanned part, of a sound elementary school program in social studies. That day has passed; today current events understandings are a necessity for the intelligent and inquiring mind, no less so for children in elementary school than for students in secondary school and for adults.[1]

Purposes of Current Affairs Instruction

The underpinnings for responsible democratic citizenship and its attendant knowledges, attitudes, and skills must be established fairly early in the child's life if they are to be well learned. One of the funda-

1. Lloyd L. Smith, "Current Events for the Elementary School," *Social Education*, XXV, No. 2, February, 1961, p. 81.

mental responsibilities of the individual citizen in a democracy is that he keep himself informed on matters that affect him and the society in which he lives. With changes occurring as rapidly as they do in the contemporary dynamic world, the matter of being well informed becomes a formidable and continuing task. It means that information gathered in or out of school to be used in the future may become obsolete by the time it is needed. For example, most adults studied Africa as a continent of possessions and colonies of outside nations. Although this is of interest historically, it is a woefully inaccurate picture of Africa today. The only way the citizen can keep himself up-to-date on the rapidly changing course of events is to develop and maintain a continuing interest in current affairs as reported via the various news mediums. If the nation expects its adults to have a permanent interest in news and current developments and have a sincere desire to keep informed, the groundwork for these attitudes, interests, and skills must be laid in the elementary school. The first major purpose of current affairs teaching at the elementary school level is, therefore, *to promote interest in current affairs and news developments.*

Intelligent consideration of current affairs requires the use of a variety of skills and abilities: (1) to read news materials; (2) to discriminate between important and less-significant news items; (3) to take a position on issues based on a knowledge and a critical evaluation of the facts of both sides; and (4) to predict likely consequences in terms of present developments. *Promoting the growth of these skills and abilities represents the second major purpose of current affairs instruction at the elementary school level.* These skills evolve over several years through the study of current affairs under the direction and guidance of capable teachers and do not appear full blown when the child enters high school or achieves voting age. It is unrealistic to hope for an adult population that can exercise critical judgment concerning current problems and issues unless individuals have at their command the fundamental skills and abilities such action demands.

The third major purpose of current affairs teaching is *to help the child relate school learning to life outside school.* The constant reference to current affairs is good insurance against the separation of school activities from the nonacademic life of the child. Good teachers recognize that printed material begins to become obsolete shortly after it is written, and there is always a gap between the information contained in books and changing developments in the world. A generous use of current affairs materials helps to close this gap. Several encyclopedias now recognize the need for timely information and publish annual supplements that include changes that have occurred during the preceding year. Because textbooks and supplementary books are not revised each year, it is necessary to depend on such sources as newspapers and magazines for the latest information on some topics. The practice of selecting topics for social studies units from the immediate surroundings and life of the child also underscores the need to use current materials.

The Program of Current Affairs Instruction

Current affairs can be included in the elementary school program in a variety of ways. The three most common methods are (1) teaching current affairs in addition to social studies, (2) using current affairs to supplement or reinforce the regular social studies program, and (3) using current affairs as the basis for social studies units. A discussion of each of these methods follows.

Teaching Current Affairs in Addition to Social Studies. Miss Hansen, who teaches fourth grade, plans to spend a few minutes each morning during the sharing period for the discussion of important news stories. She encourages children to bring news clippings from daily newspapers or to bring weekly magazines for the class bulletin board. Children are encouraged to bring news stories related to classroom work, and Miss Hansen helps interpret these stories for the children by her comments and leading questions, such as

"How do you suppose the new highway will help our town?"
"What are the explorers looking for on these expeditions?"
"Why do you suppose the animals died when they were brought here?"
"Can you show the class on the wall map the exact location of the splash-down?"

Miss Hansen uses a classroom periodical and plans to spend a half hour on it with the children each week. This consists of reading the material, or portions of it, with a discussion following. She varies the procedure from week to week and uses the suggestions provided in the teacher's edition that accompanies the classroom periodical.

Using Current Affairs to Supplement or Reinforce the Regular Social Studies Program. Mr. Ray schedules his social studies period immediately following morning opening activities for his fifth-grade class. As a part of the beginning activities, he provides time for the reporting of news articles and encourages children to report news items related to the unit under study. He and his class maintain a news bulletin board as well as a small table on which are placed news articles, magazines, current maps, or similar materials of a timely nature related to the social studies unit underway in the class. He uses current affairs materials in this way to augment other instructional resources and as a means of sensitizing his class to the need for up-to-date information in a rapidly changing world.

Mr. Ray often suggests parallels to his pupils between events that happened long ago and events that are occurring today, thereby illustrating recurrent problems in the conduct of human affairs. For example, in the study of the struggle for freedom and independence in America, he used examples from present-day affairs to show that some peoples of the world are still struggling for the right to govern themselves. When the class studied early explorers, Mr. Ray related this study to present-day exploration. In the unit on the Westward Movement, he called the attention of the class to current population movements and trends in the United States.

Using Current Affairs as the Basis for Social Studies Units. Mrs. Bell likes to develop social studies units with her sixth-grade class around topics that are currently in the news. She does this between the regular units she is required to teach during the year. During her years of experience as a teacher, she has found that units of this type must be carefully selected because it is not always possible to find a sufficient amount of instructional material suitable for children that deals with topics in the news. Units that she has taught with success in this manner in the past have dealt with alliances, such as the Organization of American States; conservation of natural resources; migration of the world's people as a result of news of newcomers to the United States; twentieth-century explorers; progress in science, medicine, and industry; and elections. When Mrs. Bell selects the unit topics carefully, she finds it possible to include much of the subject matter ordinarily included in her program under other unit titles. She feels that the use of current news happenings as a starting point for units does much to stimulate interest and discussion among her pupils.

Teaching Current Affairs Successfully

Any of the three current affairs programs described here can be used successfully. In good programs there will be time during the school day devoted to the study and discussion of current affairs that may be entirely unrelated to topics under study in the social studies units or unrelated to any other curricular area for that matter. At the same time, in guiding unit work, the teacher will not ignore current affairs relating to the topic being studied but will, in fact, seek with interest the current affairs materials that will add strength to the unit. From time to time, too, the teacher and children can plan an entire social studies unit from current news developments. Units dealing with the topics of conservation, safety, intercultural relations, weather, housing, food, elections, discoveries in science, and items of local news may, and frequently do, grow out of current affairs. When the social studies program includes these three methods, the teacher and class will use any or all of the procedures described in the following sections.

Daily Discussion of News Topics. Children enjoy discussing the news and should be given the opportunity to do so within the school program. It is a fairly common procedure for classes to have a morning meeting or sharing period at the beginning of each school day, during which time the children can report news items. Children in the primary grades frequently report only news that affects them directly: Daddy took an airplane trip, the family has a new baby, the pet cat had kittens, or other similar items of "news." As children mature, they move away from news items that are of concern only to them personally to news of more general interest. However, even primary-grade children sometimes report news of national significance if the item affects them closely. For example, if the President of the United States were to visit the community, primary-grade children would surely report the event although they, of course, would not grasp the full significance of it.

In the reporting, discussing, and consideration of daily news occurrences, elementary school children frequently report the sensational headline news that may or may not be particularly significant. Without guidance, children are likely to report murders or robberies or hold post-mortems on the previous night's television programs. The teacher must expect to get some of this from them because the newspapers, television, and radio news reports stress the sensational in lead stories. He should use these opportunities to help children evaluate the importance of news stories in terms of the number of persons affected by the event and the reasons why it received the attention it did. These experiences help the child develop his powers of critical thinking and his ability to discriminate between significant news and the sensational.

In general, the practice of reporting news should be encouraged by the teacher rather than required. Some teachers require children to bring news clippings on specified days. This usually means a hurried breakfast for the child while his mother peruses the morning or evening paper hoping to find a suitable item that she can explain to the child before he leaves for school. A better procedure is to build the child's interest in news to the extent that he voluntarily brings news clippings that he feels are important enough to bring to school. Similarly, in the reporting of news items, there will be days when there will be many items and much discussion; other days there may be none. The teacher must bear in mind that his purpose is to *develop interest* in current affairs and that this is usually not done by requiring children to spend specified amounts of time on news, whether the content justifies the time or not. The teacher's role in fostering interest is one of leadership, encouragement, and example. Worthwhile discussion and sharing of news and current affairs will be more fruitful if the teacher assumes the responsibility to help children build their discussion techniques. The reader is referred to Chapter 12 where these procedures are discussed.

As children approach the middle and upper grades, they will not only report news events but will begin to include issues on which there are conflicting points of view. This should be encouraged, and eventually the emphasis can be placed almost entirely on problems and issues rather than on simple events. In the primary grades, the current affairs material will perforce consist mainly of the reporting of events because of the immaturity of the children, their limited background of knowledge, lack of interest, and the inappropriateness of many problems in terms of the young child's life, needs, and interests. The movement from the consideration of simple events to simple issues to complex issues is a gradual one for the child; good teaching, combined with worthwhile experiences at each level, will enhance his chances of developing skill at the next level.

When controversial issues are considered by the class, the teacher will find a number of special problems presenting themselves. Some teachers are so fearful of precipitating community ill will and pressure that they avoid consideration of any and all problems that are even mildly controversial. This is unfortunate and unfair to the child who needs to develop his skills in handling problems of this type if he is to live in a world in which he is surrounded by controversy and conflicting points of view. Good sense and mature judgment would dictate that the teacher avoid issues that may cause severe and intense feeling among parents and that can cause the wrath of the community to descend on the school. It happens that problems of this type are usually not well suited for study by the elementary school child anyway. The best problems for discussion are those that are mildly controversial but that deal with material that is significant and within the realm of experience of the child. This does not mean issues must be limited to local problems. Many adults would be surprised at the extent of knowledge elementary school children have on problems of national or international import and the intelligent manner in which they are able to discuss them.

In teaching controversial issues, the teacher has a special responsibility to help children develop habits of critical judgment and open-mindedness, to evaluate sources of information, and to appraise the soundness of facts. Young children are impressionable, and the habit of insisting on getting multiple sides of a question before taking a stand can be taught to youngsters by the teacher's example. There has been some discussion of the necessity of the teacher's keeping his own stand on issues unknown to the pupils. This is not possible or entirely desirable. To be sure, the teacher does not begin the discussion of an issue by stating his own attitude to the class. It is incumbent on him to see that both sides are presented fairly and impartially and that the reasons underlying both points of view are thoroughly aired. If the class requests his feelings on an issue, he has the right to make his views known and to state the reasons for the position he takes, if he so desires. Of course, he has a professional obligation not to attempt to impose his point of view on the children on issues that are unsettled and on which there may be honest differences of opinion among well-informed persons. In such cases, the teacher might encourage children to discuss the matter with other adults whom they respect but whose views may differ from his. The child thus learns that there may be honest differences of opinion among persons who consider problems in good faith without accompanying feelings of ill will and rancor. The children will respect the teacher who is willing to take a stand on issues, who gives his reasons for feeling the way he does, and who accepts and honors the differences in the points of view of others.[2]

Use of a News Bulletin Board. The news bulletin board serves a purpose similar to the science corner in science teaching or similar to the reading table in the teaching of reading. The teacher should prepare to display interesting news pictures and news stories to which the child can turn for information concerning current affairs. Too often, news bulletin boards are tucked away in some obscure corner of the room and are largely ignored by those for whom they are intended—the children. Because items on the news bulletin board are changed frequently, it should be in a place in the room where children pass regularly. A point near the doorway is a good location for a news bulletin board because they can stop to examine it for a moment or two on their way in and out of the classroom during the school day.

The stories displayed on news bulletin boards must be selected carefully, and it must be kept in mind that they are to be read by children. It is good procedure to discuss the significance of the news articles in class before they are posted on the bulletin board. The display should contain not only the items of news of complex national and international problems, but also the items of local interest, sports stories, developments in science, people in the news, perhaps even oddities and jokes for variety and spice. When some thought is given

2. Often, school districts, states, or professional organizations issue policy statements concerning the handling of controversial issues in the schools. One such statement adopted by the Colorado State Board of Education is included in the Appendix on pages 519–520.

to the selection of the items, to the physical arrangement, to orderliness and design, to the use of eye-catching leads, the children will be enthusiastic about using the news bulletin board. As the children bring their own news clippings to class, these, too, can be placed on display. It is generally helpful to have various sections of the bulletin board specifically designated for such groupings as local news, science in the news, news of our country, and words in the news. This serves as a means of organizing the display in a meaningful and attractive way.

Use of a News Map. In the middle and upper grades, the news map can be used to teach current affairs. A world map is displayed in the center of a bulletin board allowing sufficient space around the map for the posting of current news clippings or pictures. Colored string or narrow strips of paper can then be used to connect the news story with the location of the spot where the event occurred. This has the value of combining the study of current affairs with the development of map-reading skills. Children should have a major responsibility for keeping the news map up-to-date and for handling the mechanics of its preparation. It is a special kind of bulletin board display, and much of what was said in connection with the selection and posting of material for the news bulletin board would also apply to the news map. It is also possible to subscribe to a commercially prepared news map published weekly during the school year.[3]

Use of a Classroom Newspaper. Many teachers consider the classroom newspaper or periodical an indispensable tool in the teaching of current affairs. These materials have a number of definite strengths as well as some limitations that are frequently overlooked. The limitations of classroom current affairs periodicals lie not so much in the make-up of them but in the manner in which they are used. The papers themselves are generally well prepared. Companies producing these materials have editorial advisory staffs composed of nationally recognized educators in the field of elementary education, and their editorial staffs consist of carefully selected and highly qualified personnel. Three of the better-known sources of classroom periodicals are

American Education Publications, Education Center, Columbus, Ohio 43216: *My Weekly Reader*, kindergarten through grade 6; *Current Events*, grades 7 through 8.
The Civic Education Service, Inc., 1733 K St., Washington, D.C.: *Young Citizen*, grades 5 and 6; *Junior Review*, grades 7 and 8.
Scholastic Magazines, 50 W. 44th Street, New York, N.Y. 10036: *Let's Find Out*, kindergarten; *News Pilot*, grade 1; *News Ranger*, grade 2; *News Trails*, grade 3; *News Explorer*, grade 4; *Young*

3. Newsmap of the Week, 7300 Linden Avenue, Skokie, Illinois 60076.

Citizen, grade 5; *Newstime*, grades 5 and 6; *Junior Scholastic*, grades 7 and 8.

The chief strengths of the classroom newspaper are (1) its careful attention to reading difficulty, (2) its selection of current materials that are significant yet within the comprehension of the pupil, (3) its unbiased presentation, and (4) the common background of information it presents to the class. These advantages cannot be obtained through the use of any other single source. They are designed and published for the express and specific purpose of use by pupils in a classroom, and, therefore, their writing style, readability, and illustrations are planned with this purpose in mind. They are superior to the newspaper or periodical designed for adult use.

Classroom periodicals also have some limitations of which the teacher should be aware. Even though the readability is carefully controlled, there is no published material that will meet the reading needs of every pupil in the class. Some children will find the material too difficult; others will find it too simple. The teacher, therefore, should not assume he has solved his reading problem through the adoption of a classroom periodical. There is a tendency of teachers to formalize the teaching of current affairs through the use of such a medium. One period a week is set aside for "current events" consisting of the reading of the paper followed by what is called "discussion" but amounts to the presentation of some questions by the teacher to be answered by the pupils. Overemphasis on the formal use of classroom periodicals crowds out the consideration of current affairs from the remainder of the curriculum. These materials should not be used in this manner, and such procedures represent a misuse of them.

A third limitation of classroom periodicals is that they select items of general interest either nationally or internationally and cannot deal adequately with local news. The teacher will find it necessary to turn to local sources for such news items. This is another reminder to the teacher not to depend entirely on the classroom periodical to carry the entire current affairs program.

In a sense, the classroom periodical is the "textbook" for current affairs, and its use should be governed by the same pedagogical principles that apply to the use of textbooks generally. The best use cannot be made of these materials when the teacher passes out identical copies of classroom newspapers to children and gives no more instruction than, "Read your paper, and we will discuss it when you have finished," although this procedure in various forms is fairly common in middle- and upper-grade classrooms. This lifeless approach is almost certain to dull the child's interest in current affairs.

The service bulletins that accompany classroom periodicals often suggest ways to make good use of the papers. If the best use is to be made of these instructional materials, a procedure similar to this will need to be followed:

The teacher prepares himself—
> Read the periodical and accompanying teachers' edition.
> Keep up-to-date on current affairs by regularly reading an adult newspaper and news magazine and by listening to radio and television newscasts.
> Build your own background on topics included in the classroom periodical.
> Plan how to use the periodical and vary the procedure from week to week.

The teacher prepares the classroom—
> Post related pictures, maps, and diagrams on bulletin board.
> Have additional references available.
> Place new words and terms on the chalkboard.

The teacher prepares the pupils—
> Present the periodical to the class by calling attention to a picture, a map, or a particular story.
> Discuss reasons why certain topics are in the news.
> Develop meanings of new words and terms.
> Use maps and the globe to orient pupils.
> Develop purposes for reading.
> Differentiate requirements to provide for individual differences.
> Use the bulletin board, pictures, other visual aids to motivate the class and to develop concepts.
> Plan any special activities relating to the news stories, such as reports, dramatic presentations, and panels.

The pupils read the periodical—
> Vary the reading assignments according to reading ability.
> Have specific purposes for the reading.
> Be available to assist with difficult vocabulary.
> Direct the study of slower-reading pupils.
> Have additional references on topics for more-advanced pupils.

The teacher and pupils conduct discussion and follow-up—
> Discuss the periodical in terms of the purposes established.
> Relate news stories to other classroom work.
> Have pupils present any special activities that were planned.
> Make generous use of maps and the globe.
> Synthesize and summarize ideas and conclusions reached.
> Plan further research or other creative follow-up activities.

Use of Daily Newspapers. Some teachers in the middle and

The newspaper should be a primary source of information for pupils in the upper grades. Better use can be made of it when pupils are instructed on how to read a newspaper, as the teacher in this photograph is doing. (Courtesy of the Seattle Public Schools)

upper grades find a daily newspaper helpful in promoting the goals of current affairs instruction. Newspapers may be in the classroom on a daily basis or may be brought in from time to time for specific purposes. In units dealing with aspects of communication, the newspaper is an important learning resource. Pupils will profit from classroom instruction on the use of the newspaper that focuses on items such as these:

1. The organization of newspapers, purposes of various sections, where to look for certain kinds of information
2. The nature of news stories, why some appear on the front page and others elsewhere
3. The purpose and use of headlines
4. Newspaper illustrations; wire photos, maps, charts, graphs, cartoons

5. The editorial page and its function
6. Detecting bias in news stories
7. How to read a newspaper

Use of a Variety of Activities. There are a number of learning activities that can be profitably used to study current affairs. The teacher must bear in mind, however, that activities, projects, and devices are only means of achieving the purposes of current affairs instruction and are not in and of themselves important. Properly used, any of the following activities can be applied in the teaching of current affairs:

Round-table discussions—dividing the class into five or six discussion groups, each to discuss the question, "How would a twelve-month school year affect the lives of schoolchildren?" Each group would be responsible to present to the entire class a short four- or five-sentence summary of its major ideas.

Having panel discussions—selecting five children to prepare a twenty-minute presentation to the class on some topic currently in the news. These five children would be given a few days or a week to prepare the presentation and would be the class "experts" on the topic discussed. After the presentation, the remainder of the class could ask questions, clarify points, or add to what the panel has said.

Making charts, maps, graphs—showing increases in school population, steps in an event that led to a crisis, decline or increase in employment, the number of highway accidents over a holiday weekend, the route of a recent air flight of importance, and so on.

Constructing posters, murals—to emphasize safe living, progress in preventive medicine, changes in air travel, progress into space, and other topics.

Keeping scrapbooks of news stories or pictures—clipping and keeping the headlines from the evening paper for several weeks. This helps children to distinguish between news stories that are of continuing interest and those that are transitory in nature. Collections of news clippings can be a valuable resource if the topic selected is one that is likely to be in the news for a period of several weeks or months. Careful selection of articles in the scrapbook will allow the class to follow the development of the news story on a continuing basis.

Drawing cartoons to illustrate news—can be used effectively with older children. Care must be taken to avoid having children draw cartoons that might be offensive to individuals or groups. Cartoons dealing with a community fund drive, a sports story, safety or health habits, conservation practices, good citizenship, and other topics can be used.

Giving reports—is a widely used technique for handling current affairs by having individuals report news items to the class. Chapter 12 discusses procedures for handling pupils' reports, and the reader will find specific suggestions for such procedures there.

Conducting radio news programs—can be used from time to time to dramatize news stories. Children can take turns as reporters; variety can be obtained by using a tape recorder and playing the recorded "broadcast" for the class or for other classes.

Dramatizing news events—when they lend themselves to dramatization. Not all do, but items dealing with festivals, meetings, conferences, and negotiations can be used.

Listening to live radio broadcasts—when classrooms have radios as a part of the room equipment. These can be used for listening to standard news broadcasts or for special events of interest. One teacher arranged the morning program in such a way that the class tuned in five minutes of news each day at eleven o'clock.

Viewing telecasts of special events—reporting inaugurations, visits of foreign dignitaries, advances in the space program, and other newsworthy programs can be used for in-school viewing by older children in the elementary school. Children can also be encouraged to view news programs out of school and report on these to their classmates.

The quality of current affairs instruction at the elementary school level depends finally on the teacher. All the desirable outcomes of current affairs instruction must be exemplified by the teacher himself. This is effectively stated by R. S. Kimball when he says,

> That current events can be taught successfully when a teacher is sufficiently interested to bestir himself is attested by most of the subjective appraisals as well as by the few objective studies which have found their way into print. The varying degrees of success, however, seem to indicate that the ability of the teacher, rather than the quality of the medium or the method, is the determining factor. Almost any device *can* be used effectively. The teacher's own interests, his own enthusiasms, his own understanding of what should be accomplished are the matters which determine the failure or success of current events teaching. The best available media fail of their purpose when used by a class guided by a teacher unskilled in methods of current events instruction; the poorest seem to accord some measure of success when a capable current events teacher works with his pupils.[4]

4. R. S. Kimball, "Researches in the Teaching of Contemporary Affairs and the Identification of Needed Research," *The Teaching of Contemporary Affairs*, 21st Yearbook, Washington, D.C.: National Council for the Social Studies, 1951, p. 207.

Discussion Questions and Suggested Activities

1. Can you think of historical events that remain issues to the present day? Do you think the distinction between "events" and "issues" is a satisfactory one?
2. Make a list of the standards a teacher should use in evaluating and selecting current event and current events materials for classroom use.
3. Examine sample copies of a classroom newspaper such as the *Weekly Reader*. What provisions can the classroom teacher make to insure that the use of such materials is not restricted to reading exercises?
4. What would be some of the strengths and weaknesses of a social studies program built entirely around current affairs?
5. Identify current events that would be suitable for inclusion in your resource unit (Chapter 3). Prepare a bulletin board for one of these events.
6. How can map- and globe-reading be related to the study and consideration of current affairs? What possibilities can you see for geographical and historical study related to current affairs?
7. The morning meeting, sharing period, or "show and tell" commonly include some discussion of current affairs. These periods too often become dull and routine for both the children and the teacher. Think of some ways the teacher might make the most of these periods by injecting some life and vigor into them. Develop specific methods of handling these periods in order to make them more interesting and worthwhile for the children.
8. Record a news broadcast from a local radio station. How would you use this broadcast with upper-grade children? Prepare a teaching plan for the broadcast and then present the broadcast and your lesson to your classmates.

Selected References

Brackenbury, Robert L. "A Case for Controversy," *The National Elementary Principal*, 42 (April, 1963), pp. 14–19.

Controversial Issues in the Classroom. Washington, D.C.: The National Education Association, 1961.

Crabtree, Charlotte. "Resources for Teaching About the World: Elementary," *Educational Leadership*, 21 (March, 1964), pp. 355–357.

Cummings, Howard H., and Harry Bard. "How to Use Daily Newspapers," How to Do It Series, No. 5, rev. ed. Washington, D.C.: National Council for the Social Studies, 1964.

Fraser, Dorothy M. "Current Affairs, Special Events, and Civic Participation," *Social Studies in Elementary Schools,* 32nd Yearbook, Washington, D.C.: National Council for the Social Studies, 1962.

Full, Harold. *Controversy in American Education: An Anthology of Crucial Issues.* New York: The Macmillan Company, 1967.

Kelley, Earl. "Teaching Current Issues in the Schools," *Improving the Social Studies Curriculum,* 26th Yearbook, Washington, D.C.: National Council for the Social Studies, 1955.

Mowry, Carolyn I. "Teaching Values Through Today's News," *Instructor, LXXVII,* No. 7 (March, 1968), pp. 62+.

Sheridan, Jack. "Thursday Is Current Events Day," *Social Education, XXXII,* No. 5 (May, 1968), p. 461.

Smith, Lloyd L. "Current Events for the Elementary School," *Social Education, XXV,* No. 2 (February, 1961), pp. 75–78.

Tiedt, Sidney W., and Iris M. Tiedt. "Teaching Current Events," *The Social Studies, 58,* No. 3 (March, 1967), pp. 112–114.

Wass, Philmore B. "Improving Current Events Instruction," *Social Education, XXV,* No. 2 (February, 1961), pp. 79–81.

Wesley, Edgar Bruce, and William H. Cartwright. *Teaching Social Studies in Elementary Schools.* Boston: D. C. Heath & Company, 1968.

Wilson, Richard C. "Using News to Teach Geography," *Social Education, XXIV,* No. 2 (February, 1960), pp. 56–57.

Environmental Education: Ecology

A newspaper headline tells us " 'E' IS FOR ECOLOGY—New Aim for Education—Teaching Johnny to Survive." [1] A conference of the American Trial Lawyers Association is told that legal battles to stop the ruin of the environment are absolutely necessary. *Time* magazine and *Saturday Review* introduce new sections called "Environment." These are only three examples of hundreds that might have been selected to illustrate the rise of concern throughout the land over the effects of environmental contamination on the quality of life. In a feature story for Associated Press, Saul Pett describes the situation in part as follows:

1. Seattle *Post-Intelligencer*, March 8, 1970.

We have polluted the land and the air and the water, defaced the horizon with commercial clutter and blurred our history and our symbols with dollar signs.

We have left Lake Erie beyond redemption and Lake Tahoe beyond recognition.

We have pasteurized our milk and put Strontium 90 in its source and enough waste in streams and lakes to kill 15 million fish in one year.

We have turned the New England farm of Robert Frost into an auto junk yard and built high-risers that block the view of Mt. Rainier in Seattle and the bay in San Francisco and the surf at Waikiki and countless other vistas that nourish the soul of man.

We have put enough smog into the air over Los Angeles to warn school children not to play too strenuously or breathe too keenly on the days of the dark amber clouds and enough toxics in the air over New York to make a day's walking and breathing equal to the intake of almost two packs of cigarettes.

And between the two coasts we have made eyes smart in mile-high Denver and not-as-high Phoenix and countless smaller places once idyllic.

We have put DDT in the shellfish off Martha's Vineyard . . . and human excrement in Sugar Creek, Charlotte, North Carolina.

In his story, Mr. Pett has dramatically and vividly portrayed an obviously unsatisfactory relationship between man and what was once called America, the Beautiful.[2]

The scientific study of the relationships between living organisms and the environment is known as *ecology*. The web of life, constituting the systematic and balanced relationships between living things and their surroundings, is known as an *ecosystem*. National and state leadership, along with publicity in the popular press, have given rise to a long-overdue anxiety over ecological problems relating to man. During 1969, the Gallup Poll conducted a survey for the National Wildlife Association relating to public attitudes toward environmental conditions. Of the individuals interviewed, half indicated they were *deeply* concerned about the effects of air and water pollution, soil erosion, and the destruction of wildlife on our natural surroundings. Another one third of the respondents indicated that they were *somewhat* concerned. A dramatic example of frustration and outrage over the problem was the passage of a bill by the California State Senate in 1969 by a vote of twenty-six to five banning the sale of gasoline- and diesel-powered internal-combustion engines beginning January 1, 1975! (The bill was later defeated by the California Assembly.)

The scientific data concerning the impact of modern man on his

2. Mr. Pett entitled his article "America, the What?" Seattle *Post-Intelligencer*, February 15, 1970.

environment do, indeed, provide sufficient reason to be anxious. If we continue at the present rate of contamination, there is the genuine possibility that this planet could experience something in the way of an "eco-catastrophe" in the foreseeable future. This does not necessarily mean that as a result of such a disaster the planet would be uninhabitable but that the quality of life would be reduced substantially below the present level. Danger signals can be obtained from almost any of modern man's activities but the most significant ones seem to be (1) the use of pesticides, (2) the disposition of solid wastes, (3) air pollution, (4) water pollution, (5) radiation and radioactive substances, and (6) overpopulation.

When European settlers first came to this hemisphere, the incredible vastness and abundance of this area gave no rise to thoughts of concern for the environment. There was fresh water aplenty. Forests and trees were in such abundance that they were perceived as obstacles to land use. There was no shortage of places to dispose of solid wastes. There were no internal-combustion engines or other devices creating large quantities of harmful hydrocarbons to pollute the air. The forests and streams were well stocked with wildlife and fish. What happened in the three hundred years that followed provides us with a shocking case study of unbelievable exploitation and waste and an almost total lack of concern for the consequences of this behavior. All this is now too familiar history.

The present concern for quality of living as related to environmental contamination relates to earlier efforts in the general area of conservation. The concept of conservation—meaning prudent use—has a reasonably long history in this country. Even during the colonial period some of the thoughtful men of the time (among them Washington and Jefferson) were concerned with conservation in the broad sense. During the middle of the nineteenth century, conservation efforts were institutionalized, largely as a result of rapidly diminishing forest resources. The U.S. Department of Agriculture established a Division of Forestry in 1880. Federal legislation during the last half of the nineteenth century and extending into this century encouraged conservation and conservation education.[3]

The amount of legislation dealing with environmental control has grown at a phenomenal rate in recent years. At the federal level, a few of the major measures have been the Federal Water Pollution Control Act of 1956, the Clean Air Act of 1963, amended in 1965 and 1966, the Water Quality Act of 1965, the Water Resources Planning Act of

3. A few of the major acts are these: the Morrill Act of 1862, establishing land-grant colleges; the Hatch Experiment Station Act of 1887; the Smith-Lever Act of 1914; the General Mining Laws of 1872; the Soil Conservation Act of 1935; the Taylor Grazing Act of 1934; and the Wildlife Restoration Act of 1937.

ENVIRONMENTAL EDUCATION:
ECOLOGY

1965, and the Clean Water Restoration Act of 1966. State legislatures have been particularly vigorous in dealing with environmental issues. For example, at a short, special session of the Washington State Legislature early in 1970, the following bills were introduced:

1. A bill establishing a Department of Environmental Quality
2. A Surface Mining Act (to regulate surface and open-pit mining)
3. A Nuclear Siting Bill (to plan on a statewide basis the best location for nuclear power stations)
4. A Seacoast Management Act (to provide guidelines for the use of the seacoast)
5. A Rivers and Seashore Inventory Bill
6. An Effluent Standards Bill
7. An Oil Spills Bill

It is clear that the turning point in contamination has now been reached and that man—in this country at least—will henceforth not be allowed to contaminate his surroundings with the same abandon as he has been able to do in the past. Almost everywhere in this nation local and state laws, following the lead of the federal authorities, are becoming much more strict in their control of human behavior that further contributes to environmental problems. More is being done to correct past mistakes than ever before. Similarly, educational programs are being implemented to help citizens utilize their surroundings more wisely. Recognition of the need for major remedial efforts to alleviate environmental pollution is growing.

Environmental studies are, of course, not the sole province of the social studies. The subject of environment and its use and misuse by man is such a comprehensive one that it can be studied from many points of view. It can be approached from the standpoint of science education, for, clearly, much of our polluted environment is a direct consequence of science and technology. Likewise, the subject is appropriate for health education, because research has established relationships between air pollution and respiratory ailments such as asthma, emphysema, lung cancer, and bronchitis. Certainly environmental studies have geographic, esthetic, sociological, economic, and even political dimensions. Thus the broad topic is highly appropriate for social studies programs because of its implications for human societies and human life. It is an ideal subject for interdisciplinary studies.

A program of environmental studies should concern itself with three types of broad goals:

1. It should provide the pupil an opportunity to develop a basic understanding of the dimensions of the problem, the causes and

consequences of ecological disaster, the remedial measures now underway, the need for additional corrective legislation and action, *and* similar inputs of information that bear on this important problem.

2. It should help the pupil develop an attitude of responsible concern for the quality of the environment. It should leave him with the feeling that he has a personal investment in his natural surroundings—that the environment truly is everybody's business.

3. It should provide him with the opportunity to do something himself about improving the environment. That is, if goals 1 and 2 are concerned with knowledge, thinking, and valuing, this goal constitutes the action dimension of the program.

Studies of the environment as broadly defined here should be included in the social studies curriculum in at least two ways. First, every unit studied should include attention to related environmental problems throughout the entire curriculum when the topic under study lends itself to such an emphasis. This will include most topics, as can be seen by examining the typical unit title on pages 50–54. Second, every grade should include one unit of study each year devoted entirely to the systematic treatment of environmental problems. This program should be planned on a K–12 basis in order to develop important learnings cumulatively as children progress through the grades.

Key Concepts in Environmental Education

The program of instruction that leads to understandings, awareness, and action with respect to the quality of the environment should focus on a limited number of basic ideas. These key concepts can be defined along a continuum of complexity and included in the curriculum at several points. Such a basic idea as the need for food by all living creatures can be dealt with in a simple way in the primary grades in the context of the units on family living, the local community, changing seasons, or meeting basic needs. In the upper elementary school grades this idea can be expanded and made more complex by getting into such dimensions of it as food chains and webs of life.

What gives environmental studies vitality and freshness is a spontaneity and originality not often found when teaching conventional unit topics. Because the subject is relatively new, teachers can engage in some degree of innovation that usually leads to good teaching and learning. In the past, we have had conservation units and units on outdoor education but those are not the same as the present emphasis on

Pupils of all ages can be involved in action programs relating to the environment. (Courtesy of the *Northshore Citizen*, Bothell, Washington)

the total environment and quality of living. Thus, teachers should welcome the openness of the curriculum with respect to environmental education and should seize upon the opportunity to develop imaginative learning possibilities for pupils. Therefore, the planned curriculum might provide ideas, identify emphases, suggest activities, and list learning resources but at the same time should not freeze these plans in a fixed pattern of instruction. If there is anything that will kill inspired teaching and learning in this field, it is a rigid, stereotyped curriculum lacking in any opportunity for originality and action.

The following key ideas are being suggested to provide a focus for studies dealing with the environment. They are not the only ones that could be used; indeed, they are probably not even the best ones for all locations in the country. They are, rather, a *sample* of ideas that can be and have been used as central organizing ideas for environmental studies:

1. Man is now facing critical environmental problems of his own doing.
2. The most imminent problem facing man is food shortage.
3. The problem of food shortage is presently differentially distributed around the world but could ultimately affect all mankind.
4. Some rehabilitation of the environment and greater restraint of its use are needed in order to maintain an acceptable quality of life.
5. Most of what man does has a detrimental effect on natural balances because it interferes with natural communities.
6. The earth is a self-contained, self-sustaining life-support system, consisting of an infinite number of ecosystems.
7. All living organisms fit into a complex environmental interrelationship known as a food chain.
8. The food supply for all living organisms depends ultimately on sunlight, soil, air, and water; consequently, anything that destroys these essential resources disturbs the quality of life.
9. All living organisms in some way affect and are affected by their environment.
10. Living things must have minimum space requirements for optimum development.
11. The quality of man's life depends ultimately on the natural environment that surrounds him.
12. Increase in human population, if continued at the present rate, will, in the long run, have disastrous consequences for man.
13. Waste disposal potentially is at least as severe a problem for modern man as is the fulfillment of basic food needs.
14. The effects of man's presence on his environment has esthetic as well as survival dimensions.

These ideas are suggested as providing a focus for planning instruction. The specific subject matter should and probably will, in most cases, be selected from topics relating to the local region. These studies will undoubtedly be selected in terms of the particular environmental problems relating to the region. Quite naturally, there will be a considerable overlap because many problems are common throughout the country. But case studies and examples should be drawn from the local area.

What follows is a series of specific types of environmental problems around which studies have been planned, along with a few examples of activities teachers have used successfully with elementary school pupils.

POPULATION

Pupil activities to build awareness of rapid growth

1. Using a *World Almanac* or a copy of the U.S. Census, compare the population of the twenty leading cities in 1940, 1950, 1960, and 1970. Are they still ranked in their original order? Which one has increased the most? Why?
2. Make a chart comparing the present-day population of a selected area with its population twenty years ago, one hundred years ago, two hundred years ago.
3. Make a chart comparing the present birth and death rate of a particular area with birth and death rates of 1900.
4. Use the telephone directories of 1940, 1950, 1960, and 1970 to discover growth in such things as (a) schools, (b) hotels and motels, and (c) service stations.

Pupil activities to discover population distribution

1. Using a map and reference books, compare the populations of various parts of the United States. Why do people live where they do? What areas have the fewest people? Could people be moved to those areas? Why or why not?
2. Construct a map showing areas of heavy population in the city, state, nation, or world. Identify sparsely populated areas. Have pupils give reasons for both conditions.
3. Make a chart of the most rapidly growing areas of population in the state, nation, or world. Discuss the reason for the rapid increase in these areas.

Pupil activities to understand the meaning of rapid growth

1. Have pupils use a checkerboard or other similar squares and kernels of corn and try doubling the number of kernels in each square, starting with one. How many squares can be used before there is no longer room to double again? Discuss how this relates to population growth and its implications.
2. Encourage pupils to suggest problems that would be caused by an increase of twice as many persons in their environment.
3. Find pictures of the local area ten, fifteen, and twenty or more years ago. Have pupils discover how it has changed.

LAND AND WATER USE

Pupil activities to sensitize them to the need for concern

1. Creative dramatics: A public meeting is held to protest closing of a lake to fishing. A biologist explains why it was closed. Have pupils discover what he should say. Conduct the drama and include the discussion that followed the biologist's presentation.
2. Compare reports of your state from the 1850's with those of the present day on some animal, fish, or bird. Identify the reasons for the change.
3. Collect pictures from newspapers and magazines showing misuse of land. Have pupils suggest remedial measures for improved use or what might have been done by foresighted planners to have prevented the misuse from occurring.
4. Obtain data on acres of land under cultivation in 1940, 1950, 1960, and 1970, in the local area. Have pupils find out why changes occurred.
5. Have pupils list ways that productive farmland is used for other purposes, for example, for urban sprawl, for freeway construction, as land flooded or submerged behind dams.

TRANSPORTATION

Pupil activities to understand problems of congestion

1. Construct a chart to compare the amount of space on a highway required to transport 40 persons in 40 cars as compared with that required to transport 40 persons in a bus.
2. On a local map, identify points of congestion and hours of highest congestion. Study traffic flows and suggest alternative routes.
3. Prepare a map of the local area showing existing transportation routes. Prepare another map showing an improved arrangement.
4. Show by illustration how air, water, and noise pollution are related to transportation.
5. Carry out a roadside improvement project. This could be a clean-up campaign or the planting of trees, shrubs, flowers.

NOISE POLLUTION

Pupil activities to sensitize them to the problem

1. Make a tape of various sources of noise pollution. Use this to build awareness of sounds in the environment.

2. Demonstrate instruments that measure level of sound. Measure the level of sound in and around school at various times of the day.
3. Demonstrate familiar sounds of noise pollution such as that of jet planes, stereo rock music, motors, machines, horns, and construction.
4. Take a field trip into the local area to build awareness of sound. Identify points of especially high noise pollution.
5. Make a map of the local area and label the places with most noises as found in Entry 4.
6. Prepare guidelines to reduce noise at home and at school. Develop a program of action to reduce noise.

AIR POLLUTION

Pupil activities to understand dimensions of the problem

1. Construct a map of the local region showing places of highest pollution. Explain why these areas have a high level of pollution.
2. Have pupils discover the major sources of air pollution. Present these on charts.
3. Have the class visit a meeting of the local Air Pollution Control Board. Discuss issues considered by the board.
4. Show by illustration why air pollution cannot be only a local problem.
5. Relate air pollutants to problems of health.
6. Discover effects of air pollution on vegetation.

WATER POLLUTION

Pupil activities to understand the relationship of polluted waters to recreation

1. Have pupils discover major sources of water pollution in the local area. Prepare a chart showing those sources. Discuss. Present the chart to local government officials.
2. Make a map of a specified area through which a large river flows. Find out if and/or to what extent the river becomes polluted as it flows.
3. On a map of the United States, identify water bodies that once were contaminated but that have been rehabilitated.
4. Select a water body in the local area that is not available for recreation because of contamination. Plan a strategy to have it rehabilitated. Present the plan to local officials. Begin a movement to mobilize public opinion in support of such an action.

Parents, pupils, and teachers can combine efforts in improving the quality of the environment, as is illustrated here. (Courtesy of the Shoreline Public Schools, Seattle)

The activities just listed above are provided simply as examples of things that pupils can do. They are not meaningful unless they are placed within the context of a larger study. Just to do the activity would hardly be sound teaching and would probably not lead to good learning.

Not all schools in the country have instructional resource centers that provide the teacher with the tools he needs for teaching. But in the case of environmental education, every school does have an instructional resource center immediately at hand. All that is required is an imaginative teacher who will open the door of the classroom and step outside. What better instructional center is there for environmental education than the local natural surroundings. Happily it makes no difference if the school is located in the most congested section of our largest cities or in a remote rural area. Wherever one is, he has an environment that can profitably be studied.

Former Secretary of Interior Stuart Udall is quoted as saying that the 1970's would be the "environmental decade." It appears that his prediction will be borne out if news stories, television programs, and the discourse of public officials are to be taken as indicators. Even in the field of professional education itself there is an awareness, at long last, of the importance of environmental education. Summer and weekend workshops are being offered on ecology. Special extension classes are being prepared by colleges and universities. At this writing, one state, Washington, has created a new position in the state superintendent's office called Environmental Education Supervisor, the first in the United States. With this attention being given environmental education, one can be confident that there will be an abundance of newly developed learning resources on this topic in the near future. The teacher is advised to follow the professional journals for up-to-date listings.

Activities for Conservation Education

Some schools may choose to focus on conservation education rather than on the broader topic of environment. Although it is not possible to suggest a great number of learning activities and resources for soil, water, wildlife, mineral, and forest conservation education because of space limitations, the teacher may find the following suggestions helpful. They are intended to serve as *samples* of activities that have been used with success with elementary school-age children.

Use the many good films now available on the topic of conservation. They are thoughtfully prepared, use modern photographic techniques and color to present forcefully the problem of waste and the need for better conservation practices.

Take field trips to local conservation or ranger stations, fish hatcheries, farms, and local parks.

Invite speakers to class. Persons such as the county agent, a ranger, an "ag" teacher from the local high school, a member of an outdoor or recreation club are logical men to invite.

Build library resources by increasing the school's supply of books and articles pertaining to conservation.

Relate soil fertility in various ways to plant food elements and community prosperity.

Develop and exchange correspondence with children from different parts of the country, asking for firsthand information of their local conservation problems and what is being done to correct them.

Illustrate in various ways the time needed to recover resources and the impossibility of recovering some resources lost through waste.

Familiarize the pupil with the interest and action of government (local, county, state, and national) in conservation.

Integrate conservation education of such groups as Boy Scouts and Girl Scouts, 4-H club, Future Farmers of America, Camp Fire Girls, and other youth groups with the school program.

Place instructional emphasis on new developments in conservation due to the application of scientific knowledge—new uses of resources, more productive farmland, new flood-control techniques, new energy sources.

Conduct numerous experiments dealing with conservation:
1. Collect runoff water and determine what it carries.
2. Test a sample of soil for organic matter.
3. Discover how and why grass protects soil.
4. Demonstrate the effect of rapidly falling water on soil.
5. Test the productivity of various types of soil.

Contact various agencies that have an interest in or dedication to the cause of conservation for suggestions, teaching materials, or help. Some are listed here.

American Forest Products Industries, Inc.,
    1816 N St., N.W., Washington, D.C. 20036.
American Forestry Association,
    919 17th St., N.W., Washington, D.C. 20036.
American Nature Association,
    1214 16th St., N.W., Washington, D.C. 20036.
Bituminous Coal Institute,
    1425 H St., N.W., Washington, D.C. 20036.
Conservation Education Association,
    Eastern Montana College of Education, Billings, Mont.
Conservation Foundation,
    30 E. 40th St., New York, N.Y. 10016.
Garden Club of America,
    Conservation and Roadside Committee, 15 E. 58th St., New York, N.Y. 10022.
Izaak Walton League of America,
    31 N. State St., Chicago, Ill.
Keep America Beautiful, Inc.,
    99 Park Ave., New York, N.Y. 10016.
National Audubon Society,
    1130 Fifth Ave., New York, N.Y.
National Coal Association,
    Southern Building, 15th and H Streets, N.W., Washington, D.C. 20036.

National Education Association,
  1201 16th St., N.W., Washington, D.C. 20036.
National Geographic Society,
  17th and M Streets, N.W., Washington, D.C. 20036.
National Wildlife Federation,
  232 Carrol St., N.W., Washington, D.C. 20036.
Superintendent of Documents,
  U.S. Government Printing Office, Washington, D.C. 20025.
U.S. Department of Agriculture,
  Forest Service and Conservation Service,
  Washington, D.C. 20025.
U.S. Department of Health, Education, and Welfare,
  Office of Education, Washington, D.C. 20025.
U.S. Department of Interior, Bureau of Reclamation, Fish and Wildlife Service, or National Park Service.
Wild Flower Preservation Society, Inc.,
  3740 Oliver St., N.W., Washington, D.C. 20015.
Home State: Department of Conservation
            Department of Natural Resources
Local: Office of the county agent.

Conservation education requires a multipronged approach if effective attitudes of conservation are to be developed. The inclusion of occasional units on conservation in the elementary school social studies program are, in themselves, an inadequate solution to the problem of conservation education. It requires the combined efforts of communities, parents, and schools. It also requires a sensitivity to the relationship of such attitudes as thrift, frugality, economy, and temperateness to conservation.

Discussion Questions and Suggested Activities

1. Construct a chart illustrating the web-of-life concept. Prepare questions based on the chart that would be suitable for use with elementary school pupils for the purpose of clarifying this concept.
2. Man has been described as (1) the maker of machines, (2) the domesticator of plants and animals, (3) the reshaper of the earth, (4) the hunter and gatherer, and (5) the inventor. How have each of these characteristics affected the way man uses the earth? Give an illustration of how pupils might discover relationships between the basic nature of man and his use of the earth.
3. If you have not done so, plan to visit a meeting of one of the following: (1) air pollution control board, (2) city planning com-

mission, (3) board of appeals (zoning and construction variance concerns), and (4) legislative committee on environmental problems. Make a report of your visit to your class.

4. Search out leaders of local conservation clubs. Find out what the major goals and purposes of these organizations are.
5. On what basis might one argue that no animal is really "harmful"?
6. How does man's humanitarian attitudes sometimes get in the way of maintaining a balance in natural communities?
7. What do you see as the most important *outcomes* of environmental education? Write five behavioral objectives relating to environmental education for a grade of your choice.
8. How would you respond to a pupil who asked, "Does it really matter if fish and birds are killed by water pollution as long as their loss does not affect our food supply?"
9. Select a picture that illustrates an environmental problem. Construct six reflective-type questions based on the picture.

Selected References

"America's Changing Environment," *Daedulus*, XCVI (Fall, 1967).

Carson, Rachel L. *Silent Spring*. Boston: Houghton Mifflin Company, 1962.

Dasmann, Raymond F. *A Different Kind of Country*. New York: The Macmillan Company, 1968.

Dasmann, Raymond F. *Environmental Conservation*, rev. ed. New York: John Wiley & Sons, Inc., 1968.

Dorst, Jean. *Before Nature Dies*. Boston: Houghton Mifflin Company, 1970.

Hammerman, Donald R. and William M. *Teaching in the Outdoors*. Minneapolis, Minn.: Burgess Publishing Company, 1964.

Jaffee, Joyce. *Conservation: Maintaining the Natural Balance*. Garden City, N.Y.: Doubleday & Company, Inc., Natural History Press, 1970.

Journal of Geography, LXIX, No. 5 (May, 1970). Contains a series of articles concerning environmental education.

Linton, Ron. *Terracide—America's Destruction of Her Living Environment*. Boston: Little, Brown and Company, 1970.

Michelson, Max. *The Environmental Revolution*. New York: McGraw-Hill Book Company, Inc., 1970.

Nash, Roderick. *Wilderness and the American Mind*. New Haven, Conn.: Yale University Press, 1967.

Pinchot Institute for Conservation Studies. *The Future of Conservation Education*. Milford, Pa. The Institute, 1966.

President's Council on Recreation and Natural Beauty. *From Sea to*

Shining Sea. Washington, D.C.: U.S. Government Printing Office, 1968.

Reid, Keith. *Nature's Network.* Garden City, N.Y.: Doubleday & Company, Inc., Natural History Press, 1970.

Reveille, Roger, and H. H. Landsberg, eds. *America's Changing Environment.* Boston: Houghton Mifflin Company, 1970.

Roosevelt, Nicholas. *Conservation: Now or Never.* New York: Dodd, Mead & Company, Inc., 1970.

Swan, James. "The Challenge of Environmental Education," *Phi Delta Kappan,* LI, No. 1 (September, 1969), pp. 26–28.

Udall, Stewart L. *1976—Agenda for Tomorrow.* New York: Harcourt, Brace & World, Inc., 1968.

Udall, Stewart L. "Our Perilous Population Explosion," *Saturday Review,* September 2, 1967, pp. 10–13.

Udall, Stewart L. *The Quiet Crisis.* New York: Avon Books, 1963.

Reading Social Studies Materials

Reading continues to be the most important and essential skill for learning included in the curriculum of the elementary school. The child who is retarded in reading is likely to find himself in difficulty in most of his other school work. Some learnings can be achieved visually or through careful listening, but these experiences cannot completely substitute for reading. In spite of the many changes that have occurred in teaching procedures in modern times and in spite of the introduction of new materials and media that reduce the reading requirement for some pupils, school programs still depend heavily on reading as a means of learning. The situation is summarized by Fay in a single sentence: "The evidence is clear, both from re-

11

search and from the experience of countless teachers, that after the primary grades it becomes increasingly more difficult to be poor in reading and good in the content subjects." [1] Good elementary school programs, therefore, provide time during the school day when a major effort is directed toward the development of general reading skills. During these times the child will develop a basic reading vocabulary; he will learn to use various word recognition techniques, develop independence in reading, and learn to read critically and to evaluate what he has read. He will learn to use reading as a help in solving problems and will be taught other skills and abilities that characterize the fluent, independent reader. This is all to the good, but a strong basic reading program will not be able to meet all the reading needs of children because each area of the school curriculum presents the child with a reading task somewhat unique to that special area. Helping children develop the specific reading skills and abilities associated with each area of the curriculum must, therefore, go hand in hand with other instruction in the special-subject area. This point of view is supported by almost all authorities in the field of reading who have addressed themselves to the problem.

The special reading skills and abilities needed to handle social studies material intelligently may be identified by examining textbooks and supplementary references written for children. Typically, these books have a heavy loading of complex and involved concepts, many of which the child is expected to remember as background information for ideas to be presented later. This characteristic of social studies books oftentimes precludes the possibility of entering the book at arbitrary points, because the child may lack sufficient understanding of concepts presented and developed in earlier sections of the book. Topics read about are frequently remote from the child in both time and space. He reads about places, persons, and events that had their setting many years ago—perhaps several centuries in the past. Or he may read of places, persons, or events that are contemporary but have their setting in some remote section of the world. The social studies do not always deal in absolute quantities and values, making necessary much interpretation of what is read. This calls for critical reading and analysis—not an easy assignment for young children. The vocabulary of social studies is formidable and presents a major obstacle to fluent reading. The innumerable references to quantitative concepts complicate reading as do referrals to maps, charts, figures, and diagrams. Finally, the research nature of social studies topics

1. Leo Fay, "Responsibility for and Methods of Promoting Growth in Reading in Content Areas," *Better Readers for Our Times*, International Reading Association Conference Proceedings, Vol. 1, New York: Scholastic Magazine, 1956, p. 89.

necessitates the use of reference tools, and the child is handicapped if he does not know where to find them or how to use them efficiently once they are found. Serious study of the nature of social studies reading materials will sensitize the teacher to the complex reading task the child faces as he approaches this area of the school curriculum.

It is important to emphasize that reading in the social studies is an intellectual, thinking process. Thus, problems in reading social studies in the middle and upper grades are probably a reflection of an inability to conceptualize and to handle the ideas being presented through the symbolic system of print more than the inability to handle the mechanics of reading. Once this is recognized by the teacher, he is less likely to be overly concerned about simplifying vocabulary, shortening sentences, and making other structural modifications. He will be more concerned about building meanings into concepts and terms needed to understand certain topics. For example, a middle- or upper-grade pupil may be confronted with a reading selection in which trade and commerce are discussed. This subject cannot be meaningfully presented without including at least some of the following concepts and terms: cargo, shipping, import, export, tariff, duty, hold, freight, tonnage, stevedore, boom, merchant, commercial, and barge. If these terms are eliminated from the selection, it is no longer an essay on trade and commerce.

This is not to say that the reading task cannot be simplified by careful attention to vocabulary and structural elements. The essential point is that the intelligent presentation of specialized subjects and topics in print requires the use of the terms, words, and concepts peculiar to those subjects and topics. Moreover, the reader is not going to understand the passage unless he knows the meanings of the terms, words, and concepts used. Thus, it is inevitable that pupils with limited conceptual ability are going to have difficulty reading complex social studies material, and no amount of drill on the mechanics of reading (such as sounding out words or phonetic drill) is likely to contribute much to improved reading. The problem is basically an intellectual one.

It is evident that the teacher will have to assume the responsibility of developing reading skills concurrently with other social studies learnings. Although the developmental reading program should teach the child the more fundamental and general reading abilities and skills, it is within the social studies that the child will extend and refine those special reading skills and abilities that apply to this area. Instruction should be directed toward the comprehension, interpretation, and organization of ideas, the understanding of word meanings, and the use of reference sources.

From time to time, the teacher needs to provide reading instruction to small groups of pupils in connection with work in the social studies. (Courtesy of the Northshore School District, Bothell, Washington)

Learning to Comprehend Ideas

Reading social studies with comprehension means that the reader is able to extract from the selection the essential facts and understandings, visualize details, and sense the relatedness of the facts presented. It is a process of obtaining an understanding of the meaning the author was attempting to convey when the material was written. Comprehension depends on a number of related factors, some of which reside within the reader and others that deal with the selection to be read. Because of the complexity of the psychological processes involved in comprehension, as well as the limitations of printed symbols as a means of conveying meaning, it is doubtful that the reader is ever able to obtain the exact and precise shade of meaning intended by the author. Teachers can help children read social studies materials with greater understanding, however, if proper consideration is given to the factors known to affect reading comprehension. These factors are discussed subsequently.

General Intellectual Level of the Reader.   It is axiomatic to say that the child who brings the most to a reading situation will receive the most in return. In most cases, the teacher can help increase what the child brings to the reading situation by building backgrounds of experience, increasing vocabulary, elevating the general reading ability of the child, and building a sufficient readiness. The teacher cannot, however, raise the basic intellectual ability of children and, consequently, must adjust and arrange the reading environment to suit the needs of individual pupils. As the teacher grows to know the capabilities of the various children in his class, he will be careful not to give them reading material he knows they are incapable of handling. This applies directly to the use of textbooks, because there are children in most unselected grade groups who do not have the intellectual maturity to deal with the multiplicity of complex concepts presented. It is entirely possible for the child to have the mechanical aspects of reading mastered sufficiently well to read the words involved in the selection and yet be totally incapable of gaining meaning from the passage. This, again, calls attention to the fact that "writing down" material by simplifying vocabulary is no guarantee that comprehension problems will vanish. The need in cases of this kind is to select reading material that deals with the concepts under study at a level that is within the limits of the individual child's ability. This is why the recommendation was made in Chapter 3 that, if a textbook *must* be used with all pupils, the teacher select only certain portions of it for slower-learning or slower-reading children.

Problems of reading comprehension may be less apparent with the capable children than with the slow-learning ones. The capable readers frequently find the normal social studies reading requirements at such a simple level of comprehension that they develop slovenly habits of reading. Their reading skills are sufficiently well developed for most purposes, the ideas presented seem simple for them to understand, and they experience no real challenge or difficulty. The teacher will want to provide material of sufficient difficulty to challenge the capabilities of the most able children and, at times, require them to do very careful and detailed reading when the material demands such reading.

Experience Background of the Reader.   The ability to comprehend ideas and facts depends to a considerable extent on the experience background of the reader. In any reading situation the understanding the reader obtains from the selection will be related to the background of experience that can be brought to bear on the material under consideration. The child who has visited Yellowstone National Park will find the reading material concerning Yellowstone much more meaningful than the child who has not had such an experience. He reads meaning into such words as *geyser, mud-pots,* and *canyon* that the next child cannot possibly obtain. He can relive his experiences with the pesky Yellowstone bears and almost sense the smell of sulphur coming from the boiling mud-pots. This child's ability to read the Yellowstone selection with understanding has been greatly enhanced by his personal experience with the ideas, words, and concepts presented. Generally speaking, the more experiences the child has had with the world about him, the greater will be his capacity for comprehending ideas.

As has already been noted, the social studies frequently deal with topics and concepts outside the realm of direct experience of young children. Even a study of the home state and its institutions may seem remote to a child growing up in a rural area. Because the understanding of new ideas must always be made within the context of previous understandings and experiences, the building of backgrounds for intelligent reading of social studies is extremely important. Bond and Wagner make this quite clear: "The need to build backgrounds of understanding, essential to reading is rarely more acute than in the social studies. The need to relate the material read to the experiences of the child is essential to his understanding of its concepts." [2]

The teacher must plan a number of classroom activities to help build backgrounds for better understanding. Some of these will be direct experiences, others will be vicarious. The reading comprehension of a third-grade class is likely to be improved if, in connection with its study of communication, the class visits a post office or a television studio and talks with the various persons who work there. The possibility of short field trips into the community for the purpose of extending and enriching the experiential backgrounds of children exists in every community. Teachers may also make use of motion pictures to build a common background of experience when a direct experience is impossible or impractical. When teachers properly anticipate the comprehension problems the children are likely to encounter and are sufficiently concerned with them, they will make extensive use of field trips, films, pictures, stories, exhibits, displays, and real objects. Experiences of this type will provide the moorings for the vicarious experiences obtained through reading and will assist the child in comprehending ideas.

Adjusting Speed of Reading to the Reading Task. Comprehension and speed of reading may or may not be related factors. The poor reader may read at a snail's pace and also comprehend very little of what he reads. The good reader, on the other hand, may read rapidly and have an adequate understanding of the ideas presented. Under

2. Guy L. Bond and Eva Wagner, *Teaching the Child to Read,* 4th ed., New York: The Macmillan Company, 1966, p. 282.

This teacher is building the backgrounds of experience of these pupils in order for them to gain a better understanding of what is being read. (Courtesy of the Seattle Public Schools)

ordinary conditions the difficulty of the material *as it appears to the reader* will determine the rate of speed at which it should be read. In this sense, children should be taught that rate of reading is variable, and they make adjustments in speed appropriate to the degree of comprehension necessary.

It happens that much social studies material is of such a nature that slow and painstakingly careful reading is needed to comprehend the facts presented. There are long and involved sentences, facts to remember, names, places, dates, difficult vocabulary—none of which can be skimmed over lightly. As a regular part of the social studies instruction, the teacher should devise reading situations that will require the children to vary their rate of reading for a particular purpose. This may be in the form of questions, some calling for rapid reading or skimming, others for more detailed careful reading and rereading. Commonly, the answers to names of places, persons, situations, dates, and similar factual data can be obtained through skimming, whereas answers to reflective questions will require slower, more careful reading.

Difficulty of the Topic. Some topics in social studies are more easily understood than others, and, therefore, reading comprehension is more of a problem in dealing with some topics than with others. A narrative account of lumbering in the Pacific Northwest is straightforward and relatively simple to understand. Most children can read selections of this type rapidly and keep their comprehension high. On the other hand the child may encounter a passage that explains the topic "Why Seasons Change." This is an exceedingly complex idea and will require the most careful reading the child can muster if it is to be understood. Certainly, the difficulty of the topic is associated with the reader's general intellectual level; but, even so, many topics present more problems in comprehension than others, because of their complexity. These are the ones that will require the best efforts of the brightest child and the best reader. The teacher will want to identify topics that may prove difficult and single them out for special consideration.

Word Difficulties. Vocabulary difficulties have a direct bearing on reading comprehension, and the vocabulary load of social studies materials is heavy. Because word difficulties present the serious problem they do, this entire matter will be discussed at length in a subsequent section.

Organization of Materials. Social studies reading material can be organized in such a way to make comprehension easier for the reader. Many books use topic headings, margin notes, italics, boldface type, or other techniques to call attention to significant details. Moreover, many of the newer textbooks present material at the beginning of chapters and sections that suggest things for which to look, questions to direct the reader, and other introductory material that serves as readiness for the topic to be discussed in the reading. Likewise, at the conclusion of sections, there are frequently questions, vocabulary exercises, ways to check reading skills, and things to talk about that aid the young reader in understanding the selection. Teachers should look for and use reading material organized in a manner that will be helpful in developing comprehension skills. Time must be taken to explain the organization of material to the children and to instruct them in the use of the various aids presented in selections read. In learning about the organization of the material, children are also learning skills associated with organizing their own ideas for better understanding. The teacher should not assume that because a book or selection to be read is well organized and presents many aids to the reader these aids will be used by all children. It is the teacher's responsibility to help children become efficient readers through the use of aids for a better understanding of the material they read.

The success with which children are able to comprehend social studies reading materials will depend on the extent to which the teacher is aware of the factors bearing on comprehension and the degree to which he makes allowances for them in his teaching. In this connection, he may find the following suggestions helpful.

INCREASING COMPREHENSION OF READING MATERIALS

1. Extend and enrich the background of experiences and understandings of children. This can be done through
   a. Field trips—around the school and immediate area, places of interest and import in the community.
   b. Use of authentic pictures, bulletin board displays, travel folders, study prints, models, realia.
   c. Audio-visual aids—films, filmstrips, television viewing, radio, recordings, 8 mm filmloops (single concept films), and transparencies.
   d. Language experiences—discussion, planning, creative dramatics, vocabulary-building.
   e. Recording group experiences on experience charts, log of activities, vocabulary lists.
   f. Providing a rich variety of books to allow children to read widely on topics related to the study.
   g. Relating social studies reading to other activities in the classroom such as construction, dramatization, discussion, and research.
   h. Utilizing human resources of the community.
2. Develop meanings of new words, phrases, or terms before the selection is read. Specific suggestions for this purpose may be found in the section entitled "Understanding Word Meanings" in this chapter.
3. Have children cite examples or exceptions from their own experiences that illustrate some point made in the reading.
4. Help children identify purposes for which the material is read. As a matter of principle, the children should always be instructed to "Read to find out. . . ."
5. Teach children how to use study helps, subtitles, marginal notes, pictures, and other visual materials included in all social studies books for the express purpose of aiding comprehension.
6. Provide numerous opportunities for discussion of ideas encountered in the selection. It is also helpful for the teacher to give short oral explanations of some points—these explanations should not, of course, contain concepts or words not understood by the children.

7. Following the reading, children should apply and use some of the important ideas gained from the reading. These might be
   a. Dramatizing a situation described in the selection.
   b. Constructing an interesting object described in the reading.
   c. Making or collecting pictures related to the ideas presented.
   d. Responding to questions concerning important ideas developed in the reading.
   e. Doing additional reading or research on certain ideas presented.
   f. Writing paragraphs or short selections expressing the reader's feelings concerning some issue or situation described.
   g. Having children demonstrate some process described in the reading—candle dipping, quarter notching, churning butter, a pioneer game.
8. From time to time give direct instruction for developing better comprehension and follow this with practice material that will require the child to read social studies material for varying purposes such as reading to
   a. Answer a specific question.
   b. Obtain evidence or draw conclusions.
   c. Get the general idea of the selection.
   d. Verify a statement.
   e. Obtain all the details that relate to or support an idea.
   f. Relate cause to effect.
   g. Contrast different points of view.
   h. Identify materials relevant to a generalization.
9. Provide materials of a wide range of difficulty to accommodate the varying intellectual levels found in elementary grade classrooms.
10. Teach children how to use typographical devices (italics, boldface type, spacing), punctuation marks, and connectives (*and, but, first, consequently, i.e., e.g.,* etc.).
11. Teach pupils to adjust reading speed to the nature of the material and the purpose of the reading.

Learning to Interpret Ideas

Reading comprehension in the strictest sense involves getting the facts as they are presented by the author. It happens that social studies materials oftentimes require that the reader interpret the ideas he has read. This involves making inferences, sensing relationships, noting cause-and-effect occurrences, detecting the emotional bias of the author, reading critically, evaluating the material, and being able to anticipate or predict likely outcomes from the facts presented in the selection. This ability demands summoning of the greatest power of thought available to the reader; it depends to a considerable extent on his intellectual stature, his maturity, and his experience. It requires him to go beyond the literal presentation of the facts and to sense the significance of them. This process is referred to as "reading between and beyond the lines." Consider the following example that might be a passage from a selection read by fifth-graders:

> All day long the wagon train moved slowly westward. The travelers were tired and weary from the long, dusty journey. The wagonmaster looked at his watch. It was four o'clock, but the sun was still high in the sky. Directly ahead was the river that had to be crossed. On the other side was high ground. Near the river bank was a fine grove of trees. The wagonmaster wondered if he should have the tired travelers cross the river yet today or camp on this side of the river and cross over the first thing in the morning. He decided to make the crossing that evening.

Now answer these questions: (1) In what season of the year were the people traveling? (2) Why do you suppose the wagonmaster decided in favor of crossing that evening? Notice that the material does not give the answers to either of the questions, yet the answers can be inferred from the information given. Many passages in social studies books lend themselves to questions of this type. Typically, however, the types of questions asked by the teacher or by the text call simply for the restatement of information given. Teachers who do not allow children to deviate from "what the book says" or who concern themselves only with having children get the facts or who present children with inane material that contains nothing of import in the lines, let alone between them, thereby contribute little toward the development of interpretive skills in children's reading.

Being able to interpret ideas and grasp their significance is a complex, thinking, creative process. It demands a critical analysis of the ideas presented, selecting only those that can be brought to bear on the problem at hand and projecting these data into a more generalized framework. That this type of critical thinking is difficult even for the mature adult is not to be denied. Obviously, children in the elementary school are not going to master such skills, but they can be helped to make a good beginning. This can be done by helping children draw conclusions and state generalizations, by making comparisons, by suggesting relationships, by helping children sense the need for suspended judgment, and by other similar experiences. Research in children's thinking supports the view that reasoning and problem-solving abilities begin at about age three and develop continually with increasing age and experience. Stimulating experiences in critical thinking and problem solving during the formative years of early childhood can do much to foster the growth of such skills throughout the life of the individual. The choice of the type of inferential thinking, problem solving, and interpretive situations selected would be made, of course, within the limits of the young child's maturity and experience.

There will be many occasions when the teacher will be able to assist children develop the skills and abilities needed to interpret social studies materials. The following suggestions may be helpful.

DEVELOPING INTERPRETIVE SKILLS AND ABILITIES

1. In establishing purposes for reading or constructing work-study questions, be sure to include some items that require an interpretation of the facts presented in the selection. Questions dealing with such situations as these are helpful:

   a. Tell how one set of facts shows something else to be true.

   b. Have children list similarities and differences between situations studied. In community studies, for example, the children might be asked to list similarities in the ways of living of people they are presently studying with the ways of living of people in other communities.

   c. Have children respond to cause-and-effect situations.

   d. Ask children to predict what is likely to happen next or what might have happened in a situation had some of the circumstances been altered.

   e. Include *why* type questions more frequently than those that call for *who, what, when, where,* and *how many.* Ask for information not directly stated but that can be inferred.

   f. Have children select the two or three *most important* developments that bear on the topic.

   g. Have the children check the validity of selected passages of printed material. The textbook may not serve well for this purpose, but a newspaper or magazine article will often work admirably.

   h. Give children experience in selecting statements of fact and statements of opinion. Help them learn to distinguish between fact and fiction.

2. Use literary materials to help the children develop a mental set or mood appropriate to the social studies topic under study. Children are likely to interpret materials more thoughtfully if they sense the hardships of a pioneer community, the heavy heart of a sorrowful President, the tenseness of a historical period, or the enthusiasm of a young and growing nation. Children can gain such insights

through the use of literary materials now available in great abundance.

3. Show and explain to children how the same set of facts can be used to arrive at differing and oftentimes opposite conclusions. This can usually be done with current affairs issues or with historical materials. Similarly, the teacher can utilize current television programs that deal with contemporary problems or with historical situations for this same purpose.

4. Conduct lessons that concentrate on the development of interpretive skills and follow these with practice exercises containing social studies content.

5. Have children learn about the lives of authors or historical figures to understand better their points of view or bias.

6. Use reaction stories of the type in the American Council on Education's *Reading Ladders for Human Relations* to sensitize children to their own emotional involvement in dealing with social problems.

7. Spend some time acquainting upper-grade children with terms that are emotionally charged and that tend to becloud critical reading and judgment. Upper-grade children can find examples of propaganda devices such as card stacking, glittering generalities, name calling, transfer, plain folks, band wagon, boring from within, and trial balloon.

8. Have children read or, in the case of primary-grade children, listen to selections for the purpose of deciding whether or not they would be suitable for a dramatic skit, the theme for a mural, the basis of a construction activity, a choral-reading situation, oral reading in a program presentation, or similar purposes.

9. Allow children plenty of opportunities for telling what they think of material that has been read. This can even be done and should be done with the simple pictorial material used in the first and second grades. The teacher can stimulate the children's thinking by asking questions such as "Who do you think the man is who is talking to Billy?" "What do you think will happen when Daddy leaves?" "Why is everyone happy in this picture?" "What will the family do if it begins to rain?" "How do you suppose the children feel about that?" Social studies instruction would unquestionably be more profitable for children if teachers slowed the pace, covered fewer topics more adequately, and gave children many more opportunities to do reflective and interpretive reading and thinking.

10. Have children write or draw pictures of what they think is the meaning of certain selections or passages. This procedure will usually reveal to the teacher that children commonly misinterpret material presumed to be simple and easy to understand.

Learning to Organize Ideas

The highly factual nature of much social studies material makes it imperative that the reader organize what has been read in a meaningful manner. The skillful reader will be able to read a passage, select the main ideas, identify subordinate but related facts, arrange related ideas in a sequence, identify ideas relevant to the topic under consideration, and classify information appropriately. Unless the child is able to organize his thinking as he reads social studies, what he reads is likely to be little more than a mass of detail, lacking an understandable order of importance.

The trend in elementary schools toward interdisciplinary social studies programs makes teaching the child how to organize ideas doubly important. Each of the social sciences has its own system or systems of organization. For example, history can be organized around movements, periods, trends, chronology, or topics. Geography can be studied according to regions, physical features, economic factors or studied by areas. When elements are selected from the social sciences and fused into a single study for elementary schoolchildren, as is done in the social studies, problems of organization become complex indeed. It is because teachers are unable to organize social studies ideas themselves that they sometimes find it difficult to teach a unified program. They may, for example, try to impose a historical pattern of organization on a program of instruction that contains within it elements of geography, sociology, or economics, and find this confusing. The first order of business is, therefore, that the teacher himself have a clear understanding of the organizational structure of the material at hand. He will then be able to teach youngsters how to organize it for better understanding.

The teacher should not find it difficult to plan experiences that will give children practice in organizing ideas. The following list of suggestions may help.

EXPERIENCES IN ORGANIZING IDEAS

1. In building readiness for social studies reading, acquaint the child with the organizational pattern of the material:
    a. Point out the use of paragraph headings, italicized words, marginal notes, boldface type, and other features of the selection that aid in organizing the ideas presented.
    b. Give children specific instructions to select the main ideas or the topics of paragraphs or to list the order in which events occurred.

c. Review and discuss with the children material that was read previously and that followed a similar pattern of organization.
d. Have children page through the material quickly and encourage them to ask questions relative to the manner in which the material is organized.
e. Help children understand the organization and structure of the entire book used—how it is divided into units, chapters, sections.

2. Have children write summary statements indicating what they believe to be the most important ideas contained in the selection read. In the primary grades this may take the form of a group enterprise with the teacher writing the summary statements on the chalkboard or on a chart. Children should be able to identify facts that support these main ideas.

3. If the material follows a sequence, the children may be asked to write the events in the order in which they occurred. Or, the teacher may have the events written on the chalkboard and children may be asked to number them in the order in which they occurred. With primary-grade children, this again in likely to be a group enterprise with the teacher asking, "What was the very first thing that happened? What happened next? Are you sure? Do you remember . . . ?" As the children relate the events in the proper order, the teacher writes them on the chalkboard.

4. When a selection consists of several parts, the children may be asked to suggest subtitles for the various sections. If these are already labeled in the reading, the teacher can instruct the children to "Think of another title for the part called 'The Valley of the Sun.' "

5. In highly factual accounts, the children may be asked to state specifically the facts presented. For example, they may be asked to list the persons who are involved in the production and marketing of milk, write the names of the five most important cities mentioned in the article, or give the uses of cotton that the selection describes.

6. As children become familiar with outlining procedures, they may be asked to write the most important ideas and under each one write related but less-important ideas.

7. From time to time give direct instruction on the skills of organizing materials and follow these with appropriate practice exercises. These may deal with finding the main points, recognizing sequence, making a summary statement, or separating details from key ideas.

8. Identify children who are having an unusual amount of difficulty in organizing ideas and give individual help as necessary. The teacher will first want to diagnose the specific nature of the child's problem. What specific problems of organization is the child experiencing?

Is he not able to identify ideas? Does he miss supporting details? Does he not understand the structure of the book? Is he unable to find the topic or thought of paragraphs? When the difficulty has been pinpointed, the teacher directs his teaching efforts toward the removal of the specific difficulty.

9. Teach children how to make notes on what they read, encourage them to keep notes on their research activities and discuss these with them. An inspection of the notes a child makes on his reading will help keep the teacher posted on the progress he is making in organizing social studies ideas.

Understanding Word Meanings

The vocabulary load of social studies reading material is undeniably heavy. It is one of the major causes of poor comprehension and faulty reading in social studies. Even with the more-careful grading and attention that contemporary authors have given to word difficulties, the social studies vocabulary remains a stumbling block for many children. Although a degree of simplification is possible, it is perhaps true that there are definite limits beyond which the use of a specialized vocabulary cannot be avoided. As was noted on page 313, if one is speaking or writing about social studies concepts, he is forced to use the vocabulary appropriate to that field. This is not altogether undesirable if the teacher accepts vocabulary development as one of the goals of the total social studies program. The same situation exists in other areas of the curriculum; the child must learn the language associated with mathematics, science, art, music—all of which have their own peculiar words, terms, or phrases. Vocabulary development in each of the curricular areas, therefore, must be one of the outcomes of the instructional program in all phases of school work.

The teacher can be most helpful to the child in assisting him with word difficulties if the teacher understands the nature of the word difficulties to expect. The following is a discussion of some of the types of words that cause children difficulty.

Technical Words. Technical words are words, terms, or expressions peculiar to social studies and will not be found when reading selections from other organized fields of knowledge. One cannot read social studies materials with understanding unless one has a grasp of its technical language. Technical terms are found less commonly at early grades but become evident in increasingly greater numbers as the child moves into the material written for middle and upper grades. Examples of technical words are *veto, meridian, frontier, latitude, longitude, legislature, polls, franchise, temperate, plateau,* and *hemisphere.*

More often than not, the meanings of these words cannot be obtained through contextual clues. If children are to understand them, the teacher must take time from unit activities and teach the words directly.

Figurative Terms. Figurative expressions are those that have a different connotation from the literal meaning usually associated with the words themselves. They are confusing to the young child because he is likely to visualize the literal meaning rather than the metaphorical one intended. These words and expressions are used extensively in social studies because they are vivid, colorful, and effective. The teacher must make sure the children understand them in order to avoid mistaken visual imagery and, therefore, mistaken and inaccurate understanding of the intended meaning. Examples of figurative terms are *political platform, soil bank, cold war, closed shop, iron curtain, logrolling, banana republics, open door.* Newspapers commonly use such expressions as a basis for headlines and cartoons, thereby placing additional emphasis on their literal meaning. The child may have seen the iron curtain represented in a cartoon as a huge iron wall and recall that representation as he reads his social studies material.

Words with Multiple Meanings. It is well known that some words have a number of different meanings, the appropriate one depending on the context within which the word is used. The reader is always in difficulty when he is familiar with one meaning of the word and finds it used in a situation where its intended meaning is different from the one with which he associates it. Children in the United States, for example, think of the word *state* as meaning a political subdivision of a sovereign nation. To them a state means Oregon, Wisconsin, Indiana, Georgia, or any other of the fifty states. It is easy to understand why the child is confused when he reads about the "states of Western Europe." To him these are not states, they are countries! Similarly, most American children associate the word *minister* with the clergy and interpret terms such as *prime minister* or *foreign minister* to mean church officials. Frequently, the pictures the children see of these officials strengthen their misunderstanding because the dignitaries are shown in formal dress with long, dark coats and hats resembling men of the cloth. Other examples of these words are *cabinet, belt, bill, chamber, mouth, revolution, fork,* and *range.*

Specialized Concepts Unfamiliar to the Children. Social studies materials frequently include specialized concepts that are strange to the pupils because an extensive background of information is required in order to understand them. They may be figurative terms as well, which adds to their complexity. It happens that some terms included in this category require a degree of maturity seldom found in children of elementary school age, yet they appear in the reading material of the social studies. Time and space concepts are good examples of this. Other examples of words, expressions, and concepts that may be classified as specialized and unfamiliar to children are *mountainous, wasteland, balance of power, self-rule, capitalism, democracy, nationalism, civilization, century, ancient,* and *decade.* The meanings of many of these require years of experience and teaching before they are learned, and in some cases they may never be fully understood. For most persons, an understanding of them will broaden and deepen with extended experience and greater maturity.

Terms Peculiar to a Locality. Each section of the country has its own peculiar set of expressions that are not in common use elsewhere. In most cases these expressions are known to outsiders but are not used by them. There are a few terms, however, that are neither used nor understood by those living outside the locality. It is these words that may be confusing when they appear in social studies materials. The word *truck* is sometimes used in social studies to mean *trade;* the child may interpret the word to mean a *motor vehicle* or, in some sections of the country, *to keep company.* ("I'll have no truck with him.") In certain sections, the term *meeting* means a religious gathering rather than the more general gathering of persons for any purpose. Other examples of this type of word are *borough, gandy, draw, coulee, right* (confused with "right good"), *prairie* or *section* (confused with section of land), and *run.* The teacher must alert himself to expressions and words that may have a special meaning in a specific locality and must ascertain as well as teach the meaning intended in the social studies material under study.

Confusing One Word with Another. A child in western Minnesota is familiar with the feeding habits of pheasants because this bird is plentiful in that part of the country. He knows that after the fall harvest, the birds are frequently seen picking up the remaining grain that has been left unharvested or wasted in the harvesting process. In his social studies text he reads about the peasants of Eastern Europe who, in days past, would comb the grain fields and pick up the unharvested or wasted grain. He misreads the word *peasants* and substitutes *pheasants,* obtaining a completely erroneous mental picture of what is involved. Moreover, because of this error he continues to misunderstand the entire passage and complains that it does not make sense.

Every reader has at some time or other made the mistake of confusing one word for another and has found the material lacking sense for him. A more careful rereading may make it more intelligible; a discussion of the passage with another person is almost certain to clarify the meaning. Social studies materials contain many words that are similar in appearance to other words and are easily confused if the child depends too heavily on the general configuration of the word as a recognition technique. Although this technique is a desirable one for the child to have in his repertory, he must also be taught to get meanings of words through the use of contextual clues. Examples of other words commonly confused are *alien* for *allies, principal* for *principle, longitude* for *latitude, executive* for *execution,* and *conversation* for *conservation.* As a matter of procedure the teacher would be well advised to teach at widely separated times meanings of words that are easily confused. To teach them simultaneously almost guarantees that the child will confuse one with the other.

Helping the Child Build Word Meanings. The one best way to help children with word difficulties in social studies is for the teacher to anticipate the difficulties the children are likely to have and make appropriate adjustments *before* they are placed in the reading situation. When this is done, however, words and terms should be presented in the context of a phrase or a sentence rather than in isolation. The exact manner in which this is to be done will, of course, vary from one situation to another, but the following procedures have been used with success by many teachers.

PROCEDURES FOR TEACHING WORD MEANINGS IN SOCIAL STUDIES

1. Writing key words and phrases on the chalkboard and discussing their meanings prior to the reading.
2. Having children keep lists of words they do not understand and securing help from the class or from the teacher in establishing their meanings.
3. Observing the manner in which children use social studies words in their oral reports, class discussions, and written material. This will give the teacher a clue to the words that may need explanation and clarification.
4. Having children write synonyms to social studies terms periodically to check on the extent to which words are being understood.
5. Encouraging children to get meanings of words through context. Because social studies materials contain words with multiple meanings, figurative terms, and words easily confused with others, the need for depending on contextual clues is manifest. Also encourage children to use structural clues in unlocking the meaning of words. Of special significance is the understanding of meanings of affixes.
6. From time to time, holding class discussions to bring out various meanings and derivations of words. This procedure helps condition

the child to the variations in word meanings as well as helps build his interest and curiosity in them.

7. Using visual materials to add meaning to terms that may be encountered in reading. This is standard procedure in clarifying word meanings. Even dictionaries—books solely devoted to explanation of word meanings—include many diagrams, pictures, and charts to clarify meanings. Teachers might well follow this example and use visual materials generously in helping children develop word meanings in the social studies.

8. Providing many firsthand experiences to enrich meanings for children. As previously stated, all meaning obtained from reading is based on previous experiences with reality. The greater the experience background of the reader, the greater is his capacity to gain meaning and understanding of new material. Teachers can assist in this respect by taking the children on field trips related to the unit, bringing real objects to class, or engaging children in activities within the classroom that will give them the desired experiences on which to build meanings of new words, terms, and expressions.

9. Having much reading material available to the child to enable him to read widely. Wide reading has a favorable effect on vocabulary growth, for the child encounters the same words in a variety of settings and thereby acquaints himself with their various shades of meaning.

10. Developing a wholesome attitude on the part of the children toward the use of the dictionary. This can usually *not* be accomplished by making the response "Go look it up" each time a child inquires about the meaning or spelling of a word. Rather, the children should be taught the use of the dictionary; have dictionaries easily available to them and have a good example in the teacher's use of that reference. In the primary grades it is helpful for children to make their own "dictionaries" of new words learned in connection with a social studies unit. Children can bring magazine pictures from home to illustrate the words in their dictionary.

11. Making full use of the helps for vocabulary development that appear in the text or other books used. These include not only the glossary or word list, if there is one, but also the pictures, maps, graphs, charts, and other visual material that accompany the printed material.

12. Having pupils suggest sentences using the same word but with a different meaning of that word.

13. Building recognition of acronyms commonly used in the social studies: UN, NATO, HEW, UNICEF, NAACP, and so on.

Learning to use the library and its references in order to obtain information is an essential reading skill that should be taught in the social studies program. (Courtesy of the Highline Public Schools, Seattle)

Locating and Utilizing Reference Materials

The social studies cover vast areas of knowledge, and no one single book or reference can be expected to do more than present a small segment of the many facets of social studies topics. Furthermore, much of the social studies content is of a highly factual nature, making it impossible for any one person or any one book to have all the facts. Consequently, there is need for the child to learn to locate and utilize many references and sources for the purpose of study and research in the social studies. It is perhaps more important for the citizen to know how to utilize various sources of information than it is for him to amass a great amount of factual data that are used infrequently and that become obsolete quickly.

Social studies units must necessarily make use of a wide variety of reference material. The value of such references depends not only on their availability but also on the ability of the children to make wise

READING SOCIAL STUDIES MATERIALS

use of them. The teacher's responsibility in this respect is, therefore, twofold: teaching children (1) which references to use for various purposes and (2) how to use the reference efficiently once it is found. These are continuing responsibilities of the social studies program and cannot be taught once and for all time in any one grade or any one year. A beginning will be made in the primary grades of the elementary school, but the child will continue to extend and refine his ability to use references throughout high school, college, and in his life outside school. Instruction usually will begin as soon as the child develops a degree of independence in his reading that will allow him to make use of printed material on his own.

The reference materials used in the social studies may be grouped meaningfully as follows:

Books
Textbooks
Supplementary reading books
Picture books
Biographies
Historical fiction

Special References
Encyclopedias
Maps and globes
Atlases
Dictionaries
World Almanac
Charts and graphs
Yearbooks
Legislative Manuals
Who's Who in America
Junior Book of Authors
Statesman's Yearbook

Reference Aids
Card catalogue
The Reader's Guide
Bibliographies

Miscellaneous Materials
Advertisements
Magazines and periodicals
Recipes
City and telephone directories
Labels
Guidebooks and tour books
Letters and diaries
Travel folders
Postcards
Newspapers and news clippings
Comic books
Pictures
Schedules and timetables
Pamphlets and booklets (such as those from the information services of foreign countries, Superintendent of Documents, conservation departments, historical societies, art galleries)
Weather reports
Manufacturers' guarantees and warranties
Money, checks, coupons for premiums, receipts
Reviews, government documents

It is evident that much of the instruction given on the use of references will have to be specific to the particular resource used. For example, one uses the *World Almanac* differently and to obtain different information than one does the atlas or a tour book. Moreover, the references may be utilized at varying levels of sophistication. The library may be used by primary-grade children under teacher guidance to get books, to look at magazines, or to have stories read to them, whereas upper-grade children should be able to use the library independently, making use of the card catalogue and locating books themselves. The use of the various references should be taught as the need for them arises in the social studies at a level consistent with the level of the child's understanding. The teacher will want to make a careful study of the special skills needed to utilize each of the resources correctly in order to instruct children properly in their use. A full treatment of the specific skills needed by the pupil to use references is outside the scope of this book, but the teacher will be able to find such information in any standard work dealing with the teaching of language arts or reading. Insofar as the social studies are concerned, the following suggestions will be helpful.

LEARNING TO USE REFERENCES

In the Primary Grades

1. Acquaint the children with the school library and provide pleasurable experiences for children with this facility by having them look through books, check out books, look at magazines, and have stories read to them. Enlist the help of the librarian if there is one.

2. In units on the market, harbor, post office, trains, farm, airport, and similar topics, provide a reference corner or table well stocked with easy reading and picture books related to the topic.

3. Get in the habit of saying, "Let's look it up!" when there is a question that needs answering. "Looking it up" may mean comparing a sea shell that a child has brought with the picture of one in the book of shells; finding out whether we eat the roots, stems, or leaves of broccoli; finding out about the different kinds of boats and their uses; and hundreds of other questions children wonder about during the course of the unit. It is helpful to have an encyclopedia handy for this purpose. Not all children will be able to use it, but its presence and use by the teacher provides an excellent means of developing positive attitudes toward reference materials.

4. Familiarize the children with the general make-up of standard textbooks. They learn in first grade that books have titles; they learn to use page numbers; they are taught that stories or sections of their books have titles. Gradually, in second and third grades they become more capable in their use of the table of contents as a means of finding a particular story. Provide many incidental references of this type in the regular course of instruction as well as in direct teaching as children are ready for it.

5. Identify the children who are progressing rapidly in reading and teach and encourage them to use references such as the encyclo-

pedia, magazines, pamphlets, and other material from which they can profit but that may be too complex for the majority of the class.

6. Give children experiences in helping to locate materials—finding appropriate pictures, stories, or sections of books that relate to the social studies topic.

7. Develop prerequisite competencies for efficient use of a dictionary: alphabetical ordering, use of guide words, antonyms, synonyms, multiple meanings of words. Primary-grade children could make a class "pictionary" of social studies words and terms they encounter.

In the Middle and Upper Grades

1. Make certain children know how to use the various parts of a book, namely,
   a. The title, copyright page, preface
   b. Table of contents
   c. List of maps, tables, illustrations, figures
   d. Chapter and topic titles or headings
   e. Marginal notes and paragraph headings
   f. Footnotes
   g. Index
   h. Glossary
   i. Appendix

   Take time to review or teach directly the skills needed to use a book and provide some practice in the application of these skills.

2. Take time out to teach children how to use the library, card catalogue, the *Reader's Guide,* or other aids for the purpose of locating information. Provide children with some practice in their use in addition to the functional situations in which these aids are utilized.

3. Teach the various skills needed to use *each* of the special references: encyclopedia, *World Almanac,* atlas. Provide for practice as well as application in purposeful settings.

4. Plan social studies activities that make necessary the utilization of a wide variety of references. The results of such research may be used to plan and present reports, explain a map, prepare a dramatic skit, construct a model, contribute to a discussion, prepare a written report, and so on.

5. Have children browse through the library and other sources to locate material appropriate for the unit under study.

6. Teach children how to identify key words in using reference material. Children may know how to use the references but not know what to look for with regard to the information they are seeking.

7. Teach children how to use titles of books as a guide to content and select books appropriate for the purpose.

If teachers regard the teaching of reading as something that is done in three small groups during the reading period and ignore the reading needs of children during the remainder of the school day, they may expect children to have many disappointing experiences reading social studies material. The feeling that children learn to read in the basic reading program and read to learn in the social studies, for example, is not an entirely correct concept of reading growth and development. Actually, these two processes occur simultaneously; the child improves his reading ability *as he reads to learn.* The child can extend and improve his reading skills and abilities quite apart from the basic reading program as he uses reading for a variety of purposes. In the case of the social studies, if his reading is left unguided, the child's growth in the reading skills and abilities may not occur at all or, at best, may occur in a circuitous manner. The teacher can ensure reading growth by providing instruction in the reading skills and abilities needed in dealing with social studies content.

The teacher's responsibility with respect to the problem of reading in social studies, therefore, goes beyond the matter of providing suitable materials in an adequate amount. It is evident that intelligent reading in this area demands the use of specific reading skills and abilities and that these must be taught along with the understandings, attitudes, and other skills of the social studies. As more attention is given to the development of those abilities and skills, it will become increasingly possible for children to use reading as a helpful tool for learning in the social studies.

Discussion Questions and Suggested Activities

1. Prepare a daily plan that calls for the use of a wide variety of reading resources of varying levels of reading difficulty.
2. Do you think comprehension and interpretation should be separated as they are in the text, or do you think interpretation is a facet of comprehension? Could a pupil have a high rate of comprehension and interpret very little of what he reads?
3. Make a list of the reading skills that should be developed as part of the program of reading instruction. What reading skills are best taught in the social studies?
4. List several terms that will need to be developed in the resource unit you are developing (Chapter 3). How will you use the teaching procedures presented in this chapter in building understanding of these terms?
5. Observe an elementary school classroom during several days of social studies instruction. Which techniques presented in this chapter are most frequently used? Can you point out situations in which other techniques might have been utilized?

6. What particular terms, words, or phrases are peculiar to the locality in which you live? Are any of these related to social studies concepts? How would you teach one of these to an outsider?
7. Choose one of the references listed on page 332. What prerequisite skills must the child have in order to use that reference effectively and efficiently?
8. Pick a social studies topic for a grade of your choice. Make a list of poems, stories, biographies, and other reading sources that develop a strong mental set or mood appropriate to the topic. Read appropriate passages to your classmates.
9. Examine three or four social studies textbooks for a grade in which you have an interest. How can you use the typographical and organizational format to aid the reader in comprehending and organizing the ideas presented?
10. Evaluate the following statement made by a teacher: "I nearly always initiate a unit by having the children read the appropriate pages in their textbook. This is the quickest means by which they can obtain the factual background necessary for classroom discussion."
11. How can the school librarian be of help to you in teaching pupils to locate and utilize reference materials?
12. Secure a textbook for any grade above third. Select ten consecutive pages at random from some section of the book and do a careful word-by-word reading of these pages and note all quantitative concepts. Categorize these according to definite and indefinite references to time, space, and object quantities. Do you find a somewhat heavy loading of such concepts? What effect does this have on reading comprehension? Do you find a close relationship between these concepts and those taught in the mathematics program of that grade?

Selected References

Agrast, Charlotte. "Teach Them to Read Between the Lines," *Grade Teacher*, 85, No. 3 (November, 1967), pp. 72–74.
Arnsdorf, Val. "Selecting and Using Collateral Materials in Social Studies," *The Reading Teacher*, 20, No. 7 (April, 1967), pp. 621–625.
Bond, Guy L., and Eva B. Wagner. *Teaching the Child to Read*, 4th ed. New York: The Macmillan Company, 1966.
Burrows, Alvina Truet. "Reading, Research, and Reporting in the Social Studies," *Social Studies in the Elementary School*, 56th Yearbook, National Society for the Study of Education. Chicago: University of Chicago Press, 1957.

Fay, Leo, Thomas Horn, and Constance McCullough. *Improving Reading in the Elementary Social Studies*. Washington, D.C.: National Council for the Social Studies, 1961.

Herman, Wayne L., Jr. *Current Research in Elementary School Social Studies*, Part IV. New York: The Macmillan Company, 1969.

Horn, Ernest. *Methods of Instruction in the Social Studies*. New York: Charles Scribner's Sons, 1937.

Huus, Helen, ed. *Children's Books to Enrich the Social Studies*, rev. ed. Washington, D.C.: National Council for the Social Studies, 1966.

Huus, Helen. "Reading," *Skill Development in Social Studies*, 33rd Yearbook. Washington, D.C.: National Council for the Social Studies, 1963.

McKee, Paul. *Reading: A Program of Instruction for the Elementary School*. Boston: Houghton Mifflin Company, 1966.

Michaelis, John U. *Social Studies for Children in a Democracy*, 4th ed. Englewood Cliffs, N.J.: Prentice-Hall, Inc., 1968.

Spache, George and Evelyn. *Reading in the Elementary School*. Boston: Allyn & Bacon, Inc., 1969.

Witty, Paul A. "The Role of Reading in the Social Studies," *Elementary English, 39*, No. 6 (October, 1962), pp. 562–569.

Skills for Group Interaction

The development of the skills and sensitivities that enable individuals to function in group settings and to contribute to group undertakings is important because the individual spends much of his time in group situations both as a child and as an adult. People find security in groups and use group life to solve most of their problems. It is also in groups and the relationship of one group to another that people are confronted with their most severe conflicts, often resulting in outbursts of hostility and in personal tragedy. An understanding of group life is essential to an understanding of man and of human behavior, as is indicated by Cartwright and Zander:

12

Whether one wishes to understand or improve human behavior, it is necessary to know a great deal about the nature of groups. Neither a coherent view of man nor an advanced social technology is possible without dependable answers to a host of questions concerning the operation of groups, how individuals relate to groups, and how groups relate to larger society.[1]

In a variety of ways, the total elementary school program assists the child in learning how to function in groups: in the classroom, on the playground, in the auditorium, in the lunchroom, in small study groups, in large-audience situations, and so on. But because of the nature of the social studies and the processes of instruction used in teaching the social studies, this area of the curriculum can and should contribute in a special way toward a better understanding of groups and the development of group-work skills. These skills are not easily learned and their complexity has not always been understood. Powerful forces are at work in group situations, and youngsters can be taught how to identify some of them and how to deal with them.

The term *group* as used in social psychology means something more than a collection of individuals. Krech, Crutchfield, and Ballachey, for example, give this definition of a group: "A psychological group may be defined as two or more persons who meet the following conditions: (1) the relations among the members are *interdependent* —each member's behavior influences the behavior of each of the others; (2) the members *share an ideology*—a set of beliefs, values, and norms which regulates their mutual conduct." [2] The presence of a psychological relationship causes groups to develop a solidarity—a unity or cohesiveness—resulting from working and thinking together in the resolution of problems. In this sense, a fourth-grade class at the beginning of a school year might be considered only an aggregate of individual children assigned to a particular room because of similar chronological ages. It is in a true sense a *class* rather than a *group*. This class of individuals may develop into a group as the year progresses and the children develop feelings of belonging to the class, identify with it, develop an *esprit de corps*, and grow in their concern for the welfare and success of the class. It will be a *group* to the extent that the actions of individuals are influenced by other members and the extent to which the behavior of individual members affects the group. Do individual children, for example, put forth the extra effort to conduct themselves in an exemplary fashion when the class is tak-

1. Dorwin Cartwright and Alvin Zander, *Group Dynamics Research and Theory*, Evanston, Ill.: Row, Peterson and Company, 1960, p. 4.

2. D. Krech, R. S. Crutchfield, and E. L. Ballachey, *Individual in Society: A Textbook of Social Psychology*, New York: McGraw-Hill, 1962, p. 383.

ing a field trip because they are interested in upholding the group's reputation in this respect? Similarly, is it a matter of group concern if some child or children are unthoughtful, inattentive, or disruptive on such an occasion? In some classes a group feeling does not develop quickly or easily, perhaps not at all. In others, it begins to grow and develop from the first day. Classes differ in this respect because of differences in teachers and their skill in developing group feeling, because of the personality of individual members, and because of the lack of skill on the part of individual members to solve problems through group action.

It has been only within the past thirty years that the theory of group dynamics has been subjected to serious experimental study, but during this short period a considerable amount of insight has been obtained concerning the structure of groups, how they function, their processes, and the conditions under which groups are productive. As more of this research is published and becomes known to teachers, additional principles of group processes will be applied to classroom situations—particularly in the area of the social studies.

Setting a Desirable Atmosphere for Human Relations

Children and adults become members of two quite different groups. Some groups one joins voluntarily and can leave when and if he desires. Most club groups are of this type, as are play groups, children's "gangs," and various social groups. One joins them because he shares a common problem with others, because there exists a mutual interest among members, or because he finds the association with other members to be a pleasant or profitable experience. In other words, he joins because membership in the group can fulfill some physical, social, or personal need. As long as he finds the association satisfying (fulfilling his needs), he continues in active membership or maintains a desire to continue active membership. If the member cannot fulfill his needs through participation in the activities of the group, he lets his membership lapse or simply withdraws from participating in the life of the group. The member himself decides whether or not he chooses to identify with the group.

Another type of group is that in which membership is required and from which one may not or cannot withdraw without suffering serious consequences. The family, in some cases the church, and the school are examples of this type of group. The fact that the class represents a group from which the child cannot withdraw voluntarily has significant implications for the classroom teacher. It extends into such matters as the kinds of controls the teacher may exercise over members of the group, the types of behavior that are rewarded, the methods of obtaining status, the tasks that members are asked to perform, the kind of competitive situations in which members are placed, and the overall classroom climate that prevails.

Although membership in school groups is legally involuntary, the teacher should approach the teaching task as if the pupils *did have the opportunity to withdraw if they so desired.* Pupils do, in fact, withdraw from class groups, perhaps more frequently than teachers suspect. They do not leave physically, to be sure, but they can and do withdraw intellectually and psychologically from actively participating in the life of the classroom. Active membership in a class group, therefore, is a function of need satisfaction just as it is in the case of active membership in voluntary groups. Good elementary classrooms provide an atmosphere in which children can satisfy their personal and social needs such as social recognition, prestige, status, security, and sympathetic understanding. This can best be accomplished within the context of a classroom operating on the principles of democratic leadership and control.

The term *democratic classroom* has been misunderstood and misused. In the name of democracy in the classroom, some teachers have abdicated their positions of responsible leadership and children have been given license to do almost anything. Under such conditions, children are asked to assume responsibilities for which they are not ready, resulting in frustrating experiences for both the teacher and pupils. Without adequate supervision and guidance of learning, goals are vague; no one knows quite what to do. Such confusing circumstances contribute nothing to the satisfactory achievement of the learners, nor do they help children develop competence in social skills. It is unfortunate that such extremely permissive and completely nondirective procedures are thought to be the application of democracy in the classroom.

A good summary description of democracy in the modern school has been prepared by Mork. Its simplicity in contrasting what democracy in the classroom means with what it does not mean should be helpful to the teacher in clarifying the types of procedures that delineate the character of a democratically functioning classroom. It merits careful study:

DEMOCRACY IN THE MODERN SCHOOL

It is impossible to anticipate all the opportunities for an application of democracy in the schoolroom. The following are general examples, listing some of the things that democracy in the classroom means, and some of the things that democracy does not mean. An attempt is made to make the list practical and brief, and to point up some of the *common misconceptions concerning democratic school procedures:*

Democracy in the Classroom Means

1. Establishing a reasonably natural and informal learning situation conducive to good work and study, based on a pleasant and courteous condition of mutual respect among pupils and between the teacher and pupils

2. Living in the classroom according to teacher-guided group-formulated standards that recognize the needs of age groups and individuals for physical movement, physiological needs, and controlled communication

3. Providing opportunity and direction for each child to develop according to his own capacity the skills and abilities that will enable him to participate effectively in child and adult society

4. Giving pupils opportunity to devote some of their time to study and experience in their individual areas and levels of interest

5. Providing opportunity for creative expression and utilizing the interests and abilities of all members of a group

6. Providing many practical experiences in democratic procedures, such as electing, holding of-

Democracy in the Classroom Does NOT Mean

1. Permitting an aimless, undirected, noisy, or restless room situation marked by a lack of consideration for others, nor does it mean a tense, regimented, and artificially severe room atmosphere

2. Doing what you wish whenever you wish, regardless of others, or of those in responsible positions

3. Neglecting skill subjects to the exclusive development of "projects" or "activities"—learning and doing only those things in which children recognize and express an immediate interest—holding every child to the same level of achievement

4. Expecting all pupils to pursue the same course of action and respond uniformly at all times

5. Imposing the teacher's own ideas, methods, and procedures at all times, nor permitting domination of situations by individuals or groups

6. Permitting the group to assume the responsibilities of the teacher, nor does it mean a will-

fice, participating in committee work, accepting delegated responsibility, assuming necessary individual responsibility, acceding to the will of the group, etc.

ingness to enjoy the privileges of the democracy but avoiding the individual responsibility needed to make it succeed

7. Appreciating and understanding people and groups who are different from us in color, creed, customs, and abilities

7. Ridiculing, belittling, or exploiting those who are different, nor removing the opportunities from such people even by "democratic" means

8. Teaching children to make decisions in a democratic manner, abiding by them, and accepting the responsibility for errors

8. Permitting children to make all the decisions, or having the teacher make all decisions and impose them on the group

9. Sharing schoolroom equipment and accepting individual and group responsibility for materials, tools, etc., regardless of ownership

9. Permitting the pupils to use supplies and materials carelessly, wastefully, or without consideration for the needs and desires of others [3]

In classrooms where democratic leadership is evident, one will find children developing an increasing responsibility for self-direction. The teacher-pupil relationship may be described as one of *decreasing* pupil dependency on the teacher. The teacher will give guidance and direction when it is needed but will strive to make the group independent of him for control. In situations where the teacher *increases* the dependency relationship between the pupils and himself, there is usually some evidence of disturbance when the teacher turns his back, when he leaves the room, or when a substitute teacher takes over the class. This is one sign that pupils feel the responsibility for control lies primarily with the teacher rather than with the group, as it should. Good teachers help children establish responsible control by giving them many experiences in self-control and self-management *commensurate with their age and maturity as a group*. Establishing habits of group self-control, individual responsibility to the group, and a democratic classroom atmosphere are necessary and basic conditions for teaching directed toward the development of effective group-work skills.

Classrooms in which there is a desirable atmosphere for human

3. Gordon M. A. Mork, *et al.*, unpublished material, Bemidji State Teachers College, Bemidji, Minnesota. *Used by permission.*

relations are characterized by a lack of hostility between pupils and the teacher and among the children within the group. The level of hostility and aggressive behavior in a classroom is related to what the teacher says and does. Teacher behavior can best be illustrated by such contrasts as the following:

PRACTICES AND PROCEDURES THAT TEND TO INCREASE HOSTILITY IN A CLASSROOM

1. *Negative statements by the teacher*—Here are a few examples of ridicule, sarcasm, criticism, negative, and tension-producing statements made by a teacher. Such statements to children invariably lead to hostility, emotional disturbance, selfishness, fear, and criticism of others:

"I wish you would start acting like fourth-graders instead of kindergarteners."

"Someone is whispering again, and I guess you all know who it is."

"Most fifth-grade classes could understand this, but I am not sure about you."

"Sit up straight. Don't you have a backbone?"

"Why don't you listen when I give directions? None of you seems to know how to listen."

2. *Excessively competitive situations*—Fair competition in classrooms is highly desirable. It can stimulate good work, motivate children to do their best, and help children learn the graces associated with winning and losing. It becomes undesirable when it is of the "dog-eat-dog" variety where each child is pitted against every other child whether the competitive situation is fair or unfair.

3. *Disregard for individual differences*—Classrooms where some children are made to feel "this place is not for me" contribute much

PRACTICES AND PROCEDURES THAT TEND TO DECREASE HOSTILITY IN A CLASSROOM

1. *Positive statements by the teacher*—Friendly, constructive statements by the teacher tend to reduce tension and hostility in the classroom. Here are a few examples:

"We will all want to listen carefully in order not to miss anything Sue is going to tell us."

"All of us did our work so well yesterday during our work period. Do you suppose we can do as well today?"

"It is really fun for all of us when you bring such interesting things for sharing."

"It's nice to have Bill and Sue back with us again. The boys and girls were hoping you would come back today."

2. *Successful cooperative enterprises*—The successful achievement of cooperative activities, involving all members of the class, tends to reduce hostility within the group because it demands the combined efforts of everyone in the successful attainment of a common goal. Children depend on one another in such situations and, therefore, feel a need for one another.

3. *Recognition of and adaptations made in accordance with individual differences*—In such classrooms, each child is challenged at a

toward breeding hostility in children. Such rooms are characterized by one level of acceptable performance applied to all, uniform assignments, one system of reward, great emphasis on verbal, intellectual performance.

4. *Rigid schedule and pressure*— A rigid time schedule and constant pressure associated with "hurry up," "finish your work," "you will be late," or stopping lessons exactly on time whether completed or not create insecurity in children that leads to hostility. A class that is always "one jump behind the teacher" is likely to be one where children blame others for their failure to finish, invent excuses for themselves, and seek scapegoats.

5. *Highly directive teaching practices*—Teachers who must make every decision themselves, give all the assignments, allow for very little participation on the part of children in the life of the classroom are encouraging feelings of hostility in their rooms. Such practices usually mean that teachers refer to the pupils as "my children," or in addressing the pupils, say "I want you to . . . ," or more subtly, "Miss So-and-so wasn't very proud of her class this morning."

6. *Lack of closeness between teacher and pupils*—Some teachers feel they must "keep children in their place," meaning they must remain socially distant from them. This leads to a cold, objective relationship between the children and teacher, causing the children to feel that the teacher lacks affection and warmth for them. This "holier than thou" attitude on the part of the

level commensurate with his ability. Each child feels that he "counts for something" in the classroom and that he belongs to it.

4. *Relaxed, comfortable pace*— Good teachers working with young children maintain a flexible schedule and will not place undue pressures on pupils. They will have a plan and a schedule, yet will not be compulsive in adhering to it. They will deviate from their plan and schedule now and then in the interest of the needs of the boys and girls they teach. Good teachers recognize that feelings of insecurity are related to hostility and will do everything they can to develop feelings of security in the classroom on the part of the children they teach.

5. *Pupil involvement in planning and managing the class*—Giving pupils some opportunity to plan and manage the affairs of the classroom does much to develop feelings of "we-ness," of identification with the group. Children under such circumstances are less inclined to want to think of ways to disrupt Miss So-and-so's orderly room but will work hard to make "our" room a good place to work.

6. *Warm and friendly relationship between teacher and pupils*— One of the basic needs of children is that of love and affection. They need it in their homes, in their playgroups, and in their schools. The feeling that children will not respect the teacher if he is friendly with them is in error. They are likely to respect him more if they feel he is a "human being" capable of cordial and warm per-

teacher is likely to engender feelings of hostility in some children.

sonal relationships with others. This is a mature relationship, however, not one of oversentimentalism and "gushiness." This does not mean that the teacher introduces herself to her class by saying, "My name is Miss So-and-so, but my friends call me Skippy," as one beginning teacher did in introducing herself to a class of sixth-graders.

7. *Lack of satisfying emotional experiences*—Some classrooms sorely lack experiences of an affective nature for children. Everything is deadly serious business—work, work, work. Even the music, art, storytime, or dramatic activities are made to seem like work. Little time is spent on teaching children to enjoy one another, feel the inner joy that comes from a good poem or music selection, or express their feelings in some art medium.

7. *Many opportunities for pleasurable emotional experiences*—Teachers can reduce tensions that build up in children during the course of classroom life by providing opportunities for the release of these tensions through various emotional experiences. Children have the opportunity to express their feelings orally, in writing, or through art forms. They talk together and enjoy one another's company. They prepare skits, do creative dramatics, and role-play situations to help get the feeling of the other fellow. All of these tend to reduce feelings of hostility in children.

Organizing Subgroups for Social Studies Instruction

Committee work or small-group enterprises are very effective instructional procedures in the social studies and have many values for children. It is in the small group that the children get experience with and develop skill in group processes. These experiences should begin in a limited way even as early as the kindergarten. In block play, for example, the teacher can let some children choose the things they wish to build with blocks. Some will want to build an airport, some a house, others a post office, others a supermarket, and so on. The teacher can then let each of these children choose two other children to help him build his project. The children proceed with the building and, when it is completed, tell the class or their teacher a story about their building. Early experiences in such block play will consist mainly of parallel play—three children may be building an airport but each is working to a large extent independently of the other two. As the year progresses, there will be more evidence of cooperative endeavor. Children become more conscious of what others in their

Children at the earliest ages in school are beginning to learn the skills of give and take in dealing with other human beings. (Courtesy of the *Northshore Citizen*, Bothell, Washington)

group are doing and will plan their own contribution to the project in terms of the other children and the group goal.

A good way to familiarize primary-grade children with small-group work is to have committees responsible for various housekeeping duties in the classroom. Susan's committee has the responsibility of keeping the library table neat, John's committee is in charge of the game shelf, Bill's committee is responsible for the care of the aquarium, and Betty's committee keeps the coat corner orderly. These committees can be changed and rotated from time to time to include all the children in the room. Such experiences will help prepare children for the committee work that is done as a part of the instructional program itself. Small-group enterprises in the primary grades need very careful supervision and direction from the teacher. The goals or purposes of the group should be well defined, concrete, and easily understood. Materials needed for the group to do its work must be immediately at hand. Rules and responsibilities of working on committees should be discussed, explained, and posted conspicuously in the room. All of this is done under the guiding hand of the teacher, who knows that children can learn the skills of group work only by working in groups. He does not expect mature group work from young children, nor is he crestfallen if group work is not as productive as he would like it to be. He knows group-work skills develop slowly and gradually and require practice as do any other skills.

In the middle and upper grades, small group work becomes an increasingly greater part of the social studies instructional program. Committees or small groups are used to prepare reports; discuss topics; plan activities; do construction, art, or dramatics activities; write plays; gather resources; interview resource persons; and so on. Through direct instruction and experience, children will learn responsibilities of committee chairmen and committee members and will learn that the success of the group depends on the initiative and cooperation of individuals within the group.

When the teacher organizes his teaching on the unit basis, there will be many occasions when the class will be divided into small work groups. These subgroups may be organized in a variety of ways depending on the ages of the pupils and the nature of the task to be performed. We refer, therefore, to social studies subgroups as being *task oriented;* they are formed to do things that need doing. Because of the way social studies groups are formed, they tend to be relatively flexible and short-lived. A committee may be formed to study certain aspects of a unit, such as finding out why pioneers moved westward. When the committee has obtained its information, achieved its goals, and reported back to the larger group, it can be dissolved and its members can either join other groups or work on individual activities.

Teachers who have experimented with small-group instruction commonly feel that group work breaks down either because some children within the groups do most of the work or because the children waste time and accomplish very little. This is characteristic of immature groups and is an indication that the children need more guidance in small-group activities. Actually, a group has two types of tasks that it must carry out in any cooperative endeavor. The first of these can be referred to as *achievement tasks* and have to do with the purpose for which the group was formed—to prepare a report, to construct a mural, to organize a party, to obtain reference materials, to draw a map, to construct an animal cage, or whatever the project might be. It is important that members of the group have the appropriate skills necessary to carry through the achievement task to completion. These skills are referred to as *achievement skills.* It would be unwise, for example, to send a group of fifth-graders to the library to find material dealing with their unit entitled "Men Who Made America Great" if none of the children knew how to use the library for this purpose. Similarly, pupils who do not have well-developed reading skills should not be placed on group projects that demand a considerable amount of reading and research activity. The nature of the task assigned to a committee should be consistent with the ability of the individual members who comprise the group. Because the finished product presumably represents the combined efforts of all members, each must be able to contribute in some measure to its successful completion.

The second type of tasks faced by a group may be referred to as *socialization tasks.* These involve the use of skills needed in order to function as a group: organizing, selecting a leader, designating responsibilities, deciding on controls, and various ways of working together. They are referred to as *socialization skills.* If, for example, the group sent to the library to find materials was unable to organize itself, plan how it was to go about its work, assign specific responsibilities, and decide who was the leader and how it would report its findings, its efforts would not be that of a group but rather would be that of individuals working independently. It would be trying to move in several different directions at one time, making progress as a *group* impossible.

It is obvious that achievement tasks and socialization tasks are related, and one complements the other. If a group has inadequately developed its socialization skills, it will not be able to accomplish its achievement tasks through group effort. It is in situations in which socialization skills are weak that the achievement task, or the work product, represents the efforts of only one or two members of the group. The remaining members have perhaps wasted time, withdrawn from the group, or caused a disturbance. Similarly, if the achievement task is sufficiently well defined, the problem of working out the socialization tasks becomes somewhat easier. Under certain conditions, the teacher may wish to subordinate the importance of the achievement task simply to give children the opportunity to develop socialization skills. In this manner the children develop competence in socialization skills, and group work becomes more satisfying and productive. If a group cannot work through its socialization tasks adequately, their morale deteriorates, further causing members to want to withdraw from it. Serious-minded pupils may go so far as to ask the teacher to assign them to another group because "We aren't getting anywhere in that group. The kids just waste time."

In organizing subgroups within a class, the teacher may find the following suggestions helpful:

1. Defer group work until a firm control of the class has been established and until the work habits, capabilities, and special needs of individual children are known. Beginning such activities before the teacher is entirely secure with the group or before he knows where he might anticipate difficulty is likely to lead to unhappy experiences for both the teacher and the class.
2. Begin group work slowly. Select responsible, key children for the first group and keep the group small—perhaps not more than five children.
3. Select an achievement task that is simple, well defined, and one that the group is certain to accomplish successfully.
4. Have the remainder of the class engage in individual work while giving guidance and direction to the smaller group. Either designate a leader for the small group or have the children choose a leader. Explain the nature of their responsibility and begin to discuss some of their special responsibilities when working in a small group.
5. Have resource materials the children will need available for them. Later on, as they become accustomed to working in groups, they will be able to do this themselves.
6. Meet with the small group every day for a few minutes before they begin work and again at the end of their work period to make sure things are moving along as planned. If possible, have them make a progress report to the other, larger group during the summary and evaluation that should come at the close of each social studies period.
7. Give them specific help and suggestions in how to organize their work and how to report what they are doing.
8. Have their report to the class be short, concise, and interesting. Have members of the group explain to the class how they did their work as a group. Begin calling attention to some of the responsibilities of persons working in small groups.
9. Follow the same procedure with another group of children as soon as possible. Gradually include other children, selecting some who

have had previous experience in group work and some who have not. Observe carefully the children who need close supervision and those who are responsible and work well in groups. This will help in placing children in work groups as the year goes along.

10. After all the children have had an opportunity to work in a small group under close supervision, more than one group can work at one time. Eventually, the entire class may be able to work in small groups simultaneously. When this is attempted, it should be preceded by a review of the standards of group work, goals should be clearly defined beforehand, and a careful evaluation should follow.

Factors Affecting Group Work

In order to help children become more productive in small-group work, the teacher should be alert to the conditions that bear directly on the functioning of small groups. Careful attention to each of the following factors will facilitate the effectiveness of small-group endeavors.

Extent of Teacher Guidance in Helping Children Learn Group-Process Skills. This text has repeatedly stressed the need to place children in group-work settings if they are to learn group-work skills. However, if children are only given the *opportunity* to work in groups without receiving instruction and guidance in how a group is supposed to go about its business, they may likewise not learn to function effectively in small groups. Simply dividing the class into small groups and assigning each group a task is not likely to help children grow in group-work skills. The teacher has important responsibilities in giving instruction and direction to such learnings. It should also be stressed that the teacher has a *continuing* responsibility for the guidance, direction, and supervision of small-group work. Children will need to be taught, retaught, guided, and directed many times if these skills are to be learned and maintained. Teachers do this regularly in teaching letter writing, reading, or map reading, and it should come as no surprise, therefore, that the same procedures are needed to teach the subtle and complex skills that inhere in group processes.

Before attempting a small-group endeavor with children of any age, the teacher should discuss with the class some of the responsibilities of the persons who are a part of a group. Children are quick to recognize and identify the factors that make for good group work. It is helpful if the teacher can summarize these and place them on charts that are posted in the room for the children to see. These, then, become the standards for working in groups and can be used as evaluative criteria after the children have had an opportunity to work in small groups. Such standards would vary some depending on the age

Studying together in small work groups provides opportunities to learn social as well as intellectual skills. (Courtesy of the Highline Public Schools, Seattle)

of the children involved; but, in general, they might include any or all of the following:

Group Members

1. Help the leader carry out plans.
2. Do your share of the work.
3. Work without disturbing other group members.
4. Ask other members for their ideas.
5. Select only the ideas that help the group do its best work.
6. Cheerfully take the jobs the group wants you to do.
7. Make other members of the group feel welcome.
8. Be courteous; respect the ideas of others.
9. Support the group's decisions.

Group Leaders

1. Help make everyone become a part of the group.
2. Let everyone have his turn at the "good" jobs.

3. Get ideas from all members of the group.
4. Let the group decide which ideas are best.
5. Keep the group moving to get its job finished in the best way it can.
6. Keep from being "bossy"; be a leader, not a dictator.
7. Help your group know what its job is.

Some teachers find role playing to be a valuable technique in teaching the skills needed in small-group work. By selecting four or five children to serve as group members, the teacher can demonstrate to the class what it means to "help everyone become a part of the group" or any of the standards that have been discussed. Similarly, he can demonstrate some of the responsibilities of group members. Likewise, some of the children can role-play various situations involving group work while the remainder of the class can profitably analyze the situation to determine why the group was functioning well or poorly. It is helpful to have children observe certain specific elements in the situation to be presented. For example, they might try to answer such questions as these:

1. What did individual members do to help the group do its job? What did members do that did not help the group?
2. What did the leader do to help the group get its job done?
3. How did the group find out exactly what it was to do?
4. Did the group use good resources in solving its problems?
5. Did the group seem to be working together as a team? Why or why not?
6. How could the group be helped to do its job better?

Following the role playing, the class can discuss the situation in terms of the specific points being observed. It may then be helpful to replay all or a portion of the situation to help children appreciate the forces at work in group situations. With young children it may be desirable to have an older group demonstrate such things as a domineering leader, an uncooperative group member, a member who wants only the choice tasks, the noncontributor, the irresponsible leader, the member who must always have his own way, the member who talks too much, and so on. In teaching group-work skills the teacher will want to do more than talk about what should or should not be done in group situations. Children really need an opportunity to see and experience "how it works" as well as an opportunity to experiment and try their hand at doing productive group work. Role playing can do much to sensitize them to the various subtleties and forces that come into play in small-group situations.

Size of the Group. The size of a subgroup within a classroom has considerable effect on its productivity. If groups are too large, there will be duplication of responsibilities, less opportunity for individuals to carry their share of the group effort, and a tendency for some members to fade out of the group activity, and problems of management will become more severe. On the other hand, if groups are too small, the collective talent of the group is restricted, demands on individuals may be excessive, and the work product may represent little more than the effort of one or two individuals.

In discussing group size, Thelen suggests the principle of "Least Group Size." He says, "In general the principle would seem to be: the size of a group should be the smallest group in which it is possible to have represented at a functional level all the socialization and achievement skills required for the particular learning activity at hand." [4] This implies that the size of the group is a function of the purposes for which it was formed and its objectives. The group must be large enough to have within it individuals who have the skills needed to make progress possible, yet not so large as to make group processes difficult, if not impossible. This is substantiated by Watson.

> The right size of group for any activity depends on both the maturity of the individuals and the nature of the activity. Hundreds or thousands may be spectators at a film, a TV presentation, or a spectacle; adults experienced in group work can function more successfully in large groups than can children. In general, however, working groups are composed of five to eight members. If the group is larger, some persons become performers and others spectators. At age six, spontaneous groups seldom exceed three or four children. Obviously, most school classes are much too large for good cooperative work unless broken into smaller groups. [5]

In applying this principle to group work in the social studies at the elementary school level, it means that in general the groups will be kept small, possibly not more than three to five children and rarely more than six. The achievement and socialization tasks required of elementary school pupils are not of such complexity that they could not be handled by a group this size. If the groups are larger than the number suggested, the teacher may expect more socialization problems with a corresponding deterioration of the quality of the achieve-

4. Herbert A. Thelen, "Principle of Least Group Size," *The School Review*, 57, March, 1949, p. 142.

5. Goodwin B. Watson, *What Psychology Can We Trust?* New York: Teachers College, Bureau of Publications, Columbia University, 1961, p. 15.

ment tasks. In practice this is apt to mean time wasting, rowdyism, or boredom.

Clarity of the Goals.   Teachers would find group work to be more effective if they made certain that the members of the group clearly understood what they were expected to do. This is especially important with young children who require more direction and guidance than those who are more mature. It is not uncommon to find a class dividing into small groups in a social studies unit without a clear understanding of what is to be done within the small groups. As a consequence, children begin to cause a disturbance, and the teacher is disappointed with group-work procedures.

Time spent in clarifying goals is time well spent, because goals set the direction in which learning is to proceed. Before releasing a group for independent work, the teacher should check to make certain the children understand the purposes of the group and what is expected of it. A good procedure used by some teachers is to have the group write down its goals as a first order of business. Thus, everyone knows what is to be done and begins thinking about how he can contribute toward the attainment of those goals. The group may then begin organizing itself in terms of its objectives.

Status of Members Within the Class.   Within the classroom setting there develops a prestige or status system that reflects itself in the activities of the class. This status system involves every member of the class, including the teacher. Under favorable classroom conditions the teacher is considered a high-status member; in elementary classrooms he is usually at the top of the status scale. The pupils distribute themselves status-wise on a continuum ranging from the children who are generally well accepted and highly thought of by most members to those who are almost universally rejected by the majority of the class.

Some insight into the status of various members of the class may be obtained informally by observing the children in and out of the classroom. These observations can be made in any situation where the children exercise a free choice of the partners they wish to play or work with. The teacher may observe, too, whether the preference is a mutual one or whether the child doing the selecting is simply attempting to identify with a high-status classmate. It is also possible to obtain information relative to the social structure of the class through the use of sociometric devices. More specifically, sociometric data may be used to

1. Identify leaders within the class.
2. Determine the social status or social position of any child with respect to other children.

3. Spot in-groups, cliques, or rival factions within the class.
4. Locate children who are rejected by others.
5. Obtain information that will be helpful in arranging the classroom seating pattern, forming committees, work groups, play groups.

In certain respects this method has some advantage over the observations made of play choices of children, particularly if the child is asked to indicate the child or children with whom he would most like to work. Children apparently apply a separate set of criteria to those with whom they choose to play from those with whom they choose to work. This observation was made by Bonney, who found that there were greater differences in the preferences of children for each other on the "work-with" than on the "play-with" criterion.[6] Commenting on this finding, Thelen writes: "This suggests that it is easier to find acceptance in the play group than in the work group, possibly because the special skill which would make a person desirable in the work group may be an additional requirement over and above that of congeniality, or it might be so specific as to be quite rarely found; in either case the requirements for preference in the work group are harder to meet."[7]

In securing data for a sociogram, the teacher may begin at a time when children will be working in small groups. He presents the directions to the children unceremoniously as a means of soliciting help from them in finding out with whom they would most like to work. The specific directions given the children might be as follows:

> During the next week we are going to be doing some work in small committees. In order that everyone may do his very best work, I want each of you on a committee with boys and girls you most like to work with. To help me prepare for this, please write the names of the boys or girls with whom you would prefer to work. Place first, second, and third choices on this slip of paper. I will use your choices to form the committees, and no one else will see your names.

The teacher then passes out the slips of paper upon which is reproduced a form as follows:

My name is _____
Boys and girls I would best like to work with on a committee:
First choice _____
Second choice _____
Third choice _____

6. Merl E. Bonney, "A Study of the Sociometric Process Among Sixth Grade Children," *Journal of Educational Psychology*, September, 1946, pp. 359–372.

7. Herbert A. Thelen, "Engineering Research in Curriculum Building," *Journal of Educational Research*, 41, April, 1948, p. 586.

Although this form need not be followed exactly, it is essential that children understand exactly what is expected of them and know the reasons for making the choices. It is best if the need for making the request grows out of or leads to some classroom activity and if the results subsequently are put to use in that activity. The entire procedure should be handled routinely and in a matter-of-fact fashion. The teacher can vary the procedure and situation slightly each time he obtains such data to avoid causing a discussion of the matter by the children. It is not advisable for the teacher to ask children to indicate the pupils with whom they do not wish to work or those whom they dislike. Children may not have thought much about classmates they dislike or with whom they do not want to work. The request for such information is apt to suggest to the child that there are some pupils with whom he *should* not want to work or some whom he *should* dislike. This negative approach is not likely to produce the best results in terms of human relations within the classroom.

Various methods have been devised to tabulate and diagram sociometric data. The use of a simple chart as shown in Figure 15 is a good way to begin the analysis. Each pupil's name is listed vertically and horizontally and the names are kept in the same order in each case. The vertical column is used to check each child's choice of other children; the horizontal column is used to check the number of times each child has been chosen by other children. Having ordered the data in this manner, the teacher may then proceed to construct a sociogram that can be used to gain additional insights into the social structure of the class.

In plotting the sociogram, the teacher may wish to use a system of concentric circles, placing the children who obtain the highest scores in the inner circle and those with the lowest scores in the outer circle. Various quartiles can be shown by placing 25 per cent of the class in each circle; that is, the class is divided and ranked in four groups. To place children in their proper position on this grid work of concentric circles, a small circle is used as the symbol for a boy and a triangle represents a girl. In order to tell who chose whom, arrows can be used between pupils represented on the sociogram as shown in Figure 16. Two arrows connecting pupils but pointing in opposite directions represent mutual choices. Sometimes teachers prefer to use arrows only showing the choices of children without the use of concentric circles, as represented in Figure 17. When groups are large, the lines, arrows, triangles, small circles, and concentric circles become such a complex labyrinth that the teacher may find it next to impossible to read or interpret much of value from the confusing and baffling network. The use of a chart as suggested here may be more useful than the sociogram in such cases.

	Nick	Jerry	Ruth	Bill	Jim	Susan	Jack	Diane	David	Bob	Sarah	Mary	Rand	Loren	Tim	Nell	Patty
Nick											1						
Jerry				1													
Ruth											1						
Bill												1					
Jim		1															
Susan			1														
Jack															1		
Diane			1														
David		1															
Bob				1													
Sarah																1	
Mary	1																
Rand				1													
Loren				1													
Tim		1															
Nell											1						
Patty													1				
Total	1	3	2	3	1	0	0	0	0	0	3	0	2	0	1	1	0

Figure 14. Example of a chart used to tabulate **first** choices of children in response to a "work-with" question. Second and third choices could be tabulated on the same chart, using the numbers 2 and 3 to indicate each child's preferences. Rows can be added at the bottom of the chart to show totals for second and third choices. A final row can then be added to show a grand total of all choices for all children.

It is well to remember that a sociogram yields information about a group at a *specific* time and for a given situation. Children's peer relationships change frequently, and for this reason it is recommended that sociometric data be obtained at intervals throughout the year.

The status of individual members of a work group and the social structure of the larger, parent group is important because (1) children

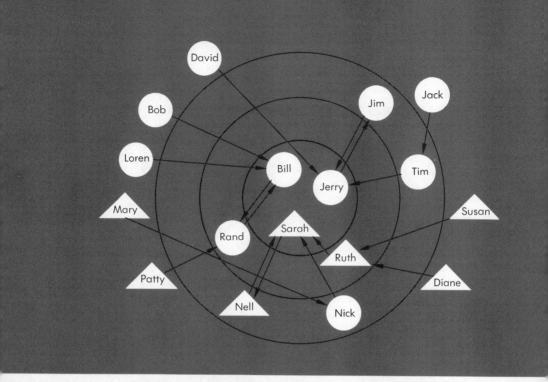

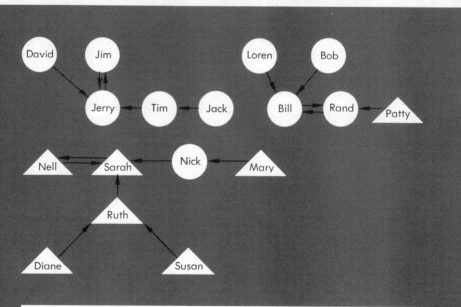

Figures 15, 16. The sociogram in **Figure 15** (top) places children receiving the most choices in the center of the diagram. The arrangement of the data in **Figure 16** (bottom) shows more vividly that the children's first choices cluster about three children.

will be interested in and attracted to groups in which they enjoy prestige and in those that enhance their social worth, (2) it affects interaction within the small group, and (3) children have difficulty divorcing ideas and suggestions from the person who made them. Immature groups are likely to adopt suggestions of high-status members in preference to those of low-status members even when the idea or suggestion itself has less merit. The teacher himself must exercise discretion in making suggestions to children because of the high status he enjoys —a "suggestion" being tantamount to a directive. It is in situations such as these that children have a genuine opportunity to exercise critical thought, subjecting each idea or suggestion to careful scrutiny and evaluating it on its own merits. The teacher must assume leadership in providing many opportunities for the group to evaluate its progress as a group. This can be done by setting up goals or standards for good group work and using them in appraising the progress the group is making. Although each class should develop its own standards, certainly such things as "Do we respect everyone's contribution? Do we consider the value of ideas rather than the person who made them?" would appear on most lists. The ability to judge contributions on the basis of their worth rather than on the basis of who made them may be generalized to the extent that the child habitually disregards nonessentials but judges ideas solely on merit.

The teacher will want to give careful consideration to the matter of status in setting up work groups. Although he will want to place children with others with whom they can work, the selection should not be left entirely to the children. When this happens, high-status children are selected first, leaving the low-status children no group wants. Even allowing children to choose the group with whom they wish to work is not entirely satisfactory. Possibly a combination of children's choices and teacher placement is the best course of action, because the teacher knows the capabilities of each child and can make a sound judgment about how and with whom each is likely to work best and make the greatest growth. Some teachers find the assignment of low-status children to group activities with high-status children has the effect of helping the low-status children obtain greater acceptance and prestige. A grouping of children that almost duplicates the "in-groups" and "out-groups" of a class rarely works out well because it does not make for good human relations within the classroom.

Maturity of the Group. The term *maturity* as applied to groups has two meanings. It may mean physical maturity of the members, or it may mean the degree of skill that a group has achieved in group-work situations. In this latter sense a group of adults may be considered an immature group if it lacks skill in group processes. Contrariwise, a group of nine-year-olds might be considered a fairly mature one if it had developed skill in the processes attendant to group action.

The maturity of a group is related to its past experiences in learning group-process skills. A group of fifth-graders that has always worked as individuals within a class, sitting in straight rows, is not likely to be ready to do productive work in small groups until each member has had an opportunity to learn the necessary socialization skills. Teachers lose sight of this when they experiment with group work occasionally and find that "it doesn't work." It does not work partly because the pupils have not been prepared for it.

Immature groups require a great amount of teacher guidance and direction. Primary-grade children working in small groups should always find the teacher close at hand to help them over the obstacles and rough spots. Similarly, middle- and upper-grade children who lack experience and maturity in group work will require much help from the teacher. With classes of this type the teacher should *institute group work gradually*, beginning with procedures that are familiar to the children. Instead of dividing the entire class into group work at one time, the teacher might better begin with only one small group. This will make it possible for him to give the group the kind of guidance and assistance it will need. As the class is ready, more groups can be added until the time when it becomes possible for the entire class to be engaged in small-group work at one time. The principle of "taking children from where they are to where they are not" applies in group work as it does in any other school learning. It is simply not possible for immature groups to be entirely self-directed. An analysis of group work skills was published by the San Diego, California County Schools. Portions of it are reproduced here:

SKILLS IN GROUP PROCEDURES [8]

Large-Group Situations

Example 1.   Participating in Class Planning
Each member helps to
   Give suggestions for the group to consider.
   Listen to proposals from other group members.
   Interpret suggestions that other members make.
   Realize that not all suggestions can be accepted.
   Decide which proposals sound most promising.
   Consider alternative plans.
   Consider the kinds of records needed for guides.

8. San Diego County Schools, *Social Studies Grades One Through Eight, Course of Study,* San Diego, Calif.: Office of the County Superintendent of Schools, 1958.

Example 2.   Thinking Through Common Problems
Each member helps to
    Define the problem to be worked on.
    Raise questions for group to consider.
    Decide what questions will have to be answered.
    Keep group thinking on the problem.
    Decide when to use expert opinion and outside resources in making decisions.
    Decide when to secure a majority vote.
    Get alternatives clearly before all the other members.
    Decide what voting procedures are appropriate.
    Decide when to delegate tasks to a committee.

Example 3.   Organizing Plans for Action
Each member helps to
    Select activities most central to the agreed plan.
    Determine responsibilities of group leaders and members of committees needed.
    Estimate people and materials needed for the job.
    Determine the number and size of committees needed.
    Determine assignments of committees.
    Decide on committee members.
    Choose the people best qualified for particular jobs.
    Plan work to make the best use of individual abilities.
    Help set standards for the job.
    Decide how to divide tasks.
    Decide on steps needed to get the job done.
    Consider materials needed.
    Explore sources of needed materials.

Small-Group Situations

Example 1.   Planning as a Committee
Each member helps to
    Talk over plans with other committee members.
    Present steps for action to the group.
    Determine chairmanship responsibilities.
    Listen to suggestions of others in making plans.
    Decide what steps the committee needs to take to get needed information.
    Decide how to keep records of committee work.
    Decide how to apportion time for the job.
    Determine responsibilities to be carried out.

Explain committee plans clearly to others.
Decide how to share results of committee work.
Decide what to do when a plan fails.

Example 2.   Working as a Committee
Each member helps to
Keep in touch with plans.
Use records as guides to action.
Find ways to resolve different opinions.
Report progress and needs during planning-evaluating periods.
Consider others' feelings.
Know what to expect from other committee members.

Evaluating Group Activities

The group can
Judge success of work on the basis of goals set up.
Determine bases on which to judge committee effectiveness.
Analyze ways tasks were carried out.
Analyze satisfactions gained from the work.
Consider future ways of working for greater efficiency.
Decide how well tasks have been carried out.
Decide when committee reports are adequate.

Being an Effective Group Member

Each member tries to
Stay open to suggestions from others.
Present fresh ideas to share with others.
Explain reasons for disagreements.
Not take offense at expression of personal feelings and opinions.
Fulfill commitments accepted.
Help to adjust plans when there are disagreements.
Decide on what share to take in carrying out a class project.
Use courteous language and gestures.
Make suggestons without offending other members' feelings.
Stand by agreements.
Plan next steps after meeting success and failure.
Know the names of fellow group members.
Know something about each member's special interests and experiences.
Decide how to apportion time for individual responsibilities.
Decide when to accept special committee responsibilities.
Decide which suggestions made in class to support.

Decide when to give up his own plans for group plans.

Find what is involved in accepting task responsibilities.

Decide when to withdraw a suggestion in favor of others supported by the group.

Share materials.

Serving as a Group Leader

The group leader tries to

Keep members informed of group decisions.

Think of possible ways to carry work forward.

Help others remember group plans.

Explain plans to others.

Help all members to contribute.

Delegate responsibility for work among committee members.

Delegate responsibility for keeping records.

Keep others' thinking on the problem at hand.

Find ways to use special talents and interests of other group members.

Get group consensus for agreements.

Manner in Which Group Work Is Evaluated. Part of the reason group work is at times ineffective is the feeling on the part of the children that it is not rewarded to the same degree that more formal aspects of classroom work are. This stems from the teacher's attitude toward the worthwhileness of group activities. If in the evaluation of unit work the rewards (recognition, praise, value statements, reports to parents, grades) go only to those who do well in paper-and-pencil activities, the child is likely to feel that group activities do not count much in the entire scheme of things. If he feels this way, the child is not likely to put forth his best efforts, because he will be more concerned with concentrating on the aspects of the unit that he considers most rewarding. Group work will be enhanced if the teacher regards it as an important part of the instructional program and rewards appropriately the children who have done commendable work in group endeavors.

Arriving at Decisions Through Discussion

One of the most widely used and most valuable techniques in social studies teaching is *discussion*. Its value lies chiefly in the fact that it represents a type of intellectual teamwork, resting on the philosophy and principle that the pooled knowledges, ideas, and feelings of several persons have greater merit than those of a single individual.

Discussion is a procedure used to arrive at a consensus regarding the solution of problems and is characteristic of democratic societies. It is basically a problem-solving activity. Discussion can serve a variety of purposes in the social studies program. It can be used in laying plans for new work, evaluating progress, making decisions concerning future action, sharing information, obtaining and gaining respect for various points of view, clarifying ideas, or inspiring interest.

Good discussion flourishes best in a permissive atmosphere where children enjoy status security. This necessitates careful guidance on the part of the teacher, who serves in the capacity of leader and guide. The teacher, of course, retains control of the class and is responsible for seeing that the discussion makes progress. He does not allow it to become sidetracked into the consideration of irrelevancies. Discussions that wander from the topic or do not progress toward solution of problems are wasteful of class time.

Because the strength of discussion is obtained from the information and viewpoint of all members of the group, it is necessary that all contribute to its progress. It is a thinking together process that breaks down if one member or group dominates it. It is the responsibility of the teacher to encourage the more reluctant children to participate because the group will profit by their contributions, too. Although there cannot be a single answer to the question of what to do with the child who dominates the discussion, skillful teachers usually take care of the matter with a statement such as "Jackie, you have given us so many good ideas today, and I know you have many more good suggestions, but we want to find out what some of the others think would be a good way to. . . ."

In good class discussions children should talk freely and voluntarily. There should be no set pattern of soliciting contributions, nor should marks be given on individual discussion contributions. It will take a while to develop effective discussions because the skills needed develop gradually. The teacher should not be disappointed if his first few attempts at discussion seem to fail. If the procedure is begun gradually and the leadership and atmosphere are conducive to discussion, the children will make progress in developing skill in this important problem-solving procedure.

The physical arrangement of the classroom may either contribute to or inhibit discussion. For example, it is difficult to interact with someone when one is forced to look at the back of his neck. When classroom seating is arranged so that all pupils face the teacher, the pattern of interaction will be *through* the teacher, that is, "pupil A–teacher–pupil B–teacher–pupil C–teacher." A preferred discussion pattern is to have pupils interacting directly with each other; this can be encouraged by having them face one another. It can be achieved also by arranging the seating in a semicircle fashion for at least some of the discussion sessions. Through careful and patient teaching, a teacher can bring pupils to a point where they interact courteously with one another—without always agreeing with each other—and do so without raising their hands to speak. Such maturity in discussion procedure, however, requires a considerable amount of good teaching, practice, and time.

As a part of the teaching process, the teacher and class should establish standards or guides that characterize harmonious, productive discussion. For example, one participating in a discussion should

1. Listen attentively when others are speaking.
2. Remain objective and not become emotional.
3. Be open-minded, respect and accept the contributions of others, but think independently.
4. Assume responsibility for contributing ideas.
5. Prepare adequately for the discussion and be able to support his ideas with factual evidence.
6. Speak loudly and clearly enough for all to hear.
7. Not be offended when his ideas or suggestions are not accepted by the group.
8. Not dominate the discussion; contributions should be stated concisely and briefly.
9. Ask for clarification of ideas he does not understand; ask for evidence to substantiate statements.
10. Recognize the problem of semantics in arriving at group decisions or in discussing a controversial issue.
11. Assume responsibility for moving the group toward its goal; help keep the group from becoming sidetracked from the central issue.
12. Have confidence in the ability of the group to come to a satisfactory decision and support the decision of the group once it has been made.

Standards such as the ones listed here are not appropriately stated for use with children, but the ideas can be discussed and understood by them when stated more simply. It is generally more effective if children themselves contribute to the setting of standards. For example, children will state ideas, such as the preceding ones, in the following manner:

1. Stick to the topic.
2. Be considerate of others' viewpoints and feelings.
3. Use facts to back up statements.
4. Ask questions when you don't understand.

5. Listen carefully while others are speaking.
6. Let everyone have his turn.

It is usually better to use positive rather than negative statements in developing standards. It is more helpful, for example, to say, "Speak clearly and loudly enough for all to hear," than to say, "Don't mumble." Positive statements help the child know what *to do,* whereas negative statements tell him what *not to do* but suggest no alternative in the way of a more acceptable course of action.

If possible, the standards for good discussion should be placed on a large chart in a conspicuous place in the classroom or written on the chalkboard. They can then be of value in reminding children of their responsibilities in a discussion and in serving as guides for evaluating progress in discussion procedures. From time to time during the year the teacher and children will want to review such standards and make revisions or additions.

Many of the same principles and procedures used in group discussions involving the entire class apply to other forms of discussion procedure. The advantage of smaller groups lies chiefly in allowing for greater participation by individual members. The teacher may find each of the following forms of discussion procedure helpful in social studies instruction.

Round-Table Discussions.   A round-table discussion usually involves a small number of persons, perhaps no fewer than three and no more than eight. Its purpose is to share ideas in an informal manner in order to gain new insights, present several views on a problem, think through a solution to a problem, evaluate a procedure or product, or generally air some problem needing further study. It requires someone to serve as a moderator to introduce the members of the discussion group, present the problem to be discussed, keep the discussion moving, solicit comments from the discussants, keep the group from getting bogged down in the discussion of unrelated points, and be responsible for summarizing results. The leader's role is one of guiding the group rather than one of dominating it. A permissive atmosphere needs to prevail and the presentations are conversational rather than oratorical.

Round-table discussions can be used in the middle and upper grades by having a group of children discuss a problem before the remainder of the class or by dividing the class into several small discussion groups that function without an audience. It is perhaps best to use this procedure with one group at a time, either with or without an audience, until the children have learned how to participate in discussions of this type. It will be necessary for the teacher to introduce the procedure to the class and to explain and demonstrate its purposes and the manner in which it works. Such points as the following need to be emphasized:

1. *Responsibilities of the moderator:* To be informed on the problem to be discussed, introduce the problem, keep the discussion moving, avoid having the group become sidetracked, ask members to explain more fully what they mean, avoid having members argue and quibble over irrelevancies, summarize and state conclusions
2. *Responsibilities of members of the discussion group:* To be well informed on the problem to be discussed, especially some phase of the problem, speak informally while avoiding arguing and quibbling, stay with the problem under discussion, have sources of information available, back up statements with facts, help the group summarize its conclusions
3. *Responsibilities of the audience:* To listen attentively, withhold questions until presentation is completed, ask for clarification of ideas, ask for evidence on questionable statements, confine remarks to the problem under discussion, extend customary audience courtesies to members of the round table

Round-table discussions may be used for any of the following purposes:

1. To discuss plans for a major class activity
2. To evaluate the results of a class activity, the merits of a film, a school assembly on citizenship, the decision of a student council
3. To make specific plans, such as the best way to present the work of the class to the parents
4. To get facts related to the unit under study
5. To discuss current affairs
6. To present differing views on a community problem or a school problem
7. To make decisions and recommendations to the class (the student council wants to know how the grade feels about a new play schedule. A committee of five children discusses this problem and presents its findings and recommendations to the class)

Panel Discussions. A panel discussion is similar to a round-table discussion in many respects, but there are also some important differences. The responsibilities of the moderator are approximately the same as they are for the moderator of the round table, as are those of the participants. The procedure is more formal than that of the round table. It usually begins with a short statement or presentation by each discussant before the panel is opened for free discussion by members.

Panels are usually more audience oriented than round tables, and frequently there is some provision made for audience questions or participation at the end of the panel's presentation. There is a greater responsibility placed on participants to prepare themselves well for their particular part on the panel, for each panelist is considered to be more or less an "expert."

Buzz Groups. The following is an example of a "buzz" group in operation.

> Mr. Hill's fifth-grade class is seated in such a way that six children have their desks placed together, with three on one side facing the three on the other. There are five such clusters in his room, plus one more in which there are only four children. The class has been studying a unit on the American West, and many children have prepared excellent diagrams, pictures, maps, and models related to the unit. It has been suggested that these materials be displayed in some way in order that other children in the school might be able to see and share them. Mr. Hill speaks to his class: "It has been suggested that these fine materials we have prepared in our unit study be displayed in some way in order that other children in the school might be able to see them. We need some good ideas for carrying out such a plan. I wonder if you could talk this problem over with the members of the class seated in your group for about ten minutes and come up with at least three suggestions for ways we could display this material for the rest of the school."
>
> The groups discuss this problem informally for approximately ten minutes. Mr. Hill then gets their attention and each group presents its suggestions. These, in turn, are written on the chalkboard and considered further by the entire class.

We have here a brief description of a buzz-group technique. It is an informal consideration of ideas or problems where the chief purpose is to solicit the suggestions, feelings, ideas, or consensus of the members participating. It is slightly more structured than informal conversation and usually has some purpose other than a purely social one. (With adult groups, however, the purpose of buzz sessions may be to help members become acquainted with one another.) The group may or may not have a designated leader and may or may not be expected to come to some conclusion.

Talking things over in a buzz session can be very helpful in clarifying ideas, getting a wide sampling of opinion and feeling, obtaining suggestions and ideas, and getting pupils to participate who might be reluctant or fearful in a more structured discussion situation. Likewise, it has some limitations. Buzz sessions can easily get out of hand and become noisy and boisterous where nothing is accomplished except the creation of confusion. There is need, therefore, for the teacher to have firm control of the class before such a procedure is attempted and to establish standards that are clearly understood beforehand.

Making Use of Pupil Reports

Pupil reports to the class are commonly utilized in social studies teaching to share information obtained through individual research and study. They serve the purpose of bringing to the group the knowledge and understanding obtained by individuals as well as of giving the child the experience of organizing, planning, and presenting the report to the class. This suggests a mutual value that accrues to the group as well as to the individual making the report. It also implies a responsibility that each must share if the procedure is to have value.

There is nothing quite so deadly or lacking in instructional value as the elementary child giving a "report" he has copied from the encyclopedia. He stumbles over every other word because he neither knows its meaning nor how to pronounce it. Because he must ask for help in reading his report, it lacks continuity, is hard to follow, and is not understood by the class. The listeners cannot follow what the child is attempting to present, become bored, and/or disruptive. Under such a set of circumstances no one likes to give reports or listen to them. They are a waste of time.

The primary responsibility for good pupil reports rests squarely with the teacher. Before instituting such a procedure he should explain how to give reports and should teach the pupils how to prepare them. Through discussion he and the class can establish standards that will be used in the preparation of reports and the evaluation of them after they are given. Examples of such standards are:

Responsibilities of the Speaker

1. Speaks in a clear voice
2. Is well prepared
3. Speaks in his own words
4. Uses charts and pictures to make his report more interesting
5. Asks for questions at the end of his report
6. Sticks to the topic

Responsibilities of the Audience

1. Listens carefully
2. Is courteous; does not interrupt the speaker
3. Asks questions only at the end of the report

Here pupils are getting practice in presenting ideas as well as in listening to others. Notice the visual aids the pupil is using to make his report. (Courtesy of the Colorado State College, Greeley)

Children can help each other improve the quality of their reports by holding brief evaluative discussions following the presentation. A good practice to follow is to ask for positive statements first—points at which the report was especially well done. Then, the children might offer suggestions concerning the way the report might have been improved. The teacher must set the stage for sincere evaluation with the attitude of helping one another, rather than only point out things that were wrong with the report. Care must be exercised so as not to make the evaluations destructively critical of a child's work.

It is the responsibility of the teacher to take an active part in assisting the child with the preparation of his report. This includes helping him select a suitable topic, suggesting references, helping him with its organization, and suggesting visual devices to use. The teacher should find a few minutes of time a day or two in advance of the presentation to sit down with the youngster and have him tell what he plans to include in his report. Once the child is prepared, he should be left alone while the report is being given unless he specifically asks for help. It is unfair to the child and the listening group to have the teacher continually interrupting and asking questions. The standards and responsibilities of good listeners apply to the teacher as well as the children. Of course, when the report is completed the teacher can ask questions, call attention to points that need further clarification, or add pertinent information to the report. He also should comment in a positive way and offer concrete suggestions as to how the child might improve future reports.

Several pupil reports should not be scheduled on the same day. It is impossible for children to sustain any degree of interest if they must listen to a dozen or fifteen reports consecutively. A better procedure is to have two or three reports at a time and spread the reporting over a period of several days.

A perennial problem with pupil reports is the tendency for the pupil to make a "bookish" report. Some teachers encourage verbalism by being too rewarding, too complimentary of reports that are well presented but are not given in the child's own words. The dependence of the child on the language of his reference material is a probable indication that he lacks an understanding of the topic. In order to combat the problem of verbalism in pupil reports, the teacher should

1. Not fully accept bookish presentations that are meaningless to the child and are simply repetitions of what has been read. This usually can be handled by a comment such as "Jackie, I know you spent a lot of time and work preparing your report, but we would have found it much more valuable and interesting if you had told it to us in your own words."
2. Encourage children to use visual material in their reports— pictures, charts, diagrams, maps, graphs, the chalkboard. These are especially effective if the child himself prepared the visual aid.
3. Ask pupils to give concrete examples of what they are describing in words they use in ordinary everyday conversation.
4. Encourage children to use more than one source for their information.
5. Be more lavish with rewards to those who avoid bookish presentations.

It is perhaps true that oral and written reports are among the most common ways pupils share ideas in social studies. In many classrooms these activities are overused and, in some cases, misused. For example, the idea of reports of any kind in the social studies is to communicate something to someone else. Oral and written reports are often ineffective precisely because the pupil has nothing to communicate; consequently, he verbalizes something he has read but does not understand. A first requirement for any report, therefore, is that the pupil have something to say. Assuming this condition has been met, the second consideration is to decide how best to communicate the ideas to others. Even though the imaginative teacher will stimulate his pupils to think of creative ways these presentations can be made, the following are suggested as alternatives to the traditional oral and written reports.

1. Dramatizing an incident, sequence, or situation relating to the topic and incorporating essential data to be communicated in the dramatization
2. Using pupils' own drawn illustrations, charts, and graphs as the basis for a presentation or using illustrations of this type found in newspapers, magazines, or other sources
3. Pretending to be a tour guide taking the class through the area studied
4. Using the overhead projector for visual aids in a presentation
5. Role-playing the part of a newscaster making an on-the-spot report
6. Interviewing a classmate who is role-playing the part of someone who is an expert on the topic under study
7. Collecting pictures, arranging them in sequence, and using them as the basis for a report
8. Writing a diary or letter that might have been written by someone in an earlier period
9. Using artifacts or realia as the basis for a report
10. Preparing and explaining a bulletin board display or diorama
11. Preparing a narration for a filmstrip
12. Doing an original narration for a motion picture film with sound turned off
13. Writing news stories that might have been appropriate to a particular period or preparing and publishing a single issue of a newspaper that might have appeared in some historical period
14. Tape-recording a presentation for playback to the class

Discussion Questions and Suggested Activities

1. Construct a poster illustrating the responsibilities of the speaker and the audience during discussion periods. How would you use this poster with a classroom of children?
2. Observe a classroom of a grade of your interest and choice. Using Mork's material on pages 342–344, give specific examples of pupil behavior that would indicate the presence or absence of a democratically functioning classroom.
3. Suggest ways a teacher might work with low-achieving pupils in order to help them obtain better status in the classroom.

4. Do you think teachers in the past have placed a greater emphasis on achievement tasks or socialization tasks as these are defined in the text? What does research say about the reasons for adults' losing their jobs? Might this indicate a need for a greater emphasis on the development of socialization skills? Must the teacher decide between the development of achievement skills *or* socialization skills or can a fine balance be struck in the instructional emphasis given to each?

5. Under what circumstances might the teacher not want to clarify in great detail the goals of a small group?

6. Prepare a presentation for your classmates on a recent magazine article or book you have read that deals with an educational problem. Utilize creative techniques such as those suggested in this chapter for such presentations.

7. What problems might the beginning teacher anticipate if he started group work before he was secure in the teaching position? How might a teacher build readiness for small-group endeavors with a group that had always worked on a whole-class basis?

8. Suggest at least one other grouping of the students included in the sociogram of this chapter.

9. What provisions can the teacher incorporate to develop more pupil-initiated verbal behavior and more pupil-pupil interaction in the classroom? In what ways can the teacher exert strong leadership without making the children unduly dependent on him? Is this desirable?

Selected References

Bany, Mary A., and Lois V. Johnson. *Classroom Group Behavior: Group Dynamics in Education.* New York: The Macmillan Company, 1964.

Bennett, Margaret E. *Guidance in Groups: A Resource Book for Teachers, Counselors, and Administrators.* New York: McGraw-Hill Book Company, Inc., 1955.

Bigge, Morris L., and Maurice P. Hunt. *Psychological Foundations of Education,* Chap. 19. New York: Harper and Row, Publishers, Inc., 1962.

Brilhart, John K. *Effective Group Discussion.* Dubuque, Iowa: William Brown Company, 1967.

Cartwright, Dorwin, and Alvin Zander. *Group Dynamics, Research and Theory,* 3rd ed. Evanston, Ill.: Harper and Row, Publishers, Inc., 1968.

Evans, K. M. *Sociometry and Education.* London: Routledge and Kegan Paul, 1962.

Flanders, Ned A. *The Effect of Teacher Influence on Student Attitudes,* Series on Individualization of Instruction, No. 3. Minneapolis, Minn.: University of Minnesota, 1959.

Fox, Robert, Margaret Luszki, and Richard Schmuck. *Diagnosing Classroom Learning Environments.* Chicago: Science Research Associates, Inc., 1966.

Gronlund, Norman E. *Sociometry in the Classroom.* New York: Harper and Row, Publishers, Inc., 1959.

Hall, D. M. *Dynamics of Group Action.* Danville, Ill.: Interstate Publishers and Printers, Inc., 1957.

Jensen, Gale E. "The Sociopsychological Structure of the Instructional Group," *The Dynamics of Instructional Groups.* Chicago: National Society for the Study of Education, 1960.

Kemp, C. G. "The Democratic Classroom," *Elementary School Journal* (November, 1960), pp. 68–71.

Lieberman, Phyllis, and Sidney B. Simon. "Vitalizing Student Research Reports," *Social Education, XXVIII,* No. 1 (January, 1964), pp. 24–26.

Lutz, Frank W. "Sociometry: Big Word for a Bright Idea," *Instructor, 83,* No. 1 (September, 1965), pp. 114+.

Margolin, Edythe. "What Do Group Values Mean to Young Children?" *The Elementary School Journal* (February, 1969), pp. 250–258.

Muessig, Raymond H., and Vincent R. Rogers. "Developing Competence in Group Participation and Human Relations," *Skill Development in Social Studies,* 33rd Yearbook. Washington, D.C.: National Council for the Social Studies, 1963.

Noar, Gertrude. *Teaching and Learning the Democratic Way.* Englewood Cliffs, N.J.: Prentice-Hall, Inc., 1963.

Rehage, Kenneth. "Group Work Skills," *Social Studies in Elementary Schools,* 32nd Yearbook. Washington, D.C.: National Council for the Social Studies, 1962.

Skeel, Dorothy J. *The Challenge of Teaching Social Studies in the Elementary School.* Pacific Palisades, Calif.: Goodyear Publishing Company, Inc., 1970.

Pupil Involvement Through Activities and Expressive Experiences

If one interprets the term *learning activity* broadly enough, it will include most of what the child does while he is in school. It embraces *intellectual* activities, such as thinking, feeling, listening, evaluating, reading, and writing; *appreciative* activities, such as the experiences the child has in literature, art, and music; *physical* activities, such as running, jumping, playing games, constructing, processing, and manipulating; or it may include combinations of all of these. When learning is defined as an interactive process between the learner and his environment, some degree of intellectual or physical activity becomes a necessary condition for learning to take place. In this sense all schools are in some measure "activity" schools. The

13

modern educator, therefore, does not have to decide whether or not there are to be activities in the curriculum but, rather, does have to decide the kinds of activities, the purposes of them, and the contribution they can best make in facilitating the child's learning. This chapter will consider some of the ways research, construction and processing, art, music, and dramatic activities can, if properly used, enhance and extend understandings in the social studies.

In the past there has been a tendency to place undue emphasis on certain types of learning activities, almost to the exclusion of others. The social studies curriculum, for example, has traditionally been dominated by verbal and linguistic activities to the extent that children did little more than read, report, discuss, write, answer questions, and recite. These practices are still common in many schools but are usually conducted more informally than they were at the turn of the century when they were the universally accepted methods of instruction. As more became known about child growth and development, about the psychology of individual differences, and about the manner in which learning takes place, there developed a reaction against this formal, academic approach to social studies instruction. And there followed a movement in education toward more physical involvement on the part of children in the learning process. This gave rise to the so-called activity or child-centered schools where teachers were encouraged to have children "learn by doing." Because of misunderstanding and/or misapplication of the activity concept, many teachers placed excessive emphasis on physical activities, and schools were criticized, with some justification, for minimizing intellectual activities. Today good schools try to maintain a balance between activities that involve the child physically and those that consist almost entirely of reading, research, writing, and discussing. In the strictest sense, activities should not be categorized as physical on the one hand and intellectual on the other, because this implies that no intellectual activity is involved in a construction, processing, art, or similar task. This, of course, is not true, because all should require the child to do careful thinking.

Learning activities, therefore, should not be regarded as a fetish but rather as mediums or vehicles used to help the learner move in the direction of established goals. Ideally, the teacher will want to select the vehicle *best suited* for the learner in attaining his goal—it is a means to an end. The selecting of appropriate means to achieve goals is a fairly common practice in the everyday lives of people outside of school. One would not, for example, use a water-color paintbrush in redecorating the exterior of his house in a weekend "do-it-yourself" project. He would in all probability select a brush of proper weight for his strength and one that would do the job most efficiently. One does not use a saddle horse to rush across country to the bedside of a dying mother, but this means of travel would be suitable if one were planning a hunting trip into the mountains of western Montana. In the classroom, the teacher will be equally selective in using various learning activities, and the selection will be conditioned by the nature and needs of the learners as well as by the goals to be achieved. For one group of children, a construction activity may be pointless; for another group under different conditions, it may hold many values. The teacher will use a great variety of learning activities to achieve his objectives —some will involve more physical activity than others but all will give impetus to careful thinking and will not be used as a way of avoiding intellectual activity.

The chief values of research, construction and processing, art, music, and dramatic activities in social studies, then, are (1) the contribution they make toward enhancing learning through the extension and expansion of meanings and understandings and (2) the extent to which they assist in promoting process learnings. Teachers must have definite goals and purposes to be achieved through the use of the activity before it is selected. With this in mind, the teacher might use such activities for any or all of the following purposes:

1. To stimulate pupil interest
2. To stimulate various aspects of thinking
3. To give direction and purpose to learning
4. To encourage initiative, exploration, and research
5. To aid in applying factual information obtained through research to concrete situations
6. To provide a setting in which to use socialization skills
7. To clarify complex procedures
8. To aid in developing an understanding of concepts and generalizations
9. To relate various aspects of the school program to one another
10. To provide opportunities for thinking, planning, sharing, doing, and evaluating
11. To provide an outlet for creative abilities
12. To provide an opportunity for recognition for the nonverbal, nonacademic child

Research Activities

The most fundamental of all learning activities are those that call for the finding and organizing of information that leads to the solution of problems. Whatever other activities the teacher may choose to use —construction, processing, music, art, dramatics, or others—doing research related to such activities is essential if they are to have meaning and validity as instructional experiences for children. For example, if a second-grade class is planning to make butter in the classroom as an activity relating to their unit on the dairy, it is presumed that the children will first *find out* how one goes about making butter, what ingredients will be needed, how much time such a process takes, what equipment is required, what temperature the cream must be in order to churn, how vigorously to churn the cream, and so on. All of this will require getting, organizing and sharing information. When this occurs in the classroom, we say children are "doing research."

Tradition has associated book reading and library work with the term *research*. Actually, if research activities are defined as those that help children secure information, it is immediately apparent that children are doing research when they ask questions of others, take field trips, look at pictures, view audio-visual material, examine and handle objects, use maps and globes, and even when they watch informative television programs. Books, of course, are important research tools, too, but they are not the only ones. Some children will depend more heavily on books in doing research than will other children, but all will take part in fact finding and information gathering in one form or another. Any of the instructional resources discussed in Chapter 4 can be used for research purposes. Research activities stress working together—defining problems, securing sources of information, and sharing the results.

Children will need a considerable amount of help from the teacher in carrying out research, and most of this help is given on an informal basis, rather than in a "one, two, three" order as is sometimes implied in discussions of problem-solving procedures. For example, to do research there must be a problem—otherwise it would have no purpose. Problems have to be pinpointed specifically for young children, simplified to the extent that the child knows exactly what he is to find out. The problem "How do people in Mexico live?" is much too broad and complex for pupils. This should be broken down into several smaller problems such as "What kinds of holidays do the people of Mexico celebrate?" or "How do the people of Mexico furnish their homes?" or "How do the children of Mexico get their education?" Sometimes in teacher-pupil planning the children will list many things they want to find out, as many as fifteen to twenty or more specific topics. Not all these are equally significant, and many are related to one another. The teacher will then try to organize the specific topics into a few major ones, including those that are less significant, with related, more important points. As an example, children may want to find out such things as "Do Mexican people have frozen foods? Do they eat three meals each day? Do they drink wine with their meals?" All of these may be gathered together under the more general problem "What kinds of food do the people of Mexico eat?" Then the specific related questions may be stated under the larger, more significant problem.

When the problem or problems have been adequately defined and organized, children will need help in finding adequate sources of information. The younger the children are, the more assistance they will need. In the primary grades, much of the research will be done through the use of nonreading resources. Children will listen to the teacher read informative selections related to the problem under study. They will gather information by asking their parents questions and sharing findings with their classmates. They will study pictures together and talk about them. They will do a considerable amount of firsthand experiencing: learning through listening, seeing, feeling, and doing. For the children who can read, the teacher will need to find books and perhaps even locate the portion of the book related to the topic. This can be done by placing a bookmark in the appropriate place. In the middle and upper grades, children should be able to locate information more independently but will still need help and guidance in finding the right book, knowing where to look for information, and how to find the right place in a book. These are times the teacher will want to teach the skills related to locating information, such as those contained in the suggestions on pages 333–334. Besides the sources that children use independently, the teacher will want to arrange for field trips, use audio-visual aids, pictures, maps, globes, resource persons, and community resources. Once the resources have been found, children begin gathering the facts and information they are seeking to answer their questions and solve their problems. In this regard, the teacher will arrange to have progress reports daily during the time set aside for planning and evaluating.

As children gather information, they will discover that some method is needed to organize, summarize, and present the material. The methods used for this purpose will, of course, depend on the age and maturity of the children. For primary-grade children it may be done by having them state the main ideas orally and having the teacher write them on the chalkboard. Children may then copy these on their own sheets of paper and keep them in their folders along with art work, pictures, and other things they have gathered in studying their topic. Or it may be done through the use of a log or a summary in the way of an experience chart, such as

We Learn About the Farm

We went to the farm.
The farmer has cows, chickens, and pigs.
The farmer sells the things he grows.
We get our food from the farm.
City people need food from farms.

Middle- and upper-grade children can be taught to organize and summarize information independently, although much of this will be done on a class basis throughout the grades. Many of these skills are taught in the language arts program in the elementary school, but they need to be tied into and applied in the social studies. Children not only will need to be taught how to select main ideas, identify subordinate but related ideas, draw conclusions, summarize data, and make notes on reading but also will need to apply these skills in purposeful ways. It is in the social studies that such an application can and should be made. In order to help organize and summarize their work, children should be taught how to use charts, graphs, maps, outlines, notebooks, 3″ x 5″ filing cards, and other devices. Presenting their findings to the class likewise presents the teacher with many opportunities to teach discussion procedures, speaking, reading, and writing skills.

Some teachers have found the use of *pupil specialties* to be helpful in stimulating individual research projects. Chase refers to a specialty as "a special assignment which deals with some person, place, event, product, or period of time. Specialties enrich the classroom program, giving the child a feeling of importance."[1] In developing his specialty, the pupil often becomes somewhat the class authority on a particular subject. This procedure has obvious values for more-capable children but is also useful with children at all levels of ability. Oddly enough, where it has been used successfully in classes, the slower-learning children show much interest in developing a specialty. Perhaps for once in their school lives, the superiority of their more capable classmates is not threatening to them, and they can enjoy the prestige that comes from knowing something the others do not.

Information obtained through research serves its most useful purpose when it can be applied. For this reason, teachers frequently stimulate research activity through the use of accompanying, related activities. For example, if the children are planning a dramatics activity dealing with Mexican life, they will need to do research to find out exactly what Mexican life is like to be able to dramatize it accurately. Or if a primary-grade group is constructing a store or a post office in

1. W. Linwood Chase, "Individual Differences in Classroom Learning," *Social Studies in the Elementary School*, 56th Yearbook, National Society for the Study of Education, Chicago: University of Chicago Press, 1957, p. 173.

their room, they will want to find out as much about it as possible in order to have their construction as nearly correct as it can be made. Teaching procedures of this type are helpful in giving the young child a definite purpose for doing research.

Construction and Processing Activities

Most children love to make things. They build villages and castles in their sandboxes; they make windmills with their tinker toys; they build boats to float in a nearby pond; they construct birdhouses, model airplanes, handicraft objects—almost anything one cares to mention. With a hammer, saw, a few nails, and some scraps of lumber, the young child is off to an afternoon of fun in his father's workroom, "making things." These natural sensory-motor play and creative-building activities are valuable for children in and of themselves. They give countless opportunities for thinking, planning, creative expression, use of tools, physical activity, and development of coordination. Children need many experiences of this type. In social studies, however, these values are only incidental to the chief purpose, which is to extend and enrich meaning of some aspect of the social studies unit under consideration. The excellence of the final product is, likewise, not the major consideration. What is important is the learning that has occurred as a result of the construction activity. This being true, authenticity, genuineness, and truthfulness in the representations are exceedingly important considerations in conducting construction activities.

There have been many abuses made of construction activities, largely because their basic purpose has been misconstrued or misunderstood. In some cases they amount to little more than keeping the children busy at something, with little thought being given to the understandings and learnings the construction is allegedly fostering. If constructions are inaccurate, contrary to truth and reality, they are detrimental to learning and would be better omitted entirely. Thirty-five years ago Horn wrote forcefully on this topic, but the misuse of construction persists.

> Lowest of all are the constructions that are largely fanciful and almost wholly erroneous. An Indian peace pipe is represented by a large bowl with enough stems so that all members of the council can smoke at once; a paper tepee typifies an Indian home in a locality where no tepee was ever built; and a drawing of a single person climbing a steep hill to reach a lone hut at the top depicts the capture of Vicksburg. Closely akin to these unbridled fabrications of the imagination are many that have become traditionally symbolic. Pointed paper hats of a pattern unknown in any age are made for soldiers of the Revolu-

Esthetic sensitivity and a desire to create can be expressed in many ways. (Courtesy of the Colorado State College, Greeley)

tionary War; paper hatchets are cut out in preparation for Washington's birthday; a frieze of jinrikishas and Fujiyamas is drawn or cut from paper to symbolize Japan; "very effective" polar bears are made by gluing cotton on patterns cut from paper; and farm life is made "real" by having city children give the conventional quack-quack for geese, cluck-clucks for hens, and baa-baas for sheep. Such enterprises are *prima facie* evidence of slovenly thought. Teachers sometimes defend or even approve them, however, on the ground that they are "real to the child" or "the child's very own," thus manifesting an indisposition to seek the truth, as well as a flagrant misconception of the healthy and vigorous use of the imagination. Such experiences not only fail to contribute to valid understanding but are an actual detriment, since they give the student concrete ideas of the ways things are *not* and discourage any effort to discover the truth.[2]

It is possible to use construction activities to motivate children's work and to establish more clearly children's purposes for doing

2. Ernest Horn, *Methods of Instruction in the Social Studies*, New York: Charles Scribner's Sons, 1937, p. 420. Copyright 1937 by Charles Scribner's Sons. *Used by permission.*

Construction activities can be used to stimulate interest and to give purpose to reading and research. (Courtesy of the Shoreline Public Schools, Seattle)

things. Let us say, for example, that a primary grade is conducting a study on the dairy farm. The teacher might suggest that the class construct a model farm in one corner of their classroom. Naturally, they want to make their model as authentic as possible; therefore, a considerable amount of research will be necessary as they proceed with the building of the farm. In fact, they cannot even begin unless they know what it is they want to do, that is, unless they have a genuine need for information. The children's purpose in this case may be to learn about the dairy farm to be able to build a classroom model of it. The teacher's purpose, however, is to have children form accurate concepts and understandings of a dairy farm; he is using the construction activity as a vehicle to achieve that goal. Under this arrangement, if the pupils achieve their goals, the teacher will have achieved his, too.

The procedure just described is a fairly common and legitimate use of construction. The one difficulty with it is that it is easy for the teacher to lose sight of his own purpose, and he, too, becomes interested in only building an impressive model. He is especially vulnerable to this if he is expecting visitors to the room, such as during an open house for parents during American Education Week. The desire to have a fine display may detract from the educational value of activities of this type.

In selecting a construction activity for a social studies unit, the teacher should make certain that

1. It is useful in achieving a definite purpose.
2. It clarifies, enriches, or extends the meaning of some important concept.
3. It requires the child to do careful thinking and planning.
4. It is an accurate and truthful representation.
5. It is within the capabilities of the children.
6. The time and effort expended can be justified by the learnings that occur.
7. It is reasonable in terms of space and expense.
8. The needed materials are available.

When the teacher has satisfied himself that a construction activity can make a definite contribution to learning in the social studies, he may have the children engage in constructing items of the type suggested here.

Toys
Model furniture
Books
Musical instruments
Costumes of foreign people, history of costumes, evolution of costumes
Simple trucks, airplanes, boats
Puppets and marionettes
Paper bag dolls
"Television" set with paper-roll programs
Working models
Paper making
Spinning wheels
Looms for weaving
Models of various homes and furnishings
Animal cages
Animals of art materials
Maps (pictorial, product, relief, floor)

Candles
Soap
Baskets, trays, bowls
Butter
Preparation of foods (making cookies, jelly, ice cream)
Ships, harbor, cargo
Trains and railroad equipment
Retail food market and equipment
Community buildings
Fruits and vegetables
Scenery and properties for stage, dioramas, panoramas
Holiday decorations
Jewelry
Pottery, vases, dishes, cups
Covered wagons, churns, butter paddles, wooden spoons, and other
    pioneer gear
Flour mill
Post office
Bakery
Gasoline station
Fire station
Dairy farm and buildings
Radio, telegraph, and other communication devices
Oxcarts
Circus accessories
Playhouses
Model villages
Purses, hot pads, table mats, small rugs
Birdhouses and feeding stations
Seed boxes, planters
Replicas of famous buildings
Dyeing cloth
Production of visual material needed in the unit, such as pictorial
    graphs, maps, charts, posters, attractive displays, bulletin boards
Weather stations
Block printing
Figures of animals or people

Assuming that the teacher has done a sufficient amount of preplanning to satisfy himself that a construction activity has a useful purpose, that materials are available, that there is sufficient space in which
to work, and that it is realistic in terms of the children involved, he
may proceed with getting the activity underway. In this connection,
the following suggestions may be helpful.

Discuss the Purposes of the Activity with the Children. The practice of having children make stores, build boats and covered wagons, or do Indian crafts without knowing why they are doing them is open to serious question. Children may not have the foggiest notion concerning the real purpose or significance of the construction. It is suggested, therefore, that at the very beginning of such an activity, the reasons for planning it be discussed and understood by all. Purposes should be reviewed from time to time during the activity.

Plan the Method of Procedure with the Children. The initial planning will take a considerable amount of time if every detail is to be taken into account. Such extensive planning is not necessary or entirely desirable, for it tends to make children impatient. Decisions must be made, however, as to the basic materials needed, major responsibilities and who will assume them, committees needed and who will be on them, where the construction will take place, where needed information may be obtained, and a general overall plan. After the construction project is underway there will be time each day to do additional specific planning. It is best to plan in a general way and get started, leaving the details for a later time.

Plan Methods of Work with the Children. Construction activities involve working in groups, the use of tools, perhaps hammering and sawing or other noisy activities, and somewhat more disorder than that found in regular classroom work. This means that unless there are some rules and standards concerning the methods of work, there is likely to be much noise, commotion, and general confusion. Therefore, before any activity of this sort is undertaken, it is recommended that the teacher and the pupils discuss and decide what the rules of work are to be. These might include

1. How to get and return materials.
2. Use of tools and equipment, including safe handling.
3. Things to remember during the work period. Such items as talking in a conversational voice, good use of materials to avoid waste, sharing tools and materials with others, consideration for others, doing one's share of work, asking for help when needed, and giving everyone a chance to present his ideas would be important considerations.
4. Procedures for clean-up time. It is well to establish a "listen" signal to get the attention of the class. It can be a chord on the piano, turning off the lights, or ringing a small bell. When the listen signal is given, children should learn to stop whatever they are doing, cease talking, and listen to whatever announcement is to be made. In this way, the teacher can stop the work of the class at any time to call their attention to some detail or get them

started at clean-up. Clean-up is one procedure that can be done in a routine fashion. When the signal is given, all work stops, children listen for directions, restore the room to its prior condition, and assemble at the circle or go to their desks.

Arrange Plenty of Time Each Day for Planning, Working, Clean-up, and Evaluation.   Before work on the construction activity is begun each day, time should be spent in making specific plans for that day. This is to ensure that everyone has an important job to do and that he knows what his responsibilities are. It also is a time when the teacher can go over some of the points the class talked about during its previous day's evaluation. "You remember yesterday we had some problem about which group was to use the tools. Which group has the tools today?" Or, "Yesterday our voices became a little loud at times. Perhaps we can be more careful about that today."

During the work period the teacher will want to move from group to group observing, assisting, suggesting new approaches, helping groups in difficulty, clarifying ideas, helping children find materials, supervising and guiding the work of the class. He will spot the children who need help in getting started, those who are not working well together, those who seem not to be doing anything, or others who may be having difficulty. The teacher will keep an eye on the time and stop the work of the class in time to ensure a thorough clean-up.

An important part of each period spent in this way is the group evaluation that occurs after the work and clean-up. During these times, the teacher will want the class to evaluate the progress it is making on the construction as well as the manner in which they are doing their work.

"Were we able to make progress on our store today?"
"How well did we remember our standards?"
"Do you think we could have done better in our clean-up? In what ways? We will want to remember that tomorrow, won't we?"
"How do you think we might change the color to make it look more real?"
"Does anyone have any ideas how Billy's group could show more action in their mural?"
"Did anyone see signs of safe handling of tools today?"
"I wonder if the mountains aren't too high on Julie's group's map? Did you check that against the picture in your book?"

The precise points discussed in such an evaluation, of course, will depend on the class and its work. In any case, some attention should be given to (1) progress on the construction, (2) methods of working together, and (3) problems that need attention the next day.

Make Use of the Construction in Some Way, Relating It to the Unit Under Study. When constructed objects are completed, they should be put to good use. In the primary grades such a project may serve very well for dramatic play activities. A market in the classroom, for example, gives the children an opportunity to play customer, grocer, butcher, checkout girl, or other personnel associated with a market. They read labels and prices, rearrange the material on the shelves, keep the store clean, and so on. In the middle and upper grades, objects made can be examined, discussed, and displayed for others to see. A mural can be used for study purposes by the entire class. A child can explain to his class the manner in which some object is constructed, its main features, how it was used, its history, why it is no longer used, and similar information. Perhaps the best constructions are the ones that can be used in some worthwhile way by the entire group in learning more about an important aspect of unit study.

Disassemble and Remove the Construction When It Has Served Its Purpose. Sometimes a construction is kept in the classroom long after the unit is completed. This usually means that it is taking up valuable classroom space that could be put to some other use. Constructions are of value only insofar as they relate to the work of the class. When they have served this purpose, they should be removed.

Closely related to construction activities are those that help the child understand the various steps or stages in the production of some material item. They deal with the *process* of changing raw materials into finished, usable items and, hence, involve *processing of materials*. These activities are used to help the pupil understand and appreciate the complexities of producing some of the basic material items most persons use in everyday living. They are commonly used to impress on the pupils the hardships, labor, skill, and ingenuity required of pioneers and primitive people in a time when it was necessary for them to produce basic materials for themselves. The most common processes used in elementary school social studies units are making butter, candles, paper, sugar, salt, bricks, natural dyes, jelly, ink, books, ice cream, and soap and weaving and dyeing cloth.

When properly handled by the teacher, processing activities have a number of values for today's children. In earlier times many of these processes were carried on in the home routinely; and children of necessity had firsthand experience with them. Today the producer and consumer are so widely separated from one another that the child has little or no opportunity to gain an understanding and appreciation of the processes involved in getting basic materials on the shelves of the supermarket or the department store.

There are some instructional problems, however, in processing materials. For example, if the teacher is expecting to demonstrate the hardships experienced by pioneers in making candles by dipping, he should not use an electric hot plate as a source of heat and an aluminum container for the wax! In most classrooms of the nation it is, in fact, impossible to duplicate conditions under which candles were made in the seventeenth century. Almost any raw material the class uses in its processing will in all likelihood *already* be semiprocessed. The child may, therefore, leave such an experience with a lack of appreciation of the complexities involved in the process—a misfire of the precise learning the teacher had hoped to put across.

Some processes require extremely careful supervision by the teacher because of physical danger to the children. Candlemaking means heating tallow, wax, or paraffin that can ignite if allowed to become too hot and cause severe burns if dropped accidentally on one's person. Soapmaking calls for the use of lye, always potentially dangerous. In one class a child drove a crochet hook through her hand while engaging in a processing activity. These points are mentioned not to discourage the use of construction and processing but to alert the beginner to the real need for careful supervision while such activity is taking place.

Classrooms utilizing construction and processing activities will require tools and equipment. In addition to some type of workbench and an adequate storage place where they can be kept neatly and safely, the following tools will be helpful

Claw hammer	Screwdriver
Coping saw	Holding devices
Crosscut saw	Pliers with side cutters
Hand drill and bits	Brace and bits
Plane	Try square
Sandpaper	Nails and screws
Tin shears	Chisel
Keyhole saw	

Lumber and other materials can be purchased as needed or brought by the children. In addition to new stock, there is need for a substantial amount of waste materials in the form of boxes of all kinds, wood, wire, cardboard, mattress crates, laths, cloth, wheels. Used pieces of wood with nails in them are potentially hazardous and must be handled accordingly.

Music Activities

Music activities make an important contribution to social studies instruction. Through the universal language of music, the child may extend his communication to other peoples, races, and cultures, past and present. Various songs and music forms are associated with periods in our national history, and many songs relate directly to heroes or great historical events. Musical expression in a sense is an emotional experience, piercing through everyday inhibitions and extending into the inner reaches of one's personality. Although the use of symbols, whether they be music or other, is admittedly a shallow means of teaching good citizenship, it is undeniably true that music inspires patriotism, love of country, loyalty, and fidelity. It is for this reason that marching bands are used in holiday parades and between halves at football games. Nation-states have used music very effectively in building a feeling of national solidarity. Music has a profound effect on individuals as well as on groups.

Music educators have worked diligently to break the shackles of the "music period" concept of music education and have consistently recommended a greater integration of music in the total life of the classroom. Music activities, therefore, not only contribute to social studies instruction but support the music program itself. The material that follows suggests some possibilities for the use of singing, rhythmic expression, listening, and creative music activities in social studies units.

Singing. For almost any social studies unit the teacher selects, he will find appropriate and related songs for children to sing. One of the chief values of singing is its affective quality; it gives the child a *feeling* for the material not likely to be obtained in any other way. Through singing, the child senses the loneliness of the voyager and of cowboys around their campfires, the gaiety of a frontier housewarming, or the sadness of a displaced people longing for their homeland. He learns the folk songs not only of his own nation, but those that are sung the world over. Singing is an experience that can broaden the child's appreciation of peoples everywhere. In the study of communities around the world, the teacher will want to use the songs of various national groups. Such experiences help the child gain a greater appreciation of and sympathy for cultural aspects of the group studied. It gives him an opportunity to learn more about a people through the language of music.

Rhythmic Expression. Rhythmic and bodily expression tend to release one from the crust of convention and formality that is built in the normal course of everyday life and provide a means of self-expression. Through rhythms, bodily expression, and folk dances, the child develops grace and poise and learns the amenities characteristic of such social activities. Folk dancing and folk games in themselves are pleasurable and legitimate social activities for children. They provide for teamwork and allow the child to participate in the activity with several other boys and girls. Folk dancing and folk games usually involve eight or more children with a continual shifting of partners. For this reason, folk dancing is well suited for children of elementary school age.

In the social studies units, the teacher will want to use the various folk dances and rhythmic activities characteristic of many countries. He will also want to use folk games and dances associated with various periods of our national history. Through activities of this type the child is helped to broaden his appreciation of people the world over who lived in the past as well as those now living in different parts of the world. He is able to trace the evolution of civilized man through his methods of rhythmic expression. Far from being solely a recreational activity for children, rhythmic expression provides a wide range of possibilities for social learnings in particular and social studies in general.

Creating. Social studies units provide many opportunities for the child to create musically. This can be done on an individual basis or as a class project and can be used with almost any topic under study by any age group. Perhaps it is not used more frequently by teachers because they feel that a considerable amount of technical knowledge of music is necessary. The need for the technical skills of music is usually greatly overestimated, but if the teacher feels insecure, he will ordinarily have someone available who does have such skills and can be of assistance. This person might be a music supervisor or teacher, the high school music teacher, or a fellow classroom teacher.

Creative music in social studies takes a variety of forms. In its simplest form it is a melody or sounds children learn to associate with the topic studied. For example, they may make sounds that make them think of a factory, a circus, or a train. Later these sounds can be used in the development of an actual melody. Children commonly produce creative verse to which they may add an appropriate melody. In the middle and upper grades such creative music activities may include the development of words and music for pageants, plays, puppet shows, or simple musicals. These original musical numbers are frequently of exceptional quality musically and are favorites of the children for years afterward—an indication of the satisfying and long-lasting quality of creative music.

Listening. Although singing, creating, and rythmic expression involve performing or *doing* aspects of music, listening places the child in the role of a consumer of music. This role deserves more attention than is usually given it, because it is the type of musical experience that continues throughout life. Long after most persons stop performing musically, they enjoy listening to music. Relating music listening to the affairs of life and living is, therefore, essential.

Listening to music is an imaginative experience for children. The teacher helps the child imagine the toys to come alive while listening to the *Nutcracker Suite* or puts him on the trail to the "clip-clop" of *The Grand Canyon Suite*. Such experiences help the child learn of mood in music and help him contrast that which is bright, gay, and lively with music that is quiet and restful. Through listening the child learns to identify the use of music by different groups and peoples throughout the world—it provides for another direct cultural contact with peoples of many lands. The teacher will have no difficulty obtaining recordings for the purposes described, for they are available in sufficient quantity and of good quality.

Creative Art Experiences

Creative art is widely used in social studies instruction because of the many activities in the units that inspire creative expression. A trip to the farm, airport, zoo, post office, or fire station all give impetus to the desire to create. Observing trucks, steam shovels, men tearing down buildings, as well as a hike to a nearby park or stream, are the types of experiences from which come the creative art work of children. Through an art medium the child may be able to symbolize his experiences, express his thoughts, or communicate his feelings, which he cannot do through the use of conventional language. For a young child in the primary grades, his picture or painting is likely to tell a whole story, and all the action is happening in the picture as it is being shared with others. For example, a first-grader's painting may show a boy playing with his dog while a jet is flying overhead and a policeman is chasing a speeding motorist. But the action is not stopped at the time the painting was made; it goes on all the time. That is, the boy is really playing with his dog and the airplane is actually flying. Children's art work tells a story; it can be very useful in recording social studies experiences.

Many parallels could be drawn between art experiences and music experiences in social studies units. Like music, art provides a cultural link with the many peoples of the world, past and present. It also places the child in the roles of creator and consumer as does music. It deals directly with feelings, emotions, appreciations, and creative abilities of children. In addition to the many desirable outcomes associated with any creative endeavor, creative art experiences have much to offer in stimulating and strengthening learning in the social studies.

Work in other areas of the curriculum, in this case art, is often related to social studies learnings. (Courtesy of the Seattle Public Schools)

In the course of the social studies unit, the teacher will use art and art mediums in a variety of ways. These are commonly used art activities in social studies:

Preparing murals
Free painting
Making illustrations
Weaving
Block-printing
Clay-modeling
Potato- or stick-printing
Chalk-, charcoal-, and crayon-drawing
Pencil-sketching

Making models
Making cartoons
Making booklets and books
Crafts related to some locality or country
Constructing dioramas to illustrate scenes
Planning and preparing exhibits
Sewing
Making designs and costumes

Making properties for plays, pageants	Wood-carving
Making puppets and marionettes	Toy-making
Soap-carving	Finger-painting
Poster-making	Indian sand-painting

Creative art expression as used in social studies may take two forms. The first of these might be described as completely personal and performed by the pupil because it expresses an idea or gives him personal satisfaction. Having the experience is its own reward, and the child need not share such a piece of art with anyone, although children often want to. Art work of this type is not evaluated in terms of the product produced but in terms of the satisfactions the experience itself gives the youngster. Any of the art mediums can be used for personal expression.

A second type of creative art expression can be thought of as *functional* in that the product is used in connection with some other activity. It might be a mural to be used as the background for a dramatic activity. It might be a model of something that will be used to illustrate an explanation. It could be a visual aid the child plans to use in making a report to the class. In art work of this type, the representation has to be reasonably accurate and authentic; consequently, the teacher will need to guard against having the children copy exactly the illustrations they find in reference materials.

The poorest of all art experiences are those that are patterned rather than creative. In such cases, the teacher dittoes a diagram of a turkey, for example, and has children color certain feathers red, others brown, and others orange. Children who follow the directions precisely and who can color within the lines are highly rewarded with teacher praise. Then the thirty-five turkeys, all alike, are posted on the bulletin board under the caption "We Do Creative Work." Such conspicuous misuse of art may also take the form of black profiles of Lincoln, hatchets and cherries, covered wagons, or Christmas trees. Teaching of this type tends to depress any creative art ability or interest in art expression that an imaginative child may have, and should be avoided.

Dramatic Activities

Dramatic representation in any one of its many forms is a popular activity with children—one in which they have all engaged during their early years. What child has not "been" a father, a mother, a teacher, a fireman, an Indian, a jet pilot, or a fairy princess during the fanciful and imaginative play of early childhood? Dramatic activities

Social Studies should provide a setting for expressive activities. (Courtesy of the Seattle Public Schools)

have great value in promoting social studies learnings. They help sharpen the child's power of observation; give purpose to research activities; give the child insight into another's feelings by putting himself in another's place; provide experience in democratic living; help create and maintain interest, thereby motivating learning and providing an excellent situation in which the teacher may observe the behavior of children.

The most structured dramatic activity is the *dramatization*. It requires a script, staging, rehearsal, and an audience. It may be used to show some historical event, to represent the growth of a movement or idea, to represent life in another period, or to demonstrate some problem of living. Children are usually involved in a considerable amount of creative work in productions of this type. They may write an original script, plan and prepare costumes, do the art work necessary for staging and properties, plan a program, send invitations, and make all arrangements attendant to the project. This means much planning, working together, evaluating, and participating.

The dramatization unquestionably has many possibilities for social learnings, but it also has many limitations. Its most serious limitation is its primary goal, which is the production itself. The learnings that it is presumably to enhance are too easily subordinated in the effort to "put on a good show." Moreover, children of elementary school age have not the technical skills needed to do much of the work necessary for this type of activity, and, as a consequence, the teacher himself makes the costumes, writes the script, or does the art work needed for the background scenery. Because this takes considerable time and effort, the teacher is tempted to use the same material year after year with different groups of children. In some communities it is generally well known that when children have Miss So-and-so they will put on some play or pageant that the teacher has been doing for years. Each season she drags out old props and costumes, and possibly even the script varies little from year to year. Such procedures cannot be justified on the basis of enhancing social studies learnings or developing creative talents of children. Even though they may be entertaining and fun for the children, from the standpoint of social studies they are in most cases a waste of time.

Another limitation of dramatizations as they are used in social studies is that they frequently are planned so far in the future that the goal lacks meaning for the participants. Children are simply unable to work up much enthusiasm in October for a pageant to be produced in May or June. They need shorter-range goals if such activities are to be related to work currently being done in the classroom. Finally, dramatizations are extremely time consuming, and one wonders if the time might not be spent more profitably on other, less elaborate activities. If and when dramatizations are used, they should be kept as simple as possible, and serious thought should be given to the limitations described here.

The least-structured dramatic activity is the spontaneous acting out or reliving of situations from life about the children. It is called *dramatic play*. As this activity is used in social studies, the term *dramatic play* is an unfortunate one because it suggests entertainment. Perhaps the terms *creative dramatic representation* or *representative living* would more accurately describe what is involved in the activity. When kindergarteners and first-graders are playing various roles of mother, father, sister, brother, doctor, and nurse in a corner of the classroom, they are engaging in dramatic play. Free dramatic play is a natural activity for young children, and they participate in it with little or no stimulation from adults. During the periods of free dramatic play, the teacher may be able to learn much about the personality of the child. It will indicate with whom the child identifies, his attitudes toward others, his willingness to share, and his emotional maturity.

As children move into the second and third grades, there is less evidence of spontaneous dramatic play. At this stage of growth, dramatic play usually requires more suggestion and stimulation from the teacher and may be profitably used to help the child understand or appreciate some phase of human relationships. These slightly more structured dramatic activities are referred to as *role playing, sociodrama,* or *creative dramatics.*

Role playing, sociodrama, or creative dramatics are used to present a specific situation for study and discussion. There is no prepared script, it is unrehearsed, speaking parts are not memorized, and properties, if used at all, are held to a minimum. Some small amount of properties may be used simply to help children remain in role. These activities are used to teach the relationship of people, to focus attention on a central idea, to help children organize ideas, to extend vocabulary, and to gain a greater insight into the problems of others by casting themselves in another's role. Because they portray problems in human relationships, they provide an excellent basis for discussion and evaluation. They should be followed by a discussion of questions of this type: "Which character did you like best? Why?" "Which one did you like least? Why?" "How do you suppose the person *felt?*" "If you had been in the wagonmaster's place, what would you have done?" "Have you ever known anyone like that?"

This final discussion and analysis requires that the situation be cut before the problem has been solved and before the outcome is a certainty. Otherwise, there would be little room left for thoughtful consideration of the problem. Klein lists the following general uses of role playing: "(1) to stimulate discussion, (2) to depict a social problem for study, (3) to train in leadership skills, (4) to train in human relationship skills, (5) to acquire insight, sensitivity, and awareness, and (6) to train in more effective problem solving." [3]

3. Alan F. Klein, *How To Use Role Playing Effectively*, New York: Association Press, 1959, p. 13.

Closely related to creative dramatics is the use of *reaction stories*. Reaction stories are brief, narrative accounts dealing with human relations that are used to uncover various attitudes and emotions. They may be written by the teacher or may be passages selected from published works. They deal with a variety of topics such as sharing, teasing, responsibility, peer pressures, respect for property, and intercultural relations. The story is read to the children, and they are asked to tell their feelings about characters, situations, what they would do under similar circumstances, what alternatives were available to the characters, and other comparable reactions. This critique and analysis is similar to the one held at the conclusion of a creative dramatics activity.

Closely related to role playing and creative dramatics are simulations and games. They have become important instructional procedures in recent years. A simulation is an accurate representation of reality. Children are simulating family life, for example, when they assume mother, father, and children roles in a family life situation. They interact with each other and conduct their affairs as if they actually were the persons whose roles are being played. Other examples of simulation are Mock United Nations, Model Legislature, Model City Council, A Day in the Life of the Mayor, Building a City, and Running a Shopping Center. Simulations rely on gaming techniques and, consequently, are sometimes referred to as "simulation games."

A teacher can devise a simulation game himself or he can purchase commercially prepared simulation games. Costs of commercially prepared games are high, some running over one hundred dollars. The precise value of these techniques is still a matter of conjecture. That they enhance interest and are highly motivating seems clear. Also, they do bring school instruction closer to reality than conventional procedures. There is little or no evidence that simulation games are more effective than other procedures in helping pupils achieve the usual objectives of social studies. Readers who wish to learn more about simulation games are referred to the bibliography at the end of this chapter.

This chapter has presented some of the possibilities for using various activities to support and enhance learning in the social studies. Any of them can be used with young children to promote growth in human relationships. Similarly, any of them can be misused and overused. Activities are of value only when viewed as means to ends and when the purposes and goals are unmistakably clear to both the teacher and the children. Activity for its own sake is rarely justified as a part of social studies instruction. The teacher or preteacher who genuinely appreciates the contribution these activities can make to social studies will extend his knowledge of the various teaching techniques associated with their use. For this reason an extensive reading list is provided at the conclusion of this chapter.

Discussion Questions and Suggested Activities

1. Cite learning activities appropriate for the introductory, developmental, and culminating phases of the resource unit you are writing (Chapter 3).
2. When you have the opportunity to visit elementary school classrooms, observe the type of constructions underway in those rooms. Are they accurate and authentic representations? What purposes was the teacher hoping to accomplish through the use of the construction?
3. Demonstrate to the class the manner in which one would proceed with a processing activity with a group of children. Explain how you would point out to children that some of the material is partially processed. Indicate the concepts being developed in this activity.
4. What special problems of supervision present themselves when children use such tools as hammers, saws, tin shears, chisels, and pliers? What would be your attitude toward the use of such tools by an impulsive and/or irresponsible child? How would you handle such a situation?
5. Locate and list as part of your resource unit poems, stories, biographies, case studies, and other literary selections that you might use.
6. Evaluate the following comment made by a teacher: "I don't use construction activities because they consume far too much time. Besides, the pupils never look on them as learning experiences but, rather, think of them as a time to have fun and to talk with their classmates."
7. Prepare an illustrated chart presenting the steps or directions for some processing activity (for example, dipping candles). Have your classmates evaluate the clarity of your directions. Demonstrate the activity to your class if time permits.
8. Either obtain or write an unfinished, open-ended story that could be used as a role-playing activity. Put the characters in a social-problem situation. What alternatives are open to major characters in the story? How might you use this story with children?
9. List resource people in your school and community who could be of assistance in the demonstration and selection of appropriate learning activities.
10. What points would you make in discussing the following state-

ment: Social studies for young children should be more activity oriented than content centered.

Selected References

CONSTRUCTION

Association for Childhood Education International. *Children Can Make It*, Reprint Service Bulletin No. 28. Washington, D.C.: The Association, 1955.

Brown, James W., et al. *A-V Instruction: Materials and Methods*, 3rd ed. New York: McGraw-Hill Book Company, Inc., 1969.

Bryce, Mayo, and Harry B. Greene. *Teacher's Craft Manual*. Palo Alto, Calif.: Fearon Publishers, 1956.

Dean, Joan. *Arts and Crafts in the Elementary School*. New York: Philosophical Library, 1964.

Endicott, Robert F. *Scrap Wood Fun for Kids: 100 Easy-to-Make Projects for Boys and Girls*. New York: Association Press, 1961.

Hanna, Lavone A., et al. *Unit Teaching in the Elementary School*, rev. ed. New York: Holt, Rinehart & Winston, Inc., 1963.

Johnson, Lillian. *Papier-Mâché*. New York: David McKay Company, Inc., 1958.

Lindsay, Zaidee. *Art Is for All: Arts and Crafts for Less Able Pupils*. New York: Talpinger Publishing Company, 1968.

Moore, Frank C., et al. *Handicrafts for Elementary Schools*. Boston: D. C. Heath & Company, 1953.

Schmidt, Alfred. *Craft Projects for Slow Learners*. New York: The John Day Company, Inc., 1968.

Scobey, Mary-Margaret. "Role of Industrial Arts in the Elementary School Program of Social Studies," *Elementary School Journal* (January, 1959), pp. 288–293.

Shaftel, Fannie R. "Industrial Arts in the Social Studies Program," *Social Studies in Elementary Schools*, 32nd Yearbook. Washington, D.C.: National Council for the Social Studies, 1962.

MUSIC

Cheyette, Irving and Herbert. *Teaching Music Creatively in the Elementary School*. New York: McGraw-Hill Book Company, Inc., 1969.

Folk Music: A Selection of Folk Songs, Ballads, Dances, Instrumental Pieces, and Folk Tales of the United States and Latin America. Washington, D.C.: Library of Congress, Music Division, Reference Department.

Garretson, Robert L. *Music in Childhood Education.* New York: Appleton-Century-Crofts, Inc., 1966.

Huffman, A. M. "Music to Enrich Social Studies," *Instructor,* 76 (February, 1967), pp. 134–135+.

Kraus, Richard G. *A Pocket Guide of Folk and Square Dances and Singing Games for the Elementary School.* Englewood Cliffs, N.J.: Prentice-Hall, Inc., 1966.

Krone, Bernice P., and Kurt R. Miller. *Help Yourself to Music.* San Francisco: Chandler Publishing Company, 1959.

Maynard, Olga. *Children and Dance and Music.* New York: Charles Scribner's Sons, 1968.

Murray, Ruth L. *Dance in Elementary Education,* 2nd ed. New York: Harper and Row, Publishers, Inc., 1963.

Myers, Louise K. *Teaching Children Music in the Elementary School,* 3rd ed. Englewood Cliffs, N.J.: Prentice-Hall, Inc., 1961.

Nye, Robert E. and Vernice T. *Music in the Elementary School,* 2nd ed. Englewood Cliffs, N.J.: Prentice-Hall, Inc., 1964.

Tooze, Ruth A., and Bernice P. Krone. *Literature and Music as Resources for Social Studies.* Englewood Cliffs, N.J.: Prentice-Hall, Inc., 1955.

CREATIVE ART

Anderson, Warren. *Art Learning Situations for Elementary Education.* Belmont, Calif.: Wadsworth Publishing Company, Inc., 1965.

Erdt, Margaret H. *Teaching Art in the Elementary School,* rev. ed. New York: Holt, Rinehart & Winston, Inc., 1962.

Gaitskell, Charles D. *Children and Their Art.* New York: Harcourt, Brace & World, Inc., 1958.

Hopper, Grizella H. *Puppet Making Through the Grades.* Worcester, Mass.: Davis Publications, 1966.

Jefferson, Blanche. *Teaching Art to Children,* 2nd ed. Boston: Allyn & Bacon, Inc., 1963.

Kaufman, Irving. *Art and Education in Contemporary Culture.* New York: The Macmillan Company, 1966.

LaMancura, Katherine C. *Source Book for Art Teachers.* Scranton, Pa.: International Textbook Company, 1965.

Lowenfeld, Viktor, and W. Lambert Brittain. *Creative and Mental Growth,* 5th ed. New York: The Macmillan Company, 1970.

Montgomery, Chandler. *Art for Teachers of Children: Foundations of Aesthetic Experience.* Columbus, Ohio: Charles E. Merrill Books, Inc., 1968.

Paine, Irma Little. *Art Aids for Elementary Teaching: A Handbook,* 5th ed. Minneapolis, Minn.: Burgess Publishing Company, 1965.

Rueschhoff, Phil H., and M. Evelyn Schwartz. *Teaching Art in the Elementary School: Enhancing Visual Perception.* New York: Ronald Press Company, 1969.

Snow, Aida C. *Growing with Children Through Arts.* New York: Reinhold Publishing Corporation, 1968.

Tritten, Gottfried. *Art Techniques for Young Children.* New York: Reinhold Publishing Corporation, 1964.

DRAMATICS

Burger, Isabel B. *Creative Play Acting: Learning Through Drama,* 2nd ed. New York: Ronald Press Company, 1966.

Chesler, Mark, and Robert Fox. *Role Playing Methods in the Classroom.* Chicago: Science Research Associates, Inc., 1966.

Crosscup, Richard. *Children and Dramatics.* New York: Charles Scribner's Sons, 1966.

Drama with and for Children. Washington, D.C.: Government Printing Office, 1960.

Durland, Frances D. *Creative Dramatics for Children.* Yellow Springs, Ohio: Antioch Press, 1952.

McCaslin, Nellie. *Creative Dramatics in the Classroom.* New York: David McKay Company, Inc., 1968.

Nichols, H., and L. Williams. *Learning about Role Playing.* Washington, D.C.: Association for Childhood Education International, 1960.

Sagl, Helen L. "Dramatic Play: A Tool of Learning in Social Studies," *Social Studies in Elementary Schools,* 32nd Yearbook. Washington, D.C.: National Council for the Social Studies, 1962.

Shaftel, Fannie R. and George. *Role-Playing for Social Values: Decision Making in the Social Studies.* Englewood Cliffs, N.J.: Prentice-Hall, Inc., 1967.

Siks, Geraldine. *Creative Dramatics: An Art for Children.* New York: Harper and Row, Publishers, Inc., 1958.

Taylor, Loren E. *Informal Dramatics for Young People.* Minneapolis, Minn.: Burgess Publishing Company, 1965.

Ward, Winifred. *Playmaking with Children,* rev. ed. New York: Appleton-Century-Crofts, Inc., 1957.

SIMULATION GAMES

Abt, Clark. *Games for Learning: Occasional Paper #7.* Cambridge, Mass.: Educational Services, Inc., 1966.

Boocock, Sarane, and E. O. Schild. *Simulation Games in Learning.* Beverly Hills, Calif.: Sage Publications, Inc., 1968.

Christine, Charles and Dorothy. "Four Simulation Games That Teach," *Grade Teacher,* 85, No. 2 (October, 1967), pp. 109–114+.

Donahay, A. "Social Studies Games: New Learning Tool," *Instructor*, 77 (August, 1967), pp. 172–173.

Ochoa, Anna. "Simulation and Gaming: Simile or Synonym?" *Peabody Journal of Education*, 47, No. 2 (September, 1969), pp. 104–107.

Rogers, Virginia M., and Marcella L. Kysilka. "Simulation Games . . . What and Why," *Instructor*, 79, No. 7 (March, 1970), pp. 94–95.

Simulation Games for the Social Studies Classroom. New York: Foreign Policy Association, 1968.

"Simulation: The Game Explosion," *Social Education*, XXXIII, No. 2 (February, 1969), pp. 176–199.

Stoll, C. S., and S. S. Boocock. "Simulation Games for Social Studies," *Audio-Visual Instructor*, 13 (October, 1968), pp. 840–842.

Towler, John, Lisa Montgomery, and Judi Waid. "Simulation Games . . . How to Use," *Instructor*, 79, No. 7 (March, 1970), pp. 96–97.

Helping Children Interpret Graphs, Charts, and Cartoons

The use of sketches, diagrams, and simple graphic portrayals to communicate ideas is as old as the written history of mankind and, strangely enough, seems to be used to a greater extent and more effectively in the twentieth century than in any other previous period. In primitive times these devices were used as a means of setting down a written record of ideas and events, because writing as we know it today did not exist. Today, graphic devices are used chiefly for persuasive purposes and as a means of simplifying some of the exceedingly complex ideas with which we must all deal. Primitive man undoubtedly selected graphic means to record his thoughts because of the simplicity of those mediums. Modern man uses them for essentially the same reasons.

Visual materials in the form of graphs, charts, and cartoons are exceptionally effective devices for conveying ideas. They are, first of all, much simpler to understand than a completely narrative account would be in relating the same information. A small chart on the pages of the child's textbook shows him the steps in the manufacturing process of plywood. He sees before him a series of sketches showing the raw wood at the beginning and the finished product at the end. The opportunity for misunderstanding is minimized because the ideas are represented in pictures. The same explanation in print would more than likely require several pages, and the opportunity for misunderstanding or lack of understanding of the process would be greatly increased over the use of a simple chart. (Who has not heard the expression "Do you want me to draw you a picture?" after a verbal explanation has been attempted!)

Graphic materials make it possible for us to understand the many statistical concepts with which we deal. The Secretary of Agriculture, for example, addresses a nationwide television audience on the current farm situation. In his discussion, he presents astronomical figures regarding the millions of tons of rice, cotton, wheat, and corn produced by the nation's farmers and compares current figures with production in previous years. He also discusses the amount of money paid by the government in subsidies. These figures run into hundreds of millions of dollars. It is impossible for most persons to comprehend such large numbers, make intelligent comparisons, and see relationships when the numbers are conveyed verbally or even in print. Through the use of carefully constructed graphs and charts, the Secretary reduces these complex statistics to intelligible quantities and presents them in such a manner that they can be understood by the average layman. Persons who have the responsibility to inform the public have learned that graphic devices are far superior to the spoken or written word alone in conveying meaning.

It is unfortunately true, however, that graphic devices can be used equally effectively for promotion of selfish ends as well as portrayal of unbiased objective information. This intensifies the need for critical judgment on the part of citizens. Our votes, loyalties, dollars, values, beliefs, in fact everything we do, is bargained for on a competitive market. In general, if we make intelligent and responsible decisions, we examine critically what each competitor has to offer and make our selection on the basis of what is best for us personally and for the society in which we live. Through experience and education, we learn to discriminate between the valuable and the valueless, between the good and the bad, and between the reputable and disreputable sources of information. We do not always make wise decisions, but in any case, the final decision is ours to make. That we find decision making difficult should not surprise us, for we are subjected daily to a tremendous volume of misleading and conflicting persuasive information, much of it in the form of very convincing graphic materials. This tends to cloud our sense of critical judgment, and we find ourselves being less objective than we should like. If the citizen did not discount much of what he reads and hears in the way of advertising, oratory during political campaigns, sales talk in major purchases, "scientific proofs" of all sorts—well documented with charts, graphs, and other "facts" —he would find himself deceived at every turn. He sometimes becomes either fearful and submissive—an easy prey for the huckster— or cynical, bitter, and suspicious of everyone. Because it is not likely that practices along these lines are going to change suddenly in the foreseeble future, the child needs to learn how to live intelligently in a world of persuasive materials. As the individual citizen becomes more discriminating in his choices, the likelihood of deliberate misrepresentation will be minimized. Because many of our daily decisions are made on information we obtain through the medium of charts, graphs, and cartoons, the need to know how to read, interpret, and understand them is especially important.

Teaching Children the Use of Graphs

The use of graphs is perhaps the best means of comprehensively representing the great amount of statistical data that surrounds us. In this age of statistics, it often happens that we are less interested in the figures per se than we are in using them for comparisons with other figures. The citizen wants to know how much of his tax dollar is spent for various items in order to determine whether that amount is greater or less than it was in the past or to see the relationship of individual budget items to one another or to see the way the items compare with budgets of other countries. Because the numbers are extremely large, such comparisons are difficult to make. But if the data are shown graphically, the relationships can be seen at a glance. The greatest strengths of graphs lie in the fact that they make statistical data easy to comprehend, that in them relationships are easily seen, and that it may be possible to discern trends that are occurring. It is important to recognize that graphs represent data as they actually are and do not indicate the reasons for the conditions that the graph represents. One needs to be extremely cautious in inferring causal relationships from the data presented in graphs. Everyone can think of examples where concomitance and coincidence have been mistaken for causation.

In the past, it was thought that children below the middle grades could not comprehend graphs, but more recently it has been found that this is not true. When the content of graphs deals with experiences the children themselves have had or are having, they are able to see the relationships the graph is attempting to portray. In the first grade, the children can grasp the idea of a simple bar graph recording daily temperature. They can keep a bar graph or simple pictorial graph showing money that they are collecting for the March of Dimes, United Good Neighbor, or similar drives. In the third grade, children can keep a graphic record of spelling words, mathematics scores, or money in the school savings plan. The bar graph can be understood by young children, particularly if it uses pictorial symbols. An extremely simple bar graph of this type may be constructed to show the number of boys and girls in the room. Initially there should be a one to one relationship between the number of stick figures on the graph and the number of children in the room. Later this same graph can be modified to show that one stick figure on the graph can be used to represent more than one child in the classroom. Both graphs and charts are generally more effective if the material is presented in pictorial or semipictorial fashion than if it is completely abstract. This especially applies to their use with younger children.

Young children can also grasp the relationships shown in an area graph. A simple area or circle graph showing the manner in which they divide their time on various activities can be understood by them. This type of graph is constructed on a percentage-of-area basis and, therefore, the children must have a substantial understanding of mathematics in order to construct them. The children are rarely ready for this below the upper grades. When children construct area graphs freehand, they are usually inaccurately drawn because the children cannot depict the area relationships with precision. For example, if a child wishes to show the relationship of two quantities, one being twice as large as the other, the area of the two figures used must, of course, maintain this same relationship. In using pictorial symbols such as bags of money, he is not able to draw them exactly enough to keep this relationship accurate. If area graphs are used in the lower grades, they need to be carefully explained, and children should not be asked to construct them until they have a clear understanding of the arithmetic involved. Figure 18 represents another way that circle graphs can be misleading, even when they are well constructed.

The most accurate of graphs is the line graph, ordinarily used to show changes in quantity through measured amounts of time. Children can be taught the basic features of this graph and can construct it in the middle grades. It is an excellent device to show changes in temperature during various months of the year, the increase in the number of telephones, automobiles, homes with electricity, tractors, population changes, and similar data. It frequently happens that more than

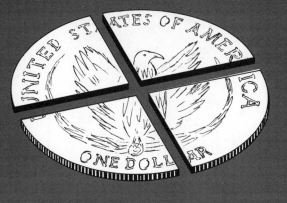

Figure 21. The drawing illustrates how the popular "pie" graph is sometimes used to create an incorrect impression. Because the sketch is shown in perspective, the sizes of the sections are distorted. Thus, sections that seem to be farthest from the viewer appear smaller than those in the foreground, although arithmetically they represent equal amounts.

one set of related data can be shown on one graph. For example, from 1920 to the present there has been a continual increase in the number of automobiles. During the same time, the number of horses used for transportation has declined. Both these variables can be shown on the same graph with one line ascending and the other line descending.

Because the steepness of the slope of the line is usually interpreted as an indication of the rapidity of the change, the middle-grade child should be familiarized with the manner in which bias may be brought into the construction of the graph. This can be demonstrated by placing the same data on conventional graph paper and then on a grid work where the "squares" are rectangular in shape. The slope of the line will vary considerably depending on the nature of the grid used and is an important consideration in the interpretation of these devices. Figure 19 illustrates this point.

Perhaps the best way for the child to learn about the construction and interpretation of graphs is for him to make them and use them himself. Here is a middle-grade child giving a report to his classmates on the growth in population of his home state during the past one hundred years. Why not construct a graph to show these data? Or suppose the question of distance between some city such as New York and other important cities of the world is discussed. Would not a

HELPING CHILDREN INTERPRET GRAPHS, CHARTS, AND CARTOONS

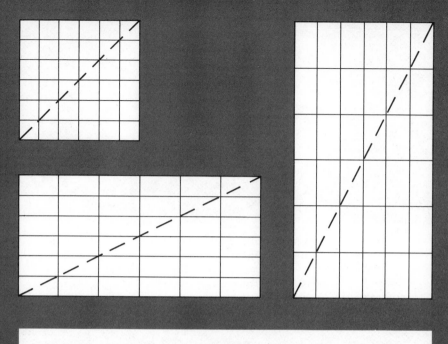

Figure 20. It is important for children to learn that graphs can create false impressions. In the line graphs above, the same data were used on three different grids, resulting in varying steepness in the slopes of the lines. Consequently, although the facts are the same, the rate of change appears markedly different.

graph show these data about as vividly as any medium that could be selected? Graphs can be of immeasurable help in clarifying much of the statistical data that grow out of the social studies unit. A few examples of the uses of graphs in this respect might be to show differences in temperature, growth of product use, production output, increasing use of resources, reduction in diseases, length of important rivers, sizes of cities, loss of topsoil through erosion, increasing speed of travel, growth in use of telephones, amount of money made by various concessions at a school carnival, progress of an animal experiment in nutrition, how a family or community spends its money, or the number of serious accidents from various causes. Situations such as the ones suggested give the children valid reasons for making and using graphs as well as constitute a useful source of information on topics studied in the unit. Figure 20 illustrates simple graphs that could be constructed by pupils.

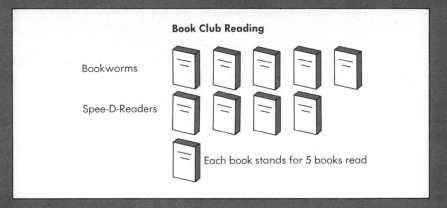

Book Club Reading

Bookworms

Spee-D-Readers

Each book stands for 5 books read

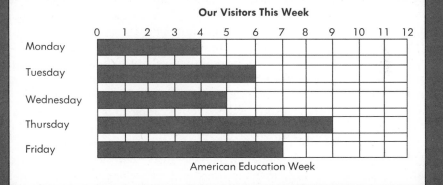

Our Visitors This Week

	0	1	2	3	4	5	6	7	8	9	10	11	12
Monday													
Tuesday													
Wednesday													
Thursday													
Friday													

American Education Week

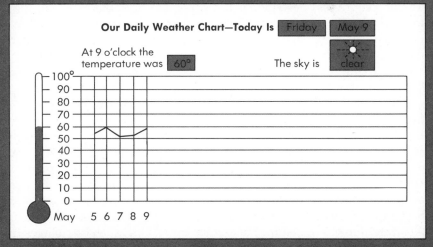

Our Daily Weather Chart—Today Is Friday May 9

At 9 o'clock the temperature was 60° The sky is clear

May 5 6 7 8 9

Figure 18. The graphs shown here were used with success with young children. The resourceful teacher will help children understand simple graphs by utilizing data from the everyday life of the classroom.

The teacher may expect that some formal and direct teaching of graph reading will be necessary. This is one facet of the social studies that can and should be closely related to mathematics instruction. A good way to begin is for the teacher to have very simple data concerning something within the experience of the children of the class. He places these data on the chalkboard along with the grid that will be used. With the class he discusses the purpose of the graph, the need for the grid, the intervals used and how these are determined. The importance of the accuracy of the data will be stressed, although it will be emphasized that the graph is intended to show relationships rather than accurate statistics. Emphasis will also be placed on such things as the need for equal intervals, a title for the graph, and for visual simplicity. As the various features of the graph are explained and discussed, the teacher will place the data on the grid until the graph is completed. The teacher and the class should then discuss the essential facts about graphs, about graph reading and construction, and list these points on the chalkboard. Immediately following this demonstration the teacher should have additional sets of data at hand, graph paper, and other necessary materials and have the children themselves construct graphs. These, in turn, are displayed, discussed, and evaluated in terms of the essential facts about graphs that were placed on the chalkboard. The teacher will then turn to graphs that appear in the children's books and those from magazines brought to class. These, too, are discussed and evaluated. The class can then be encouraged to bring graphs they find in magazines and newspapers in order that they may be studied and displayed appropriately in the classroom. The procedure just described is not presented with the intention that the teacher will follow it exactly but, rather, is presented as an indication of the need for *systematic* teaching of the complex skills of graph reading and interpretation.

After children have acquired a basic understanding of graphs and know how to make them, they should be encouraged to make and use graphs frequently in summarizing and reporting work done in connection with unit study.

Graphs can be constructed to represent *quantity comparisons*, such as the amount of forest land today as compared with that of 1900, the production of a specific product by different countries, the amount of working time needed to earn basic needs in selected countries, the size of farms in various parts of the world, and so on. Some variety of a bar graph can be used for this purpose. Pupils can also use graphs to illustrate *changes in quantity over a period of time*, such as changes in population, land use, miles of highways, cost of basic commodities, growth in air travel, time needed to produce something, and the number of people in a certain occupation at various times. The line

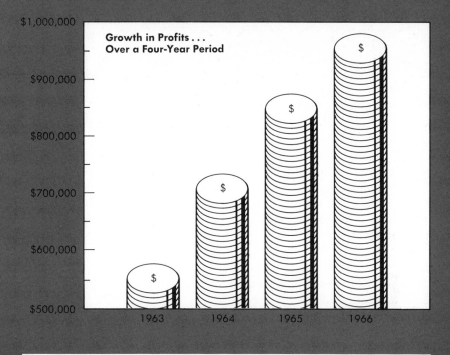

Figure 19. How much larger were profits in 1966 than in 1964? The chances are that you have said "about twice as large." This graph illustrates how wrong impressions are conveyed when pictorial graphs are improperly constructed. Careful examination of this graph will show that the 1966 profits **are not even** twice those of 1963. The basic error in this graph is that it does not show the first $500,000 of profit. A more accurate perception of the growth in profits can be made if the correct position of the base line is established. Can you locate the place on the page where the base line should be?

graph is most appropriate to show data of this type. Finally, pupils can construct graphs to show *proportional parts of anything*, usually expressed in percentages, such as land use, budgets, costs, expenses, occupations of persons in an area, resources, and minerals. The circle graph can be useful in presenting such information. The need to keep the data simple and based on the child's experience is essential. It is a good procedure to have children use graph paper rather than to have them construct their own grids, because of the time consumed in preparing the grid. The construction of graphs by children should focus on the information being portrayed by the graph rather than on artistic perfection. Even though the teacher should hold the children to high standards of neatness and orderliness, there is little justification for making art lessons out of graph construction.

In addition to presenting data, graphs should also serve as a stimulus to careful, reflective thinking. This comes about when pupils are helped to see relationships in the data or can relate the graph data to other information already known and draw inferences. The kinds of questions the teacher asks has much to do with the extent of pupil thinking that comes about as a result of such inquiry. Examine the following questions, for example, and note the ones that could be answered by reading facts presented by the graph and those that call for more reflection, for interpretation, and for the combining of information from other sources. These questions would be appropriate for late middle and upper grades and, obviously, do not all apply to the same graph:

1. What product is measured on this graph?
2. What countries are compared?
3. What period of time is covered?
4. Which country had the largest production? The least?
5. In what ten-year period did production rise most rapidly?
6. Why do you suppose there was such a sharp change after 1960?
7. What does the graph tell you about cotton production in the Southern states?
8. Why was there so little oil produced before 1930?
9. From the countries shown on the graph, in which part of the world would you say people had the longest life expectancy? Why is this so?
10. How do the temperatures shown on the graph compare with local temperatures at different times of the year?
11. Which country has the most people? Which has the most land? Which country has the greatest population *density?*
12. According to the graph, how much land is in crops? How much is not usable? What does the graph tell you about life in that country?

Teachers can easily devise similar questions of various types for inquiry with graphs in connection with unit study. Genuine understanding of graphs, of course, comes only after continued careful study. The best teaching of graphs will occur when the teacher provides many opportunities for their construction and reading associated with the regular social studies instruction and provides the children with specific instruction in their construction, interpretation, and use.

Teaching Children the Use of Charts

Within recent years there has been a noticeable increase in the use of charts in and outside of school. Like graphs, their value lies in the representation of complex ideas with which we must deal in modern living. They do this by providing a degree of concreteness to ideas and by focusing attention on the relationship between facts. They are widely used in advertising, appear in the daily newspaper in great numbers, and are used extensively in the business world as well as in government. Modern social studies textbooks make extensive use of *narrative, tabulation, relationship, pedigree, classification, organization,* and *flow charts.*

The *narrative chart* is widely used to show developments in a procedure, to compare developments, or to illustrate events along a time dimension. It often depicts steps in a procedure, such as how a bill becomes a law, how automobiles are assembled, or how a newspaper goes to print. The narrative chart may also be used to portray developments, such as the history of the use of the wheel, changes in the structure and design of trains through the years, or changes in dress styles during the past century. In order to illustrate events that occur along a time dimension, it may be used to depict events that led to the outbreak of World War II or the hazards encountered by a group of pioneers on their way to the Oregon country. In the last case, it may combine the use of a map and a chart and is sometimes called a map-chart. The narrative chart is so named because it tells a story. It is frequently used in social studies textbooks and is a very effective learning device. It is easy to read; the eye can freely follow the story step by step. (See Figure 22.)

The *tabulation chart* is usually a listing of data in table form in order to facilitate making comparisons: the labor leader wishes to show the income of various occupations over a period of five years. These data are listed side by side and the comparisons can be made by the reader. A chart in the social studies book may show the minutes of labor required to earn enough to buy various essentials for living such as bread, shoes, clothing, and shelter in the United States, Great Britain, China, and the U.S.S.R. The encyclopedia may present in table form the number of telephones per capita in several countries of the world. All of these are forms of the tabulation chart. Its purpose is to present data in a form that facilitates comparison of the items.

The *relationship chart* may take many forms, but its chief purpose is what its name implies—to show relationship. A chart showing the manner in which gas and oil lines lead from the oil well to the nearby

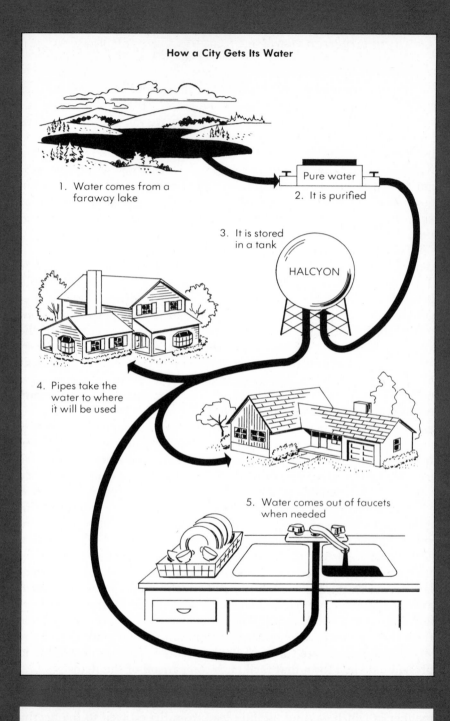

How a City Gets Its Water

1. Water comes from a faraway lake

2. It is purified

3. It is stored in a tank

4. Pipes take the water to where it will be used

5. Water comes out of faucets when needed

Figure 22. An exceedingly simple narrative chart—one of several types of charts used in social studies instruction.

chemical plant, synthetic rubber plant, refinery, storage tanks, and transportation facilities needed to market the resultant materials would be an example of this type of chart. A diagram showing the inter-relatedness of various aspects of our transportation system would be another example. Most teachers are familiar with the relationship chart used to show the various forces brought to bear on the life of the young child; the home, school, and community are usually represented by concentric circles surrounding the child. Still another example would be a chart showing the voting record of various senators and representatives and identifying them with specific bills or issues. In a sense, all charts show relationship of factors presented.

A chart designed to show developments that have a single origin is called a *pedigree chart*. It is sometimes used to show lineage of a family (genealogy) and thus becomes a family tree. It can be used to show the development of movements, such as the struggle for freedom, the extension of the franchise, or the growth of organized labor and to show the development of political parties that had a single origin but have since developed in many directions. Children enjoy making charts of this type as they trace the history of their own ancestry. It serves as one way the child can identify himself with the past as well as familiarize himself with his own family background. Children usually find this interesting.

Closely related to the pedigree chart is the *classification chart* that organizes and groups data in such a way that relationships can be seen easily. A meat-packing company furnishes a chart showing the manner in which various cuts of meat are classified. Here, the child can see how meat is rated as choice or commercial and can see that it may be classified in terms of the animal from which it comes, such as beef, pork, veal, and mutton. These, in turn, can be subdivided into steaks, roasts, chops, and other cuts. A chart can be constructed to show community workers who help keep us well. These can be subdivided into doctors, dentists, nurses, and city or county health officers and inspectors. We use classification charts whenever we begin categorizing various types of data.

Every schoolchild is familiar with the *organization chart*. It is designed to show schematically the internal structure of an organization such as the school, community, state or federal government, a corporation, or a student council. Almost everyone recalls the chart showing the division of the federal government into three branches, the executive, legislative, and judicial. These are generally shown by a series of three rectangles on the same horizontal level that represent equal status. These, in turn, have lines extending from them, and the various subagencies are represented by other rectangles. At the apex of the chart is a single rectangle representing the electorate with direct lines extending to each of the three departments of government. Many organizations have a complex structure, and the use of organization charts makes an understanding of their structure easier.

When one is attempting to show a process that involves a change at some central point or series of points, a *flow chart* is used. Generally, a series of arrows is used to indicate the flow of materials into the central point of interest where it is altered, exchanged, or modified in some way and is then shown leaving the critical point. Thus, into the meat-packing plant go cattle, pigs, sheep, and calves and out come cuts of meat—ham, bacon, pork chops, roasts, and by-products. Into the schools of the nation go boys and girls from all walks of life and out come the citizens of tomorrow. Into a factory go various raw materials and out come the finished products. The flow chart is exceedingly helpful in clarifying social studies concepts that involve processes of the type just described. (See Figure 23.)

In social studies, the teacher will want to make extensive use of the charts that appear in books, in free and inexpensive materials, and in newspapers and magazines as well as make use of charts that are made in the classroom by the teacher and children. The best charts are simple, vivid, and concrete; but it is a mistake to assume that because a chart has these characteristics it will be easily understood by the

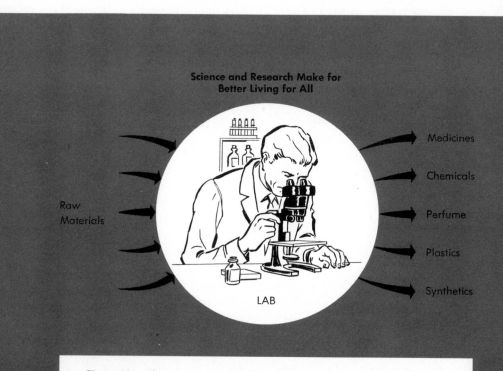

Science and Research Make for Better Living for All

Raw Materials

LAB

Medicines

Chemicals

Perfume

Plastics

Synthetics

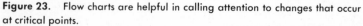

Figure 23. Flow charts are helpful in calling attention to changes that occur at critical points.

children. Time must be taken to teach youngsters how to read and interpret charts. One way this can be handled is to call the attention of the class to a chart that appears in their books or one large enough to be displayed in the classroom where all can see it. Through inquiry the class discovers the general nature of the chart, its title, and the subject with which it deals. The class learns how relationships are shown, where the chart begins, and how it is to be read. They look carefully at the sketches used, particularly if the principals appear in caricature. At the conclusion of the instruction, a generalization or conclusion should be stated. In short, the instruction should follow a systematic pattern, and the teacher should not depend on simply making occasional and incidental references to charts if their maximum value as instructional aids is to be realized. In addition to the direct instruction that is given from time to time, the teacher will want to utilize every opportunity to use charts in a meaningful way in the regular unit work of the class.

Informal Charts

In addition to formal and commercially prepared charts, the teacher will find the use of informal charts indispensable in teaching social studies. Informal charts are the ones developed and constructed by the teacher or by the children. They are commonly placed on wrapping paper, oak tagboard, newsprint, "butcher" paper, chart paper, or the chalkboard. They may contain diagrams, sketches, pictures, or other illustrative material or may simply be written accounts of experiences or activities related to the unit under study. Michaelis groups informal charts of this kind into the following categories:

Experience charts for reading and discussion based upon study trips, experiments, constructions, and other firsthand experiences.

Group standards charts for use in work periods, discussion, dramatic play, making reports, committee work, and cooperating with others.

Sequential charts such as time-lines, charts, records and logs of activities, calendar of events, sequence of activities, and records of progress.

Direction charts for use in construction, field trips, map making, processing materials, describing use of references or tools and materials, and carrying out other activities.

Creative expression charts to record songs, poems, and stories.

Vocabulary charts for listing frequently used terms and concepts related to the unit.

Organization charts to summarize committee organization, organization for a trip, or organization of various institutions or groups studied in units.

Information charts to clarify basic facts needed for various activities.
Classification charts to record such items as types of boats, dwellings,
food, shelter, clothing, weapons, utensils, and arts and crafts.[1]

When charts are constructed for use with primary-grade children
it is essential that the mechanics and make-up of the charts conform
exactly to the patterns that are being taught in the basic language arts
program. For example, the style of lettering used should be exactly the
same as that used by the children in manuscript writing; capital letters
and punctuation marks should be used only where they are used in
ordinary writing; and the reading vocabulary should follow as closely
as possible the vocabulary being developed in the basic reading program. Careful attention should be given to the format to facilitate
ease of reading: uniform margins; well-spaced letters, words, and
lines; natural phrases of appropriate length; and sharp, clear lettering.
Phrases should not be broken at the end of a line such as:

The fresh milk is kept in
a cooler.

But rather:

The fresh milk is kept
in a cooler.

Middle- and upper-grade children can be encouraged to make and
use charts in connection with their reports, committee work, and
displays. As was true with graphs, the children need be less concerned
with the artistic perfection of the chart than with the manner in which
it conveys ideas. Simplicity, vividness, concreteness, and accuracy of
the idea presented are more important considerations than artistic
finish. Before chart making is undertaken, the teacher and the class
will want to establish guidelines for the construction of them, and the
products should then be evaluated in terms of those criteria.

Teaching Children the Use of Cartoons

Almost everyone enjoys the humor of good cartoons. Cartoons
seem humorous to us because we see a part of our own experience
reflected in them and because they deal with situations commonly
known to all of us. They exaggerate, the subjects are presented in
caricature, and they are designed to show all the vices or virtues associated with a particular character in our culture. They give us a chance
to laugh at ourselves and thereby add spice and variety to living.

1. John U. Michaelis, *Social Studies for Children in a Democracy*, 4th ed., Englewood Cliffs, N.J.: Prentice-Hall, 1968, p. 397.

Figure 24. This cartoon illustrates remarkably well how much the reader must bring to such illustrations if they are to have meaning for him. Rather than using word symbols either in the diagram or in a caption, the cartoonist has relied totally on the illustration itself to communicate the message. What message does this cartoon convey to readers?

If the cartoon is presented to young children and they are asked why the lion is crying, they will respond, "because his foot hurts" or "someone hurt him." Older children, unfamiliar with the symbolism attached to the cartoon, will say, "it is a cartoon during 'Be Kind to Animals Week,'" or "he misses his freedom now that he is all caged up" or "he lost his mate."

The meaning of this cartoon becomes clear when the reader (1) knows that the lion has long been used as a symbol to represent Great Britain; (2) knows that the cartoon appeared immediately following the death of Sir Winston Churchill; and (3) has sufficient maturity to associate (1) and (2) in a meaningful relationship. In other words, the cartoon summarizes a vast amount of information and knowledge **that the reader already has**, and structures it in a new relationship or a new experience by providing the necessary visual clues. (Cartoon reprinted by permission of William Morris Agency, Inc. Copyright © 1965 by Bill Mauldin.)

When dealing with social or political matters, however, cartoons may be anything but funny—especially to the person or group represented in them. The same techniques of symbolism, the use of familiar situations, exaggerations, satire, and caricature are used to present forcefully a *single point of view*. The cartoon does not allow the reader or the person portrayed in the cartoon an opportunity for rebuttal. Recognition of the fact that only one point of view is represented in cartoons is exceedingly important in their interpretation. Older children need to be taught the general make-up of cartoons that deal with social and political problems and need the experience of critically evaluating them. It is well for the children to present an opposite point of view from the one presented in the cartoon.

The symbolism used in cartoons causes much confusion in the minds of some children. When the characters are portrayed as animals, the children tend to associate those animals with various national groups. Cartoons use stereotypes of people that add little to the type of international understanding we are attempting to foster and encourage in the social studies program. Figurative terms such as *iron curtain* are represented as walls of iron, leading the child to believe that such a wall exists in a literal sense. Cartoons usually demand a high level of understanding on the part of the reader of the issues involved if they are to tell their story accurately; thus, the child needs to be instructed and helped in developing the skill of interpreting cartoons. (See Figure 24.)

The material presented in this chapter is not intended to create the impression that learning to read and understand charts, graphs, and cartoons will be completed in the elementary school. Proper use of these devices calls for the application of many subtle interpretive and comprehension skills. Moreover, life experience is important in understanding their meaning. Therefore, all that can be hoped for at the elementary school level is an introduction and systematic presentation of such devices and a confining of their use to the situations clearly within the realm of experience of the young child. When this is done, a good groundwork will have been established for an extension of an understanding of them at the junior and senior high school levels.

Discussion Questions and Suggested Activities

1. Construct a line graph, a bar graph, and an area graph that summarize data that are appropriate to the topic of your unit (Chapter 3).
2. Prepare a poster showing how graphs can convey false impres-

sions. Obtain samples of such graphic material from newspaper and magazine advertising.

3. Construct samples of the various formal and informal charts discussed in this chapter. Observe the presented suggestions for the construction of such charts.

4. What types of misunderstandings are likely to develop when principals in charts and cartoons appear in caricature? How can good use of these materials prevent such misunderstandings from developing?

5. Find a cartoon that might be suitable for teaching purposes in a grade of your interest and choice. Present the cartoon to your classmates and indicate points you would want to make in using it with children.

6. Begin a collection of charts, graphs, and cartoons for the grade level at which you plan to teach.

7. Because graphic materials are used to show relationships rather than exact quantities, to what sources might the pupil turn if he wanted to obtain exact amounts?

8. Examine reading and mathematics textbooks to find other suggestions for the development of skill in making, understanding, and using graphs, charts, and cartoons.

9. What are some of the advantages and limitations in using the chalkboard for the construction of graphs, charts, and cartoons?

10. Show by specific illustrations how the reading, interpretation, and use of graphs, charts, and cartoons can be taught as a part of a social studies unit. Does this approach conflict with the need to teach the meaning and use of these devices in a systematic fashion?

Selected References

Brown, James W., Richard B. Lewis, and Fred F. Harcleroad. *A-V Instruction: Materials and Methods*, 3rd ed. New York: McGraw-Hill Book Company, Inc., 1969.

Dale, Edgar. *Audio-Visual Methods in Teaching*, 3rd ed. New York: Holt, Rinehart & Winston, Inc., 1969.

East, Marjorie. *Display for Learning: Making and Using Visual Materials*. New York: Holt, Rinehart & Winston, Inc., 1952.

Erickson, Carlton W. H. *Fundamentals of Teaching with Audiovisual Technology*. New York: The Macmillan Company, 1965.

Eulie, Joseph. "Creating Interest and Developing Understanding in the Social Studies Through Cartoons," *Peabody Journal of Education*, 46, No. 5 (March, 1969), pp. 288–290.

Glenn, William H., and Donovan A. Johnson. *Adventures in Graphing*. St. Louis, Mo.: Webster Publishing Company, 1961.

Harvill, Harris. "The Use of Posters, Charts, Cartoons, and Graphs," *Audio-Visual Materials and Methods in the Social Studies*, 18th Yearbook. Washington, D.C.: National Council for the Social Studies, 1947.

Liechti, Alice O., and Jack Chappell. *Making and Using Charts*. Palo Alto, Calif.: Fearon Publishers, 1960.

McCune, George H., and Neville Pearson. "Interpreting Material Presented in Graphic Form," *Skill Development in Social Studies*, 33rd Yearbook. Washington, D.C.: National Council for the Social Studies, 1963.

Michaelis, John U. *Social Studies for Children in a Democracy*, 4th ed. Englewood Cliffs, N.J.: Prentice-Hall, Inc., 1968.

Naslund, Robert A., and Jack McClellan. *Graph and Picture Study Skills*. Chicago: Science Research Associates, Inc., 1966.

Stutz, Frederick H., et al., "Interpreting Material Presented in Graphic Form," *Skills in the Social Studies*, 24th Yearbook. Washington, D.C.: National Council for the Social Studies, 1953.

Wittich, Walter A., and Charles F. Schuller. *Audio-Visual Materials: Their Nature and Use*, 4th ed. New York: Harper and Row, Publishers, Inc., 1967.

Teaching Pupils How to Use Globes and Maps

Social studies has a special responsibility to teach youngsters the skills of reading and interpreting globes and maps. Even though this has been one of the purposes of social studies instruction for many years, the need for skill in the use of these tools has taken on additional importance in modern times because of the course of world events. Since 1945, Americans have maintained a continuing contact with nations of the world—some of them well known, others obscure. Because international affairs demand the attention of the American citizen to the extent that they do, he has genuine need for skill and facility in the use of the basic tools of geography: globes and maps.

Teachers in secondary schools and colleges have long expressed disappointment concerning the student's inability to read and interpret maps and globes. The feeling exists that map and globe reading and interpretation should be taught in the elementary schools in order that the pupil may apply these abilities and skills when needed in the later grades. It happens, however, that globe and map reading and associated interpretive skills and abilities are not taught to completion at any one school level. The child is introduced to them fairly early in the elementary school on an informal basis, and each succeeding year should bring an extension and refinement of these skills and abilities. Map reading is a developmental process, just as is conventional reading, and is one that can continually be improved throughout life. This being the case, all elementary teachers can expect to shoulder responsibility for the teaching and maintenance of these learnings just as they do in the case of reading, mathematics, and other skills.

Nature of Globes and Maps

Globes and maps use combinations of colors and symbols to represent all or a portion of the earth. Because the earth is spherical in shape, the globe is a very small model of it and is, therefore, the most accurate representation of the earth available in the classroom. The difficulty with the globe, however, is that to represent an area the size of one of our states with any amount of detail, a globe would have to be so large that it would be impossible to carry around or keep in a classroom. It is much more convenient to take a small section of the world map, such as a single country or a state, enlarge it, and place it on a sheet of paper that can be displayed on the wall of the classroom or can be conveniently rolled up and stored out of the way when not in use. As a consequence, man has for centuries been experimenting with ways to show accurately the round surface of the earth on flat paper. But because the earth is round and maps are flat, there is no way of representing the earth's surface on a map without making some adjustment in the representation. This can be demonstrated to children very vividly by securing a six-inch rubber ball, cutting it into two hemispheres, and having children try to flatten it out on a table top or on their desks. The hemispheres will not lie flat and cannot be made to lie flat unless they are cut in some way. If the hemispheres are cut into gores and tacked down, the surface of the ball no longer looks as it did before. Similarly, flat maps do not look as the surface of the globe does because adjustments had to be made in the process of representing a round surface on a flat one. For this reason it is important to remember that no map is accurate in every respect and that all maps contain some distortion of the areas represented.

GRID WORK

Globes and maps use a system of coordinates or grids in order that directions can be established and places located accurately. The grid work consists of a series of east-west and north-south lines referred to as parallels of latitude and meridians of longitude, respectively. The parallels of latitude encircle the earth in an east-west direction and are used to measure distances in degrees north and south of the equator. The meridians of longitude encircle the earth in a north-south direction, converge on both poles, and are used to measure distances in degrees east and west of the prime meridian or Greenwich meridian. Parallels of latitude become shorter in length as they approach the poles, whereas meridians of longitude are all the same length. The nature of this imaginary grid work over the earth is extremely important to understand when consulting maps and globes. In the process of projection, the grid is usually modified, thus resulting either in shrinking or stretching some areas out of their actual shape. If a land area lies between the boundaries of a given latitude and longitude, it must be presented in that location irrespective of the arrangement of the grid. When the North and South poles, which are single points, are extended to the width of the map as they are in the Mercator projection, distortions in the polar areas are severe.

The need for the grid work as a means of locating places on the earth may be demonstrated to children by using a playground ball twelve to sixteen inches in diameter, preferably one that has no lines on it at all. The teacher can begin the demonstration by taking a piece of chalk and placing an X mark on the ball in some place. He can then ask the children to describe the location of the mark exactly. This, of course, is impossible to do unless there are other previously established points of reference on the ball. For example, if the children say that the X is on the upper half of the ball, the ball can be turned about, making the statement incorrect, because then it is on the lower half of the ball. Children quickly discover the need for well-defined reference points and, if measuring is involved, the need for a point of origin. Locating the X becomes easier and more exact, for example, if we have a North Pole, a South Pole, and an equator. The location can be made even more precise by adding a meridian or north-south line. The more north-south lines one has to work with, the more precisely one is able to locate points. This is the manner in which places are located on the surface of the earth if their location is to be pinpointed exactly. However, precise location of places on a map or globe in terms of degrees should not be attempted below the seventh or eighth grades. Middle-grade children can become accustomed to the use of coordinates in locating places by using simple road maps as shown in Figure 25.

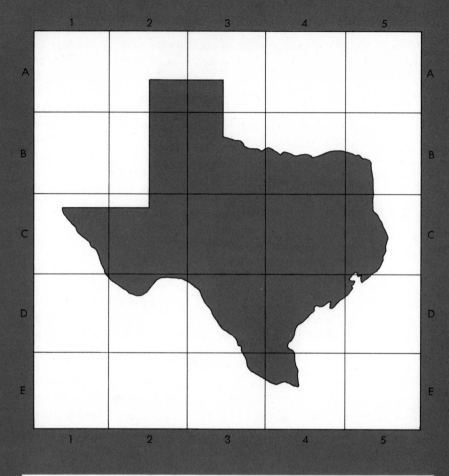

Figure 25. Middle-grade children can learn to use a grid in locating places by using road maps that have coordinates of the type shown in this diagram. Teachers or students can enlarge smaller maps by marking them into grids and then transposing the material to be enlarged onto a grid of larger scale. For example, the teacher may make an enlarged version of a home-state map to place on a wall or bulletin board. What learning experiences can you think of to use such enlarged maps?

SCALE

Any portrayal of the earth on either a map or a globe is, of course, a graphic reduction from its actual size. This is accomplished through the use of scaling—reducing everything in an equal amount. Through the use of different scales it becomes possible to show an area of the earth's surface on different-size pieces of paper. A map of North America can be placed on the page of a child's textbook or on a large wall map. All maps and globes prepared for school use should have the scale indicated on them.

There are three commonly used methods of expressing scale on maps. One is known as the inches-to-miles method. This means every inch on the map represents a specified number of miles on the ground, that is, "one inch equals a hundred miles." Although this method seems not too complex, it has one serious shortcoming—using one unit of measurement for the map (inches) and a different one for ground distance (miles). On one map the scale may be one inch equals fifty miles, on another it may be one inch equals two hundred miles, on a third it may be one inch equals four hundred miles, and so on. In order to avoid the inches and miles confusion, a graphic scale can be used.

The child can place an edge of a piece of paper between the two points on his map, mark them, and lay the edge along the scale in order to find the distance in miles. This is the easiest scale to understand and to use and can be taught in fourth grade. Later in the grades the children can also use the inches-to-miles scale. Figure 26 illustrates a graphic scale.

A much more complex method of expressing scale is through the use of a representative fraction. It is expressed as a ratio between units on the map and similar units on the ground. Hence, the representative fraction 1/10,000 means that one unit of *anything* on the map stands for ten thousand of the *same units* on the ground. For example, one inch on the map would represent ten thousand inches on the ground. If one were interested in finding distance in miles, he would then convert inches to miles. This method should not be taught in the elementary school except perhaps as an enrichment activity for gifted children.

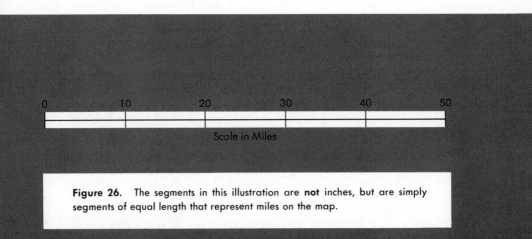

Figure 26. The segments in this illustration are **not** inches, but are simply segments of equal length that represent miles on the map.

Pictorial

Semipictorial

Completely abstract

Figure 27.   The above diagram illustrates varying degrees of abstraction in symbols that could be used to represent a church.

Symbols

Maps and globes use a variety of symbols to represent places and things. Learning to read maps and globes involves learning this special language of maps and globes—knowing the meanings of the symbols used. If everything could be represented by a picture of the real object, map reading would be relatively simple. More frequently than not, however, the symbol used bears no resemblance to the object represented and the reader cannot understand or interpret the map unless he is familiar with the symbols used.

Map symbols vary in abstraction ranging from those that are pictorial and least abstract to those that bear no resemblance at all to the object being represented. (See Figure 27.)

The use of pictorial or semipictorial symbols will simplify map reading for young children. The younger the children are, the less ab-

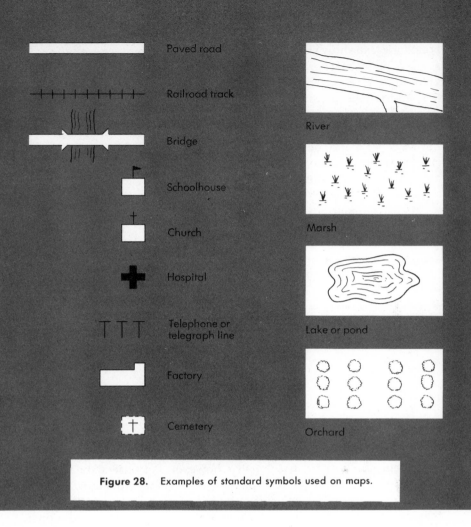

Paved road

Railroad track

Bridge

Schoolhouse

Church

Hospital

Telephone or
telegraph line

Factory

Cemetery

River

Marsh

Lake or pond

Orchard

Figure 28. Examples of standard symbols used on maps.

stract should be the symbols used. In map making and map reading in the primary grades, pictorial and semipictorial symbols should be used almost entirely. It is helpful, too, if the symbols are not only pictorial but also three dimensional. That is, small models of churches, homes, schools, and other objects placed on the map on the classroom floor will make map reading more meaningful for primary-grade children. As they move into the middle and upper grades, children can learn to use conventional map symbols as illustrated in Figure 28.

COLOR

Many maps and globes use color for a variety of purposes, the most common being to indicate land elevations; to represent political

TEACHING PUPILS HOW TO USE
GLOBES AND MAPS

boundaries; to show rainfall, population, and temperature; and to show similar data. Confusion regarding the meaning of color on maps is well known. Children oftentimes think the color used on the map is the actual color of the area represented. Consequently, they come to believe that Montana is orange, Iowa is yellow, or Florida is green. Sometimes countries and their territorial possessions are shown in the same color, but on other maps they may not be represented in this way. As a result, children who have learned that "countries and their possessions are shown in the same color" may develop erroneous ideas when consulting maps where such a color scheme is not used.

As used in map reading, color should be taught as a special kind of symbol. This means that one should consult the legend or key of the map to be sure that he knows what the colors stand for and how they are used. In the primary grades children can understand that the dark blue areas on their globe represent water and that the brown areas represent land. They begin to learn that color on maps is used for purposes other than simply decorative ones. The special uses of color to represent data on maps can be taught gradually as the child moves into the middle and upper grades.

Legend

Maps and globes have a legend that is the key to the symbols, scale, and other data represented on them. The person skilled in the use of maps will turn immediately to the legend to learn the special meanings of the symbols used. As a matter of procedure, the map maker may use any symbols he chooses as long as they are explained in the legend. The common practice, however, is to use standard map symbols. Early in the grades, pupils can become acquainted with a legend and accustomed to using it by including a legend on the maps they themselves make in the classroom. In the middle and upper grades the teacher should call the attention of the class to legends on maps from time to time and note the information given. (See Figure 29.)

Instructional Experiences with the Globe

The globe is an object that has adorned classrooms for decades. The twelve-inch, metal meridian globe colored in various shades of dull green and suspended from the ceiling by a system of pulleys, although rarely used, was as much a trade-mark of American elementary education as the Little Red Schoolhouse itself. But like the Little Red Schoolhouse it, too, has given way to a modern counterpart. The globes and maps prepared for the schoolchildren today are excellent learning devices and are constructed for classroom use. Most

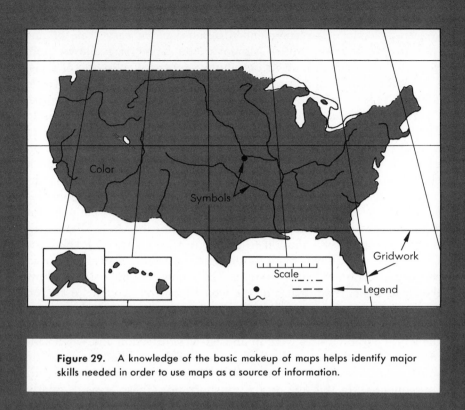

Figure 29. A knowledge of the basic makeup of maps helps identify major skills needed in order to use maps as a source of information.

globes come in a simplified form for younger children and in standard models for more mature pupils. The wise use of color makes them vivid and attractive to the child. These learning tools are no longer tucked away in some corner or suspended out of reach of the pupils but are at the level of the child—intellectually and physically—and are easily accessible to him.

Because the globe is the most accurate representation of the earth available to the schoolchild, every elementary school classroom should have one. In grades one, two, and three a simplified twelve-inch globe is generally recommended because small children find this size somewhat easier to handle than the larger, sixteen-inch one. For primary grades, the globe selected should have a minimum amount of information on it. It should not use more than three colors to represent land elevation or more than two colors to represent water depth. Only the largest cities, rivers, and water bodies should be shown. Globes that have a great amount of information on them are a maze of detail for the young child and confuse him. In the middle and upper grades, a sixteen-inch globe is recommended because of its easy scale of one inch to five hundred miles. Moreover, its larger size allows more detail to be shown without its becoming a confused collection of facts. Globes for middle- and upper-grade children will ordinarily use seven colors to represent land elevations and three to represent water depths.

The chief value of the globe in grades one, two, and three is to familiarize the children with the basic roundness of the earth and to acquaint them with this small model of the earth. Most adults have an east-west orientation to the world, perhaps because they have dealt chiefly with maps rather than with globes. Once these relationships become fixed in one's mind, it is difficult to visualize the true global relationships of the major land areas to one another. On a wall map, for example, the Soviet Union appears to be east of the United States, although the globe will show it to be north. (See Figure 30.) Thus, the United States is constructing its defensive warning system not in an easterly direction but in the Arctic. The globe will immediately show the closeness of many parts of the world formerly thought to be "on the other side of the world." The east-west orientation that many adults have to the world is a vestige of sailing days when most of the world's trade routes were in an east-west direction and when sailing ships were limited to the open waters of the middle latitudes. The rough and unnavigable waters of the Arctic were thought of as inconsequential. In this age of air transportation, these areas, formerly ignored and relegated to positions of unimportance, have become extremely significant not only because of their strategic value but also because they are on the most expeditious transportation routes of the world. The globe is the instrument to use in order to understand these global relationships. Early contact with the globe is very important in this respect.

The primary-grade child is not subjected to formal lessons on the use of the globe. If the globe is in the classroom, it will provoke his curiosity and he will want to know more about it and how to use it. His father speaks of places in the news, and the child wonders where they are. He hears of earth satellites and wants to know how they go around the earth. A child has just joined the class; his family has recently moved to this country from Germany, and he wants to show the class the location of his former home. The teacher will use situations such as these, and hundreds more like them, to acquaint the young child with the globe and with the fact that he can "find" places on it.

While the teacher is at it, he will help children discover other things about the globe. He will have them learn that there is a difference between water and land areas and that these are represented by different colors. The line that separates the water and the land is called

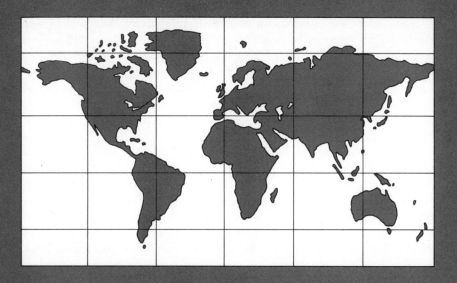

Figure 30. Notice how differently a world map and a globe portray global relationships. In the Space age we need to think of the world more as it is shown by the globe than the map.

the sea coast; in some places it is straight and smooth, perhaps suitable for bathing; in other places it is jagged with many zigzags, and the water rushes against the rocks with a mighty roar. He may show them pictures of each of these to help the children visualize different kinds of coast lines. With his imagination stimulated by the teacher and supported by pictures or illustrations, the young children will almost hear the tide rushing in and see the gulls flying overhead. In like manner, the teacher extends their understanding of other concepts— oceans, cities, rivers, mountains. He shows the children that most of the brown areas that represent land are on the half of the earth that has the North Pole and tells them it is here that most of the people of the world make their home.

In addition to the incidental references made to the globe in the normal course of classroom living and exploration by the children, the teacher will use the globe in teaching when the opportunity presents itself. This may come during social studies activities or at any time during the school day. In the stories that are read, the children from time to time will want to find where Pedro, Elle-Kari, Eva, or Noriko-San live. The children will find that some of these book friends "live" close to them, whereas others are far away. Some live where it is warm the whole year round, others where it is cold most of the time. But Ching lives where it should be warm but it is not, because his home is high in the mountains, and that makes it cold. Thus, the globe can be used in a great variety of ways to lay a good foundation for more formal aspects of the teaching of these skills later on as well as to introduce children to basic geographical concepts so important to the understanding of the world as the home of man.

The following are examples of the *types* of learnings and experiences that can be planned with the globe for pupils in the lower grades:

1. Pupils learn that the globe is a very small model of the earth. Good models look exactly like the real thing but are smaller. The globe is a good model of the earth.
2. Show the children how land areas and water bodies are represented on the globe. Have children find land areas and water bodies. Names of these need not be taught at this level, but children might already know the large water bodies such as the Pacific and Atlantic oceans. Similarly, they might be familiar with North and South America, Africa or the Antarctic, and these can be pointed out. Explain that all water bodies and land areas have names.
3. Have children discover that there is considerably more water than land shown on the globe. Ask children to find the half of the globe that has most of the land. Explain that this is the half on which we live and is the part of the earth where most of the world's people make their homes.
4. Show children the location of the North Pole. Explain that most

of the land of the world is on the same half of the world as the North Pole. We call this the northern half.

5. Show children the location of the South Pole. Explain that most of the water areas of the world are on the same half of the world as the South Pole. We call this the southern half.
6. Most primary children will have heard of planets. Explain that our earth is a planet.
7. Show children how they can find their country, their continent, their state, and possibly their city on the globe.
8. Use the globe to find places that are familiar to the children— places they have visited on vacations, places in the news, homes of book friends and visitors from other countries, or places in the world from which some circus or zoo animals are brought.
9. Encourage children to handle the globe and to find places on it themselves.
10. Answer questions the children ask concerning the globe in simple, nontechnical language.

As the child moves into the middle and upper grades, instruction in the use of the globe should take two forms. First, the teacher should take time out from regularly scheduled unit activities to do direct teaching of the skills needed in reading and interpreting the globe. Second, in unit work and other classroom activities there should be constant reference to the globe and maps. Both of these aspects of instruction are important, and one should supplement the other. To hope that children will become skillful in the use of a globe or maps simply by making incidental references to them when the occasion presents itself is wishful thinking. At the same time, formal lessons in the use of these devices without application of the newly acquired skills in purposeful situations is equally ineffective. The best arrangement is to provide for systematic instruction in the use of map- and globe-reading skills as a part of unit activities, reinforcing this with direct teaching of these skills as the need arises. For example, in a unit on "Life in the Northeastern States," an essential learning is that this is an industrial, manufacturing region. Its growth in this respect is related to the geography of the area: the irregular coast line providing good harbor facilities, the many rivers and streams with waterfalls to provide power, the relatively unproductive farmland of the New England section, the fishing ground lying offshore, the accessibility of raw materials, marketing facilities, and so forth. Maps and globes are necessary tools of instruction for studies of this type, and there should be constant reference to them in the course of such a unit. This is a time when the teacher will want to show the children how to make better use of them. That is, in addition to developing a better under-

Map making has added value for pupils when they use maps for further study, as is being done here. (Courtesy of the Shoreline Public Schools, Seattle)

standing of the geography of this region and its relationship to the life of the people who inhabit the area, the children should also be developing greater skill in their use of maps and globes. To this end the teacher will make use of product maps, weather maps, and maps showing the location of natural resources. The class will make a careful study of what makes a good harbor and how one can recognize such a condition on a map. The globe will show the location of this region with reference to the markets of Western Europe. The class will examine the water and land transportation routes and relate this to map study. The teacher will explain how to interpret the surface features of the area from the colors on the map. Such teaching should be supported by the generous use of pictures, filmstrips, and films. Procedures of the type described can be an important part of many if not most of the units undertaken in the social studies.

Globes can give such information as distance, direction, relative and exact location, and size and shape of areas more accurately than flat maps can. Whereas maps may be used to find distances between points only under certain conditions, the globe represents distances accurately and true to scale at all points on the surface of the earth. It is a simple procedure for the child to place his plastic ruler on the globe and measure directly the distance between two points in question. He can then refer to the scale and determine the actual distance in miles between the two places. The air routes of the world use great circles because these are the shortest distances from place to place on the earth's surface. If he uses nothing but flat maps, it is difficult for the child to understand the concept of great circle routes, and, therefore, of airplane routes. The globe can help to simplify this for the youngster. In this connection, the slated globe (sometimes called the project globe) is useful because it is possible to write on the surface of it with a piece of chalk. Such globes should be twenty-two inches in diameter in order to be large enough to write various information on their surface.

It is important for the child to be able to conceptualize distances between points on the earth, because he is living in an age when world travel is commonplace. He needs to understand distances in terms of time as well as in miles. More and more, we are making references such as "It is x number of hours to Paris, or Tokyo, or Lagos." Only infrequently do we hear references to these places in terms of the number of miles they are from us. Even in large American cities, commuters say they live "thirty minutes from the office" rather than state the number of miles. Absolute distance is less important to us than the amount of time it takes to cover the distance using modern means of transportation.

In this connection, it is necessary to note that many previously unknown areas have become extremely important in terms of modern-day transportation. A globe, for instance, will show the shortest route to the Orient from Minneapolis to be over Alaska and the Aleutians. On a Mercator projection, this route appears as an arc. To the child, this would appear a much greater distance than a straight western flight over the Pacific. Globes are indispensable in helping children understand concepts such as these.

Globes are helpful, too, in establishing concepts of direction. It is not difficult for the child to think of north as being in the direction of the North Pole if he is using a globe. On the other hand, this may

What map skills can be learned through the construction of a globe such as the one shown here? (Courtesy of the Highline Public Schools, Seattle)

be very confusing to him if he has had experience only with a flat map and his teacher has told him that "north is at the top of the map." Furthermore, the relative direction of various parts of the earth can be better understood through the use of a globe. Many Americans are surprised, for example, when they learn that all the British Isles lie in a more northern latitude than do any of the forty-eight mid-continent states of our country; that Boston has nearly the same latitude as Rome; that our most westerly state is not Hawaii but Alaska; that Moscow and Glasgow have approximately the same latitude, both being farther south than any city of Norway or Sweden. These facts are not important except to demonstrate that one perceives the earth differently on a globe than on a flat map.

A definite advantage that globes have over maps is that they show size and shapes of areas exactly as they appear on the earth's surface, whereas maps frequently do not. The classical examples of distortions in size and shapes of land areas are Greenland on the Mercator projection and Australia on the polar projection. On the Mercator projection, Greenland appears as a very large area—larger than South America. On a polar projection, Australia appears to have a greater east-west distance and a shorter north-south distance than is actually the case. Notice the different shapes North America takes on various maps as illustrated in Figure 31. A globe will show all of these map shapes and sizes to be inaccurately represented. Therefore, a globe should be constantly used with maps to prevent wrong conceptions regarding size and shape of the earth's areas. Maps must always make some adjustment in representing the earth's surface because they are flat and the earth is round.

The child, therefore, will be introduced to the use of the globe early in the primary grades through informal and incidental ways leading to more direct instruction in its use in middle and upper grades. He will learn the basic nature of the globe and how it can be used to get information concerning direction, distance, and size and shape of areas, as well as the location of places precisely and accurately. It is an important tool in developing a global view of the world and in teaching basic geographical concepts. It needs to be used in conjunction with flat maps to ensure the growth of accurate conceptions of the earth.

Instructional Experiences with Maps

During the time the child is extending his knowledge and is developing skill in the use of the globe, he should also be learning how to use flat maps. Ordinarily, the child will not have the use of conventional wall maps before third grade except in an incidental way. In the first and second grades, the child may have been given a jigsaw-puzzle map of the United States, and he is able to recognize it as a map of his country and identify various states, lakes, cities, and so forth. The family may have planned an automobile trip where his father made use of road maps. He may have seen the "weather man" use a map on the nightly television weather forecast. He may have seen maps in newspapers, magazines, or travel folders. The notion that our country or any part of the world can be shown on a map is, therefore, not an altogether new idea to most children.

One does not begin the teaching of map reading to children by introducing them to conventional printed maps except to show them what a map looks like. There are a number of exceedingly complex skills involved in map reading and interpretation; therefore, early experiences with maps should be kept very simple. This can best be

Figure 31. A land area such as North America may take a variety of shapes on maps, depending on the projection that is used. A classroom globe shows shapes and areas more accurately than maps and should be used in conjunction with the study of wall maps.

done through the use of diagrams and maps that the teacher and the class make of their immediate vicinity. These experiences may take the form of a layout on the classroom floor using blocks and other objects for houses, streets, trees, and public buildings. It can be done on a sand table, if there is one, or the map can be drawn on a large piece of wrapping paper on the classroom floor. Where the floor material will permit it, masking tape can be placed on the floor itself to represent boundaries, streets, or roads.

A fundamental skill in map reading is to learn that a symbol represents a real and actual thing. The symbol may be arbitrarily chosen and bear no resemblance to the object represented, or it may be one that would suggest to the reader what is intended. A school might be represented by a small circle or by a small square with a flag placed on top. It is easier to associate the flag and square with a school than to associate the circle with it. The flag and square are, therefore, less abstract. With young children, it is better to use pictorial or semi-pictorial symbols of this sort than to use completely abstract ones. In teaching map-reading skills to children it must be remembered that both reading and interpretive skills are involved, and the interpretive skills depend heavily on maturity and background knowledge. Primary-grade children will do less with interpretive skills than they will with reading skills.

The idea of objects representing other objects, people, or things is not new to the children; they have substituted symbols for the actual things many times in the imaginative play of childhood. The teacher can begin by explaining to them that they are going to draw a map of the schoolroom, schoolyard, or some segment of the immediate vicinity. It is best if this can be done on the classroom floor, so the layout can be oriented exactly as it appears in relationship to the classroom; this sidesteps the matter of orientation to directions at this early stage. Trees, doors, playground equipment, parking areas, and other objects appear in relation to other objects, and only the major ones should be included. The purpose of this type of experience is simply to show children that it is possible to represent space symbolically and that symbols stand for real things. Their map should have a title and a key to tell what the symbols stand for. This is the first experience in the development of skill in comprehending the significance of symbols, and it will be continued and extended as long as maps are used.

As the children become ready for more-abstract symbols, they will be introduced, taught, and used, as will conventional map symbols. As a part of this instruction in the middle and upper grades, it is extremely important for the teacher to make generous use of pictures and other visual aids that will help the child visualize accurately the area represented by a map symbol. It is very helpful, too, to take children to some high point of vantage in the community where they can look down on an area and see what it actually looks like from above. In most localities it is possible to purchase inexpensive aerial photographs of the local community, and these can be used by the class in studying map symbols and in making their own maps of the local area. Some map companies have prepared wall charts designed to help children visualize things represented by map symbols; these are excellent devices for teaching this skill to middle- and upper-grade children. The teacher also should take advantage of the many fine photographs in social studies textbooks to acquaint the pupils with the appearance of various areas, landscapes, surface features, land and water forms, and man-made things that are represented symbolically on maps.

For reasons of simplicity, the matter of orientation to direction may be avoided in the first contacts children have with diagrams or maps, but the need for development of the skill of orienting a map properly for direction will become apparent immediately if their classroom layout is rotated. Being able to note and read directions is prerequisite to serious map study and should be introduced fairly early, perhaps in second grade. Children learn the cardinal directions first, through direct teaching. They learn the direction of north, south, east, and west by having these directions pointed out to them. They quickly learn which wall of the room is north, south, east, and west because the teacher has placed labels on the walls for all to see. They learn that if one knows the direction of north, he can place the other directions; for if he faces north, the direction of south will be to his back, east to his right, and west to his left. To extend their ability to orient themselves, children should be taken outdoors and directions pointed out to them. If this is done at noon on a sunny day, the children's shadows will point in an approximate northerly direction. After the children have this basic orientation to direction, subsequent map work should include reference to direction, and should become increasingly more complex as pupils mature.

Finding directions on conventional wall maps can be facilitated with the aid of a globe and perhaps should not be taught below fourth grade. When this concept is introduced to children, it should be done through reference to north-south and east-west grid lines. They are taught that north is in the direction of the North Pole and that south is in the direction of the South Pole. The poles can be easily found by following the north-south lines because they converge on the poles, and all globes and wall maps show these lines. The east-west directions can be found by following the east-west lines or parallels, for they encircle the earth in that direction. Generalizations such as "north is at the top of the map" and "south is at the bottom of the map" should *not* be taught to children because they are not correct and because they serve to confuse the child when he uses various map projections. Similarly, references to north as "up" and south as "down" should not be taught in connection with either maps or globes. When we speak of the earth, the term *down* means toward the center of the earth and *up* means away from the center of the earth, and both terms should be taught only in that way. The matter of associating up with north introduces many serious instructional problems as children learn more of the geography of the earth. For example, if north is up, how can so many of the world's rivers flow north? The children will invariably ask why we say "way down South" or "the Land Down Under"; these can be explained as being colorful expressions and figures of speech similar to "way out West" or "out at sea" that have crept into our language but have nothing at all to do with direction itself. (See Figure 32.)

Teachers who are concerned about helping children develop the skill of noting directions will frequently take time to have children point out and discuss directions on the map the class is using. In the middle and upper grades the teacher will duplicate maps on various grids and have the children place directional data on them. When this is done he will want to emphasize the need to use east-west and north-south lines. This will give the children experiences noting directions on various map grids as well as keep the teacher up to date on the progress children are making in the development of this skill.

Map reading also involves the skill of being able to recognize and use scales. Children can be taught the need for scaling by indicating to them that maps must be small enough to bring into the classroom or carry around. We cannot make maps as big as the area we wish to show because that would make the map so large it could not be used. It must, therefore, be made smaller, and everything on the map must be made smaller in the same amount. Just as a photograph of the family shows everyone smaller in the same amount, so must the map; otherwise, it would not give a true picture. Children should learn that maps are precise and accurate instruments. In primary grades, the scaling is not done in the mathematical sense, but the reductions are made in a relative way. In middle grades, when children have had sufficient background in mathematics, they can deal with graphic reductions more precisely. They learn that wall maps have the scale printed on them and are taught how to read the various ways in which scale can be indicated. The experiences children have using map scales provide a good time for the teacher to call their attention to distances between various places. Children can be helped to visualize these distances through an appreciation of the amount of time needed to

Figure 32. This map illustrates why generalizations such as "north is at the top of the map" are incorrect. East-west lines or parallels of latitude have been omitted in order to draw attention to north-south directions. What questions might you pose to pupils studying this map?

traverse the distances in question by air travel. These times may be obtained from commercial airlines.

When the children have learned the meaning of map symbols, are skillful in orienting themselves to direction on a map, and can recognize and use map scales, they are then well on their way toward an understanding of the language of maps. This does not mean, however, that they find them especially useful or that they regard them as a

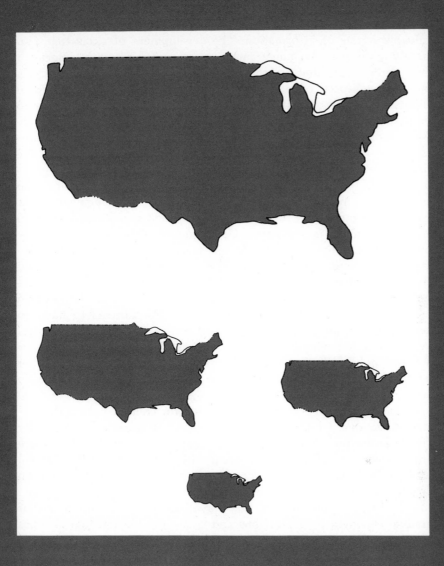

Figure 33. Children should learn that scale is used to reduce the size of the area represented on a map. An area such as the United States can be drawn on various sizes of paper by using a different scale.

TEACHING PUPILS HOW TO USE
GLOBES AND MAPS

valuable source of information. The development of skills that deal largely with map language must be accompanied with associated interpretive skills that are the most difficult to teach. Proficiency in interpretive aspects of map use will vary considerably with individual children. The person skillful in map use has developed the ability to visualize what an area actually looks like when he sees it on the map. As he looks at the map color, he in a sense "sees" the rugged mountains of our West, the waving grain fields of western Montana, the rich farmlands of the Midwest, and the rolling countryside of Virginia. Because the child cannot visualize places he has not actually seen except in an imaginative way and because he cannot personally visit all places in the world, the generous use of additional visual material along with maps is suggested. Good quality pictures are especially important, and the class should see several of an area in order to avoid fixing one picture of the area in their minds. Filmstrips and slides, of course, can be used for the same purpose, and motion pictures and television are also excellent aids. As was previously noted, in early stages of map reading, an excellent procedure is to have an aerial photograph of the local area as well as a conventional map. When these are placed side by side, the child can see how the area actually looks and how it is represented on a map. Stories and other narrative accounts also are helpful in assisting the child to visualize areas represented on maps.

The use of color has caused confusion for children trying to visualize elevations. Children seem to feel that all areas represented by one color are precisely the same elevation, not recognizing that there are variations in elevations that occur within the limits of the interval used by the color representation. (See Figure 34.) Moreover, children develop the mistaken notion that elevations occur abruptly where colors change. Conventional color symbols give no impression of gradual elevation or depressions and create the illusion that changes are abrupt. The use of a relief map is helpful in showing that changes in elevation occur gradually. Comparing colors of a wall map with elevations on a relief map helps children gain a better understanding of map color as used to represent elevations. It is important to remember, however, that relief maps use two scales—one for vertical distances and another for horizontal distances. If the horizontal scale were used for vertical distances, the elevations would be imperceptible on a relief map of the size usually found in elementary classrooms. Maps are now available that combine shaded relief with altitude colors; this adds a third dimensional effect to the mountains and valleys. Oblique shading and blending of color from one elevation to the other gives a graduated effect to land elevations that more accurately portray the surface of the earth. Such maps are becoming fairly widely used

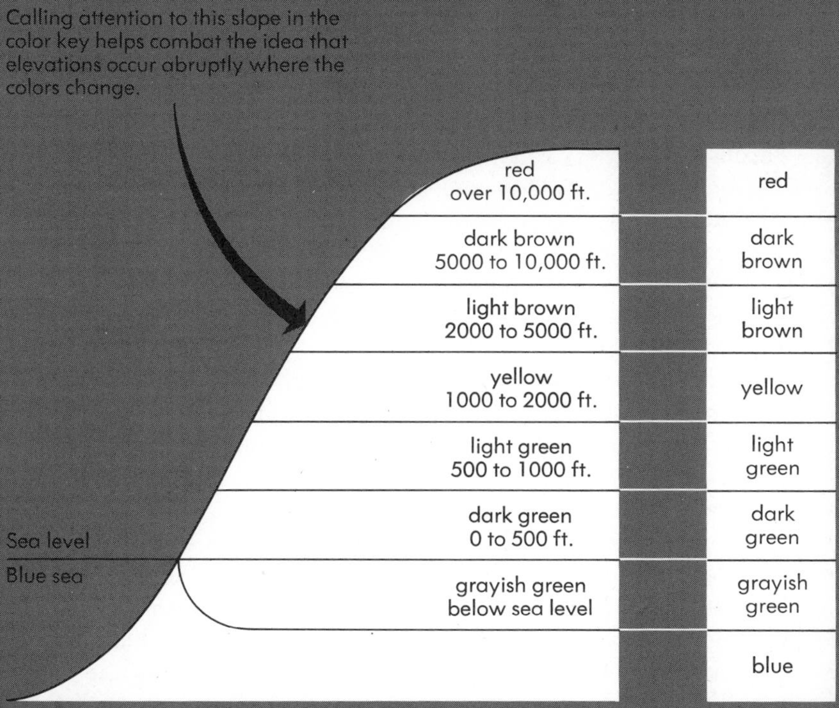
Calling attention to this slope in the color key helps combat the idea that elevations occur abruptly where the colors change.
red
over 10,000 ft.
dark brown
5000 to 10,000 ft.
light brown
2000 to 5000 ft.
yellow
1000 to 2000 ft.
light green
500 to 1000 ft.
dark green
0 to 500 ft.
grayish green
below sea level
Sea level
Blue sea
red
dark brown
light brown
yellow
light green
dark green
grayish green
blue

Figure 34. This diagram shows two methods of illustrating keys to colors used to express elevations on classroom maps. Some teachers find it helpful to construct a three-dimensional papier-mâché model of the key shown on the left.

in children's textbooks. Children must also be taught that color may be used to designate political divisions such as states, nations, territories, and possessions and that the color chosen is an arbitrary one having nothing to do with the way the area actually looks. Pictures of state boundaries, for example, will illustrate that if it were not for the boundary marker, one would not know when he passed from one state to the next.

Sometimes pupils find land-form maps difficult to understand. The usual land forms shown are plains, plateaus, hills, and mountains; each is represented by a different color. The difficulty in using these maps arises when the pupil mistakenly thinks of the colors as representing elevations in absolute amounts. For example, there are high mountains and low mountains, yet on a land-form map they appear in the same color. Some high plateaus are actually higher in absolute elevation than some low mountains. Some hills may be lower in elevation than plateaus and plains. Pupils need to learn that land-form maps only show where the plains, plateaus, hills, and mountains are located, not how high they are above sea level.

Through years of experience with maps, the child will develop skill in the location of places and become familiar with the shape and size of better-known ones. This he must do if he is to become efficient in the use of maps and globes. Moreover, he must learn to point out places precisely. In pointing to Chicago on the map of the United States, for example, he will point it out exactly—not by sweeping his hand across the general location of Chicago, thereby including parts of Iowa, Illinois, Wisconsin, Michigan, and Indiana. But the location exercises must go beyond simply pointing to places and objects that appear on the map. What information can be obtained from the map that might account for the large settlement of people in the Chicago area? What features tend to encourage or discourage settlers? Such factors as natural transportation routes, waterways, waterfalls, mouths of rivers, coast lines, temperature, gaps in mountains, and outlets for products of the surrounding areas will immediately become apparent as being important in the matter of population density and settlement. Why do certain areas of the Red River Valley in Minnesota and North Dakota experience frequent spring flood problems? The facts that the Red River is a north-flowing river and its head waters thaw while the sections farther north are still frozen help explain this recurring problem. What is the relationship of the grazing lands of the West to the farmlands of Iowa to the meat processing plants of South St. Paul, Chicago, and Kansas City? Map study, along with some knowledge of the geography of these areas, will help answer questions of this type for children. They gain insights into geographical relationships by having a helpful teacher who can assist them in seeing possibilities for interpreting and making inferences from facts gained through map study.

Certainly, a knowledge of the various kinds of information maps can yield will help the teacher see many possibilities for interpreting the language of maps. The types of information that can be read directly or inferred from map study can reasonably be classified as follows:

Land and water forms—continents, oceans, bays, peninsulas, islands, straits

Relief features—plains, mountains, rivers, deserts, plateaus, swamps, valleys

Direction and distance—cardinal directions, distance in miles and relative distance, scale

Social data—population density, size of communities, location of major cities, relationship of social data to other factors

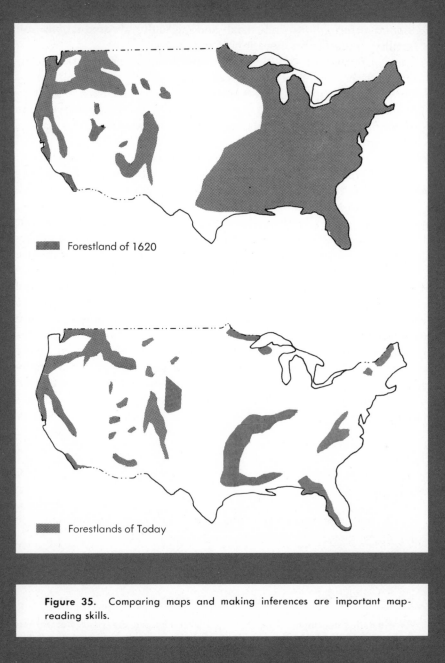

Forestland of 1620

Forestlands of Today

Figure 35. Comparing maps and making inferences are important map-reading skills.

TEACHING PUPILS HOW TO USE GLOBES AND MAPS

Economic information—industrial and agricultural production, soil fertility, trade factors, location of industries

Political information—political divisions, boundaries, capitals, territorial possessions, types of government, political parties

Scientific information—location of discoveries, ocean currents, location of mineral and ore deposits, geological formations, air movements

Human factors—cities, canals, railroads, highways, coaxial cables, telephone lines, bridges, dams

The importance of the gradual and continuous nature of the development of globe- and map-reading skills cannot be overemphasized. They are simply not taught once and for all time but are developed steadily and gradually throughout the child's school life.[1] Moreover, there are big differences in the ability of individual children to understand and make use of maps and globes. For these reasons, it is unwise to set up minimum standards of expectation that apply to all children at each grade level. What is really important at the elementary school level is to introduce the child to these helpful tools of learning and to teach him how to use them at a level of complexity consistent with his degree of maturity and understanding. With this in mind, it is possible to indicate in a general way what might be expected of the *average* child at a given grade level, if one keeps in mind that many children will go much beyond such expectations while other children will fall short of them. The program of the Denver Public Schools may be taken as an example of expectancies of this type:

A SUMMARY OF MAP AND GLOBE SKILLS

Grades K–6

By the end of the sixth grade, children should have acquired the following map and globe skills:

A. Skills that should be introduced in kindergarten and grades one, two, and three and then reinforced in grades four, five, and six:

1. For a detailed development of suggested learnings and experiences at various grade levels, *see* R. M. Harris, *The Rand McNally Handbook of Map and Globe Usage*, Chicago: Rand McNally, 1967; Gertrude Whipple, "Geography in the Elementary Social Studies Program: Concepts, Generalizations, Skills to be Developed," *New Viewpoints in Geography*, Washington, D.C.: National Council for the Social Studies, 1959; Zoe Thralls, *The Teaching of Geography*, New York: Appleton-Century-Crofts, 1958; Helen McCracken Carpenter, ed., *Skill Development in Social Studies*, Washington, D.C.: National Council for the Social Studies, 1963, pp. 322–325.

1. Use relative terms of location and direction, such as *near, far, above, below, up,* and *down.*
2. Develop an awareness of cardinal directions in the classroom and the neighborhood.
3. Use terms of intermediate directions, such as *southwest* and *northeast.*
4. Use cardinal and in-between directions while working with maps.
5. Understand that north is toward the North Pole and south toward the South Pole on any map or globe.
6. Understand the use of the compass for direction.
7. Use the north arrow on the globe and map.
8. Orient individual, textbook, or atlas maps correctly to the north.
9. Use parallels and meridians in determining directions.
10. Construct simple maps, properly oriented as to direction.
11. Recognize home, city, and state on a map of the United States and on a globe.
12. Identify continents, oceans, large islands, the equator.
13. Recognize land and water forms on simple globes and on a variety of simple maps.
14. Use a highway map for locating places by number and key.
15. Interpret and use abbreviations commonly found.
16. Use key and map vocabulary with accuracy.
17. Use two or more globes or maps to gather information about the same area.
18. Recognize the location of major cities with respect to physical and directional setting.
19. Trace routes of travel of different means of transportation.
20. Develop a visual image of major land and water forms, the United States, and other map patterns studied.
21. Read maps of various types that show elevation of land form.
22. Learn to make simple sketch maps to show location.
23. Use small objects to represent large ones, as a model or photograph to represent actual size.
24. Make simple large-scale maps of a familiar area, such as the classroom or the neighborhood.
25. Determine that the distance on a map is not the true distance but represents the true distance.
26. Understand that real objects are represented by pictures or symbols.
27. Use legends on different globes and maps.
28. Compare two maps of the same area, combine information, draw conclusions based on data.

29. Recognize that there are maps and globes of many varieties for many purposes and learn to select appropriate ones for the purpose at hand.

30. Infer man's activities or way of living from physical detail and from north or south distance from the equator toward the poles.

B. Skills that should be introduced in grades four, five, and six:

1. Relate low latitudes to the equator and high latitudes to the polar areas.

2. Use longitude and latitude in locating places on wall maps and globes.

3. Use an atlas to locate places.

4. Identify time zones of the United States and relate them to longitude.

5. Understand the reason for and use of the International Date Line.

6. Compare the actual length of a block or a mile with distance on a large-scale map.

7. Compare the same area in maps of different sizes.

8. Compare maps of different areas to note that a smaller scale must be used to map larger areas.

9. Estimate distance on a globe; use latitude, great circle routes.

10. Understand and use map scale as a representative fraction, statement of scale, or bar scale.

11. Develop the habit of checking scale on maps and globes used.

12. Identify symbols for water features to learn source, mouth, direction of flow, depths, and ocean currents.

13. Visualize the nature of areas shown through color-contour and visual-relief maps and globes.

14. Interpret elevation of land from flow of rivers.

15. Interpret dots, lines, colors, and other symbols in addition to pictorial symbols.

16. Develop the ability to use all parts of a simple atlas.

17. Read into maps and globes relationships suggested by data shown, such as factors that determine the location of cities.

18. Recognize differences in map projections and distortions in any representation of the earth other than the globe.

19. Use maps and globes to explain the geographic setting of historical and current events.

20. Draw inferences from a variety of special-purpose maps.[2]

2. Adapted from *The Social Studies Program of the Denver Public Schools*, Division of Instructional Services, Denver Public Schools, Denver, Colorado, 1966. Used by permission.

Selecting Classroom Maps

The types of maps available to children unquestionably have much to do with whether or not they will be used. If too much information is crowded into the surface of a small map, the result is confusing to children. Most map companies producing maps for elementary schools offer a simplified series for lower grades and a standard elementary series for upper grades. The maps commonly used today combine political and physical data on one map. There is less need for maps that show only political or only physical data than there is for those showing both. Although wall maps, which are produced by reputable companies specifically for elementary grades, usually are well constructed and suitable for children, the teacher should be extremely careful when selecting maps found in magazines, travel folders, and free material. Maps in the *National Geographic Magazine,* for example, are excellent in many respects but may be too complex or contain too much detail for young children to handle. Even a critical examination of commercially prepared maps for use with elementary schoolchildren will reveal great differences in quality and suitability.

In appraising the suitability of maps, these standards might be applied:

1. Is the map content adequate for the grade in which it is to be used? The map should convey complete and accurate information, yet it should not be cluttered with detail that is not used in the grade. In general, the simplest map that will adequately do the job is desired over a more complex one.
2. Does the map fit into a developmental sequence of globe and map-reading skills? Are the scale, projection, color use, and symbols appropriate for the maturity of the pupils who will use the map?
3. Is the map easy to read? Can it be seen from across the room? Are its colors used in a pleasing and functional way? Are standard map symbols used? Is the key one that children can understand and use?
4. Does the map lend itself to a variety of uses in building map-reading skills? Single-purpose maps are of less value to the teacher than those that can be used for multiple purposes. Political-physical maps are often more useful than those showing only one or the other of these data.
5. Are the mechanics of the map such as to make for easy handling? Can it be conveniently displayed? Can it stand the heavy use it will get in the classroom?
6. Is the map publisher a reputable and dependable concern, familiar with the needs of elementary classrooms?

Beginning with the fourth grade and above, classes should have the following wall maps easily available for use:

1. A political-physical map for each continent.
2. At least one political-physical world map.
3. A slated, washable map of the United States and the world. (Usually the United States is printed on one side and the world on the reverse side of this map.)
4. A political-physical map of the home state.
5. A map of the town or city (a quality service station map may suffice here).
6. A polar projection world map.
7. A plastic relief map of the United States.
8. A population-density map of the United States.
9. If additional money is available, it is recommended that classrooms also have world maps showing population, rainfall, vegetation, land-use patterns, and resource distribution and have charts that picture various map symbols.

Devices such as the twenty-two-inch slated globe, a miniature planetarium, charts that picture map symbols, and maps that are used only occasionally can be conveniently shared by several rooms. This practice makes it possible to have a greater number of different types of map materials available, and it helps keep costs down. The basic maps used daily should be stocked in every classroom in third grade and above and should be easily accessible to the children. Instructing the children in the proper care and use of maps will help keep the maps in good condition for several years. When maps become obsolete because of changes in data, they should, of course, be replaced.

This list includes some of the better-known producers of globes, maps, or map-reading materials:

1. A. J. Nystrom and Company, 3333 Elston Ave., Chicago, Ill. 60618.
2. C. S. Hammond and Company, Inc., 515 Valley St., Maplewood, N.J. 07040.
3. Denoyer-Geppert Company, 5235 Ravenswood Ave., Chicago, Ill. 60640.
4. Rand McNally & Company, P.O. Box 7600, Chicago, Ill. 60680.
5. George F. Cram Company, Inc., 730 E. Washington St., Indianapolis, Ind. 46206.
6. Hagstrom Company, Inc., 311 Broadway, New York, N.Y. 10007.
7. National Geographic Society, 16th and M Streets, N.W., Washington, D.C. 20036.

8. American Geographical Society, Broadway at 156th St., New York, N.Y.
9. Farquhar Transparent Globes, 5007 Warrington Ave., Philadelphia, Pa.
10. Keystone View Company, Meadville, Pa.
11. McKinley Publishing Company, 809–811 N. 19th St., Philadelphia, Pa. 19180.
12. Jeppesen & Company, 8025 E. 40th Ave., Denver, Colo.
13. Replogle Globes, Inc., 1901 N. Narragansett Ave., Chicago, Ill. 60639.
14. Weber Costello Company, 1900 N. Narragansett Ave., Chicago, Ill. 60639.
15. W. H. Olson and Company, Inc., Providence, R.I.
16. Panoramic Studios, Inc., 179 W. Berks St., Philadelphia, Pa.
17. Science Research Associates, Inc., 259 E. Erie St., Chicago, Ill. 60611: *Map and Globe Skills Kit* (learning materials organized that pupils may work independently and at their own rate on such topics as "Learning to Read Globes and Projections," designed for use in grades 4 through 6).

For a list of maps approved for public sale, the teacher should write to Army Map Service, Corps of Engineers, U.S. Army, Washington, D.C. Another excellent source of inexpensive relief maps is the U.S. Geological Survey, Distribution Section, Federal Center, Denver, Colorado.

Discussion Questions and Suggested Activities

1. Plan specific map- and globe-reading experiences that can be used with children in conjunction with the resource unit that you are developing (Chapter 3).
2. What are some of the advantages and disadvantages of having children draw maps?
3. Obtain a Mercator projection and present a "lesson" to your classmates explaining that the shortest route from Panama to Tokyo passes over the central part of the United States, western Canada, Alaska, and the Aleutians. Have a classmate present the same idea using a classroom globe or a slated globe if one is available. Which of these two aids would you recommend if this idea were being presented to children?
4. Prepare a series of posters showing map symbols and accompany each symbol with a photograph of the object being represented.
5. What desirable educational outcomes can you cite for children's experiences in making relief maps when it is well known that such

maps always badly distort surface elevations? Would you say that the making of relief maps by children in the elementary school is a valuable experience that contributes to the development of map-reading skills? Do you feel that it is possible for much map making by children to amount to little more than "busy work"? How might the teacher guard against map-making exercises becoming a waste of time?

6. Examine several conventional wall maps and evaluate them in terms of the criteria presented in this chapter.

7. Make a list of words or phrases related to the understanding of maps and globes that are misleading (for example, up, down). For each entry suggest an alternate word or phrase that would be more accurate.

8. What map- and globe-reading experiences could be correlated with current affairs activities? Should map- and globe-reading skills be taught separately or as components of other units of instruction? Defend your point of view.

9. Can you give specific examples of misunderstandings that are likely to occur if the teacher uses only conventional wall maps instead of using wall maps and a globe at the same time?

Selected References

Bacon, Phillip. "A Straight Line Isn't Always the Shortest Distance," *Grade Teacher, 83,* No. 2 (October, 1965), pp. 104+.

Douglass, Malcolm P. *Social Studies: From Theory to Practice in Elementary Education.* Philadelphia: J. B. Lippincott Company, 1967.

Gengler, Charles R. "The Application of Geographic Terms to Map Symbolism," *Journal of Geography, LXVI,* No. 7 (October, 1967), pp. 394–396.

"What You Need to Sharpen Map and Globe Skills," *Grade Teacher, 84,* No. 2 (October, 1966), pp. 106–109+.

Hanna, Paul R., *et al. Geography in the Teaching of Social Studies: Concepts and Skills.* Boston: Houghton Mifflin Company, 1966.

Harris, Ruby M. *Handbook of Map and Globe Usage.* Chicago: Rand McNally and Company, 1967.

Herman, Wayne L., Jr. *Current Research in Elementary School Social Studies,* Part VII. New York: The Macmillan Company, 1969.

Kennamer, Lorrin. "Developing a Sense of Place and Space," *Skill Development in Social Studies,* 33rd Yearbook. Washington, D.C.: National Council for the Social Studies, 1963. .

McAuley, J. D. "Second Grade Children's Growth in Comprehension of Geographic Understandings," *Journal of Geography,* LX, No. 1 (January, 1966), pp. 33–37.

Marine, Helene. "Using Audiovisuals in Map Reading Readiness Instruction," *Audiovisual Instruction, 13,* No. 1 (January, 1968), pp. 48–51.

Michaelis, John U. *Social Studies for Children in a Democracy,* 4th ed. Englewood Cliffs, N.J.: Prentice-Hall, Inc., 1968.

Preston, Ralph C. *Teaching Social Studies in the Elementary School,* 3rd ed. New York: Holt, Rinehart & Winston, Inc., 1968.

Raisz, Erwin J. *Principles of Cartography.* New York: McGraw-Hill Book Company, Inc., 1962.

Resnick, Abraham. "The Student-Made Outdoor Map," *Journal of Geography,* LXVI, No. 4 (April, 1967), pp. 164–166.

Rushdoony, H. A. "Children's Ability to Read Maps: Summary of the Research," *Journal of Geography,* LXVII, No. 4 (April, 1968), pp. 213–222.

Sabaroff, Rose. "Improving the Use of Maps in the Elementary School," *Journal of Geography,* LX, No. 4 (April, 1961), pp. 184–190.

Towler, John O., and L. D. Nelson. "The Elementary School Child's Concept of Scale," *Journal of Geography,* LXVII, No. 1 (January, 1968), pp. 24–28.

Whipple, Gertrude. *How to Introduce Maps and Globes: Grades One Through Six,* How to Do It Series, No. 15. Washington, D.C.: National Council for the Social Studies, 1967.

Building Worldmindedness

It is unlikely that any single event in human history had as profound an effect in providing a feeling of worldmindedness and world identity than did the moon landings by the American astronauts. Throughout the world, human beings watched or listened, hoped or prayed for the safe return of the men, and contemplated the concept of the oneness of mankind. The event truly did mark "one giant leap for mankind" as was so aptly put by Mr. Armstrong.

Barring some global catastrophe, it is likely that worldmindedness will continue to grow among the people of this planet. This has many implications for social studies instruction. Today international relations are dominating the attention of our nation. It could hardly be

16

otherwise given the realities of the modern world. Consequently, social studies programs are being planned to equip the young citizen to deal thoughtfully and intelligently with problems of international import.

The people of the United States as well as others throughout the world have a sincere desire to maintain peaceful relationships with other nations. Their experiences in World War II, and the development of atomic weapons of war, have made people everywhere fearful of the consequences of another international conflict. One of the chief purposes of the organization of the United Nations was "to save succeeding generations from the scourge of war, which twice in our lifetime has brought untold sorrow to mankind."[1] If this statement and others like it correctly represent the sentiments of responsible, rational men—and there can be little doubt that it does—it seems incredible that mankind continues to expend fantastic amounts of the world's resources on the machinery of war. An interesting observation of this phenomenon was made by Dr. Jerome D. Frank:

> As a psychiatrist, I have been struck by certain parallels between the behavior of nations today and the behavior of mental patients. In particular, we seem to alternate between what General Omar Bradley has termed "a colossal indifference to danger" and frantic intensification of the very behavior which brought it about. Thus, in our efforts to lessen the danger, we increase it. An individual who behaved in this way would be a psychiatric patient.[2]

Perhaps what mankind really needs is therapy on some kind of mass scale, but better education directed toward an understanding of the problems and peoples of the world seems to be a more realistic alternative.

The type of education that will lead mankind to a more rational approach to international relations will need to be of a particular type. Increased amounts of education apparently does not do the job, for as Goodlad has noted, "the people who soon may bring down upon themselves a holocaust are—or will have been—the *most* educated of all time."[3] In modern times it has not been the nations who were ignorant, illiterate, and uneducated that have led the world down the path to war. Quite the contrary, it has been nations with highly developed educational systems.

There can be little doubt that we live in a world fraught with danger. What is more, this is likely to increase as modern instruments

1. From the Charter of the United Nations.

2. Jerome D. Frank, "Sanity and Survival," *Social Education*, XXVI, No. 7, November, 1962, p. 367.

3. John I. Goodlad, *Some Propositions in Search of Schools*, Washington, D.C.: Department of Elementary School Principals, 1962, p. 7.

of destruction become available to more and more nations. Even a tiny nation, armed with modern weapons, constitutes a threat to the entire world. To ignore the real danger that exists or to minimize it could result in disastrous consequences for all of mankind. But if nations can spare themselves from destruction during this delicate time of the present, perhaps more sensible approaches to human relations will eventually prevail. Perhaps through educational programs directed toward the understanding of others and toward a search for world peace, a more satisfactory method of resolving international disputes can be found than man's oldest and least effective method, war.

Teaching for worldmindedness, therefore, is essential if man is to survive. Such programs cannot be allowed to become based on sentimentalism and naive optimism. The harsh realities of the world are ever present and must be faced. Teachers will want to help pupils develop feelings of good will, mutual trust, and understanding of others, but at the same time, it must be understood that these feelings cannot be one-sided in their application. No matter how strongly men of good will of *any* nation long for peace, it cannot be a realizable goal so long as huge sections of the world's people are taught to hate and distrust others. As has been said many times, we deal with the world the way it is, not as we wish it to be.

The policy of the United States as a government and the personal philosophy of most Americans toward people of other nations is one that supports peaceful and harmonious relationships between people of all countries. This policy has been announced publicly in a variety of ways countless numbers of times. What is more, the behavior of Americans as a nation as well as individually has given testimony to support our policy. This is not to say that the actions of our government or of individual Americans in dealing with people of other countries has in all cases been faultless. It is precisely because there have been instances of poor judgment in our relationships with others that our policies and intentions can be misconstrued or distorted. Moreover, because the United States is a rich and powerful nation, in a position of world leadership, the actions of its government and individual citizens come under constant and extraordinarily careful scrutiny by the rest of the world. A diplomatic blunder or the thoughtless actions of a private citizen traveling abroad committed by a small, obscure nation might go almost unnoticed in the stream of world events; the same actions by the United States or one of its citizens could precipitate an international crisis. Heavy responsibilities are thrust on those who find themselves in leadership positions, and the standard of expectation for performance is correspondingly high. Teaching for worldmindedness in American schools is crucial, therefore, when viewed in this context. American schoolchildren must be sensitized to these realities, for it is they who will be representing the United States to the rest of the world in the years to come and who will be the decision makers of the future.

Framework for a Program to Develop Worldmindedness

Although the need for educating children along the lines of world-mindedness is evident, the precise manner in which it should be included in the school curriculum has been a matter of some controversy. Teachers are likely to view with concern the inclusion of additional material to an already demanding teaching load. Parents and various lay groups may express apprehension over such teaching—fearful that the schools will develop feelings of worldmindedness at the expense of building fundamental loyalties to and understanding of their own country. Others are openly hostile toward the inclusion of any teaching directed toward world understanding because they feel it is prejudicial to the American way of life. It is, therefore, necessary to clarify the manner in which instruction in worldmindedness is to function in the school curriculum.

Teaching for worldmindedness should not and need not conflict with developing within the child a basic loyalty to and love for his own country. The two concepts can and should be complementary rather than hostile to each other. For example, a person does not love his family any less because he has an understanding of and sympathy for the problems of his community. Similarly, one need not love his own country less because he has a better understanding of the world community. The primary goal is to develop worldminded Americans. It begins with the individual and his relationships with other individuals and groups he meets face to face.

When education for world understanding is regarded as one of the broad goals of education, it becomes immediately apparent that the addition of a new subject to the curriculum is not necessary. Rather, it should represent an *extension and broader interpretation of what is already taught in most schools*. If this is to occur, however, somewhat substantial shifts in emphasis will be necessary in dealing with conventional topics. In the following passage, the late Hilda Taba noted certain inadequacies in existing school practices:

> Although living in a world of vastly expanded horizons requires vastly extended selectivity and capacity to understand, there is little in the usual curriculum of our public schools that is addressed directly to developing a cosmopolitan sensitivity, to seeing the "culturally other" in its own right. To be sure, there are factual surveys of the geography and the economy of other lands; these have been introduced under the mistaken assumption that knowing the rivers and resources of a coun-

try produces an objective insight into the compelling forces in its culture. Such information alone, no matter how pertinent, does not produce insight into the dynamics of the people and into the core values by which they live.[4]

Teaching for world understanding can occur through experiences the child has in music, art, science, literature, reading—in fact, in almost any of the various curricular areas. This was clearly demonstrated in a project designed to improve the teaching of world affairs conducted in the public school system of Glens Falls, New York. This three-year project was sponsored by the National Council for the Social Studies and is known as Improving the Teaching of World Affairs (ITWA). It utilized the total resources of the Glens Falls school system in a full-scale effort to improve education about world affairs. Within the existing curriculum framework, the project sought to develop a "heightened awareness of and increased sensitivity to the large world"[5] through every subject at every grade throughout the system. The Project report continues, "The heart of the program is not in a curriculum guide, nor a set of lesson plans, valuable as these are, but rather in a point of view. We believe that instruction in all grades and subjects can reflect, in one way or another, a world point of view."[6] Almost any unit or topic in the social studies can be broadened and taught from the standpoint of worldmindedness by an aware, informed teacher.

In order to broaden instruction as described in the previous paragraph, teachers will need greater freedom in planning their units than has been the case in the past. They will also have to be imaginative in exploring and discovering new avenues to a world view. For example, at the primary-grade level, when children are studying homes and home life, is perhaps the time to begin developing the understanding that people all over the world need homes and that they build them in a variety of ways. Or, when the food market is studied, some time might be devoted to an examination of food markets around the world. Units on transportation and communication can, likewise, be expanded to familiarize the child with these functions on a broader basis than the local community. Almost any topic has within it such possibilities for teaching global relationships, and it is up to the teacher to discover and develop them with his pupils.

If a school accepts the education of boys and girls for worldmind-

4. Hilda Taba, *Curriculum Development: Theory and Practice*, New York: Harcourt, Brace and World, 1962, pp. 73–74.

5. Harold M. Long and Robert N. King, *Improving the Teaching of World Affairs: The Glens Falls Story*, Washington, D.C.: National Council for the Social Studies, 1964, p. 18.

6. *Ibid.*, p. 61.

edness as one of its primary purposes, a first step is to determine the general objectives to be achieved. These can be stated in terms of behavioral changes or as aims and purposes. It is likely that any program designed to develop international understanding would concern itself with concepts such as these and would state its specific objectives accordingly:

1. The interdependence of peoples
2. The need for peaceful relations among nations
3. Basic similarities and differences in peoples due to geographic, cultural, and historical considerations, to include an elementary understanding of the ways of living in the modern world
4. The philosophy and practice of respect for the dignity of the individual irrespective of race or other factors over which he has no control
5. The need to develop a sensitivity to and respect for the cultures of other peoples

Experiences to Help Build Worldmindedness

Basically, programs devoted to fostering worldmindedness are characterized by providing children with opportunities to apply their learnings within the setting of their everyday life. Such learnings take root and grow in classrooms where children are practicing fundamental principles of democratic group living. There is no point in attempting to develop respect for the people of a far-off land when pupils reject a classmate because she is of Japanese extraction. Building a readiness for international understanding begins with the development of respect for individuals with whom the child lives in his day-to-day activities, a willingness to give consideration to the needs, points of view, and characteristics of his classmates and neighbors.

A second-grade teacher who was interested in having the pupils develop a sensitivity to others, started by having the children study themselves. They prepared "Guess Who" riddles about themselves. "I have light hair and have a tooth missing in front; who am I?" This was followed by having each child draw a picture of himself; these drawings were placed in a class book. These procedures stimulated much discussion of the differences and similarities in people. The children became intensely interested in the study, and under the skillful guidance of the teacher were able to conclude that everyone is "a little bit different, but we all do many of the same things and are very much alike."

Single experiences of the type described are not likely to do much in shaping attitudes of acceptance, nor is the statement of a generalization by the children an indication that the teaching has been effective. But let us assume that children will have many experiences intended to engender attitudes of acceptance of others and that these will be extended throughout the several years the child is in the elementary, junior high, and senior high school. The effect of the sum total of these experiences is likely to have a strong influence on the attitudes of a substantial number of them. Even though such teaching is particularly susceptible to verbalism in the form of broad generalizations to the effect that "people everywhere are different, yet the same in many respects," not all such conclusions by children should be discarded as sheer verbalism. One teacher, for example, was struck with the sincerity of her first-graders when, after examining and talking about shoes of children from seven different countries, a child was moved to say, "Our shoes are different, but our feet are the same."

The specific kinds of experiences a teacher will plan with pupils depend on the make-up of the group with which he is working. Having children draw pictures of themselves, for example, might be completely inappropriate in some classrooms, for it might draw attention to physical features that would embarrass some. What will "work" for one teacher with a particular group may or may not be appropriate for another teacher or for the same teacher with a different group. Perhaps more important than the specific experience itself is the classroom setting in which it takes place. Teachers who are concerned with developing attitudes of acceptance of others and thereby helping pupils develop international understanding will begin by reducing hostile feelings within the classroom.

A classroom climate that permits the growth and development of attitudes of acceptance is a necessary but not a sufficient condition for teaching worldmindedness. There is also the need for accurate and authentic information of the peoples of other lands. Most social studies programs make provision for the study of foreign countries or communities. In grades three or four it might be a single country, such as Mexico, or a series of several communities of the world. In grade five it might be England or other countries of Western Europe. In grade six it might be Latin American countries, Canada, India, Japan, or others. Just which countries or communities are to be selected for study presents some problem because they cannot all be studied, and, therefore, choices have to be made. Kenworthy suggests that the following criteria might be applied in selecting countries for study in a *twelve-year* program:

1. World powers
2. Countries of the future
3. Neighboring nations

4. Countries that represent cultural areas
5. Countries of the ancestors of the pupils
6. Countries representing emerging nations
7. Countries of our Western heritage
8. Countries against which the pupils have prejudice or little up-to-date information
9. Countries representing different forms of government and economy and religions
10. Countries on which adequate materials are available.[7]

A systematic and comprehensive study of countries or communities is not attempted in the primary grades. Children at the primary-grade level are sensitized to persons in other lands through informal, although planned, experiences largely of a firsthand nature. One first-grade teacher had a friend who taught six-year-old children in England. She developed a system of correspondence between the two classes that grew into correspondence between the parents of the children from both groups. Some families exchanged photographs and small gifts. Throughout the year, as letters, pictures, and other articles were received, they were shared with the class and provided the children with an intensely stimulating contact with another country. Several of the families continued writing their English friends on a permanent basis, and, in one case, the American family visited the family in England.

Another first-grade teacher used dolls of different countries as a lead to building an awareness of children in other lands. The class talked about the dolls as though they were people: "Does she have a home? Does she have parents as you do? Does she get hungry as you do? But her clothes are not like yours. Yes, but she does have clothes! Why are her clothes different? Because it is cold (or warm) where she lives. But this little doll's face is brown. Maybe she doesn't get hungry. Oh, yes, she gets hungry, needs clothes, becomes angry and happy just as the others." This presentation, of course, was accompanied by stories and other planned activities, including classroom visitors from England and Morocco who answered the children's questions about schools, games, bicycles, language, homes, and foods.

A second-grade teacher's class became interested in a group of children in a Korean orphanage through the teacher's husband, who was stationed in Korea. The initial contact was made through correspondence and led to a number of exceedingly interesting and worthwhile experiences for both groups. The groups exchanged small toys and gifts. The American children prepared an original skit to tell the Korean children about themselves. Because the activity took place in

7. Leonard S. Kenworthy, *Social Studies for the Seventies*, Waltham, Mass.: Blaisdell Publishing Company, 1969, pp. 453–454.

December, the children included the singing of Christmas songs in their skit. The material was tape-recorded, sent, and played for the Korean children, who in turn recorded material of their own and sent it to the American group. The project had many side values for the American class, for the teacher used this opportunity to have the children learn about the post office, how material had to be wrapped for overseas shipment, how much money was needed for postage, what size packages were acceptable for shipment, and so on.

Teachers who experiment with activities of the types cited are not interested in having the children make intensive studies of the countries or communities but are attempting to build an awareness in children of the need for desirable human relations at the international level. Taba suggested that "The development of cosmopolitan cultural sensitivity requires conditions similar to those required for teaching feelings and values—using experiences which evoke feelings, such as reactions to literature and life incidents, and enhancing contact and interaction of individuals from different cultural backgrounds." [8] Many specific situations or activities could be selected for this purpose; but, whatever experiences are planned, it is recommended that the principles discussed below be observed.

Principles for Selecting Activities to Build Worldmindedness

Use Experiences from the Everyday Lives of Pupils to Initiate Such Projects. These experiences might include the return of a parent from an overseas assignment, the presence of a foreign visitor, a curio from another country that some child brought to share with the class, a story or television program about children in other lands, or a news item familiar to the children. Successful activities of this type usually begin in class discussions under the guidance of an alert teacher who can identify experiences of children that lend themselves to such a study.

The Experiences of Children Must Result in Information About Other Peoples That Is Accurate and Authentic. Misguided teaching resulting in erroneous concepts of other peoples, the development of stereotypes, or overemphasis on those aspects of the lives of others that are drastically different from our own is worse than none at all. In order to get up-to-date information about the group being studied, the teacher might consult the local library or local travel bureaus, write to the appropriate embassy in Washington, D.C. or the local consulate, or request information about the country through the United Nations.

8. Taba, *op. cit.*, p. 74.

Persons from other countries can be an important data source for pupils who are making culture studies. Here we see a visitor from India showing the class a garment worn in her country. The pupils as well as their teacher, who is modeling the sari, and the visitor are obviously enjoying the lesson. (Courtesy of the Shoreline Public Schools, Seattle)

Another good source of information is through interviews with persons who were or are citizens of the country—exchange students attending American colleges and universities, foreign brides, or persons who have recently come to the United States and are seeking citizenship.

Instruction and Experiences for Primary-Grade Children Should Be Kept Simple, Child-Like. Difficult concepts relating to international understanding, geography, and intercultural relations should be avoided in teaching young children. One of the major purposes of these studies at the primary-grade level is to develop the concept of friendliness and neighborliness among the peoples of the world. Experiences planned should be simple ones, dealing with ideas and things that are consistent with the experience and maturity of the young child. Specifically, this means experiences concerning the way children in other lands live, play, dress, and eat. The primary-grade child can understand that everyone needs a home, a family, and friends, must go to school, and feels sad, happy, or angry at times.

Some Provision Should Be Made for Direct Contact with the Life of the Group Studied.   One of the best learning experiences for young children in making a study of people in other lands is to have direct contact with a person from the country, especially a child their own age, who can answer questions about the clothes they wear, their school, games, celebrations, homes, foods, stories, and similar ways of living. Other types of contacts include material things that have come from other countries. These are especially interesting to children if the items are similar to something they use in their own lives each day. A doll, an article of clothing, a musical record, a book, and a toy are examples of items that help children understand that there are differences in the *ways* of doing things but that children everywhere do many of the same things. With help from the teacher and their parents, even primary-grade children can carry on correspondence with children abroad, which invariably leads to the exchange of photographs and other objects. Teachers who wish to have their classes or individual pupils correspond with children in other lands may obtain information and addresses from the following sources:

American Junior Red Cross, 17th and D Streets, N.W., Washington, D.C. 20036.
Caravan of East and West, Inc., 132 E. 65th St., New York, N.Y. 10021.
International Friendship League, 40 Mount Vernon St., Beacon Hill, Boston, Mass. (*All ages*)
Letter Writing Committee, People-to-People Program, World Affairs Center, University of Minnesota, Minneapolis, Minn. 55455.
Letters Unlimited, G. J. Raymond, 5718 Wigton Drive, Houston, Tex. (*Ages 10 through 25*)
Pen Friends Division, The English-Speaking Union, 16 E. 69th St., New York, N.Y. 10021. (*Ages 9 through 16*)
Student Letter Exchange, Waseca, Minn. (*Ages 10 through 20*)
World Mailbag, 2 Hillcrest Rd., West Nyack, N.Y.
Youth Pen Pal Exchange, Box 6993, Washington, D.C. 20020. (*Ages 10 through 20*)

Make Generous Use of the Story and Literature Resources Related to Life in Other Lands.   Storybook material dealing with children's lives in other lands is increasing in abundance each year. Typically, these little books are vividly illustrated, and primary-grade children get as much from the pictures as from the story as the teacher reads it to them. As children advance to the second and third grades, some of them can read the stories themselves. The teacher will find a generous listing of materials in any of these sources:

Best Books for Children, 1969 or later ed. New York: R. R. Bowker Company.

Books for Friendship, 4th ed. Mary E. McWhirter, ed. Philadelphia, Pa.: American Friends Service Committee, 1968. (160 N. 15th St., Philadelphia, Pa. 19102)

Eaton, Mary K. *Subject Index to Books for Intermediate Grades,* 3rd ed. Chicago: American Library Association, 1963.

Eaton, Mary K., and Eleanor Merritt. *Subject Index to Books for Primary Grades,* 2nd ed. Chicago: American Library Association, 1961.

Huus, Helen. *Children's Books to Enrich the Social Studies: For the Elementary Grades,* Bulletin No. 32, rev. ed. Washington, D.C.: National Council for the Social Studies, 1966.

Kenworthy, Leonard S. *Social Studies for the Seventies.* Waltham, Mass.: Blaisdell Publishing Co., 1969, pp. 473–501.

Turner, Robert K., "Children's Books about the United Nations," *Junior Libraries,* 7, No. 3, November, 1960.

United Nations Plays and Programs, rev. ed., Aileen Fisher and Rabe Oliver, compilers. Boston: Plays Inc. (8 Arlington St., Boston, Mass. 02116) For intermediate grades and above.

The program of instruction for worldmindedness in the middle and upper grades represents an extension upward of many of the same practices, procedures, and principles discussed with respect to the program in the primary grades. Because of the increasing maturity of the children, better-developed reading skills, the nature of the curriculum content in these grades, and the greater abundance of resource material available, a more direct approach can be taken to the study of people and life in other lands. In addition to the principles discussed in connection with the primary-grades program, the following material would apply to the middle and upper grades.

Make Use of a Wide Variety of Up-to-Date Learning Resources. With the great amount of material available in the way of books, pictures, films, filmstrips, magazine articles, television programs, and resource persons, there seems little need for the teacher to depend entirely on a single source for information about the country or community studied. The textbook and encyclopedia may be good sources for factual data concerning the country—its geography, production, transportation systems, methods of producing goods, and so forth—

but even though that information is quite necessary, it does not give the pupil an opportunity to learn much about the everyday lives and feelings of the people who live there. This can be accomplished through stories and literature, art, music, folk songs, pictures, films, filmstrips, viewing slides, talking with people who have lived there, or listening to someone who has visited the country recently.

It is perhaps true that there is much misinformation obtained by pupils in the study of other countries in the middle and upper grades. Teachers sometimes center unit activities around customs of the country that are very unusual or even traditional, yet these are represented as life in that country in modern times. The story is told of the American child who visited the Nethelands with her parents and was surprised to learn that people in that country wore leather shoes. It is not proper to make sweeping generalizations about life in an entire country, because it is impossible to make generalizations with any degree of accuracy. For example, how can one describe a Japanese home? To do this, one would have to describe several different kinds of housing: fishing huts along the coast, farm homes in rural areas, modern homes in some of the large cities, and apartments. The kinds of homes the people of Japan live in depend on where they live, what they do for a living, and how much money they can spend for housing. We see, therefore, that great differences exist within a single country, and to continue to think of entire groups of people as a single type is a serious error. Lives of people in other lands should be taught as they are today, not as they were a hundred years ago.

Involve Children in Activities That Require Action by Them Rather Than Depend Entirely on a Verbal Approach. It was noted earlier that instruction intended to develop attitudes of greater acceptance is particularly vulnerable to verbalism. One way to combat this tendency is to have children apply what they have learned in carrying out some action. Such projects may take a variety of forms: exchanging letters with children abroad, participating in the Junior Red Cross program, planning and preparing dramatics activities, sending CARE packages abroad, visiting foreign restaurants, making maps, learning elements of a foreign language, learning games and dances of another country, collecting money for UNICEF, preparing murals or exhibits for others to see, visiting various churches in the community, collecting stamps or coins from various countries, and sharing their learnings with other children or their parents.

Help Children in the Middle and Upper Grades Explore More Deeply Some of the Reasons for the Differences in Ways of Living. People everywhere are products of their backgrounds—historical, geographical, sociological, psychological, and religious factors help explain how and why people live the way they do. Children in the

Social studies programs should provide pupils the opportunity to handle objects and artifacts from other cultures. (Courtesy of the Shoreline Public Schools, Seattle)

middle and upper grades can begin to sense these relationships. They can learn, for example, how the presence of natural barriers such as mountains has tended to isolate people and that these barriers usually stabilize borders between nations; they can see the cultural impact of missionaries, explorers, and colonists; they learn that modes of dress or types of homes people select are related to climatic conditions of the region; they can understand why island people turn to the sea for their livelihood and why desert people move toward water and food. In studying other cultures, pupils need experiences that will help them perceive the world through the eyes of the people of that culture, insofar as that is possible. They need to imagine how the world would look to them if they were a member of the culture studied. When children begin to see even partially how others view themselves and the world, they come to understand some of the basic reasons for differences in ways of living, and the differences tend not to seem unusual to them. Rather, they come to the conclusion that people the world over are resourceful, logical, and show considerable ingenuity in dealing with environmental factors and forces.

Teach About the United Nations and Its Specialized Agencies. Whether schools should teach about the United Nations has been a highly controversial issue in some communities in the United States. Because under our educational system such issues are resolved at the local level, teachers will need to decide whether to include the United Nations in their programs in terms of the policy of the district in which they teach. As a nation, we support the United Nations and are members of it. It has its headquarters within the boundaries of our country. Our national policy is to trust that it will continue to be a strong force in averting wars and in settling international disputes equitably and peacefully.

Many American elementary schools teach about the United Nations and its specialized agencies. This teaching occurs at several grade levels. Wilhelmina Hill, in reporting on teaching about the United Nations, lists the following activities as the ones most frequently followed by elementary schools:

1. Observing special days through assembly programs with songs, folk dances, and explanations of the nature and work of United Nations.
2. Preparing bulletin board displays for U.N. Day.
3. Giving U.N. programs for PTA's.
4. Writing to children in other countries which belong to the United Nations.
5. Reading books about the United Nations.
6. Watching television programs about the United Nations or its personalities.
7. Discussing current events relating to the United Nations.
8. Viewing films, filmstrips, and slides about the United Nations.
9. Exhibiting dolls representing U.N. member nations.
10. Making a painting or model of the U.N. headquarters.
11. Discussing U.N. problems and accomplishments in class.
12. Participating in pupil "Security Council" or "General Assembly" meetings to gain some idea of procedures and debate techniques used in the real United Nations.
13. Writing own versions of a "human rights charter" and comparing it with U.N.'s *Universal Declaration of Human Rights.*
14. Making a mural for a class or school "Security Council."

15. Writing creatively of peace and peoples, freedom, and children's own ideas about the world.
16. Listening to music of other lands.
17. Meeting visitors from other United Nations countries.
18. Locating U.N. member countries on globe and wall maps.
19. Visiting U.N. headquarters by classes or with parents, and sharing these visits with others through talks, pictures, and exhibits. (Even Hawaii reports that many teachers and pupils have visited the U.N. buildings.)
20. Using songs, poems, games, informal dramatizations or conversations in the languages of one or more other member countries.[9]

Imaginative teachers will develop their own appropriate activities for their classes. However, the ones listed below have been used successfully and may provide suggestions that will get the new teacher started:

1. Have a returning Peace Corps volunteer come to the classroom and discuss his experiences with the class.
2. Have pupils construct an international cookbook, game book, book of holidays, national sports.
3. Invite foreign-born local residents to the classroom to display traditional national costumes or skills.
4. Set aside one bulletin board for current events in other countries around the world. Associate such countries with their map and globe location.
5. Have pupils write to embassies, consulates, airlines, or travel bureaus for material on countries being studied.
6. Develop simulated situations and instructional games to teach about other countries. This can be combined with role playing for additional insights. Topics such as city life, education, agricultural problems, and government would be appropriate for this activity.
7. Teach folk songs, national anthems, poems, dances, and games of other countries at the time they are being studied.
8. Study the origin, growth, and change of languages. Examine the derivation of specific words.
9. Develop dramatic activities based on legends, myths, or stories of other peoples around the world.
10. Study contributions to American culture made by immigrants.
11. Have pupils prepare a travel brochure on a country, continent, or region; role-play the part of a tourist representative from that country telling about a fifteen-day tour of the country.

9. *Teaching About the United Nations in the United States*, Bulletin No. 18, Washington, D.C.: U.S. Department of Health, Education, and Welfare, 1960, pp. 28–29.

12. Enter into correspondence with a class in another country.
13. Have children organize an International Club as a means of sponsoring all-school activities with an international emphasis.
14. Develop a tape exchange with children of another country. See pages 138–139 for address of contact.

Basic to sound programs of education for world understanding in the elementary school is the staffing of classrooms with teachers who are themselves worldminded. This area of study is a relatively new field, and teachers are perhaps less well prepared to teach it than they are some of the material that has had a longer history in the elementary curriculum. Fortunately, the teacher need not avoid teaching world understanding because he lacks adequate background; there are many good resources to assist him in gaining the information he needs to develop a global perspective. The bibliography at the end of this chapter contains an extensive list of books and materials the teacher can use for this purpose. To guide the teacher in this self-study, the following description of the worldminded teacher may be helpful. Kenworthy describes the internationally minded teacher as one who should be

1. . . . an integrated individual, on the way to becoming a mature person.
2. . . . an expert in democratic human relations.
3. . . . rooted in his own country and culture.
4. . . . appreciative of and concerned about other countries and cultures.
5. . . . informed about the contemporary world scene and its historic background.
6. . . . an informed participant in efforts to strengthen the United Nations and to promote international community.
7. . . . conversant with methods and materials for creating internationally-minded children and youth.
8. [committed to] . . . a faith or philosophy of life which undergirds all his efforts to produce world-minded boys and girls and to help create a better international community in his day.[10]

There is becoming available an increasing amount of resource material dealing with teaching for worldmindedness. Each month the professional journals are likely to carry listings of sources of such materials; the alert teacher will encounter little difficulty securing

10. Leonard S. Kenworthy, *The International Dimension of Education*, Background Paper II, World Conference on Education, Washington, D.C.: Association for Supervision and Curriculum Development, 1970, pp. 106–108.

teaching aids, reading material, and teaching suggestions on this topic for very little if any cost. The following is a listing of some of the better-known sources:

Asia Society, 112 E. 64th St., New York, N.Y. 10021.

Audio-Visual Aids for International Understanding, World Confederation of Organizations of the Teaching Profession, 1227 16th St., N.W., Washington, D.C. 20036.

Instructor, 79, No. 2, October, 1969, pp. 74–78. Bibliography of materials for teaching worldmindedness.

Kenworthy, Leonard S., and Richard A. Birdie. *Free and Inexpensive Materials on World Affairs.* New York: Teachers College Press, Columbia University, 1968.

UNESCO Publications Center, P.O. Box 433, New York, N.Y. 10016.

UNICEF, 833 United Nations Plaza, New York, N.Y. 10017.

United Nations Association of the United States of America, 345 E. 34th St., New York, N.Y. 10017.

United Nations Publications, United Nations, Room 1059, New York, N.Y. 10017.

U.S. Committee for UNICEF, 331 E. 38th St., New York, N.Y. 10016.

World Affairs Materials, Brooklyn College, Brooklyn, N.Y. 11210.

The teaching for worldmindedness is filled with many possibilities and challenges for the modern classroom teacher. Vastly improved learning resources, coupled with the closeness of the world's people because of modern technology, can make this an exciting and adventuresome experience in learning for American schoolchildren and their teachers. The outcomes of this instruction are of an importance to transcend any yet conceived in the field of education. When the goals of teaching for world understanding are ultimately achieved, children everywhere will sincerely feel that "a foreigner is a friend I have yet to meet." [11] There is no field more fertile for the teacher of vision and the one dedicated to the service of humanity.

Discussion Questions and Suggested Activities

1. Find examples in the unit you are developing (Chapter 3) where you can provide learning experiences to promote worldmindedness.
2. Collect a number of study prints and magazine pictures concern-

11. General Carlos P. Romulo in an address delivered at Minneapolis, Minnesota, to the Minnesota Education Association, October, 1953.

ing a major culture of the world. Share the collection with your classmates. Tell how you would use these pictures with children.

3. Cite ways that pupils in your community might have firsthand encounters with people from other countries.

4. Develop a realia kit for a unit on a major country of the world (use Kenworthy's guidelines in your selection). How can these items help pupils understand the ways of life in this country?

5. What is the meaning of the term *ethnocentrism?* How is it related to prejudice, insularity, and narrow-mindedness? Is this similar to *provincialism?* Do ethnocentrism and provincialism contribute to the development of international understanding?

6. What evidence can you find to indicate that insecurity leads to hostility and aggression? Do you believe that a teacher contributes to intercultural education and international understanding when he makes every effort to reduce the causes of insecurity on the part of children in the classroom?

7. Why do you think the motives of the United States have been misunderstood in its efforts to help underdeveloped areas of the world? What are some of the reasons that the prestige of the United States has suffered abroad in spite of the efforts of this nation in behalf of international understanding? What steps might the United States take to break down stereotyped notions of Americans that many people of the world have?

8. What would be the advantages of a mass student exchange at the college level between various nations of the world? Do you think that this would promote the cause of world peace?

9. What are some of the pitfalls to be avoided in teaching pupils about another culture?

10. Using the criteria of Kenworthy presented in this chapter, prepare a list of approximately ten countries that you feel should be studied in the elementary school. List and describe learning activities for a country of your choice.

Selected References

Banister, Richard E. "A Social Studies Program for the Space Age," *The Social Studies*, LVI, No. 5 (October, 1965), pp. 166–172.

Becker, James M., and Howard D. Mehlinger, eds. *International Dimensions in the Social Studies*, 38th Yearbook. Washington, D.C.: National Council for the Social Studies, 1968.

Boulding, Kenneth E. "Education for the Spaceship Earth," *Social Education*, XXXII, No. 7 (November, 1968), pp. 648–652.

Brown, Ina Corine. *Understanding Other Cultures*. Englewood Cliffs, N.J.: Prentice-Hall, Inc., 1963.

Hamilton, Dorothy W. "Educating Citizens for World Responsibilities, 1960–1980," *Citizenship and a Free Society*, 30th Yearbook. Washington, D.C.: National Council for the Social Studies, 1960.

Humphreys, Mary B., ed. *Approaches to the Study of International and Intercultural Relations*. Chicago: Foreign Relations Project of the North Central Association of Colleges and Secondary Schools, 1968.

Instructor (October, 1969), pp. 53–85. Contains a number of very practical articles and learning activities on international understanding.

Keach, Everett T., Jr. "International Education in the Elementary Schools—Some Problems and Prospects," *The Social Studies*, LIX, No. 6 (November, 1968), pp. 243–247.

Kenworthy, Leonard S. *The International Dimension of Education*. Washington, D.C.: Association for Supervision and Curriculum Development, 1970.

Kenworthy, Leonard S. *Social Studies for the Seventies*. Waltham, Mass.: Blaisdell Publishing Co., 1969.

Long, Harold M., and Robert N. King. *Improving the Teaching of World Affairs: The Glens Falls Story*. Washington, D.C.: National Council for the Social Studies, 1964.

Morris, Donald N., and Edith W. King. "Bringing Spaceship Earth into the Elementary School Classroom," *Social Education*, XXXII, No. 7 (November, 1968), pp. 675–680.

National Education Association, Research Division. *Teaching About Other Countries and Peoples in the Elementary School*. Washington, D.C.: The Association, Department of Elementary School Principals, June, 1960.

Renaud, Mary, ed. *Bringing the World into Your Classroom: Gleanings from Glens Falls*. Washington, D.C.: National Council for the Social Studies, 1968.

Shane, Harold G., ed. *The United States and International Education*, 68th Yearbook, National Society for the Study of Education. Chicago: University of Chicago Press, 1969.

"International Relations: Ideas and Issues," *Social Education*, XXXIV, No. 1 (January, 1970), pp. 19–62+.

Strickler, Mervin K., Jr., ed. *An Introduction to Aerospace Education*. Chicago: New Horizons, Publishers, 1968.

Thompson, Elizabeth M. *Resources for Teaching About the United Nations*. Washington, D.C.: National Education Association, Committee on International Relations, 1962.

Turner, Ralph E. "World Affairs in the Balance: Some Observations on the Cultural Crisis of Our Time," *Citizenship and a Free Society*, 30th Yearbook. Washington, D.C.: National Council for the Social Studies, 1960.

Tyler, I. Keith. *Television for World Understanding*. Washington, D.C.: National Education Association, Division of Educational Technology, 1970.

Evaluating Pupil Achievement and Teacher Effectiveness

Evaluation of learning may properly be thought of as the method or methods used to determine the extent to which previously established goals, objectives, or purposes have been achieved. It is the process of comparing the outcomes of instruction with the anticipated or stated objectives. Evaluation, therefore, always involves identifying values sought and establishing expectations. If the values sought are not stated as instructional objectives, they are implicit in the tasks that are called for in the evaluation exercise. As the term is used here, it presupposes that the participants in the evaluation have established some values and that these have been stated as anticipated outcomes or as aims, objectives, or goals.

17

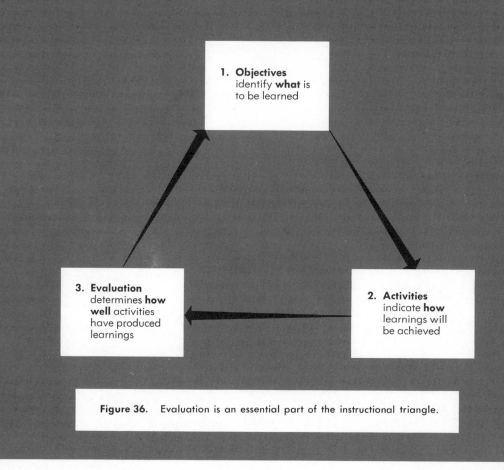

Figure 36.   Evaluation is an essential part of the instructional triangle.

The boxes in the figure read:

1. **Objectives** identify **what** is to be learned

2. **Activities** indicate **how** learnings will be achieved

3. **Evaluation** determines **how well** activities have produced learnings

Earlier chapters of this book have repeatedly stressed the importance of continuous evaluation and the need to consider evaluation as an essential part of the teaching-learning process. This is necessary because a threefold relationship exists among objectives, teaching procedures, and evaluation. Compatibility must be maintained in this relationship, for what occurs in one part of this instructional triangle directly affects the other two parts. (See Figure 36.) It would be inconsistent, for example, for a teacher to state objectives dealing with the development of group-work skills, social sensitivity, and democratic values and at the same time to utilize teaching procedures that are authoritarian and evaluate only subject-matter outcomes with the use of a paper-and-pencil test at the end of the unit. Because objectives, teaching procedures, and evaluation are related to the extent that they are, evaluation should not be regarded as something that is reserved for the end of the unit but should occur often while the unit is in progress. At the time the teacher is stating objectives for the unit, he should be thinking of ways he will evaluate outcomes. He will then utilize teaching methods that are in harmony with such plans and if necessary will modify any or all of these three aspects of the instructional process during the course of the unit. This reconstruction of goals and purposes is essentially what is meant by the term *emerging goals*. Because the chief purpose of evaluation is to make certain that recognized goals are being achieved, this can best be accomplished if evaluation is conceived as an integral part of the teaching itself. In this way evaluation provides feedback to the teacher about how effectively he is teaching as reflected by how well pupils are learning. If evaluation is deferred until the unit is completed, there is not much the teacher can do to bring about an improvement of learning. He cannot go back and reteach the unit in an effort to attain objectives that have been neglected. He can only use the information to guide his future planning and teaching. This represents a limited use of evaluation.

Appraising Pupil Growth in Social Studies

When teachers are concerned about the progress of the individual pupils in their classrooms, the teachers find themselves spending a considerable amount of time evaluating, diagnosing, and appraising the status of individual learners. Actually, most teachers are making evaluations almost continually without being aware of it. Whenever they make a judgment that has to do with the values sought in the social studies unit, they are evaluating. This can and usually does happen several times each day. Evaluative procedures have not always included the more informal methods of evaluation in use today but have depended on measuring instruments—tests—almost exclusively. Perhaps for this reason, tests and evaluation are erroneously thought of as synonymous. Testing is only one of several evaluative devices, techniques, or procedures used in appraising pupil progress and growth.

Most schools now accept the broader concept of evaluation and do not rely entirely on objective tests for appraising the child's learning. Because social studies deal with many dimensions of behavior that are for the present impossible to quantify, the teacher depends heavily on judgment in making evaluations of children's growth. For this reason the evaluative procedure needs to be scrutinized carefully and frequently. Some of the more commonly used techniques and devices are described on the following pages.

Group Discussion. Group discussion can be used to appraise the progress of the class in terms of plans and standards previously established. Discussion will activate thinking along the lines of self-evaluation; it helps clarify and remind children of learning goals; it is helpful in establishing an attitude of looking forward to progress and growth. As a matter of teaching procedure, it is a good plan for the teacher to reserve some time near the end of every social studies period for the class to discuss its progress and to make plans for the next day's work. As was noted earlier, this helps children crystallize their thinking, helps identify concepts needing further study, and reminds them of the things they are learning in social studies. In addition to the daily discussions of the progress of the class, this technique can also be used in a variety of other situations, a few examples of which are

1. As a follow-up of a major class activity such as a field trip, a school service project, a dramatization
2. As a method of evaluating group reports, unit projects, creative dramatics activities
3. As a means of improving small-group endeavors
4. As a means of evaluating behavior of the class at a school assembly, in the lunchroom, or on the playground
5. As a method of working out some problem of human relations within the classroom
6. As a means of bringing to light attitudes that may be held by pupils
7. As a means of verifying information obtained through individual study

The use of discussion as a technique of evaluation necessitates the identification of standards to be attained and a knowledge of what is expected on the part of the pupils. This means that in most cases the teacher and the class will have to decide on standards that apply in a given situation. For example, if a class is about to engage in an activity calling for small committees, the following standards may be agreed on:

1. Work quietly, so others may work, too.
2. Know where the materials are.
3. Arrange with other groups to borrow materials.
4. Speak quietly to other committee members.
5. Stop work as soon as the bell rings.
6. Arrange and clean up the area after work.

Specific work standards of the type just described should be posted on a chart in the room for all to see and ought to be referred to and used when the work of the class is being evaluated through discussion. Verbal agreement on standards is not sufficient for young children—

they forget from day to day just what the standards are. Posting the standards and discussing them without "harping" on them, helps remind children of their responsibilities and enhances learning. Knowledge of progress is a strong force in the motivation of learning and a knowledge of areas in which improvement is needed helps give direction to learning. The use of class discussion as an evaluative technique can serve both of these purposes admirably.

Observation. By observing each child, noting especially his comments, relationships with peers, attitudes, feelings, and new interests, the teacher may notice changes in behavior in and out of the classroom.

Observation is among the best techniques available to the teacher in learning about children, appraising their growth, and sensing their needs. Although all teachers use this method of pupil appraisal, not all are equally skillful in its application. It is perhaps true that much of what is called observation of pupils might better be described as a disorganized set of impressions the teacher obtains during the course of instruction pretty much on a catch-as-catch-can basis. The teacher who makes the most of observation is the one who knows what he is looking for, systematizes his observations in some manner, and makes some attempt to objectify the data so obtained. To this end it is suggested that the teacher

1. Spell out exactly and unambiguously the traits to be evaluated in this manner and state evidences of these in terms of child behavior. For example, if the teacher desires to observe a child's behavior to determine whether or not he is growing in his *consideration for others*, he might look for such things as the following:
Does the child
   a. Show respect for the ideas and feelings of his classmates?
   b. Abstain from causing disturbances that make it impossible for others to do their best work?
   c. Carry his fair share of the work load in a small group?
   d. Enjoy giving a classmate an "assist" when needed?
   e. Display sensitivity to injustices that may occur in the course of life in and out of the classroom?
   f. Return borrowed materials? Obtain permission to use materials that belong to others?
   g. Observe rules established by the group?
   h. Fulfill his responsibilities on time? Avoid doing things that hold up the progress of the class?
2. Rather than observing "in general," select certain pupils for intensive observation and study. This intensive observation might be

limited to certain specific situations. For example, just what happens to Billy when he is placed on a committee to do some project in connection with a social studies unit? How can the situation be changed to help him develop more responsible habits of work in a group situation? The purpose of observations of this type, of course, is to gain insight into the child's behavior and not to sharpen the teacher's eye for minor infractions of room rules.

3. Not depend on memory as a device to record observations. Keep a written record of data obtained through observation and maintain this record over a period of time to establish a definite pattern in the child's behavior. At best, observation is a highly unreliable method of appraising growth, and without a record of the observations, it is of little value indeed. The written record may take the form of anecdotal accounts, a check-list system, or a rating device. Data of this type are extremely helpful in interpreting and reporting the progress and growth of children to their parents.

Check Lists. Check lists may be constructed from previously established specific goals and can be used either by the teacher or by the children themselves in evaluating progress. It is a good practice for classes to work out short check lists cooperatively and apply them to their work individually. They may be used when children are giving reports or short talks to call attention to clarity of speaking, new information presented, use of visual material, extent of preparedness, and other responsibilities of the speaker. A similar check list can be devised to cover the responsibilities of the listening audience. An example of a self-evaluation sheet developed by a teacher with his class is reproduced in part in Figure 37.

In addition to the check lists developed and used by the children for self-appraisal, the teacher can devise similar check lists for his own use in recording the behavior of children. As previously noted, this procedure adds objectivity and reliability to the teacher's observation of his class. The specific points to be checked would be the behavior characteristics that provide evidence either of the presence or absence of the trait under study. Commercially prepared behavior-rating scales may be used for the same purpose.

Conferences. Conferences with the child are helpful in assisting him to establish a sense of self-evaluation leading to increasing self-direction. The teacher-pupil conference can be of great help in discovering particular learning problems and difficulties children are having, gaining insight into their feelings about their school work, becoming aware of special personal-social problems the children may be having, and as a method of assisting every child individually in a very personal way. The quality of instruction in the elementary school

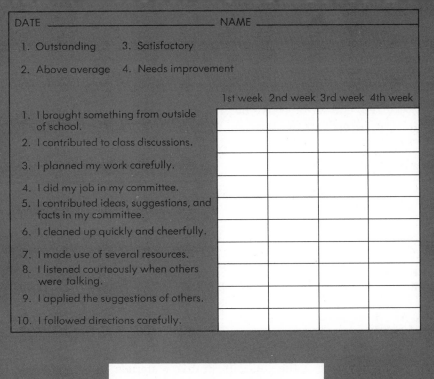

DATE _____ NAME _____

1. Outstanding   3. Satisfactory

2. Above average   4. Needs improvement

	1st week	2nd week	3rd week	4th week
1. I brought something from outside of school.				
2. I contributed to class discussions.				
3. I planned my work carefully.				
4. I did my job in my committee.				
5. I contributed ideas, suggestions, and facts in my committee.				
6. I cleaned up quickly and cheerfully.				
7. I made use of several resources.				
8. I listened courteously when others were talking.				
9. I applied the suggestions of others.				
10. I followed directions carefully.				

Figure 37. Self-evaluation sheet.

would unquestionably be markedly improved if the teacher could spend an hour each day in ten-minute individual conferences with children. As matters now stand, teachers find little time during the school day that can be used for such purposes. But, for the children who appear to need the personal contact with their teacher that a conference can give, time should be found.

A conference will be of little value if the teacher does all the talking and the child all the listening. In fact, it might be said that the conference will have a detrimental effect if it results in greater feelings of insecurity on the part of the child. Scoldings, threats, and admonishments have no place in the type of conference under discussion. The thought, rather, is a friendly, helpful approach that results in greater feelings of personal worth on the part of the child along with some constructive and concrete helps for improving his work. This is the guidance and counseling approach to teaching and is one with which elementary teachers should be thoroughly familiar because of their close working relationship with pupils.

Anecdotal Records. An anecdotal record is a description of some incident or situation in the life of the child. A collection of such descriptions of pupil behavior kept over a period of time, therefore, provides the teacher with a documentary account of changes of behavior that have occurred or are in progress. It is another way of systematically recording observations. Anecdotal records should indicate the date and time of the incident, the circumstances under which it occurred, and an objective description of the situation. If an interpretation is made of the incident, it should be kept separate from the description of the actual happening.

⟨Work Samples.⟩ The practice of saving samples of pupils' work by the teacher is similar to the parent who cuts notches on the inside of a closet door recording the height of his child at various ages. Both the parent and the teacher know that growth is occurring but because of their continuous contact with the child on a day-to-day basis, growth and progress are imperceptible. They need, therefore, a specific example of the child's status at one point in time in order to judge his growth or progress at a subsequent time. The greater the time interval between the two samples, the greater should be the evidence of change.

Work samples that are saved for this purpose are usually written material and may include a report, a story, a classroom test, an explanation, a booklet, or a research project. The teacher might also want to save map work of the child, illustrative materials he has prepared, art work done in connection with the social studies, or a small construction project. The tape recorder can also be used to obtain a sample of the child's spoken word. For example, children find it revealing and profitable to hear reports privately that they have made to the class at various times during the school year. The same device can be used by the entire class to evaluate their progress in discussions, dramatizations, and similar speaking situations involving the entire group. Care must be taken, however, to ensure that such procedures do not call attention to speech disorders that specific children may have.

Experience Summaries. Experience summaries placed on charts are used to abstract learnings and to record a particular learning experience. They are ordinarily constructed cooperatively by the teacher and the class and are used to record and evaluate a single or specific experience rather than a series of experiences. For example, when the group returns from its trip to the dairy farm, the children can summarize some of the important things they have learned as a result of the trip and place these on a chart in the classroom. The chart may then be used to evaluate the extent to which they found out the things they set out to learn in planning the trip.

⟨Diaries and Logs.⟩ Diaries and logs are similar to experience summaries except that they are kept on a continuing basis. Each day the class can summarize its progress and record it on a chart or in a notebook it keeps. This provides a running account of work in the unit and is very helpful in reviewing and checking on previous plans and decisions as the unit progresses. In the final phases of the unit, the class, by referring to its log, can recall many details of its work that would otherwise be overlooked or forgotten. In the primary grades, the teacher will have to assume much of the responsibility for recording the material to be placed in the log, although children can and should assist in deciding *what* is to be recorded. In the middle and upper grades, individual children or committees can assume much of this responsibility if they are given some help and guidance by the teacher.

Sociometric Devices. Sociometric devices are used to evaluate growth in social relations, and/or to observe changes in the social structure of a group. In order to be used effectively for either purpose, they should be applied more than once to the group. Data collected in this manner indicate the structure of the group at the time the data were obtained and in terms of the reason for which the children made their choices. Social relationships change, and with young children these changes occur frequently. The younger the children are, the less stable their friendships are. As an example, a first-grader's "best pal" one day may be ignored by him the next; the third day he may be his best pal again. Such unpredictability of friendship patterns would have a devastating effect on a sixth-grader. Sociometric devices are, therefore, less reliable at lower levels than when the children are older and more consistent in their choices of children with whom they wish to work or to play.

Carefully administered, sociometric devices will be helpful to the teacher in appraising the extent to which (1) peripheral children have won greater acceptance by the group, (2) leadership roles have shifted, (3) preferences of children for one another have changed, and (4) strong in-groups have become more flexible. Assuming that the teacher has in mind the direction in which these changes would be most desirable and beneficial in terms of human relationships in the class, he is able to evaluate the progress the class has made over a period of time. Specific directions for the application of sociometric devices can be found in Chapter 12.

Teacher-Made Tests. Classroom tests constructed by the teacher are usually used to appraise the child's growth and progress in the more factual outcomes of social studies instruction. Even though paper-and-pencil tests can be used successfully with primary-grade children, their value increases as the child moves into the middle and upper grades. These tests are of maximum value when they are constructed to test basic understandings, concepts, and knowledges rather than simply the facts related to the topics under study. Too frequently questions dealing with *who, what, when, where,* and *how many* take precedence over more reflective and penetrating items such as those

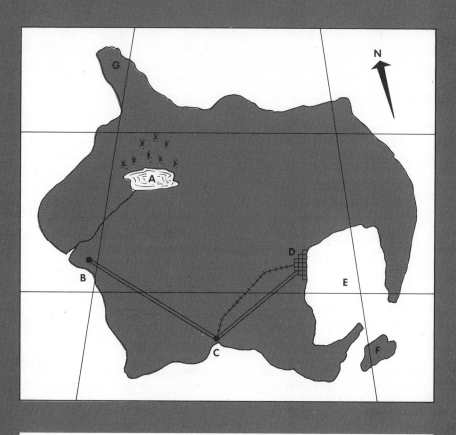

Figure 38. Teachers can devise tests of this type to evaluate growth in map-reading skills:

Underline the correct answer:

1) The land north of **A** is (a swamp), (a desert), (mountainous).
2) The mouth of a river is located near letter (**A**), (**B**), (**C**).
3) The city at **D** is perhaps a (capital), (seaport), (mining town).
4) The river flows (from southwest to northeast), (from northeast to southwest), (from east to west).
5) An island is marked by the letter (**A**), (**B**), (**F**).
6) A railroad runs between (**B** and **C**), (**D** and **B**), (**D** and **C**).
7) The letter **E** marks (a bay), (a peninsula), (an island).
8) A peninsula is shown on this map at (**B**), (**G**), (**C**).
9) A delta might be found just north of (**C**), (**A**), (**B**).
10) The letter **G** is due north of (**C**), (**A**), (**B**).

that call for knowing *why, for what reason,* and *how we know.* An important requirement of any good test is that it should enhance and encourage desirable study habits. Overemphasis on recall of minutia and inconsequential details inevitably leads to rote memory of facts without understanding their significance or without relating them to the basic and underlying key ideas. When the teacher makes use of conventional objective-type test items such as multiple choice, alternate response, completion, recall, and matching, he should make certain their construction is technically correct. Many of the standard works on measurement and evaluation discuss in detail the advantages and limitations of various objective-type test items as well as suggestions for their construction.

Teacher-made tests are particularly valuable in evaluating growth in certain social studies skills. Tests designed to measure the child's skill in using a map—locating places, identifying map symbols, reading the legend, understanding scale, interpreting map data, recognizing land forms—are a necessary part of instruction in the use of maps. An example of this type of teacher-made test appears in Figure 38. Similarly, short tests can be designed to evaluate the child's ability to use reference material, to read social studies materials, to understand the vocabulary of social studies, to evaluate news stories, to distinguish between fact and opinion, and other social studies skills.

In addition to their use in evaluating growth in understandings and skills, teacher-made tests can also be used to gain valuable insights into the child's attitudes and beliefs. When used for this purpose, they may take a different form than the traditional classroom test. Some teachers find it helpful to present the child with a problem or situation and ask him to respond to it orally, by drawing or by writing. Usually children are asked to tell how they *would feel* if they were the principal in the story or what they *would do* if they found themselves in such a situation. The following examples illustrate how such testing situations were used at two levels.

First-Grade Level

A first grade teacher posted a picture of a toddler with his mother in a supermarket. The child reached up and pulled out an orange from the display and the entire pyramid of oranges tumbled to the floor. The picture showed the child with an orange in his hand, oranges all over the floor, a distressed storekeeper standing nearby, and a very surprised and embarrassed mother. Beneath the picture the teacher had written the following story:

EVALUATING PUPIL ACHIEVEMENT AND
TEACHER EFFECTIVENESS

Baby wanted an orange.
He pulled one out.
Down they all came.
What will Mother do now?

The class discussed the picture and read the story. Many related having similar experiences that led to a discussion of conduct in stores. The feelings of Mother were discussed as was the fact that the storekeeper would have additional work. Some children with younger brothers or sisters indicated that small children always do things like that and are "pests," whereas others felt they had some responsibility for teaching and helping younger brothers and sisters. The teacher found the children's responses to "What will Mother do now?" particularly interesting because of the degree of severity with which they thought Mother should deal with Baby. Some thought he should be severely spanked on the spot, others felt Mother should scold, others thought he was too young to know better and should not be punished at all.

Sixth-Grade Level

The teacher displayed a picture taken from the cover of a popular magazine showing an exceedingly awkward, gangly, oafish rookie reporting in uniform to a baseball dugout. Some members of the team seated in the dugout are whispering to one another and gesturing in the direction of the rookie. The children were asked to write (1) what they would do if they were a member of the team and (2) how they would feel if they were the new player.

Although methods of the type just described are helpful in gaining a better understanding of children, the teacher is cautioned against overestimating the significance of such responses if they are taken singly. The understanding of a child can be likened to a giant jigsaw puzzle—the more parts the teacher can fit into place, the more complete the picture becomes. A single part taken by itself is meaningless. Data collected with the intent of understanding children and evaluating their growth must be obtained from a wide variety of sources and pieced together carefully if valid judgments are to be made concerning the child's progress. Teacher-made tests represent just one of many sources the expert teacher will use.

In constructing specific items to evaluate certain kinds of learnings, the teacher may find the suggestions of Maxine Dunfee helpful as presented in the Thirty-fifth Yearbook of the National Council for the Social Studies. A few examples of the types of items she suggests are these:

To test for *factual information*—
 Arranging in order the steps in a process
 Matching events with periods of time
 Supplying key words missing in statements of essential facts
 Matching vocabulary and definition
 Placing events or persons on a time line
To test for *understandings*—
 Matching causes and effects
 Supplying a generalization to be drawn from a given set of facts
 Stating the most important ideas learned
 Selecting a conclusion to be drawn from a chart, diagram, or graph
To obtain insights into *attitudes* of pupils—
 Responding to statements in terms of strength of belief, feeling, or
  opinion by indicating degree—always, sometimes, never
 Responding to statements that imply prejudice or lack of prejudice
  by indicating state of agreement—I agree, I disagree, I am un-
  certain
 Matching attitudes with likely resultant actions
 Writing endings to stories that describe problem situations
To test for *skills*—
 Interpreting an imaginary map, locating physical and cultural fea-
  tures and answering questions calling for interpretation of infor-
  mation provided
 Supplying a missing step in directions for doing something that
  involves a skill
 Demonstrating how to conduct a meeting, how to give a good re-
  port, etc.
 Using a table of contents or index to locate specified information [1]

Pupil-Interest Inventories. Pupil-interest inventories are useful in identifying particular likes and dislikes of children, types of learning they feel most satisfying, activities they would like to repeat, out-of-school activities, clubs, hobbies, and so forth. The instrument used to obtain this information can take a variety of forms. The teacher may simply be interested in obtaining facts related to the life of the child. A series of direct questions is prepared and the child responds to them in yes-no fashion. For example,

To be answered "Yes" or "No":
 1. Do you play a musical instrument?
 2. Are you a member of the Cub Scouts, Brownies, or Bluebirds?
 3. Have you ever ridden in an airplane?
 4. Do you have color television in your home?

1. Maxine Dunfee, "Evaluating Understandings, Attitudes, Skills, and Behaviors in Elementary School Social Studies," *Evaluation in Social Studies*, 35th Yearbook, chap. 8, Washington, D.C.: National Council for the Social Studies, 1965, pp. 165–167.

5. Do you have a library card?
6. Have you been to the Science Museum during the past year?

The same direct question procedure can be used to have children indicate whether they like or dislike various situations, activities, or things —although responses dealing with children's *feelings* (as opposed to responses to the preceding questions of fact) are likely to be less reliable.

To be answered "Yes" or "No":
1. Do you like to play baseball?
2. Do you enjoy clubs such as Cub Scouts, Brownies, or Bluebirds?
3. Do you think it would be fun to have a garden?
4. Do you have a favorite TV show?

Or,

Write L if you like the activity and D if you dislike it:
1. Playing a musical instrument.
2. Reading a book.
3. Watching TV.
4. Helping around the house.
5. Going to the library.

The questionnaire can also be organized in terms of paired comparisons:

Underline the part of each sentence that tells what you would do if you had a choice between the two activities presented:
1. Would you rather go fishing or read about an exciting fishing trip?
2. Would you rather have a new football or a chemistry set?
3. Would you rather watch a True Science program on TV or watch a "Western"?
4. Would you rather go to the library or build a model airplane?

Questionnaires of a less general nature can be prepared and used at the conclusion of a unit to find out which activities children enjoyed most or felt were most worthwhile for them. As an illustration, the teacher might list the activities as follows and have the children mark those they liked very much L and those they did not like D:

1. Making individual booklets on the unit.
2. Working in committees.
3. Dramatizing important events.
4. Writing summaries.
5. Doing map work.
6. Seeing films and filmstrips.
7. Reading different books.

8. Collecting pictures to go with the unit.

9. Taking the field trip.

10. Hearing the resource people.

Standardized Tests. Standardized tests are helpful in obtaining an objective measure of progress and growth in the more tangible outcomes of social studies instruction—those amenable to measurement procedures. This means they cannot be used to evaluate many of the broader goals of social studies instruction, because they are usually confined to the measurement of growth in subject-matter knowledge or to the measurement of the child's growth in skills. Standardized tests have a valuable contribution to make in the appraisal of a child's growth in social studies, but, to supplement them, the teacher will want to utilize many of the informal devices and techniques previously described.

Standardized tests gain their strength by providing the teacher with an objective yardstick to measure growth in learning. Furthermore, the teacher can compare the progress, growth, or achievement of his group or of any child in the group with other children of the same age and grade. The chief obstacle to their wise use, however, is that teachers have a tendency to regard the grade norm as a standard all must achieve if their progress is to be regarded as satisfactory. In other words, teachers feel that all children must attain a grade score on the test equal to their present grade status. *This is a completely erroneous approach to the use of standardized tests.* The teacher should recognize that the grade norm represents an *average* performance. For many children this level of achievement expectation will be too low; for others it will be too high. The teacher can reasonably expect the range of achievement in any unselected grade group to range from two to four grades below, to two to four grades above the grade norm. This range will be less in the lower grades but becomes wider as the children move into the higher grades. Just what constitutes an adequate and satisfactory performance on the test will depend on factors resident in individual children. Standards or levels of achievement expectation, therefore, should properly be established in terms of the capabilities of individual children and should not be dictated by the norms of a standardized test.

Published tests in the social studies differ in the extent to which they emphasize various social studies outcomes. Some are almost entirely subject-matter tests or tests designed to measure the child's status with reference to understandings and knowledges. These tests can be of value only if the content of the test and the content of the social studies curriculum are the same. The test will lack validity to the extent that it lacks congruity with the curriculum. For example, if the teacher were administering a test that was heavily loaded with

EVALUATING PUPIL ACHIEVEMENT AND TEACHER EFFECTIVENESS

items about life in early America, the children would not do well on it unless the material had actually been taught. It would be inconsistent and improper to use such a test if the class had studied a series of units dealing with their home state that year. It should be emphasized that decisions on the curriculum content should come first and that the selection of the test should come second, rather than the other way around. In selecting a test, the person making the selection should ascertain that its content is compatible with the curriculum in the particular school in which it is to be used.

To side-step the issue of building a social studies test to fit the diverse programs now operating throughout the country, some test makers have placed emphasis on skills rather than on content. Somewhat the same social studies skills should be developed in the grades irrespective of the topics studied. Children should be learning to read maps, to use basic reference materials, to read social studies material with understanding, and so on. Moreover, many of the subject-matter outcomes tend to be somewhat short-lived, because the rate of forgetting factual material is high, whereas mastery of the skills tends to be more permanent. Some teachers feel that standardized tests in the social studies are most useful for measurement of more permanent learnings such as skills and prefer to evaluate subject-matter outcomes through the use of tests they themselves construct.

The following is a partial list of standardized tests that contain sections dealing with elements of social studies or that are entirely devoted to the measurement of social studies outcomes.

1. Stanford Achievement Test, Harcourt, Brace and World, Inc., New York, N.Y.
2. Coordinated Scales of Attainment, Educational Publishers, Inc., Minneapolis, Minn.
3. Metropolitan Achievement Tests, Harcourt, Brace & World, Inc., New York, N.Y.
4. SRA Achievement Series, Science Research Associates, Chicago, Ill.
5. Sequential Tests of Educational Progress: Social Studies, Level 4, Grades 4–6, Educational Testing Service, Princeton, N.J.
6. Iowa Every-Pupil Test of Basic Skills, Houghton Mifflin Company, Boston, Mass.
7. California Tests in Social and Related Sciences, California Test Bureau, Del Monte Research Park, Monterey, Calif.
8. Tests of Critical Thinking in the Social Studies, J. W. Wrightstone, Bureau of Publications, Teachers College, Columbia University, New York, N.Y.
9. American School Achievement Test, Part 4—Social Studies and Science, Public School Publishing Company, Cincinnati, Ohio.

'It follows logically that if varied outcomes are expected from social studies instruction, a broad basis of evaluation must be utilized as well. Effective evaluation depends in no small measure on the teacher's ability to select the appropriate means of appraising pupil growth in accordance with the established goals. The teacher should constantly look for evidences of growth in the child's ability to enter into class discussion, plan, lead, answer questions, assume responsibility, show consideration for others, share, take part in group endeavors, and apply his learning to everyday living. The primary goal is continuous progress and growth in the many dimensions of human relationships for each child.

The teacher's choice of the particular means of evaluation for each learning is, therefore, a matter of utmost importance. In making the choice, he should recognize that soundness of any evaluative technique, device, or instrument rests on two basic assumptions, namely: (1) The method of evaluation consistently produces similar results. (In the field of measurement the technical term *reliability* is used to define this quality of measuring instruments.) (2) The technique, device, or instrument does, in fact, evaluate pupil growth in the particular value being considered. (In the field of measurement the technical term *validity* is used to describe the extent to which an instrument measures what it purports to measure.)

If the teacher uses standardized tests, the test manuals will usually state indices of reliability and provide data relative to the test's validity that were obtained in the standardization. It is also possible for the teacher to compute indices of reliability and validate his own tests through the use of statistical procedures. Because of the complexities involved in such operations and the lack of technical knowledge of measurement on the part of most classroom teachers, these indices are rarely obtained on teacher-made tests. Most teachers depend on "face" validity and assume reliability; they exercise their best judgment in determining whether the test measures what it is supposed to measure and whether it will do so consistently. The evaluative technique, device, or procedure will lack reliability and validity to the extent that the teacher's judgment is in error in this respect.

When the teacher begins to use evaluative techniques and devices other than tests, the problems of determining reliability and validity become even more severe. How consistent are teachers in their observations of children? Does a child's behavior in a given situation really indicate the extent to which he is socially sensitive under other conditions? Are classroom discussions truly an indication of changes in pupil behavior in life outside the classroom? Does the fact that children's friendships change frequently have anything at all to do with the reliability of sociometric devices? How often do children act the way they do and say the things they do because they know it will please their teacher, although their basic behavior remains unchanged? These questions and many more like them are the sort the teacher should ask himself as he uses the various evaluative techniques.

In general it may be said that any evaluative device or procedure should be as objective as possible. Objectivity strengthens reliability directly and validity indirectly. Some method should, therefore, be used to systematize and objectify the informal procedures that are used. It is better, for example, for the teacher to observe specific elements of a child's behavior than simply to observe the child with nothing especially in mind for which to look. It is better for a class to evaluate its work if they have a set of standards, criteria, or values from which to work than it is simply to talk about how well they did. Check lists, rating scales, or similar devices are helpful in maintaining objectivity and ensuring that certain aspects of the evaluation are not omitted inadvertently. It is also recommended that evaluative statements be supported by several actual examples of situations that demonstrate evidence of changed behavior on the part of the learners.

The educational literature dealing with evaluation of pupils' learning stresses the importance of obtaining evidence of changed behavior on the part of the learner attributable to the effects of an instructional or educative experience. In the main, this is a sound approach to the evaluation of learning—it has been recommended several times throughout the text. But using observation of behavior without fully understanding the reasons that lie behind the behavior can be a misleading indicator of the extent to which learning has occurred or of whether school instruction accounts for such learning. The following example illustrates this point vividly.

Let us assume a young child, Billy, has had an adjustment problem in school. He was uncooperative, disruptive, and bullied other children. The teacher arranged a conference with the mother at which time the problem was described and discussed. The mother seemed submissive and in broken English assured the teacher that the home would do what it could to help. That evening she related the teacher's comments as best she could remember them to Billy's father, who became furious and severely punished the child. Moreover, he promised the child to expect to be dealt with similarly should he hear of any more such "foolishness" in school.

Satisfied that she had "really gotten some place" with the mother, but really not expecting much help from the home, the teacher decided to engage the class in a dramatic play activity, with the thought of giving Billy an opportunity for "more satisfying experiences with others." This activity was repeated on several successive days and the teacher noticed that the child's behavior had changed remarkably. She said to herself, "Billy was able to reorganize his self-concept through a series of successful and satisfying experiences with others made possible through dramatic play activity." She decided to write an article for a professional journal on the subject.

Now it may very well be that the teacher's conclusion was a correct one; it also may be that the child's school experiences had nothing at all to do with his "new look." If the change was a permanent one, it was perhaps the result of a changed attitude on the part of the teacher as a result of the conference with the mother, plus the experiences in school, plus the experiences at home, plus other circumstances, conditions, or experiences of which neither the home nor the school were aware. The social life of the schoolchild is multidimensional and is influenced by many factors and a multiplicity of experiences in and out of school. The teacher can rarely, if ever, be absolutely certain that a child behaves or reacts the way he does *because* he has had a given school experience.

Teacher Self-Appraisal in the Social Studies

When the teacher is appraising the growth of pupils in the social studies, he is indirectly evaluating his own effectiveness as a teacher. If he satisfies himself that the outcomes of instruction were reasonably consistent with his original purposes and objectives, he assumes that his teaching was at least satisfactory. But using pupil progress as the sole criterion in evaluating one's teaching procedures can be both misleading and in serious error. Suppose, for example, the teacher set very limited goals for his social studies instruction—let us say, the mastery of certain facts related to the unit under study. His evaluative procedures, of course, would reflect such purposes as would his method of teaching. If it happens that the children demonstrate a knowledge of such facts as have been taught, the teacher assumes his teaching has been effective. If an outsider were making the evaluation and was concerned with some of the broader goals of social studies, such as understandings, attitudes, and skills, he might not be as favorably impressed with this teacher's effectiveness.

In self-evaluation, pupil progress is not a satisfactory criterion if used alone, because it is the teacher himself who establishes purposes, does the teaching, and evaluates outcomes. Although he may claim to get "good results," his purposes might be such that the "results" are not worthwhile even when achieved. It is evident that if pupil growth is to be used as a criterion of teacher effectiveness, measures of pupil growth on a wide variety of outcomes will be needed. Furthermore, this approach concerns itself only with ends and not with the means used to achieve them. Throughout this volume it has been stressed that in the social studies, instructional procedures are themselves related to certain important goals and outcomes. Therefore, the *way* a teacher achieves his goals may be at least as important as the goals themselves and in some cases even more so.

How, then, is the teacher to know how effectively he is teaching children the social studies? Perhaps what he will need to do is to obtain a set of standards or criteria and in an honest and objective way apply them to his own teaching. Such a procedure will have validity to the extent that the criteria accurately represent good social studies teaching procedures and the accuracy with which the teacher applies them to his teaching. If the teacher is sincerely interested in self-evaluation, he will not simply answer "yes" or "no" or "Oh, I do that all the time!" to items on such an evaluative device but will try to give specific examples to support his responses. In order to do a more thorough analysis of his teaching, the teacher may want to use an audio- or video-tape recording of his lesson. He can then replay the tape, study the interaction pattern, observe his movements, expressions, and teaching style. The following criteria may be of value to the teacher in making a self-evaluation of his teaching procedures in the social studies:

1. Is the classroom climate or atmosphere one that enhances and fosters the growth of skills and abilities in human relationships? (As evidenced by sincere friendliness, mutual helpfulness, and good will among pupils and between pupils and teacher; absence of hostility, rude remarks, and ill feelings; presence of a "we" feeling among pupils; pride in the classroom and the work of the class; good class spirit; absence of strong in-groups or cliques; absence of nervousness, emotional upsets or outbursts, impulsive behavior as a result of tension, pressure, or insecurity.)

2. Is there a good balance among outcomes dealing with the development of knowledge and understandings, attitudes, and skills? (Is the major instructional effort directed toward fact gathering or is there concern for developing meanings that underlie facts? Does the program emphasize subject matter *and* the social development of children or does it emphasize one at the expense of the other? What ways are used to develop children's attitudes? Are skills taught in a systematic and functional way? Are children *applying* what they are learning to their everyday lives? What evidence is there that the teacher evaluates not only subject-matter outcomes but also attitudes and skills?)

3. What provisions are made to accommodate the wide range of

individual differences known to exist in unselected grade groups? (Is there variety in reading materials, in classroom activities, in quality and quantity of required work, in the level of difficulty of ideas, and in the supervision of the children's work? Are differences accepted by the teacher? Does each child make some contribution to the work of the class? Is every child given some recognition for work well done? Are standards of acceptability or excellence of work determined on an individual basis or must all pupils measure up to a single standard? How does the program help meet the particular needs of the pupils in the class?)

4. Is the social studies program designed in such a way as to relate to the out-of-school lives of children?
(Are children encouraged to talk about their interests, problems, and concerns? Does the teacher make use of community resources and local resource persons? Is the teacher considering growth and development characteristics of children in planning social studies experiences? Does the teacher draw on the experiences of children in planning and teaching the social studies? In what ways does the social studies program make a difference in the lives of the children?)

5. What evidence is there that the children are growing in their ability to use democratic processes and procedures?
(Are opportunities provided for children to develop self-control, self-evaluation, cooperative planning abilities? Do children share in planning some of the specifics of the unit? Do children go about their work in responsible ways? Does the class become disorderly and boisterous when the teacher is not supervising it closely? What specific instances can be cited to show that children are developing concern for others, respect for property, attitudes of acceptance, respect for American ideals, self-direction?)

6. Is the instructional program conceptually oriented with a focus on basic organizing ideas?
(Does the unit deal with a broad topic with concepts relating to several of the social sciences, or is it a single subject-matter unit, such as history or geography? Are children able to participate in unit activities both intellectually and physically? Is a wide variety of instructional resources drawn on or is there heavy dependence on a single textbook? Are children given opportunities for planning and evaluating each day? Are there many opportunities for discussing and sharing ideas and information? Are activities and tasks problem oriented? Do children know what the problems are? Does the teacher employ appropriate inquiry procedures?)

7. Are studies conducted in sufficient depth to allow pupils to gain a reasonable degree of understanding of the topics studied?

(Are many units undertaken each year in a survey approach or are fewer units selected and studied intensively? Do pupils have time to reflect on topics studied and to come to some conclusions themselves? To what extent does the program deal only with descriptive information? Does the teacher feel compelled to "cover" the book or does he develop selected units thoroughly?)

8. What changes in pupil behavior indicate that the goals and purposes of the program are being achieved?

(Are a wide variety of techniques and devices used to evaluate pupil growth in social studies? Does pupil behavior in and out of the classroom indicate growth in human relations skills and abilities? In what way?)

Improving the Social Studies Program

In addition to the appraisals made of pupil growth in social studies, schools should engage in study and evaluation of the total program on a continuing basis. This procedure should be conceived as a cooperative, in-service study of the strengths and limitations of the program with the intention of improving it. Usually projects of this type get guidance and direction from local leadership, but outsiders may be called in for specific assistance or to be used as resource persons.

Evaluation of a social studies program may properly be regarded as a process of self-evaluation, and as such must involve all members of the teaching staff. Teachers participate individually in the instructional aspects of the program and, therefore, should also participate in the evaluation, which is intended to improve instruction. This differs sharply from practices of an earlier period when programs were evaluated chiefly by supervisors or administrators. It is important to keep the rating of teachers separate from the evaluation of the instructional program. Rating usually is used to establish various degrees of teaching excellence for the purpose of promotion, salary considerations, retention, removal from probationary status, or some similar purpose. Evaluation, on the other hand, has as its major purpose the improvement of instruction and as such should be disassociated from the appraisal of the competence of individual teachers.

There are basically two approaches that can be taken to the evaluation and improvement of the social studies curriculum. The first of these might be described as a complete and comprehensive study including every aspect and many of the details of the program: goals, teaching methods, materials, evaluative techniques, grouping, selection of content, and so on. Such a study is usually undertaken when a major curriculum change is anticipated and can take as long as two to five years to complete. It may be directed by a central steering committee, chaired by someone who devotes full time to the direction of the project. There is no set pattern of procedure to be followed in conducting studies of this type.

The second approach to evaluation and improvement of the social studies program of instruction is much less comprehensive than the first. It consists of short-term evaluative projects aimed specifically at the improvement of some one aspect of the social studies curriculum. These evaluative and in-service projects are designed to examine and improve elements of an existing program believed to be fundamentally sound. A single project of this type usually does not involve the entire staff at any one time, but there may be several under way concurrently that lead to wide staff participation. The examples that follow show how this approach functions.

Study Groups Formed to Meet Specific Needs. Teachers on the job are continually beset with instructional problems growing from their own professional inadequacies and often welcome the opportunity to obtain help with such problems. For example, a new curriculum guide calls for the teaching of the home state in the fourth grade, but many teachers may come from outside the state and have an inadequate background of information on the home state. Or perhaps there is a group of primary-grade teachers who cannot seem to institute unit procedures in their teaching. Perhaps there is a lack of familiarity on the part of the staff with instructional resources. Study groups can be organized to help meet these needs of teachers in the system, and the result will be more effective social studies teaching. Study groups of this type may take the form of *workshops, grade-level meetings, lectures, college courses for credit, institutes,* or *conferences.*

Opportunities for Professional Growth. Some of the same procedures discussed in the preceding section on "study groups" can be used to provide teachers with other opportunities for professional growth. The difference between the two lies chiefly in purpose. Professional-growth activities are usually based on interests of teachers rather than on their immediate teaching needs. A teacher may feel, for example, that she has no serious needs with respect to her teaching yet may look forward to the opportunity to take part in a professional-growth workshop in order to improve her teaching, to gain new insights, or simply to secure the inspiration and stimulation that come from activities of this type. Some systems encourage teachers to participate in professional-growth activities by allowing credit for attendance that can be applied toward more favorable salary consideration.

System-Wide Committees.   Because the amount of time individual teachers are able to spend on curriculum problems is necessarily limited, some systems establish special committees to study intensively some specific problem relative to the social studies curriculum. Such problems might include the use of community resources in the social studies, the consideration of new materials—textbooks, maps, globes, audio-visual materials—articulation from grade to grade, emphasis given to conservation, possibilities and needs for curriculum revisions, recent trends in social studies teaching, or any number of other problems. Such committees meet regularly during the year, keep the staff posted on their progress through bulletins, and make recommendations and suggestions for the entire staff to consider. Sometimes committees of this type are charged with the responsibility of preparing a handbook or other curricular material for publication and use by the system.

Consultant Service.   Many systems provide consultant service to the teacher who needs help with instructional problems in the social studies. The practice that is gaining favor in recent years is to have the consultant available on an invitation basis. This means that the teacher must request the visit and, unhappily, that the consultant may not receive an invitation from the rooms where he is most needed and could be most effective. However, this procedure has much to be said in its favor. Consultants are completely removed from rating, hiring, or recommending teachers. Some systems even prohibit any discussion of individual teacher's problems between the consultant and the principal. The situation is such, therefore, that the teacher need not feel insecure in requesting the consultant's help and that a professional relationship can develop between the consultant and teacher. The consultant's job is simply and solely to give to the teacher whatever service and help he needs to improve his teaching. To this end the consultant might help the teacher learn how to organize his class for group work, demonstrate teacher-pupil planning, sensitize the teacher to individual differences, call the teacher's attention to new instructional resources, help with the organization and planning of a construction activity, demonstrate the use of dramatic play, or help with some detail of unit procedures. The consultant can and should be an important force in the evaluation and improvement of social studies instruction.

Staff Meetings.   A certain number of staff meetings are of necessity the "nuts and bolts" variety—the assignment of playground duty, which group uses the south door, when the book requisitions are due, time of dismissal on Veteran's Day. But the regular meetings of the school staff should also provide time for the consideration of the unique curricular problems that bear directly on the instructional program in the school. For the social studies this means that staff meetings might be used for such activities as learning more about the special needs of the boys and girls who attend the school, exploring instructional resources in the immediate community, planning ways to resolve special problems relative to the school and school site, organizing service projects, coordinating the work of the school safety patrol or the student council, considering ways of improving citizenship, conservation or safety education, arranging for maximum use of instructional resources in the school, sharing teaching ideas and procedures with others, arranging visitations between teachers or between schools, utilizing resource persons, or planning small school research projects. The local school staff is charged with the responsibility of putting the social studies curriculum into operation, and it is not likely that the staff will be able to fulfill this responsibility unless it meets regularly for evaluation and discussion of the manner in which the program is functioning and how it can be improved.

Research Projects. Schools really concerned with the improvement of instruction in the social studies encourage teachers to maintain an experimental outlook in their teaching. The attitude may reflect itself in somewhat sizable research projects sponsored and directed by the system with teachers participating or by encouraging and supporting smaller research activities that can be carried out by individual teachers or schools. Suppose, for example, a system is considering placing a greater emphasis on world understanding in its social studies program. Rather than move forward with such plans on a system-wide basis, certain teachers or schools might be selected to experiment with the proposal for a year or two with the idea of discovering ways it might be implemented, the units especially adaptable to such an emphasis, the grade levels in which such teaching seems most effective, the resources available, the special problems that might be encountered if the idea went into effect on a system-wide basis, and other ideas. The findings of these research projects then are used to improve the plan or possibly to reject it as inadvisable. Or suppose a teacher has devised a new method of presenting geographical concepts to young children. He might be encouraged to plan a suitable experimental design and to use it on a trial basis. If the idea seemed to have merit, other teachers would be encouraged to try it, also. The progress of such projects would be made known through curriculum bulletins or other communication organs of the system and ultimately might be adopted throughout the district.

In the past decade, vast sums of money have suddenly become available for research and development in the social studies. This is all to the good, for it is through research studies of a scientific nature that we-will get the most reliable answers to problems of social studies education. There is great need for research in the field of social studies, and a greater number of school systems should allow and encourage teachers to pursue research activities. In practice, too frequently the opposite occurs. The new teacher is presented with a detailed teaching guide or preplanned units of study, along with a "helping" teacher. It is made clear to the inductee that "in this system we do it this way." A degree of structuring is, of course, necessary in any system that expects to follow a developmental sequence of instruction in the social studies for boys and girls. However, the greatest hope for improved social studies instruction lies in imaginative, creative, research-oriented teaching, and this can only occur when teachers are given a measure of freedom in their teaching. The school systems that place a premium on the spark of imagination that leads to new and better ways of teaching are likely to be the ones that will have the most to offer the boys and girls of today who will become the men and women of tomorrow.

Discussion Questions and Suggested Activities

1. In what ways does the evaluation that comes near the close of a unit or that comes near the end of a school year differ from the evaluation that is made daily in connection with social studies units?
2. Show by actual example how objectives, teaching procedures, and evaluative procedures are related. Under what circumstances would one be changed in terms of the other two?
3. Many situations in the course of teaching a social studies unit call for the setting up of standards: discussions, reports, group work, field trips, room conduct. Identify several of these situations and write standards that could be applied and used with children of a specific age. In practice would these be developed in advance by the teacher or would they be worked out cooperatively by the teacher and the pupils? Might the teacher work out a tentative list in advance that he could use as a guide?
4. What behavior characteristics would indicate that a child was making progress in the development of each of the following: (1) responsibility, (2) cooperation, (3) self-direction, (4) social relationships, (5) open-mindedness, (6) creativeness, (7) critical thinking, and (8) problem solving? Can you identify any published tests that purport to measure any of the above characteristics?
5. Refer to a standard work on measurement and test construction to find out the advantages and limitations of various objective-type

test items: multiple choice, alternate response, simple recall, completion. Use this information and construct a classroom test that could be used as a part of the resource unit that you are developing (Chapter 3).

6. What types of information might a teacher be able to obtain in a teacher-pupil conference that would be difficult to obtain through use of formal testing techniques?

7. Acquaint yourself with the various published standardized tests in social studies, including the personality and behavior-rating scales. Consult the manuals for these instruments and check what the authors have to say concerning the validity and reliability of their instruments as well as their descriptions of the standardization group. Compare this with what you find on the tests in O. K. Buros' *Mental Measurements Yearbook.*

8. List several techniques that a teacher might employ to evaluate his effectiveness as a teacher.

9. What are some ways that an outside "expert" in social studies or curriculum can be of maximum service to a staff that is making a study and evaluation of its social studies program of instruction? What are some disadvantages of bringing in outsiders?

10. Examine a basic social studies textbook for a grade in which you have a special interest with a view toward analyzing the methods of evaluation it suggests and recommends. Do you find a good balance in emphasis among objectives dealing with knowledges, attitudes, and skills?

11. Take the test that you constructed in Question 5 and evaluate the cognitive level of the questions that you asked. Use the Bloom *Taxonomy of Educational Objectives: Cognitive Domain* found in Appendix C for categorization purposes. Do some of your questions ask the students to apply, analyze, synthesize, and evaluate?

Selected References

Association for Supervision and Curriculum Development. *Evaluation as Feedback and Guide.* Washington, D.C.: The Association, 1967.

Berg, Harry D., ed. *Evaluation in the Social Studies,* 35th Yearbook. Washington, D.C.: National Council for the Social Studies, 1965.

Bloom, Benjamin S., ed. *A Taxonomy of Educational Objectives* (Handbook I: Cognitive Domain). New York: Longmans, Green & Company, 1956.

Buros, Oscar K., ed. *The Sixth Mental Measurements Yearbook.* Highland Park, N.J.: Gryphon Press, 1965. Contains reviews of social studies tests.

Dimond, S. E. "Evaluating Concepts and Attitudes," *Instructor*, No. 76 (March, 1967), pp. 103+.

Douglass, Malcolm P. *Social Studies: From Theory to Practice in Elementary Education.* Philadelphia: J. B. Lippincott Company, 1967.

Ebel, Robert L. *Measuring Educational Achievement.* Englewood Cliffs, N.J.: Prentice-Hall, Inc., 1965.

Fox, Robert, *et al. Diagnosing Classroom Learning Environments.* Chicago: Science Research Associates, Inc., 1966.

Fraser, Dorothy McClure, ed. *Social Studies Curriculum Development: Prospects and Problems*, 39th Yearbook. Washington, D.C.: National Council for the Social Studies, 1969. Chap. 7: Roland F. Payette and C. Benjamin Cox, "New Dimensions in Evaluation of Social Studies Programs."

Gronlund, Norman E. *Measurement and Evaluation in Teaching.* New York: The Macmillan Company, 1965.

Gross, Richard E., and Dwight W. Allen. "Problems and Practices in Social Studies Evaluation," *Social Education, XXXI*, No. 3 (March, 1967) pp. 207–208+.

Herman, Wayne L., Jr. *Current Research in Elementary School Social Studies*, Part VIII. New York: The Macmillan Company, 1969.

Krathwohl, David R., Benjamin S. Bloom, and Bertram B. Massia. *Taxonomy of Educational Objectives* (Handbook II: Affective Domain). New York: David McKay Company, Inc., 1964.

Medley, D. M., and H. E. Mitzel, "Measuring Classroom Behavior by Systematic Observation," in N. L. Gage, *Handbook of Research on Teaching.* Chicago: Rand McNally and Company, 1963.

Michaelis, John U. *Social Studies for Children in a Democracy*, 4th ed. Englewood Cliffs, N.J.: Prentice-Hall, Inc., 1968.

Payne, David A. *The Specification and Measurement of Learning Outcomes.* Waltham, Mass.: Blaisdell Publishing Co., 1968.

Phillips, Ray C. *Evaluation in Education.* Columbus, Ohio: Charles E. Merrill Books, Inc., 1968.

Preston, Ralph C. *Teaching Social Studies in the Elementary School*, 3rd ed. New York: Holt, Rinehart & Winston, Inc., 1968.

Organizing Ideas from the Disciplines Appendix A

The following list of organizing ideas from the disciplines has been compiled from published lists prepared by social scientists. They are stated as major generalizations. This material is based on but not excerpted from these sources:

Report of the State Central Committee on Social Studies to the California State Curriculum Commission. Sacramento: California State Department of Education, 1961.

Fraser, Dorothy McClure, and S. P. McCutcheon, eds., *Social Studies in Transition: Guidelines for Change.* Washington, D.C.: National Council for the Social Studies, 1965.

Berelson, Bernard *et al., The Social Studies and the Social Sciences.* New York: Harcourt, Brace & World, Inc., 1962.

A Conceptual Framework for Social Studies in Wisconsin Schools, Madison, Wisc.: State Superintendent of Public Instruction. 1965.

Billings, Neal, *A Determination of Generalizations Basic to the Social Studies Curriculum.* Baltimore: Warwick and York, Inc., 1929.

Teaching the Social Studies, The Illinois Curriculum Program, Bulletin C-7. Springfield, Ill.: Superintendent of Public Instruction, 1962.

Walsh, H. M., *A Teaching Model for Culture Studies,* unpublished Ed.D. dissertation, University of California, Los Angeles, 1962.

History

1. The affairs of human societies have historical antecedents and consequences; events of the past influence those of the present.
2. Human societies have undergone and are undergoing continual, although perhaps gradual, changes in response to various forces.
3. Several civilizations have risen and fallen in the history of human societies; many have contributed to existing civilizations.
4. The methods of rational inquiry have increased man's knowledge of the world and have greatly accelerated the accumulation of new knowledge.
5. Man's struggle for freedom and human dignity has occupied a relatively brief period of time as compared with the total span of his existence.
6. In the modern world, historical events have a significance that reaches far beyond the limits of the state or province or the place of their origin.
7. Guidelines for understanding thought and action in contemporary affairs can be derived from the historical backgrounds of society.
8. The early history of a country has a definite bearing on the culture, traditions, beliefs, attitudes, and ways of life of its people.
9. Human beings in different stages of civilization react differently to similar environments.

Geography

1. Geographic factors influence where and how people live and what they do; man adapts, shapes, utilizes, and exploits the earth to his own needs.
2. The global location of a nation or a region contributes to its importance in international affairs.
3. People living in similar natural settings throughout the world have similarities, but many differences in ways of life can be noted.
4. No nation-state is an island unto itself; all have some contact with others; hence, the nations of the world are interdependent.
5. The choices made by people in adapting to (or in adapting) their environment depends on cultural values, economic wants, the degree of technological insight and on such physical factors as climate, water, soil, and landscape.
6. Resources and resource use are related to the level of cultural, technological development; industrial societies place heavy demands on the earth's resources.
7. Places on the earth have a distinctiveness about them that differentiates them from all other places.

8. Areas of the earth develop bonds, interconnections, and relations with other areas.
9. Successive or continuing occupance by groups of people, as well as natural processes and forces, results in changing and changed landscapes.

Economics

1. The economy of a country (or region) is related to available resources, investment capital, and the educational development of its people.
2. The wants of man are unlimited, whereas resources that man needs to fulfill his wants are scarce; hence, societies and individuals have to make choices as to which needs are to be met and which are to be sacrificed.
3. Decisions concerning what will be produced are generally made on the basis of what society considers of most worth (for example, production of war material and consumer goods); cultural tradition; desire for economic growth; and similar considerations.
4. In any society, consumers outnumber producers of goods and services.
5. The interdependence of peoples of the world makes exchange and trade a necessity in the modern world.
6. The standard of living is related to productivity and to the extent to which people have direct control over the affairs of their government.
7. Increased specialization in production has led to interdependence among individuals, communities, states, and nations.
8. In the complex, modern industrialized society of today, government plays an important part in the economic life of society.
9. Most modern societies perceive economic welfare as a desired goal for their members; universally, poverty is devalued as a human condition.
10. Economic resources can be used in various ways; different nations have developed different economic systems.

Anthropology

1. Every society, however primitive, has formed its own system of beliefs, knowledge, values, traditions, and skills that can be called its culture.
2. Culture is socially learned and serves as a potential guide for human behavior in any given society.
3. Although all mankind is confronted with the same psychological

and physiological needs to be met, the manner in which these are met differs according to culture.

4. A society must continuously evaluate and modify its culture in order to adjust to changing conditions; failure to do so leads to social disorganization or to the absorption or exploitation of the society by more aggressive and rapidly developing cultures.

5. Man's cultural adaptations result in great diversity in ways of living and allow him to be highly versatile in selecting where and how he will live.

6. The art, music, architecture, food, clothing, sports, and customs of a people help to produce a national identity.

7. All human beings, since long before the beginning of written history, have been members of the same biological species.

8. Nearly all human beings, regardless of racial or ethnic background, are capable of participating in and contributing to any culture.

9. Certain social functions such as communicating; producing, distributing and consuming goods and services; educating; recreating; governing; conserving resources; and expressing religious and aesthetic feelings are primary activities of all organized societies.

10. The increased and more frequent contacts of persons from various cultures made possible by modern-day transportation and communication systems are resulting in extensive cultural diffusion, cultural borrowing, and cultural exchange.

Political Science

1. Every known society has some kind of authority structure that can be called its government; such a government is granted coercive power.

2. A stable government facilitates the social and economic development of a nation.

3. All societies have made policies or laws about how groups of people should live together.

4. Each society has empowered a body (that is, tribal council, city council, state assembly, parliament) to make decisions and establish social regulations for the group that carry coercive sanctions.

5. The decisions, policies, and laws that have been made for a given society reflect and are based on the values, beliefs, and traditions of that society.

6. Throughout the history of mankind, man has experimented with many different systems of government.

7. The responsibilities of governments can be grouped into five large categories: (1) external security; (2) internal order; (3) justice; (4) services essential to the general welfare; and, under democracy, (5) ensuring freedom.

8. The consent of the governed is to some extent a requirement of all governments, and without it a government will eventually collapse; but in a democracy, consent of the governed is clearly recognized as a fundamental prerequisite of government.

9. A democratic society depends on citizens who are intellectually and morally competent to conduct the affairs of government.

10. Certain factors are necessary for democracy to succeed. These include (1) an educated citizenry, (2) a common concern for human freedom, (3) communication and mobility, (4) a degree of economic security, (5) a spirit of compromise and mutual trust, (6) respect for the rights of minority groups and the loyal opposition, (7) moral and spiritual values, and (8) participation by the citizen in government at all levels.

Sociology

1. The family is the basic social unit in most cultures and is the source of some of the most fundamental and necessary learning in a culture.

2. Social classes have always existed in every society, although the bases of class distinction and the degree of rigidity of the class structure have varied.

3. The trend toward urbanization within the United States as well as in the rest of the world has accentuated problems of social disorganization, interpersonal relationships, and group interaction.

4. Population growth is presenting mankind with one of the most challenging problems of modern times.

5. Every society develops a system of roles, norms, values, and sanctions to guide the behavior of individuals and groups within the society.

6. In order to meet individual and group needs, societies organize themselves into subgroups that, in time, become institutionalized; individuals are members of several such subgroups or institutions.

7. The satisfaction of social needs is a strong motivating force in the determination of individual behavior.

8. All societies develop systems of social control; conflicts often arise between individual liberty and social control in societies where both values are sought.

9. Status and prestige are relative to the values sought by a social

group; behavior that is rewarded in one social group may be suppressed in another.

10. The social environment in which a person is reared and lives has a profound effect on the personal growth and development of every individual.

Controversial Issues

The following *Statement on Teaching About Controversial Issues* was adopted by the Colorado State Board of Education on February 10, 1965.

For purposes of this statement, controversial issues are defined as those problems, subjects, or questions about which there are significant differences of opinion, for which there are no easy resolutions, and discussions of which generally create strong feelings among people. Although there may be disagreement over what the facts are and what they mean, subjects usually become controversial issues because of differences in the values people use in applying the facts.

Controversy is inherent in the democratic way of life. It is essential, therefore, that the study and discussion of controversial issues have an important place in education for citizenship in a free society. Students can develop into free men with informed loyalty to democracy only through the process of examining evidence, facts, and differing viewpoints; through the exercise of freedom of thought and moral choice; and through the making of responsible decisions. These procedures are as characteristic of, and essential to, a free society as authoritarian indoctrination is to totalitarianism.

Each pupil has the right and need, under competent guidance and instruction, to study issues appropriate to his interest, experience, and ability. He must have access to relevant information, and he has the obligation to examine carefully all sides of an issue. He has the right to form and express his own point of view and opinions without jeopardizing his position in the classroom or in the school.

Each teacher has the right and the obligation to teach about controversial issues. It is his responsibility to select issues for study and discussion which contribute to the attainment of course objectives, and to make available to students materials concerning the various aspects of the issues. He also has the obligation to be as objective as possible and to present fairly the several sides of an issue. Although he has the right to express his own viewpoint and opinions, he does not have the right to indoctrinate students to his views.[1]

1. *Statement on Teaching About Controversial Issues,* Colorado State Board of Education, Denver, Colorado, 1965. *Used by permission.*

Questions to Encourage Reflective Processes

Appendix C

The types of questions teachers ask relate directly to the intellectual processes required of pupils. If teachers are concerned about helping pupils build thought patterns that include reflection, critical thinking, inquiring, forming hypotheses and tentative conclusions, questions must be framed calling for the use of such intellectual operations. Nevertheless, the preponderance of questions asked in social studies instruction is of the fact type, requiring only the retrieval of information that has been presented in print or presented verbally by the teacher. The following questions are samples of other types that can be utilized. These questions are grouped according to the classification of objectives suggested by the Bloom *Taxonomy*.[1]

> I. Those requiring depth of comprehension—"*Translate* what is learned from one level of abstraction to another, one symbolic form to another or one verbal form to another."[2]
>
> **Examples**
>
> 1. From the product map on page _____, what can you say about

---

1. Benjamin Bloom, *A Taxonomy of Educational Objectives: Cognitive Domain* (Handbook I), New York: Longmans, Green & Co., 1956.

2. *Ibid.*

a. The way population is distributed in this region?

b. The importance of farming in this area?

c. The location of factories and manufacturing plants?

d. The size of farms west of the Mississippi as compared with those east of the Mississippi River?

2. Study the map on page _____. A ship moving from Montreal, Canada, to Duluth, Minnesota, would be about nine hundred miles west of Montreal at its destination. Use the map to find out how many miles the ship actually traveled. How many different directions would the ship have traveled on the journey? How much higher above sea level would the ship be in Duluth than it was in Montreal? How does that compare with the length of your school building? A football field?

3. Study the two pictures posted on the bulletin board. How would you describe the differences in the surface of the land in these two pictures? What is the most important idea shown in each of the pictures? How can you tell the season of the year in which the picture was taken?

4. For each of the following give what you think the actual *number* is:

a. It took a *long time* for the Pilgrims to cross the Atlantic. Number of weeks: _____

b. There are *high mountains* in the western part of our country. Number of feet high: _____

c. *Long ago* the pioneers first came to this part of the country. Number of years ago: _____

d. The new mine brought *many people* to Leadsville. Number of people: _____

"Interpret what is learned by explaining, summarizing, re-arranging." [3]

Examples

1. In certain parts of the world neighboring countries either grow a single crop or mine a single mineral that they sell or trade. Such countries often have few factories and do little manufacturing.

a. Would such countries trade with each other or with countries in other parts of the world? Why?

3. *Ibid.*

    b. What problems might people in such countries have in making a living?

    c. Where in the world do we find countries of the type described in the preceding paragraph?

    d. How would countries such as the United States be of help to nations that depend on a single product for their income?

2. In studying the map on page _____, how many of these large cities are located on large rivers or lakes? What does this tell you about the importance of water transportation to the growth of these cities? Is this true in other parts of the United States that you have studied?

3. Why are there no roads or railroads in the area shown on the map on page _____?

4. Study the photograph on page _____. What do the number and size of the highways tell you about this area?

"Extrapolate, going beyond the given information to determine implications, consequences, and effects." [4]

Examples

1. Today, states have laws to protect wild animals and birds. Some animals can be hunted only during a part of the year. Even then only a few of them can be killed. Other animals cannot be hunted at all. The state conservation department sees that these laws are obeyed.

    a. Why is it that some animals can be hunted only during a part of the year?

    b. What time of the year should animals not be hunted?

    c. Why is it that sometimes hunters are allowed to kill only male animals?

    d. Why is it that some animals cannot be hunted at all?

2. How do you suppose the people in cities A, B, and C are affected when the area marked "heavy snowfall" has two weeks of very warm weather in early March?

3. In a medium-sized city, a large company needed to hire fifteen thousand more workers. Would the population of that city increase by fifteen thousand or by more than that number? How can you tell? What problems would such a city face in taking care of this many more people?

4. *Ibid.*

II. Questions requiring application of information—". . . going a step beyond translation, interpretation, and extrapolation, showing how information will be used, given a situation in which no method of solution is specified."[5]

Examples

1. Mr. Jones read the following paragraph in his evening newspaper: "The Lindberghs' children are Kristina, Wendy, Lars, Leif, and Erick. With names like that, they can always move to Ballard if they weary of commuting."
   a. What would you say is the nationality background of the people of Ballard?
   b. Are these American children or children of another country? Why can't you tell by the information given?

2. Study the map on page _____ and answer these questions (various points are identified as A, B, C, etc.):
   a. At what place would you expect to find a seaport?
   b. If one were building a highway from A to B, he would probably build it through the mountain at point ___.
   c. If there is a large city at A and a medium-sized city at B and C, you would expect to find the greatest amount of traffic between which two cities? Why?
   d. If you lived in the area shown on the map and you wanted to fly to Chicago, you would probably board your plane at an airport located near which city? Why?

3. How have people in this region built their homes? What are some other ways they *might* have built them? Why do you suppose they have chosen the ways they have to build their homes?

III. Questions requiring analysis—"Identify and classify the elements involved in a problem; show relationships among elements and determine their connections and interactions; discover the organizational principles involved, the arrangement and structure of a body of information or a problem."[6]

Examples

1. What features of the land appear to be most important to the people who live in this area? Which occupations appear to be most important? What principal tools and machines do these

5. *Ibid.*
6. *Ibid.*

people use? Do the answers to these three questions tell you something about the way of life of the people who live there? In what way?

2. What sort of education do the people receive? Do most of the people know how to read and write? What kind of religious education is given the children? What things done by children are rewarded or punished by the family? Do the answers to these questions tell you something about the type of person who would be considered the ideal person in this group? Describe such a person.

3. What does the road map on page _____ tell you about the relief of the land in the area shown?

4. How many different types of communication are discussed on pages _____ in your text? In what ways has the invention of new methods of communication helped people improve their way of living?

IV. Questions requiring synthesis—"Re-combine previously learned information with new information into unique or original ideas, a plan or prepared set of operations."[7]

Examples

1. From what you know of this area, what direction would you say the camera was facing when the picture on page _____ was taken?

2. Suppose the settlement of the United States had been from west to east instead of east to west, as it was.
   a. Where do you think America's large cities would be located?
   b. What routes do you think settlers would have followed? Would they have been the same as those used by early settlers moving west?
   c. Would it have been easier for people to move east than it was for people to move west? Why do you think so?

3. What happened here?
   It was a tiny village in 1898, but two years later it had a population of thirty-five thousand. For two years a continuous line of men crawled over Chilkoot Pass. Since then it has gone down in population. Today it has only about eight hundred people. However, it continues to live with the memory of its dramatic past.

7. *Ibid.*

a. Why did this town rise so rapidly in population and then lose its people?

b. Where do you suppose this town is located?

4. Through use of illustrations, pupils respond to such questions as

a. Where would you sell this product?

b. Where will the population grow most rapidly?

c. Which place is likely to make changes most easily?

d. Where is this place?

Index

International understanding. See Worldmindedness